Prices and Quantities

ARTHUR M. OKUN

Prices and Quantities: A Macroeconomic Analysis

THE BROOKINGS INSTITUTION
Washington, D.C.

Library of Congress Cataloging in Publication data:

Okun, Arthur M
   Prices and quantities.
   Includes bibliographical references and index.
   1. Macroeconomics. 2. Inflation (Finance)
I. Brookings Institution, Washington, D.C. II. Title.
HB172.5.038   339   80-70076
ISBN 0-8157-6480-4
ISBN 0-8157-6479-0 (pbk.)

1 2 3 4 5 6 7 8 9

THE BROOKINGS INSTITUTION is an independent organization devoted to nonpartisan research, education, and publication in economics, government, foreign policy, and the social sciences generally. Its principal purposes are to aid in the development of sound public policies and to promote public understanding of issues of national importance.

The Institution was founded on December 8, 1927, to merge the activities of the Institute for Government Research, founded in 1916, the Institute for Economics, founded in 1922, and the Robert Brookings Graduate School of Economics and Government, founded in 1924.

The Board of Trustees is responsible for the general administration of the Institution, while the immediate direction of the policies, program, and staff is vested in the President, assisted by an advisory committee of the officers and staff. The by-laws of the Institution state: "It is the function of the Trustees to make possible the conduct of scientific research, and publication, under the most favorable conditions, and to safeguard the independence of the research staff in the pursuit of their studies and in the publication of the results of such studies. It is not a part of their function to determine, control, or influence the conduct of particular investigations or the conclusions reached."

The President bears final responsibility for the decision to publish a manuscript as a Brookings book. In reaching his judgment on the competence, accuracy, and objectivity of each study, the President is advised by the director of the appropriate research program and weighs the views of a panel of expert outside readers who report to him in confidence on the quality of the work. Publication of a work signifies that it is deemed a competent treatment worthy of public consideration but does not imply endorsement of conclusions or recommendations.

The Institution maintains its position of neutrality on issues of public policy in order to safeguard the intellectual freedom of the staff. Hence interpretations or conclusions in Brookings publications should be understood to be solely those of the authors and should not be attributed to the Institution, to its trustees, officers, or other staff members, or to the organizations that support its research.

Foreword

IN RECENT YEARS the U.S. economy has been plagued by chronic and worsening inflation that has persisted despite substantial slack in operating rates and high unemployment levels—the condition termed stagflation. In the past, traditional techniques of macroeconomic management owed their success in combating either inflation or unemployment to the responsiveness of wages and prices to changes in aggregate demand. Wage and price increases could be moderated by restraining aggregate demand, or employment could be increased by stimulating it. During the past decade, however, the same policies have not been effective, and the nation has not been able to contain inflation even in periods of economic slack.

It now seems clear that the economists' traditional model, which presupposes short-run price and wage flexibility, is no longer valid for most of the industrial world, and hence inflation responds only weakly to shifts in macroeconomic policy. In this volume, Arthur M. Okun seeks to explain that loss of responsiveness by analyzing how modern labor and product markets work and how their structure leads to the observed macroeconomic behavior. Many, often divergent, models of economic behavior have been advanced during the past decade, based on job search, expectations, and other recent developments in economic theory. Okun examines these models critically, rejecting some and building on the insights of others. His interpretation of microeconomic behavior and macroeconomic performance provides a basis for the design of policies to deal with stagflation.

A central feature of Okun's analysis is implicit contract theory, which recognizes that efficiency-maximizing decisions by business firms reflect long-term considerations as well as short-term changes in markets. The establishment of long-term relations in labor and product markets—by implicit contracts—reduces costs, but such contracts also complicate the task of managing the economy as a whole. The growing importance of implicit contracts has increased the number of markets in which wages and prices are less sensitive to short-run changes in the demand for labor and goods. For that reason, restrictive macroeconomic policies have the

vii

seemingly paradoxical effect of reducing output and increasing unemployment while doing little to slow inflation. Moreover, the adverse effects of external shocks to the economy, such as restrictions on the supply of oil, are magnified by public and private arrangements that have evolved to protect workers and producers from the consequences of inflation.

Okun describes the mechanics of the long-term relations between employers and employees and between customers and suppliers and shows how the resulting practices in price and wage setting affect overall economic management. He characterizes the contracts in career labor markets and in customer product markets as analogous to an *invisible handshake*. Within this framework, Okun shows why traditional monetary and fiscal policies alone are unable to cope with stagflation and how government policies such as indexation, increases in indirect taxes, and excessive regulation exacerbate inflation. He also recommends specific policies to address today's problems. It was Okun's hope that economic policymakers would be encouraged to move in these new directions to prevent even more damage to the economy.

The book was virtually completed before the author's untimely death on March 23, 1980. The manuscript was prepared for publication by his colleagues at Brookings under the supervision of Joseph A. Pechman, director of the Brookings Economic Studies program. Okun had completely revised and edited the first seven chapters in response to comments on the manuscript received at a series of staff seminars in the summer of 1979. The material constituting the seventh (and last) chapter of Okun's original manuscript is here divided, as Okun intended, between chapters 7 and 8. He left chapter 8 not quite finished; only minor editorial changes were made in it to preserve as much as possible of the original language. Okun prepared the bibliographical notes and the figures for the first six chapters. Footnote references were added to the text of chapters 7 and 8, but no attempt was made to prepare bibliographical notes for these chapters. The figures in chapter 8 were prepared by Martin Neil Baily and Barry P. Bosworth.

Handwritten notes on copies of the manuscript in Okun's files indicate that he would have made a number of further revisions had he lived to complete the book himself. Because Okun's skills as an economic analyst and a writer are legend, his colleagues were reluctant to alter the manuscript even in places in which Okun himself had clearly indicated his dissatisfaction. They agreed that it would be better to publish the book as Okun left it rather than attempt to guess at the changes he might have made. Even without his final revisions, Okun's book stands as a major contribution to macroeconomic analysis.

Many persons were helpful during the preparation of this volume. The author was particularly grateful to his colleagues at Brookings and to William Fellner of the American Enterprise Institute for comments and suggestions at the staff seminars. Individual chapters of the manuscript were carefully reviewed by Henry J. Aaron, Martin Neil Baily, Katharine L. Bradbury, David W. Breneman, Ralph C. Bryant, Andrew S. Carron, Owen J. Evans, Howard K. Gruenspecht, Robert W. Hartman, Lester B. Lave, Robert Z. Lawrence, Thomas M. Lenard, James P. Luckett, George L. Perry, Walter S. Salant, Juliet B. Shor, and Karen A. Swiderski. Nancy J. Delaney and J. Edward Shephard provided research assistance and verified factual content. The manuscript was edited by Karen J. Wirt and typed by Jacquelyn G. Sanks; Florence Robinson prepared the index.

The work on this project was supported by grants from the Andrew K. Mellon Foundation and the National Science Foundation. The views expressed here are the author's alone and should not be ascribed to these foundations or to the trustees, officers, or other staff members of the Brookings Institution.

BRUCE K. MAC LAURY
President

December 1980
Washington, D.C.

Contents

Tables

Figures

I

The Literature
and the Real World

THE DECADE of the seventies was an unhappy time for macroeconomic performance and for macroeconomists. Capitalist industrial countries generated far less growth and suffered far more inflation than in the fifties or the sixties. They experienced persistent inflation, often in the face of excess supply, that defied the standard lessons of economic textbooks. Some industrial nations fared better on price stability at the expense of growth; others that accepted less deterioration of growth displayed inflation records that were generally worse than average; some managed to compile abysmal records on both fronts. So the strategy of policy is everywhere subjected to agonizing reappraisals.

The State of Macroeconomics

What was in the mid-sixties a developing synthesis and an emerging consensus on macroeconomic policy and analysis has crumbled. Just as the consensus was Keynesian (to be sure, post-Keynesian after a generation of refinements and amendments), so the counterreaction has been anti-Keynesian. The monetarists, led by Milton Friedman, expressed their skepticism and pessimism about the future of the "new economics" of the Keynesians when it looked most successful, in about 1965. As economic performance deteriorated, their earlier views seemed prophetic. Some eclectic observers who found events disturbing abandoned the Keynesian paradigm of macroeconomic analysis and naturally turned to the competitive product supplied by the monetarists.

But the monetarist model has not dealt successfully with the phenomenon of chronic inflation, either ex ante by means of prediction or ex post by explanation. It has a mixed record of accounting for speedups and slowdowns in the growth of nominal GNP. It also has failed to account

1

for the unusual "split"—a bloated inflation component and a shriveled real component—in the growth of nominal GNP in slack economies. Indeed, the monetarists were particularly enthusiastic in predicting prompt disinflationary benefits from slower growth of nominal GNP. As such, they have been especially optimistic, and thus especially wrong, about the consequences of recession and slack for inflation.

The plain fact is that no school of economists has a satisfactory theory of inflation. We all operate, more or less, with a view of lagging and shifting short-run Phillips curves. That model continues to point to a disinflation that does not, in fact, take place. Why, after the 1970 recession, did the U.S. inflation rate become no lower than 3 percent—and then only with the artificial influence of controls and only for a brief respite? Why did the American economy remain at essentially 6 percent inflation after mid-1975, following the most severe recession in nearly forty years? The annals of the National Bureau of Economic Research reveal no comparable inflationary recession. Why did inflation in the United States accelerate so dramatically in 1978 when indicators of resource use for labor and capital were comparable to earlier tranquil periods like 1964 and 1972?

Economists keep chasing the shifting econometrics of the shifting Phillips curve. The lags in response to excess demand have to be short, but those in response to excess supply grow increasingly longer in successive estimates. The estimate of the full-employment (or equilibrium or "natural") utilization rate is progressively revised downward. If the unshakable maintained hypothesis is that inflation is the product of excess demand, the analyst has to find that demand was excessive most of the time to keep the inflation in orbit. Models of expectations proliferate in which people are supposed to look forward by looking backward over a decade. Allegedly, people see the stubbornness of inflation, expect it to keep churning, and turn that into a self-fulfilling prophesy. But where and when did that stubbornness originate?

To be sure, four or five consecutive years of objectively defined excess demand were experienced during the late sixties. Neither the growth record nor the 4 percent inflation record of the Vietnam War period poses a serious puzzle. Indeed, it is entirely consistent with the standard Phillips curve analysis that was at the time a respected element of the post-Keynesian synthesis and that neatly fits the facts of the entire 1954–69 period. To account for that experience, one does not need to strain for evidence of long lags in wage-price responses, of structural deterioration in labor markets, or of inflationary psychology. The mystery began when the excess demand ended. I argue below that the prolonged, traditional excess-demand inflation of the late sixties compounded the problems of the seventies by dislodging arrangements and institutions that previously stabilized the price level. But that argument has to swim against the tide. It has to recognize that the trade-off deteriorated throughout the industrial world, not merely in the United States, and it has to cope with the fact that the American economy experienced more severe periods of excess-demand inflation in several other wartime eras, which apparently did not produce a derailing.

Something has to be different now. The difference in what exists today must stem from what has happened in the past. The intensity of inflation that is maintained in a weak economy simply must reflect the inflationary history that preceded it. Some insidious ratchet has gone into operation, giving inflation a far greater degree of persistence than it ever had before. But who threw the ratchet into the soup? In searching for the villain, the question arises of whether the fiscal-monetary process or the price-wage process has changed. Yet both these suspects have good alibis; it takes a great deal of ingenuity to write even a plausible indictment against either. Policymakers accepted (more accurately, opted for) more recession and more slack in the seventies than they did after the Second World War or the Korean War. Private decisionmaking shows no evidence of a major increase in monopoly power in either labor or product markets or of anticompetitive structural changes that would account for the resistance of prices and wages to excess supply.

Even more fundamentally, economists cannot explain adequately why and how much inflation matters. Clearly, it matters a great deal to the American public. Even when it was well predicted and not accelerating, 6 percent inflation was highly disturbing to the citizenry. Yet many economic models imply that only the unanticipated component of inflation can cause any significant welfare loss.

Economists sometimes get along remarkably well in the absence of a theoretical framework. A few of them sensed the major inflationary implications of food, fuel, and devaluation in 1973–74, even though they could not produce such results with analytical models. Even those who were surprised by that episode have learned from experience. Everybody now knows enough to disaggregate and to take account of special factors. No professional economist will ever again insist (as some did early in 1974) that a major rise in the price of oil cannot raise the price level since it merely pushes other prices down. But when they proceed ad hoc without an underlying theoretical framework, the lessons do not get properly generalized. People can learn the truth about the inflationary effect of decisions made by the Organization of Petroleum Exporting Countries and yet fail to realize that the same truth applies to hikes in indirect taxes, farm price supports, or minimum wages.

It is my conviction that the price-wage process is the place to look for an understanding of persistent inflation. The sluggishness in the response of prices and wages to imbalances in supply and demand accentuates fluctuations in output and employment. Because prices do not carry the main burden of adjustments, quantities are obliged to carry the load. The theory of inflation and the theory of fluctuations in the real economy face a single task—to explain the split of nominal GNP growth between the real and the price components.

The domain of this book is what Keynes described as the aggregate supply function. He labeled it, but he never really analyzed it with the same perceptiveness or enthusiasm that he devoted to aggregate demand. For years after the Phillips curve was grafted to the main body of Keynesian thinking about aggregate demand, economists seemed to have a workable set of macroeconomic tools that gave the right answers to the big questions of practical relevance. The macro framework clearly had missing linkages and even glaring inconsistencies with micro analysis. Many economists recognized these defects, and some worked to correct them. But their efforts seemed to be mainly an intellectual venture to improve the logic of economics and reunify the micro-macro compartments, rather than to increase relevancy in explaining the key characteristics of short-run macroeconomic fluctuations. Recent experience has made clear that the building of a sturdy micro-macro bridge is essential not just to link the two sides of economics, but to make the macro side viable once again.

For the short run, the aggregate supply function is concerned basically with how prices and wages behave as functions of GNP (nominal or real). It is intended to explain how a given rise in nominal GNP, determined by aggregate demand, is split between output gain and price increases. Viewed from the income side, the questions are how variations are compounded of changes in factor productivity, factor inputs, and factor prices (mainly wages). I basically ignore the intriguing long-run issues of supply here—the role of technology, capital formation, work incentives, and the like in determining output at full employment. Similarly, I have little to say in this book about the basic building blocks of aggregate demand—the consumption function, the marginal efficiency of capital, and the liquidity preference function. The shapes of these functions and their stability are still controversial and unsettled issues, which are extremely important both for understanding economic fluctuations and making fiscal and monetary policy. But the basic determinants of aggregate demand are not much in dispute. The framework of the demand side is generally acceptable and readily usable. The supply side lacks an equivalent framework to organize our thinking about interactions between prices and quantities.

In developing the supply side of the story, I believe I was on the right track in stressing customer product markets and career labor markets in my article, "Inflation: Its Mechanics and Welfare Costs" (*Brookings Papers on Economic Activity, 2:1975*). That piece was an early sketch; this book is an attempt to turn it into a portrait. It is an attempt to generalize and formalize the concepts into a way of thinking about the world. Also, unlike its predecessor, it uses an interrelated and symmetrical framework to analyze fluctuations in real activity and in the inflation rate.

The Heritage of Classical and Keynesian Theory

The observed character of short-run fluctuations in aggregate output is palpably inconsistent with the classical microeconomics of competitive equilibrium. That inconsistency is most clearly evident in a simple model of an economy that produces one commodity, with labor as its only variable input and capital as a fixed factor in the short run. Suppose that homogeneous labor is hired in a perfectly competitive market and produces a given output as determined by a short-run production function. The demand curve for labor, with the wage measured in units of output, is then technologically determined; indeed, it is identical to the marginal product curve of labor, *MP*. Diminishing returns give it a negative slope. So long as the supply curve of labor, *S*, is a function of the real wage, whether positively, vertically, or negatively sloped (provided that it is less negatively sloped than demand), equilibrium in the labor market lies at the intersection of the supply and demand curves. As figure 1-1 below shows, the intersection determines the real wage, the level of labor input (employment), and, in turn, output.

The short-run equilibrium can be disturbed only in two ways. The

Figure 1-1. *Labor Market Equilibrium in a One-Good Competitive Economy*

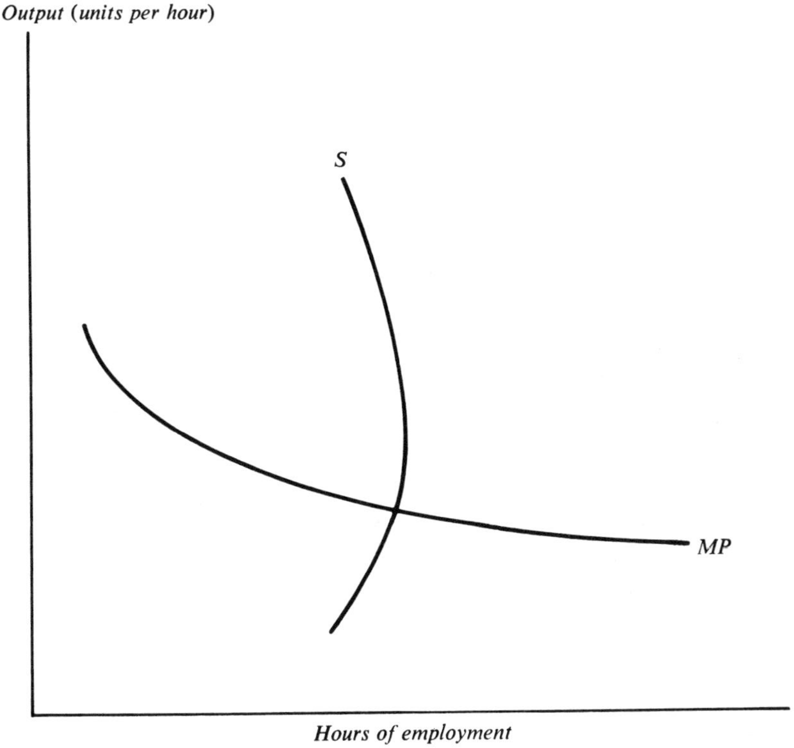

Output (units per hour)

Hours of employment

supply curve of labor may shift, reflecting a change in the labor-leisure preferences of the working-age population, or the demand (marginal product) curve may shift, reflecting a change in technology. Changes in the stock of capital or in the size of the working-age population are ruled out of the short-run analysis as long-run phenomena.

Similarly, supply and demand curves for the commodity determine conditions in the product market. Given perfect competition in that market, the supply curve of output is simply a transformation of the demand curve for labor from a labor input to an output scale. If, for example, the marginal physical product of labor is five units of a good per hour, clearly the real marginal cost of output, MC/W, is one-fifth of an hour of labor. Real marginal cost is therefore the reciprocal of marginal product: $MC/W = 1/MP$. Both demand for labor, D_N, and supply of output, S_G, must be unaffected by equal proportionate changes in wages, W, and prices, P (that is, both are homogeneous of degree zero in W and P) and can be expressed as functions of the ratio between the two—either the real wage or, as Keynes preferred, the price measured in wage units. Thus, $S_G = S_G (W/P)$ and $D_N = D_N (W/P)$.

The demand for a good, D_G, is a more elusive animal. It has a relation to the supply of labor, but the two are not necessarily tied together in the way that the demand for labor and the supply of goods are. To the extent that real wages influence the choice of leisure, they must influence the demand for goods in the opposite direction. Because people who decide to work less are presumably deciding to consume less, consumption and leisure are jointly determined in the individual's optimization. Given the supply of work that is forthcoming and the profit generated by the stock of capital and the amount of labor being applied to it, people translate real income into demand for goods whenever they decide either to invest in or to consume a basic commodity. (Think of it as grain, which can be eaten or used as seed.) The demand for goods can differ from the volume of real income only because people can consume and invest, in sum, either more or less than their incomes. If that were not the case, factor supply and demand for goods would be linked closely in trades for the commodity. For anyone to spend on the commodity more or less than income (to save without investing, dissave without disinvesting, or invest without saving) requires the existence of a "financial market" for loans or securities. That market, in turn, creates a third price—the price of loans or the interest rate—to go along with the price of labor (the wage) and the price of goods.

Then, the demand for goods can shift while the supply of labor remains the same, and such a shift necessarily changes the demand for, or the supply of, loans. Presumably a weakened demand for goods, which implies a larger supply of loans, a weaker demand for loans, or both, means a much lower interest rate on loans. That rate in turn bolsters the demand for goods (investment in the commodity and current consumption), thus equilibrating D_G and S_G. Therefore, although the change in the demand for goods can alter the interest rate, it cannot affect overall output, employment, or the real wage in equilibrium.[1] Those are all basically determined in the labor market. Fluctuations in the demand for goods cannot account for cycles in output.

---

1. This abstracts from the conceivable influence of a lower interest rate in reducing the supply of labor by encouraging people to take leisure now because the return to saving is lower.

In the one-good competitive economy, the IOUs of some well-known economic agents whose promises to pay are viewed as absolutely reliable might circulate as commodity money and might be held, even though they carry a zero interest rate, because of their convenience as a means of exchange. It strains the imagination to try to introduce a money other than a commodity standard into this world. But if the model is to say anything about the price level, it must have a dollar unit and not just a goods unit; and then it must have a supply of money that will obviously influence the dollar price of the good. Once money is held, economic agents can increase their demand for goods by reducing their desired holdings of money (as well as, or instead of, reducing their net supply of loans). That attempted disgorging of money must increase the dollar price of the product. Because the real wage that maintains equilibrium in the labor market is unchanged, the nominal wage rate must rise in parallel with the product price, leaving output and employment unchanged.

Similarly, if an added supply of money is dropped like rain upon the system, people will adjust. In part, they may raise their net supply of loans in the financial market, lowering the interest rate on securities (non-money). That in turn raises D_G, encouraging substitution of the good for money and thus raising the price of the good. In part, they may directly raise their demand for goods as a result of the added money, again raising the price of the good. And again, the dollar wage must rise proportionately (unless the labor-leisure margin is altered). Under a broad class of assumptions, the full equilibrium of all markets, following a one-time change of g percent in the supply of money, involves g percent changes in prices and wages, and no change in the interest rate. That is a quantity-theory world. The validity of that quantity-theory condition determines whether a change in the money supply alters the interest rate. Regardless of whether it holds, a change in the money supply cannot alter output and employment in short-run equilibrium.

The model does not guarantee the existence of an equilibrium, or its stability, for any or all three markets. But it does indicate that, if the equilibrium is stable, changes in technology and in the labor-leisure margin are the only explanations for equilibrium fluctuations in output and employment!

The macroeconomic practitioners who relied on the classical model did not try to spin a cyclical theory of laziness or of innovation. Instead, cycles were attributed to disequilibria. One or more of the three market sectors must fail to do its job of adjusting the price to maintain the balance of supply and demand. Sometimes the interest rate on loans was seen as the source of the problem. More often wages and labor markets were the prime suspects. There lay the sluggishness that made shifts in the demand for goods turn into changes in output and employment. If wages adjusted rapidly enough, there would be no problem. So there were proposals to improve the competitive behavior of labor markets and suggestions for monetary policy to offset fluctuations in aggregate demand and thereby reduce the burden placed on labor markets to accomplish large and prompt adjustments in the money wage. The prescription and the analysis were ad hoc efforts outside the framework of the classical model. They were pragmatic ways to recognize the cyclical baby, while still maintaining the bathwater of a model that had no room for business cycles.

Keynesian Wage Floor

In the *General Theory,* Keynes attempted to alter the fabric of classical microeconomics to fit real-world macroeconomics. The big new element was the assumption of downward inflexibility of wage rates. I would guess that the Keynesian wage floor has been subjected to more Talmudic exegesis than any other passage in the entire literature of economics. At one level, Keynes presented that inflexibility as an empirical generalization, stipulating that the nominal wage was an equilibrium level or a floor level, whichever was larger. The wage floor was taken as an institutional characteristic, which neither had nor needed a full theoretical explanation. In suggesting that workers would accept a decline in the real wage associated with a rise in prices but not with a fall in money wages, Keynes said: "Whether logical or illogical, experience shows that this is how labour in fact behaves."[2]

At another level, Keynes attempted to give the assumption some behavioral justification. He found good, sound reasons to account for a pattern of behavior by workers that seemed irrational—for "money illusion" (as others besides Keynes have called it). He stressed that "reductions of money-wages . . . are seldom or never of an all-round character"; and "any . . . who consent . . . will suffer a *relative* reduction." He concluded: "The struggle about money wages primarily affects the *distribution* of the aggregate real wage between different labour groups."[3]

2. John Maynard Keynes, *The General Theory of Employment, Interest, and Money* (Harcourt, Brace, 1936), p. 9.
3. Ibid., p. 14.

The rationality of concern for relative wages was further amplified by James Tobin. The unsynchronized determination of wages in various firms and industries creates a relative wage problem that inhibits employers from cutting wages. Once declines in wages become extraordinary, any that do occur are perceived adversely by workers and have undesirable effects on morale. Those negative responses of workers are ultimately recognized by employers and give them added reasons to refrain from wage cuts. So the package becomes tied together in an institutional constraint, given a basic predisposition against wage reduction. This is a plausible story, even though it cannot be deduced from a basic utility function!

If it is difficult to understand the origins of the wage-floor assumption, it is easy to see where it leads, and in fact where it led both Keynes and other economists. First, it became part of Keynes' argument against a policy strategy of promoting wage reductions as a cure for the depression. In this part of the brief he stressed that wage cuts simply would not happen; in another part, he argued that they would not necessarily be beneficial even if they could be made to happen.

Second, the wage floor was a remarkable simplifier of theory. Given that assumption, wage inflation can be ruled out of the underemployment world. There, wages remain at the floor level; there is no wage inflation, so there is no need for a theory of wage inflation. Within that range, fluctuations in labor markets are reflected only in *quantities* (employment). Beyond that range, when aggregate demand is high enough to make the demand for labor at the floor wage exceed the supply, quantity variation disappears. As Keynes put it, at full employment, "aggregate employment is inelastic in response to an increase in the effective demand for its output."[4] Thus the supply curve linking nominal wages to employment is a right angle; and right-angle functions are a pleasure for any theorist. The world has an underemployment zone, an inflation zone, and a single point between those zones that represents noninflationary full employment, as the top panel of figure 1-2 indicates.

Third, the wage floor preserved most of the classical microeconomics —for demand in labor markets and for both supply and demand in product markets. By dropping what he described as the "second postulate of the classical theory" (that labor supply is determined by the real wage), Keynes was able to maintain the first: "The wage is equal to the marginal

4. Ibid., p. 26.

Figure 1-2. *Aggregate Supply as a Function of Wages and Prices*

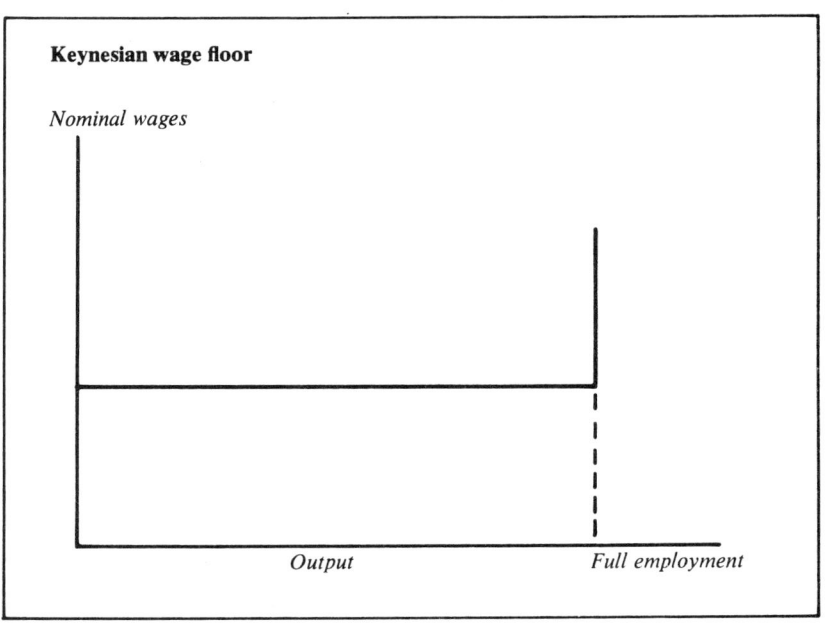

Keynesian wage floor

Nominal wages

Output   *Full employment*

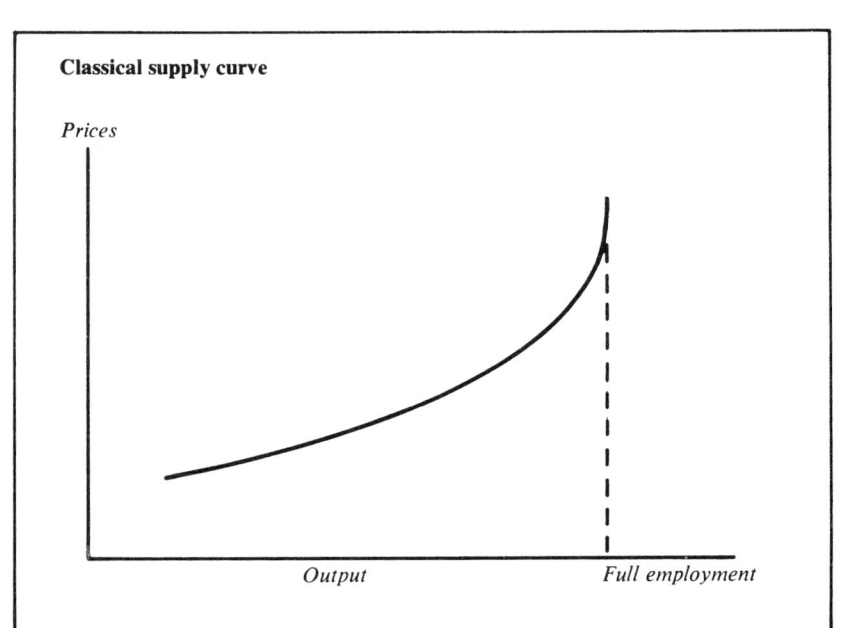

Classical supply curve

Prices

Output   *Full employment*

product of labour."[5] So in product markets the short-run marginal cost could still be equated to price. Keynes had to modify the classical framework because the persistence of underemployment was inconsistent with full microeconomic equilibrium in both product and labor markets. He altered it in the most conservative way possible, amending only one of the four functional relations that underlie labor and product market equilibrium. Only the classical supply curve of labor had to be overhauled.

Wage inflexibility was not Keynes' only explanation of why output and employment remain at levels below full employment. He offered a variety of other explanations—the liquidity trap, the marginal efficiency trap, and an expectations trap (falling prices lowering real aggregate demand through expectations of further declines). In principle, these traps can explain the persistence of output and employment at levels below full employment without self-correcting tendencies. But if they are combined with a fully classical view of labor and product markets, they imply unrelenting downward pressure on wages and prices in the underemployment zone. Only the wage floor can provide the rationale for an "equilibrium" in the wage level, while output and employment remain depressed.

The traps are essential to Keynes' story. Both the liquidity and marginal efficiency traps suggest that monetary policy may have a limited potential (in particular, less than fiscal policy) to bring the economy out of depression. But the traps are fifth wheels in the combined explanation of underemployment persistence and sluggish downward wage-price adjustments. For that dual purpose, the wage floor is central—both necessary and sufficient. Relying on the wage floor (and ignoring the traps), one has a basic explanation for persistent underemployment in slack, recession, or depression. Output and employment fall so much and stay down so long simply because prices do not fall enough when product demand declines. Indeed, prices do not decline enough because of the downward rigidity of wages, but that rigidity should be taken as a fact of economic life, to be neither deplored nor destroyed.

Keynesian-Classical Product Market

In the Keynesian world that retained the classical product market and the classical demand for labor, the wage floor is the only drag on price

5. Ibid., p. 5.

flexibility. Prices must vary cyclically in relation to wages. In the bottom panel of figure 1-2 the aggregate supply curve, scaled in terms of prices rather than wages, is not a right angle. Instead, it rises rather smoothly at an accelerating rate up to the full-employment level of output and then becomes vertical. The continuity of that function follows from the downward sloping marginal product curve—that is, from the theory of diminishing returns of production.[6] At lower rates of utilization of capital, the marginal product is higher; for given money-wage rates, the marginal costs must also be lower, and hence so must prices.

Keynes finessed the issues of price variation and of the shape of the supply-price function by insisting on deflating both output and input by "wage-units." That same device also eliminated the analytical complication (but socially welcome phenomenon) stemming from a rising trend of productivity, which held down unit labor costs relative to wages and therefore provided a margin for increasing wages to be consistent with stability of prices.

It is instructive to consider the shape of the supply-price function for an economy governed by a Cobb-Douglas production function:

$$Q = AK^a N^{1-a},$$

where Q is output; A, a scale factor; K, the stock of capital; N, employment; and a, the elasticity of output with respect to capital. For the short run with the capital stock fixed, production is governed by $Q = A'N^{1-a}$, where $A' = A\bar{K}^a$. A drop in output of 1 percent in such a world is associated with a reduction in marginal costs of $a/(1-a)$ percent. Because a is typically estimated to lie between one-fourth and one-third, each 1 percent drop in output should be associated, given money wages, with a drop in prices between one-third and one-half of 1 percent. Thus prices should fluctuate substantially in a procyclical pattern even with money wage rates held constant.

According to classical production theory, the average product of labor, as well as its marginal product, declines as output increases. Productivity—output per hour worked—must be highest in the slump and lowest in the boom. Furthermore, with the classical demand curve for labor still operative, the real wage rate must equal the marginal product, and hence fluctuate countercyclically. As Keynes put it, "An increase in

6. Because the analysis here is short-run, change in plant scale or entry of new firms is precluded.

employment can only occur to the accompaniment of a decline in the rate of real wages."[7]

Although other forms of the production function might render a different verdict, the Cobb-Douglas form insists that the total real wage bill should move in parallel with output, and labor's share of income remains $(1 - a)$, regardless of the level of employment. The real value of gross profits and aggregate wages moves proportionately throughout the cycle, although net profits can be more volatile cyclically because of depreciation and other fixed costs on capital.

The Model and the Facts

The wage-floor model fails to accord with the facts of the real world in several important ways.

EITHER-OR. The right-angle aggregate supply function in terms of wages is clearly wrong in its prediction that expansion will raise *either* wage rates *or* employment, but not both. Employment gains and money wage increases are not either-or matters in the real world; on the contrary, they tend to go hand in hand. Yet empirically the change in the quantity of employment does account for most of the variation at very low levels of employment, and the change in wage rates accounts for most at extremely high levels. Thus the right angle can be a useful first approximation, subject to refinement by rounding its corners.

The rounded corner can be derived by disaggregating the labor market into various sectors, with imperfect substitutability, each subject to its own wage floor. Then once any sector reaches its full-employment point in a general economic expansion, any further growth in demand that comes its way generates wage increases, while other sectors still respond to the expansion with gains in employment. The proportion of full-employment sectors grows as the aggregate employment level rises, generating a smooth Phillips curve.

NO INFLATIONARY PROCESS. Even if a smooth curve existed, a higher level of employment would appear to generate a one-shot increase in wage rates rather than a continuing process of inflation. Yet the Phillips curve approach, which became a standard component of the post-Keynesian synthesis, slipped a derivative from the Keynesian aggregate supply function and related the rate of change of wages to the level of the

7. Ibid., p. 17.

unemployment rate. Tobin supplied the theoretical underpinning of "perpetual sectoral disequilibrium [and] stochastic macro-equilibrium."[8] He emphasized the continuous nature of disturbances that create new disequilibria in various sectors, even though aggregate demand is stable. The merry-go-round turns, and the wage level is kept off balance. The economy contains some sectors with excess supplies of labor in which wages are not falling, and some with excess demands in which wages are rising. For a given degree of dispersion among sectors, the fraction of those experiencing excess demand will be greater the higher the level of employment. So, not only the wage level but the rate of wage increase can be related to the level of employment. I examine this phenomenon in detail in chapter 6.

NO STAGFLATION. Even with the Phillips curve approach and Tobin's sectoral wage floors, the amended model of the *General Theory* has no room for chronic inflation. The aggregate wage level can advance throughout the cycle, but wage increases in a recession should be confined to those few sectors that nonetheless experience excess demand. The model cannot explain the observed experience of the recession and slack periods of the seventies when wages rose in virtually all sectors. Accounting for that puzzle is a major task of the analysis in chapter 3.

FRICTIONAL UNEMPLOYMENT. Furthermore, the model really has no room for frictional unemployment. While Keynes recognized its existence, his labor market models implied that supply and demand would equate without friction whenever the market-clearing wage exceeded the floor wage. On the other hand, when the wage-floor constraint was operative, the unemployment that resulted was "involuntary" and not frictional. By definition, frictional unemployment requires a departure from the perfect auction, continuously clearing market.

Keynesians, like Keynes himself, have shrugged their shoulders or waved their arms about this defect. Although frictional unemployment is admittedly an important feature of the real world, a model that cannot account for it may be thoroughly adequate to explain cyclical unemployment. Economists analyze many micro phenomena by relying on a perfectly competitive model that rules out any rationale for advertising; similarly, they can analyze many aspects of labor markets with an auction model that rules out frictional unemployment. Just as they drop the paradigm of a perfectly competitive product market when they need to explain

8. James Tobin, "Inflation and Unemployment," *American Economic Review,* vol. 62 (March 1972), p. 11.

advertising, so they must turn to an alternative framework of labor market analysis to explain frictional unemployment.

Productivity, Real Wage, and Share Paradoxes

Of the various empirical shortcomings of the Keynesian wage-floor model, its predictions about productivity, real wages, and factor shares over the cycle are glaringly inaccurate. According to the model, the movement of both productivity and real wages should be countercyclical. Combined with a Cobb-Douglas production function, the model also implies that labor's share of income should be noncyclical. In sharp contrast, empirical research strongly suggests that real wages are essentially noncyclical, productivity procyclical, and labor's share countercyclical.[9]

Keynes' views on the countercyclical movement of real wages were challenged by John Dunlop, Lorie Tarshis, and Richard Ruggles shortly after the publication of the *General Theory*. Keynes responded to such criticism by conceding that he had probably accepted too much of the classical story and insisting that none of the propositions they were contesting were central to the conclusions of his theory. That was true, but the concession left the *General Theory* without a microeconomic underpinning or a macroeconomic distribution theory.

The cyclical behavior of real wages, productivity, and labor's share has been explored in a vast number of econometric studies in the past forty years. It is fair to summarize the consensus as finding no detectable significant cyclical pattern in real wages. Meanwhile, the procyclical pattern of productivity movements has been solidly established in dozens of empirical studies. Relative to trend, labor's share of income is highest in slumps. Its distinct countercyclical pattern is evident to the naked eye in the national accounts time series. It holds for GNP, national income, and private product. That necessarily implies a procyclical pattern for the share of gross property income (as well as that of net profits).

Salvaging the Model

A number of attempts have been made to perform a salvage operation that preserves the spirit of Keynesian theory—as well as the spirit of

9. Labor's share is the real wage (W/P) divided by productivity (Q/N), or NW/QP. Given this linkage, there are only two independent paradoxes from which the third (whichever one chooses) derives.

classical theory subject to the wage-floor modification—while changing the assumptions to eliminate the erroneous predictions about real wages and productivity.

FIXED LABOR. One salvage tactic emphasizes that a portion of labor input is fixed rather than variable. If total labor input has a sizable overhead component (which cannot be used to substitute for variable labor), the average product of total labor can be rising as output expands, even though the marginal product of (variable) labor is declining. In that event, strong expansion creates a bonus in *average* labor productivity by spreading overhead labor. Moreover, the real wage bill for fixed labor becomes a higher fraction of total real income in the slump, which explains the countercyclical movement of labor's overall share.

The assumption of fixed labor cannot, however, alter the implied countercyclical pattern of real wage rates that Keynes posited, at least not for variable labor. The real wage of overhead labor can be noncyclical; but that of variable labor must be governed by a marginal product that falls with rising output.

In any case, the concept of fixity for the labor factor is tricky. For capital goods, fixity has obvious sources: the absence of perfect markets for the resale of used plant or equipment and substantial sunk costs from the installation of capital facilities. But because workers are dismissed rather than resold and are not physically bolted down, those explanations cannot apply with equal force to labor. Indeed, some phenomena that are casually attributed to overhead labor are more accurately viewed as the results of nonclassical properties in the production function. For example, labor may be needed to maintain overhead capital: a worker may be needed merely to lubricate an idle machine. In that case, the employment of such a worker is necessary in a slump, although the reason he is needed stems not from any fixity in the labor factor, but rather from a production function in which capital and labor are complementary (and not substitutive) in the short run. Another reason for nonvariable labor stems from indivisibilities in specialized assignments or hierarchical organizations: a firm has one chief counsel in prosperity or recession; if it carves up its sales territories in a particular way, it may have one salesperson covering New Jersey throughout the cycle. But in these cases the overheads stem from the costs of revising the hierarchy or the sales territories rather than from sunk costs of labor input.

The kind of labor fixity most analogous to the ownership of a machine with an imperfect resale market is associated with a contractual obligation of the firm to keep a worker employed for some stated period. Such tenure arrangements are, in fact, rare for nonprofessional workers; moreover, they are inconsistent with the competitive view of the labor market taken by this model. So are collective bargaining contracts, which produce fixity of wage rates although not of employment. A number of significant costs of varying employment will have an important role in the story of labor markets developed in chapters 2 and 3, but they rarely create overheads analogous to those stemming from explicit tenure contracts.

PRODUCT MONOPOLY. The introduction of monopoly elements in product markets is another salvage tactic. It helps because, under conditions of monopoly, firms can be operating when their marginal costs are constant or declining. Hence the marginal physical product of labor need not be declining, even though its marginal revenue product must be falling with rising output to permit competitive equilibrium in the labor market. For a profit-maximizing monopolist, the ratio of price to marginal cost must be equal to $[1 + 1/(e - 1)]$, where e is the absolute value of the price elasticity of demand for the product. Because marginal cost is the wage divided by marginal product, it follows that P/W must equal $[1 + 1/(e - 1)]$ divided by the marginal product, and W/P must equal the marginal product multiplied by $(1 - 1/e)$.

If the marginal product of labor is constant rather than falling as output expands, and if e is also constant, W/P will remain constant. The real-wage paradox is thus resolved. If, in addition, the average product of labor rises as output expands, the labor-share paradox is also resolved.

This is not the only way, however, in which average productivity can be procyclical. Procyclical productivity can also emerge from the monopoly model if marginal costs decline with rising output. Suppose a monopolist firm is producing in the range of output in which marginal costs are falling, while it hires labor at the going wage in a competitive labor market. An economy dominated by such monopolist firms will display procyclical marginal productivity and also, as the real world does, procyclical average productivity. But if e remains constant over the cycle, then W/P, real wages, must vary procyclically, rising during the expansion as marginal productivity increases. For W/P to remain constant over the cycle, the degree of monopoly $(1/e)$ must rise in the expansion enough to offset the rise in marginal product. Similarly, the degree of monopoly must fall in an offsetting fashion during the slump. The elasticity of demand must be lowest in the boom and highest in the slump. So the degree of monopoly must be sufficiently procyclical to offset the procyclical variation of marginal product. But that is an incredible explanation; it requires synchronous offsetting movements of two variables that have very different underlying determinants—the technologically determined marginal physical product of labor and the market-determined effective degree of monopoly.

SUMMARY OF INGREDIENTS. With a sufficient display of ingenuity, a "quasi-Keynesian" model can be concocted that is consistent with the cyclical facts on productivity, real wages, and factor shares of the factors of production. The least unpalatable recipe calls for the following ingredients: the wage floor, monopoly (or monopolistic competition) with horizontal marginal cost curves, constant elasticity of demand (effective degree of monopoly) over the business cycle, and some overhead labor.

These analytical pyrotechnics really illustrate that anything goes under conditions of monopoly. In the absence of a priori information constraining the shape of cost curves or the pattern of cyclical fluctuation in the effective degree of monopoly, any observed pattern of productivity, prices, and wages can be consistent with short-run profit maximization by the monopolist.

Product Market Disequilibria

The resulting analytical concoction remains classical only in the sense that it preserves continuous short-run profit maximization—and rules out product-market disequilibria. But why should one cling to the maintained hypothesis that product markets are always in equilibrium in the short run? Perpetuating the hypothesis preserves the principle of conservatism about, and respect for, the classical model that has served economists so well for so long in so many dimensions. But it is difficult to find any other virtue. In particular, empirical evidence pulls the analyst in the opposite direction. Some situations of firms in a slump seem as "involuntary" as the unemployment of workers. The hallmark of U.S. recessions since the Second World War has been the liquidation of inventories, and the need for such inventory adjustments can arise only from a previous disequilibrium in the product market.

The model of a competitive product market can readily be tailored to permit disequilibria. Suppose that product prices are announced by sellers at the beginning of each market period and are not altered during that period. Similarly, in the labor market, wages are announced by firms at the beginning of the market period and also remain fixed for that interval. At the beginning of this period, firms put some workers on their payrolls and set a production schedule designed to meet anticipated product demand; but they can change their quantities of output and employment during the course of the period in light of any surprises about product demand.

Now suppose that, in some particular period, firms experience unexpected declines in the demand for their products, and these disappointing sales tend to produce an undesired growth of inventories. Hence they are encouraged to cut back their outputs. Similarly, they trim employment because they cannot sell the output of marginal labor. Although the productivity of labor is as high as ever and prices have not gone down, the marginal revenue product of labor is, to use Robert Clower's words, no longer the "effective" (but merely the "notional") demand for labor.[10]

This type of model provides added insight into the workings of the wage floor. Even with the weak demand in product markets, employers would be willing to maintain employment if they could make barter deals to pay their workers their marginal physical product (a deal that is easy to imagine in a one-commodity world). These employers can afford to pay the previously established wage in physical units; they cannot afford to pay it in dollars. The problem is not that the real wage is too high; it is that the demand for output is too low.

The disequilibrium in product markets is attributable to downward inflexibility of *prices*. At least temporarily, there is a price floor, analogous to Keynes' wage floor, with respect to downward shifts of demand. Both these floors can be viewed as sources of lagged disequilibrium responses in a dynamic model rather than as features of a static equilibrium. In this view, depressed employment occurs through a movement to a position off the marginal product curve for labor, rather than a movement along the curve. Hence the real-wage and factor-share paradoxes are resolved; because of the price floor, a noncyclical real wage can emerge even with diminishing returns to labor. But the productivity

10. Robert Clower, "The Keynesian Counterrevolution: A Theoretical Appraisal," in F. H. Hahn and F. P. R. Brechling, eds., *The Theory of Interest Rates* (London: Macmillan, 1965), pp. 118–20.

paradox is not resolved because employment and production are viewed as readily adjustable despite the fixity of prices and wages.

The "Fixprice" World

The "fixprice" model of John Hicks generalizes the "price floor" and carries it to the logical extreme where price and wage variations in both directions are ignored. The fixprice method is not intended to provide an explanation of wage-price paradoxes, but rather to establish an analytical simplification to finesse them. It begins with a short-run justification for viewing prices and wages as given. In a world of price makers, rather than auctioneers and price takers, it takes time and resources to change prices and even to reconsider them. At least for some interval of time and for some range of variation in demand, it is reasonable to take prices as fixed and to focus solely on quantity variations.

In practice, the period to which fixprice has been applied goes far beyond that justification. Many familiar Keynesian tools—such as multiplier analysis—essentially assumed fixed prices as well as wage floors. Although most followers of Keynes did not adopt his proposal for wage-unit deflation, they generally ignored the cyclical variations in prices that were implied by the Keynesian model, as in the bottom panel of figure 1-2, even when wages were constant. So they adopted the either-or aggregate supply function for prices as well as wages.

Obviously it is safe to ignore movements in prices and wages (or, more accurately, in prices and unit labor costs) if they are tiny. But it also is reasonably safe to ignore nontrivial movements as long as they can be considered independent of aggregate demand. An upward trend of prices can be significantly different from zero inflation, and yet be of no major analytical concern if it is essentially exogenous or predetermined. That was basically the justification for the fixprice method of macro analysis in a period such as 1958–65. The prevailing inflation rate of roughly 1½ percent was an upward trend visible to the naked eye, but its steepness was not seriously altered by the recession in 1960 or by the strong expansion in 1964.

In fact, the boundaries of the territory for the fixprice method are wider than that. Even when aggregate demand does influence prices, inflation may be safely ignored provided that it is not a major social concern and that it does not have major feedbacks on real economic activity. The period from 1933 to World War II exemplified such a situation. At that time, price movements were clearly responsive to the rate of change (although not the level) of real economic activity. Between 1933 and 1937 the price level rose on average about 3 percent a year; then, with renewed recession, it fell in 1938–39 by a few percentage points. But who cared? Certainly the concern about inflation was not the operative constraint on stimulative fiscal and monetary policies. Inflation was not curbing the recovery of real activity through monetary effects. Interest rates on short-term government securities remained a mere fraction of 1 percent, and those on corporate bonds fell throughout the expansion.

The fixprice method was, indeed, limited to peacetime use. It was shelved during the Second World War and again in the Korean War. But the analytical approach came back because serious inflation disappeared. Inflation even vanished before the Korean War ended; with an unemployment rate of 3 percent and inflation of 2 percent, the experience of 1952 remains one of the most remarkable and least well-explained phenomena in American economic history.

In short, the fixprice method served economists reasonably well in peacetime for more than a generation. The price level fluctuated little or mattered little, and multiplier-accelerator analysis provided reasonable answers. Macroeconomists used a kit of tools that traced the effects of fluctuations in demand on quantities, largely ignoring the behavior of prices. Macroeconomics moved a world apart from microeconomics, which focused on price variations as crucial.

The macroeconomic practice emphasized particularly the fixity or exogeneity of price and wage levels for the short run. That turned the standard micro doctrine on its head. As Hicks has suggested to me in private correspondence, the standard microeconomic view that price variations play the largest role in the short run and quantity variation the largest role in the long run can be traced back to Alfred Marshall's threefold division of time intervals into a market period, short run, and long run. As a prototype for the market period, economists used the sale of fresh fish, where producers would sell the fixed amount that they had on hand for whatever price it would fetch. Hicks reports that Marshall's lecture notes incorporated another possibility, never written up in *Principles,* which allowed for "customary pricing." In that variant, based on price making rather than price taking, the market period had a completely horizontal—rather than completely vertical—supply curve. Had Marshall decided differently, the fixprice method might have had its place in microeconomics.

Plan of the Book

In fact, for both product and labor markets, models that focus on price takers and auctioneers and that assume continuous clearing of the market generate inaccurate microeconomics as well as misleading macroeconomics. Recent experience makes it clear that price and wage variations must be recognized—and not ignored as they are by the fixprice method; but they must be analyzed along with quantity variation in a world of price making and wage making and of searching and shopping. This challenge has been accepted by the builders of search models for the labor market.

I discuss and appraise their product in chapter 2. There I develop a "toll" model that encompasses the long-term career relationships between firms and workers. I then explore in more detail in chapter 3 the arrangements governing wages and employment in the labor market. In chapter 4, I turn to product markets and distinguish a small category of auction markets that fits the classical model from a broad class of markets that do not. In the latter, prices and quantities are influenced by customer relationships that have some of the same elements as career employment relationships and by a shopping process that is analogous to search in the labor market. In chapter 5, I examine asset markets, with emphasis on the limitations of the auction paradigm of classical theory for various types of assets and debts. In chapter 6, I put the labor and product markets together and show how they operate to create inflation inertia. In chapters 7 and 8, I discuss the social costs of inflation and the policy implications of the analysis, assess the scope of discretionary fiscal and monetary policy in affecting both prices and quantities, and stress the significance of other public policies that influence costs and prices.

Bibliographical Notes

Among the many post-Keynesian expositions of the Keynesian model and its relation to the classical heritage are the following: Alvin H. Hansen, *A Guide to Keynes,* Economic Handbook Series (McGraw-Hill, 1953); Gardner Ackley, *Macroeconomics: Theory and Policy* (Macmillan, 1978), especially chaps. 4, 5, 10, 11, 12; Lawrence R. Klein, *The Keynesian Revolution* (Macmillan, 1947); James Tobin, "Money Wage

Rates and Employment," in Seymour E. Harris, ed., *The New Economics: Keynes' Influence on Theory and Public Policy* (Knopf, 1947), pp. 572–87; and James Tobin, "Keynesian Models of Recession and Depression," *American Economic Review,* vol. 65 (May 1975, *Papers and Proceedings, 1974*), pp. 195–202.

An early probing discussion of real wages and factor shares over the cycle can be found in Michal Kalecki, *Essays in the Theory of Economic Fluctuations* (London: Allen and Unwin, 1939), chaps. 1 and 3. A cyclical pattern in the degree of monopoly is posited by R. F. Harrod, *The Trade Cycle* (Oxford: Clarendon, 1936), pp. 17–22, 75–88; and sharply questioned by Joan Robinson in her review of that book in *Economic Journal,* vol. 46 (December 1936), pp. 691–93. A number of aspects of the fixity of labor are perceptively analyzed by Walter Y. Oi, "Labor as a Quasi-Fixed Factor," *Journal of Political Economy,* vol. 70 (December 1962), pp. 538–55.

Criticisms of countercyclical real wages in Keynes' *General Theory* appear in John T. Dunlop, "The Movement of Real and Money Wage Rates," *Economic Journal,* vol. 48 (September 1938), pp. 413–34; Lorie Tarshis, "Changes in Real and Money Wages," *Economic Journal,* vol. 49 (March 1939), pp. 150–54; and Richard Ruggles, "The Relative Movements of Real and Money Wage Rates," *Quarterly Journal of Economics,* vol. 55 (November 1940), pp. 130–49. For his reply, see J. M. Keynes, "Relative Movements of Real Wages and Output," *Economic Journal,* vol. 49 (March 1939), pp. 34–51.

The modern empirical research on the cyclical behavior of real wages includes Ronald G. Bodkin, "Real Wages and Cyclical Variations in Employment: A Re-Examination of the Evidence," *Canadian Journal of Economics,* vol. 2 (August 1969), pp. 353–74; and Edwin Kuh, "Unemployment, Production Functions, and Effective Demand," *Journal of Political Economy,* vol. 74 (June 1966), pp. 238–49. Studies that focus on the markup of prices over labor costs include William D. Nordhaus, "Recent Developments in Price Dynamics," in Otto Eckstein, ed., *The Econometrics of Price Determination,* a conference sponsored by the Board of Governors of the Federal Reserve System and Social Science Research Center (The Board, 1972), pp. 34–43; Otto Eckstein, "A Theory of the Wage-Price Process in Modern Industry," *Review of Economic Studies,* vol. 31 (October 1964), pp. 269–71; and Robert J. Gordon, "The Impact of Aggregate Demand on Prices," *Brookings Papers on Economic Activity, 3:1975,* pp. 613–62.

The productivity paradox is discussed and the voluminous literature in this area is well summarized in Ray C. Fair, *The Short-Run Demand for Workers and Hours,* Contributions to Economic Analysis, 59 (Amsterdam: North-Holland, 1969). An important contribution to that literature is Frank Brechling and Peter O'Brien, "Short-Run Employment Functions in Manufacturing Industries: An International Comparison," *Review of Economics and Statistics,* vol. 49 (August 1967), pp. 277–87.

A thoroughgoing theoretical formulation and exposition of Keynes in terms of product and labor market disequilibria is developed by Axel Leijonhufvud, *On Keynesian Economics and the Economics of Keynes: A Study in Monetary Theory* (Oxford University Press, 1968), chap. 2. An article by Robert Clower also contributes to that interpretation; see "The Keynesian Counterrevolution: A Theoretical Appraisal," in F. H. Hahn and F. P. R. Brechling, eds., *The Theory of Interest Rates* (London: Macmillan, 1965), pp. 103–25. Robert J. Barro and Herschel I. Grossman, in their "A General Disequilibrium Model of Income and Employment," *American Economic Review,* vol. 61 (March 1971), pp. 82–93, explicitly note (on p. 87) that their "result differs from the conventional view that employment and real wages must be inversely related."

The development of the fixprice method appears in John Hicks, *Capital and Growth* (Oxford University Press, 1965), pp. 76–83.

II

The Labor Market

IN CHAPTER 1 it was shown that an analytical framework that assumes the continuous clearing of labor markets tends to rule out the existence of unemployment and thus of depressed output. The Keynesian wage floor is an ingenious device that permits a type of excess supply to exist without creating downward pressure on the wage. The model can have it both ways: equilibrium in one sense and disequilibrium in another. Unemployment emerges, but only for the quasi-disequilibrium world of less than full employment. More recently, a variety of "search models" has been developed by economists in order to supply a rationale for some unemployment to persist at all times and why it varies cyclically in ways that do not depend on a wage floor. These models eliminate the auctioneer who clears the neoclassical labor market; hence, unsatisfied labor supplies (and demands) become the usual state of affairs. In this chapter I argue that the search paradigm goes only one step further toward explaining the key cyclical characteristics of employment and wages, and I propose a more promising analytical route. The search model is the place to start this search.

Simple Search Model

I begin by inspecting in detail the assumptions and implications of a simple search model to see just how it changes the unemployment story. I offer a bare-bones model that represents my own way of capturing the spirit of the recent literature. In this model, the labor market has no auctioneer or organized exchange; otherwise, it has all the characteristics necessary to produce a neoclassical competitive equilibrium: a large number of unorganized workers and of relatively small firms that act independently; labor of homogeneous quality—any worker will have the same productivity (which is known costlessly by the employer) and will be given the same tools and the same task; and, similarly, homogeneity of jobs in all nonpecuniary respects, like pleasantness and social status.[1]

With no auctioneer to process bids, the transactions must be arranged bilaterally between buyer and seller. Suppose that the arrangements take the following form: prospective workers apply for jobs to individual firms; the firm, in turn, gives the applicant a wage offer, which may be zero (that is, no offer at all) or any positive number; the applicant must decide whether to accept it; the acceptance of an offer is promptly followed by employment; and following the rejection of an offer, the applicant either continues the search by trying another firm or else drops out of the job market.

To put the model into a specific time context, I assume that applicants can sample one firm each per "day" and that they must sacrifice wages or leisure for that day. At this point, I ignore any other transactions or search costs; and, in particular, assume that the firms incur no cost of hiring—an assumption with important implications, as subsequent sections will make clear. Finally, I assume that searchers must sample firms randomly; they have no clues about which firms are making good offers. But they do have information that allows them to know (or to think they know) the distribution of wage offers for the entire labor market. In effect, they know the cards in the deck but recognize that it has been thoroughly shuffled.

Within this framework, consider an applicant who is offered a job starting tomorrow at some specified wage. The applicant must now decide whether to accept or reject the offer. Accepting it means starting to work tomorrow. Rejecting it means applying for work elsewhere tomorrow or, in principle, dropping out of the labor force. But, because of the assumption that the applicant knew the distribution of job offers, the dropout option can be eliminated, assuming that the applicant's labor-leisure tastes are unchanged. If the "lottery" presented by the distribution of wage offers made it worthwhile for a particular searcher to apply for a job today, it will also be worthwhile to apply for work tomorrow.

Thus the applicant will try again if the present offer is disappointing, and hence the direct cost of rejecting the offer in hand is the next day's wage. The benefit of rejecting that offer is the increase in wage income for the future that might be conferred by obtaining a better offer the next

1. Workers and jobs could be taken as costlessly gradable, rather than homogeneous, without changing any important results. But in that case, the analysis would have to consider multiple submarkets or a "representative" submarket.

Figure 2-1. *Hypothetical Distribution of Wage Offers*

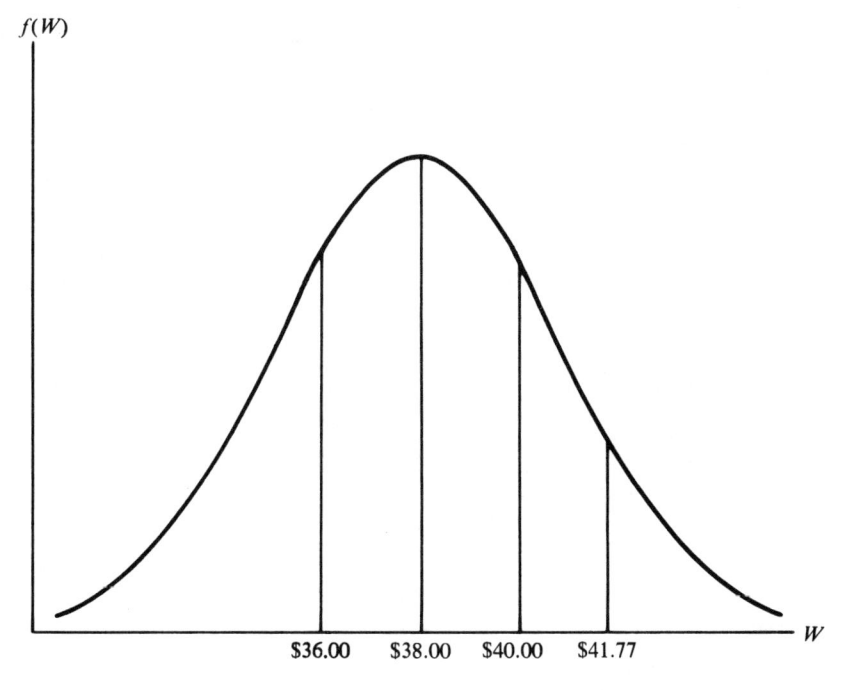

$f(W)$

$36.00 $38.00 $40.00 $41.77

W

day. (It is reasonable to suppose that the applicant has no inherent preference between spending a day searching or working.) Knowing the distribution of wage offers in general, the applicant will know in particular the probability that the next day's application will yield a better offer than the one in hand. It will be possible then to calculate the expected margin of wages by which better offers will surpass the offer in hand.

The "Acceptance Wage"

Suppose the wage-offer distribution is that shown in figure 2-1; and suppose that an applicant is weighing a current offer, W, of $40 a day. That offer is well above the average of that normal distribution. But it still leaves a probability, π, of 0.25 that the next application will elicit a better offer; one-fourth of the distribution has $W > $40. Among all the superior job offers with $W > $40, the average is $41.77—an extra daily wage, X, of $1.77.

In addition to those considerations, the applicant deciding whether to accept or reject the $40 offer must know how many days' worth of value to attribute to the extra wages from any superior job. That depends, in turn, on two predictions: how long any particular wage premium (or deficiency) of a particular job will last, and how long the job itself will last before the applicant or the employer terminates it. In effect, the searcher must attach a horizon, h, of some number of days to any wage premium.[2] In the example, because one-fourth of all jobs pay more than $40 and the mean wage of those superior offers is $41.77, the expected value of the next day's search (one more offer) is $(0.25)($1.77)(h)$. The searcher must ask whether it is more profitable to spend the next day in searching or in working for $40. If $h = 100$, search has an expected value of $44.25 and beats work; if $h = 50$, work beats search. The dividing line is at $h = 90.4$; above that, it is worthwhile to reject the $40 offer in order to search the next day.

In general, for every wage offer there is a probability, π, that it will be exceeded on the next day; an extra wage premium associated with the average of superior offers, X; and a horizon, h, associated with that wage premium. Whenever $W < \pi X h$, the offer will be rejected. Whenever $W > \pi X h$, it will be accepted. The level at which $W = \pi X h$ is the acceptance wage, W^*, the minimum offer that the applicant will find acceptable.

Clearly, below-average wages will be accepted by searchers who have short horizons, but only by them. For example, a wage offer of $36 is below three-quarters of all elements in the distribution of figure 2-1 and $\pi = 0.75$. The average wage for all offers exceeding $36 is $39.26, so $X = \$3.26$. The $36 offer will be acceptable only to applicants with horizons shorter than 14.7 days. Searchers who expect wage differentials and jobs to be long lasting will be especially selective in choosing a job. They will set higher acceptance wages and be willing to search longer. The expected length of search—or duration of a spell of unemployment— will be greater the higher the acceptance wage of the applicant. In fact, it will simply be the reciprocal of the value of π associated with W^*. In the case of $W^* = \$40$ where $\pi = 0.25$, the average spell will be four days—the searcher should, on average, require four drawings to obtain an offer in the top quarter of the distribution.

In this world, the workers with jobs also know the distribution of wage

2. A few other simplifying assumptions should be made explicit: the time-horizon is sufficiently short that the discounting of future income payments can be ignored; searchers do not need to worry about running out of money to sustain their search activity (or otherwise experiencing increasingly adverse income effects along the way); and they maximize expected values, implying no risk aversion.

offers. By assumption, they can apply for offers elsewhere only by sacrificing a day's wage from their present jobs. In fact, because they know the distribution, they can decide once and for all whether it is worth searching. If their acceptance wages as searchers exceeded their present wages, it is worth quitting. There is no reason for a job attachment. Indeed, the "quit-or-stick" decision of the employed worker on a given job is no different from the reject-or-accept decision for that job by a searcher with the same horizon. Turning down a new job and quitting an old job have exactly the same costs of searching elsewhere in the labor market and the same opportunities for improving on the current wage offer. Indeed, it is a hallmark of the simple search model that workers have no reasons for job attachments that would make them behave any differently from searchers obtaining the same wage offers. As shown below, the assumptions needed to fulfill that requirement are extremely restrictive and implausible.

Wage Offers by Firms

Consider the demand side of the story. How do firms decide on their wage offers? They recognize that their supply of labor consists of those current employees who continue to offer their services and of new applicants who accept wage offers. The symmetry of the quit-or-stick decision and the reject-or-accept decision suggests that the acceptance rate of applicants and the "nonquit" or stick rate of current employees can be taken as the same fraction, α. The daily flow of applicants to the firm can be regarded as exogenously determined; some fraction of the total pool of unemployed in the community samples that firm's offer on any given day.[3] The value of α will be a rising function of the wage rate set by the firm, given the wages paid by other firms. Today's supply of labor to the firm, N_1, is equal to α multiplied by the sum of yesterday's employees, N_0, plus today's flow of new applicants, A_1:

$$N_1 = \alpha(N_0 + A_1).$$

Because N_1 is proportional to α and α is a rising function of W, N_1 must be a rising function of W. At some wage rate and its corresponding α, the

3. In principle, one must suppose that searchers have some clues on the relative size of firms so that more applicants show up at large factories than at tiny grocery stores. But such niceties need not detain us, given the assumption that all firms are relatively small.

Figure 2-2. *Profit-Maximizing Employment Level of a Firm Faced with an Upward-Sloping Supply Curve*

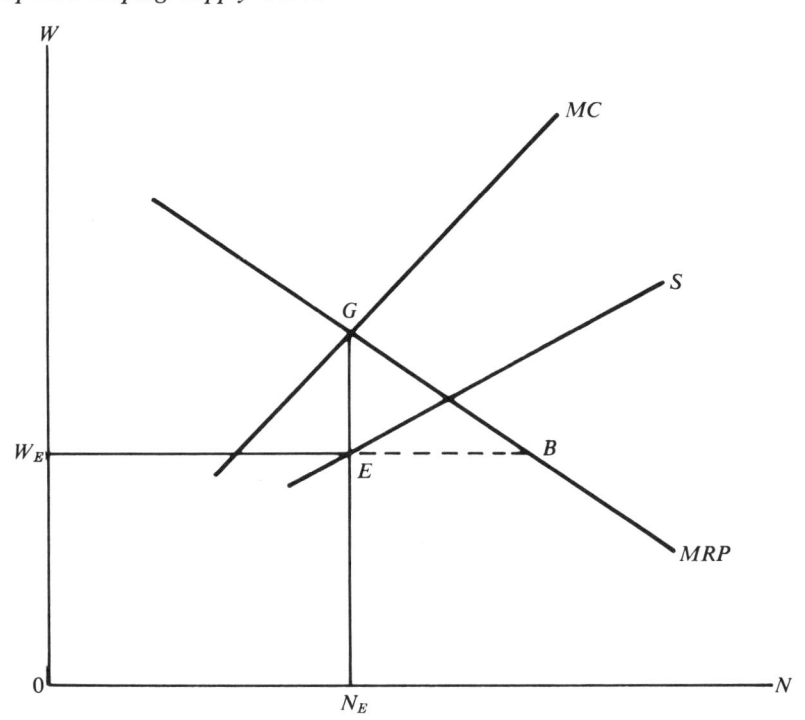

acceptances by new applicants exactly match the quits of current employees, making $N_1 = N_0$. At any higher wage, $N_1 > N_0$, indicating that labor supplied to the firm increases over time, and at a lower wage it contracts.

A hypothetical relation between the labor supply and the wage rate is illustrated in figure 2-2. The slope of the supply curve is the change in W that is required to bring about a unit change in the work force in one day. The daily elasticity, e, of that labor supply is higher the flatter the curve—it is the reciprocal of the slope multiplied by W/N.

As in the neoclassical work, the firm optimizes by equating the marginal cost of an extra worker with the marginal revenue product of that worker. Because the supply curve of labor is upward sloping, the marginal cost of labor is the wage multiplied by $1 + 1/e$. In a competitive auction market, e would be infinite, and the marginal cost of labor would be equal to the wage and constant. In the search market, there will be a determinate optimum even if the marginal revenue product of labor does not decline because the marginal cost of labor rises.[4]

In figure 2-2 the marginal cost curve of labor is necessarily positively sloped, as implied by the supply curve; the marginal revenue product curve is drawn sloping downward, but it could be horizontal or even positively sloped (so long as it is less positively sloped than *MC*). The *MC* and *MRP* lines cross at point *G*, leading to an optimum wage and employment back on the supply curve at point *E*.

The firm sets the wage on the basis of its expectations about the number of quits and willing applicants. Thus far I have assumed that the firm really knows its supply curve, but some aspects of surprises are worth noting. Suppose that, after posting its wage for a particular day, it elicits more willing applicants (or fewer quits) than it expected. It will then be profitable to hire all the applicants whose marginal revenue product exceeds the wage. It will be willing to move to point *B* in the figure if the supply of applicants turns out to be surprisingly large. If the firm expected that large number of applicants, it would have set a lower wage; and presumably it will adjust the wage downward in the future. But just as a monopolist happily fills orders that were not expected, the employer who faces a positively sloped supply curve of labor gratefully hires unanticipated applicants. The firm has "latent vacancies" at the going wage. Hence the model implies that firms will be hiring at their posted wage virtually all the time. Only if there were a huge surprise, with applicants pushing beyond point *B* in the figure, would the firm stop hiring all comers. This implication of the model supports the kind of offer distribution drawn in figure 2-1, which excluded wage offers of zero. In short, this world would not have no-help-wanted signs, even if the possibility of moderate surprises in supply is incorporated.

Implications of the Model

When the demand and supply sides are pulled together, the model successfully accounts for unemployment as a normal phenomenon. The substitution of search for market-clearing accomplishes that objective.

4. For simplicity, I assume that the firm is certain about the supply curve of labor and can treat applications and acceptances as nonstochastic. If either uncertainty about the distribution or the stochastic nature of searchers' decisions must be considered, complications arise.

By assumption, information about specific wage offers is acquired only by search, and search takes time. Information costs maintain some level of unsatisfied supplies; those who keep searching will experience what can be described as "frictional" unemployment.

A second contrast between simple search and auction worlds is that the search world must violate the "law of one wage" that necessarily rules an auction world. The maintenance of frictional unemployment depends on a spread in the distribution of wage offers, whereby equally qualified workers receive different rates of pay in equally pleasant jobs. Otherwise, search is unnecessary, and unemployment (or at least any spell lasting longer than one day) vanishes.

Third, monopsonistic elements must enter into the search labor market as surely as they stay out of the competitive auction market. Even with atomistic firms, employers in the search world face a rising supply curve of labor in the short run; they cannot have all the workers they might want at a particular wage. This monopsony has the same character as the monopoly that Kenneth Arrow attributed to a competitive market that is out of equilibrium.[5]

A fourth feature of the search world is that its adjustments are necessarily dynamic. The wage rate of a firm does not determine its *level* of employment, but rather its incremental flows through time. With higher wages, firms attract an increased rate of inflow of workers rather than a one-time increment of labor. Similarly, if they lower their wages, they will suffer gradual attrition, rather than a one-time loss.

The cost of obtaining information by search influences the significance and quantitative importance of these distinguishing features of the search market. The more readily information is collected, the less the auctioneer is missed. The search market approaches the neoclassical auction market as the cost of search approaches zero. Consider an alternative set of assumptions that imply a much lower cost of search: for example, workers can apply to two firms (rather than one) in a day; applications are guided toward high-wage firms by specific low-cost information from help-wanted ads, employment services, or hearsay; and some opportunities arise for applicants to shop the labor market without actually losing

5. See Kenneth J. Arrow, "Toward a Theory of Price Adjustment," in Moses Abramovitz and others, *The Allocation of Economic Resources: Essays in Honor of Bernard Francis Haley,* Stanford Studies in History, Economics, and Political Science, 12 (Stanford University Press, 1959), pp. 45–50.

a day's pay.[6] In general, for a given distribution of wage offers, workers would split the benefits of more favorable conditions for search in two directions: by setting higher acceptance wages and by reducing time spent unemployed. As a specific example of this, consider the worker with the 90.4-day horizon who is facing the distribution of figure 2-1. That worker has an acceptance wage of $40 and an average spell of unemployment of four days, given the opportunity to obtain one wage offer per day. If, instead, such a worker can obtain two wage offers a day, the cost of the next drawing is only half a day's pay. Then it turns out that the acceptance wage is $41.09; at that wage, $\pi = 0.149$, implying that 6.7 job offers must be obtained per spell of unemployment and 3.4 days must be spent in that spell. The acceptance wage exceeds the earlier $40, and the average spell of unemployment falls well below four days.

While it is instructive to consider the impact of a set of new rules for search on wages and unemployment duration for a *given* distribution of wage offers, the distribution will in fact tend to change in the face of these new rules. As a result of the lower cost of search to the employee, firms will encounter a more elastic supply of labor. Those paying at the top of the distribution will get more acceptances per day, and those paying below-average wages will experience a reduced supply of employees. The same types of reductions in search costs that permit workers to be more selective in choosing jobs also lead employers to shade their wage offers closer to the average of the distribution. Hence the dispersion of the wage distribution will be narrower when the costs of search are lower. That, in turn, implies a smaller gap in behavior between the search world and the auction world. As the dispersion of wage offers approaches zero, the search world approaches the auction world.

The gap between the search and the auction world also depends on the stability of the labor demand of individual firms over time. Some wage differentials might be maintained even if the marginal revenue product function for every firm remained constant indefinitely. Some firms might

6. The entire logic of the search models rests on the assumption that on-the-job searching is much less efficient than searching while jobless. Otherwise, people would take the first job offer and keep looking for a better one. Yet there is neither compelling factual evidence of that differential efficiency, nor obviously persuasive reasons why it should prevail. Lloyd Reynolds has reported that some employers would not accept applications from workers who had jobs elsewhere; he conjectured that such a practice might reflect a "gentlemen's agreement" against labor piracy. See Lloyd G. Reynolds, *The Structure of Labor Markets: Wages and Labor Mobility in Theory and Practice* (Harper, 1951), pp. 51–52.

adopt personnel policies of paying low wages, accepting small work forces of people with particularly short horizons. Others might develop a combined strategy of personnel and product marketing associated with high wages, high acceptance rates, and low turnover of employees. However, if the marginal revenue product functions of firms never shifted, long-run wage differentials and consequently both wage-offer dispersion and the volume of frictional unemployment would be small. To the extent that changes in technology and in the demand for output affect various firms differently and shift marginal revenue product curves differentially, they will increase the dispersion of wage offers. Firms experiencing upward shifts in marginal revenue product will find it worthwhile to raise wages in order to expand employment over time, and those with the opposite experience will hold wages down and aim for attrition of their work forces. The increased dispersion of wage offers brought about by such relative shifts makes search more valuable and increases the level of frictional unemployment. If these shifts raise employment demands for some firms and lower them by an equal aggregate amount for others, they will be consistent with constancy in the aggregate demand for labor; thus they can generate the "stochastic macro-equilibrium" that Tobin described. Within such a macro equilibrium, the extent of dispersion depends on how much the composition of labor demands typically shifts from day to day and week to week. The more unstable it is, the more workers and firms need the costly information obtainable only through search, and the more the auctioneer's services are missed.

Responses to Shifts

Because the optimum wage and employment for a firm depend on the marginal revenue product curve and the labor supply curve, shifts in those curves will generally change the firm's decisions. From the vantage point of a single firm, a rise in the demand for its output that raises the marginal revenue product of labor in the relevant range leads it to offer a higher wage and to increase employment. Figure 2-3 shows how such a shift (from MRP to MRP') leads to a change in the firm's position from E to E'. Alternatively, with MRP unchanged, a reduction in the supply of labor to the firm (from S to S''), which might result from increases in wages paid by other firms, would lead it to raise wages and lower employment, shifting from E to E''.

Suppose, however, that all firms experienced stronger product de-

Figure 2-3. *Optimizing Adjustments by a Firm to a Shift in Product Demand or Labor Supply*

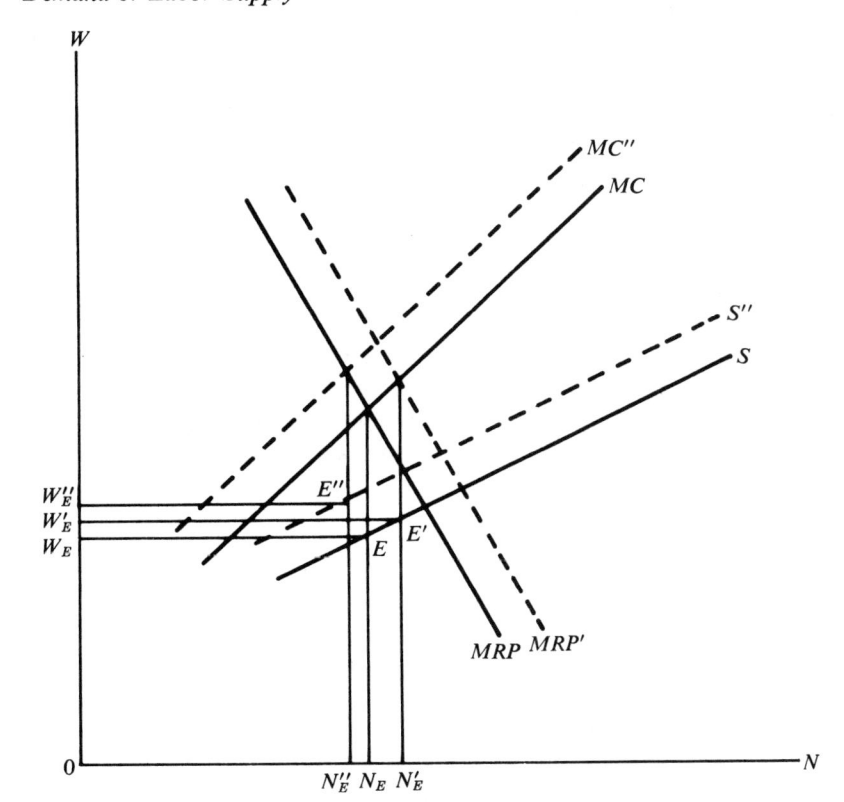

mand and thus an increase in their marginal revenue product of labor and that all were led, acting independently, to raise their wages by an equal proportion, say 2 percent. Now every applicant encounters wage offers that are 2 percent higher than they were previously. The pay that must be sacrificed to search one more day also is increased by 2 percent; and so are all the returns to be gained by finding a superior wage offer, that is, for any p, the corresponding X increases 2 percent. There is no clear reason for h to change meanwhile; if it does not, W^* will also rise 2 percent. Given the assumption that searchers recognize the upward shift in the distribution of wage offers, everyone's acceptance wage rises 2 percent. Neither the quit rates of workers nor the acceptance rates of searchers are changed. The higher level of wages does not reduce unemployment. The acceptance decision turns on relative wages—not on the absolute level of wages (whether in nominal or real terms). People compare the offer they have currently with the prospects of getting better offers by continuing to search. In the example, the bird in the hand and the bird in the bush become equally more attractive, and the choice between them is unchanged. So long as people are assumed to know the distribution of wage offers, the search model cannot explain any decline in unemployment resulting from a general rise in aggregate product demand. A decline in unemployment can occur only as the result of either a reduced dispersion of wage offers or a reduction of the required time spent searching to obtain a job offer. There is no reason in the framework of this model for a cyclical upswing to generate those changes.

Indeed, the higher wage offers may increase participation in the labor force by inducing some people now engaged in home activity to begin searching in light of the opportunities for a higher wage. That effect will emerge if the supply of labor is positively related to the real wage and if consumer prices do not rise in parallel with the increases in the nominal wage. Such a response of new entrants to the higher distribution of wage offers will tend to increase employment, but it cannot reduce unemployment. Indeed, any sudden inflow of entrants would raise unemployment temporarily until they receive offers that meet or beat their acceptance wages.

The "Stale Information" Amendment

To account for cyclical fluctuation in unemployment, which is the outstanding feature of the cycle, the simple search model sketched above must be amended to allow for imperfect information about the *distribution* of wage offers, a plausible revision of the assumptions. It is difficult to imagine how people could ever know (or even think they know) the distribution of wage offers without knowing anything about the location of particularly good offers. It strains credulity to suppose that, when some firms set higher wages, workers learn immediately just *how much* the distribution has shifted but get no clues whatsoever on *which* employers created the shift.

It is more realistic to assume that people have collected *some* information about recent wages paid in particular locations, that they assess the present state of the labor market by relying on this body of knowledge. They must evaluate today's wage offers in terms of a perception of the wage distribution (and its key characteristics that generate π and X

for any W) based on *past* experience and information. In particular, when the distribution of wage offers improves, they do not learn immediately about that shift; and they do not revise their acceptance wages at once. Meanwhile, they view higher wage offers as better relative offers, even if in fact those are merely better absolute offers in the same relative place of an improved distribution. The lagged perceptions result in estimates of π and X for any W that are too low. Hence a larger fraction of wage offers meets or beats their acceptance wages. Searchers will have higher rates of job acceptance in the improved environment, thereby reducing average search time and level of unemployment.

Suppose that, unbeknownst to searchers, the entire distribution of wage offers depicted in figure 2-1 shifted to the right by 5 percent. Searchers still attach values of $\pi = 0.25$ and $X = \$1.77$ to a $40 offer, when π is now 0.487 and $X = \$2.45$. The job seeker with a horizon of 90.4 days would still accept the $40 offer when in fact an extra day of search is worth $107.86. (With full information, that searcher's W^* should move up 5 percent to $42, where $\pi = 0.25$ and $X = \$1.86$.)

The assumption of stale information is the key to the cyclical nature of unemployment in a search world. It is the underpinning of the celebrated Friedman-Phelps analysis about how people are fooled by changing labor market conditions. Their point is that information lags lead people to search less than optimally when labor markets tighten (and unduly long when they ease), thereby shrinking (swelling) unemployment.

Shifts in labor market conditions do not remain secret for long, however. If a new higher distribution of offers is maintained, information about it will gradually filter through. If the relative dispersion of wage offers remains unchanged, job seekers will scale up their acceptance wages in proportion to the rise in the average offer; the average search period will return to its old and still optimal level; and unemployment will rise to its previous frictional level. Only if demands keep rising cumulatively can the process of fooling continue, and even then searchers may begin to extrapolate the trend of improving wage offers and try to offset the lag in their information. As Abraham Lincoln once pointed out, the potential for fooling is limited.

The Friedman-Phelps insight is important; again and again in the analysis below, information lags force today's decisions to be based on yesterday's data. The reasoning points to misperceptions resulting from information lags concerning wages—not from lags in price information and not from any irrationality or "money illusion." People search for too long or too short a time insofar as they have stale information about relative wages, regardless of whether they are correctly informed about consumer prices. The choice between accepting a given offer or continuing to search for a better one depends on the perception of the distribution of wage offers—not of the market basket that any particular wage offer will buy. To be sure, for choices between work and home activity, real wages may enter the story. Thus misperceptions about prices, as well as about nominal wages, can influence participation rates, but not unemployment rates.

Moreover, while the pioneering search models in the macro literature invoked the stale information feature, the characteristic is really an amendment to, rather than a natural component of, the simple search framework. The "clean" assumption about the information available to searchers is full knowledge about the distribution of wage offers and no information about the location of particular offers. While that assumption is unrealistic, it is tractable and has clear implications. Once the anchoring assumption of full information about the distribution is lifted, it is not obvious where the model will drift. Are people supposed to operate with expectations about today's distribution of wage offers that simply are based on the distribution that actually obtained last month or last year? Or are they supposed to have imperfect information even about past distributions? In general, what are they supposed to know and how are they supposed to find out?

In all likelihood, people begin a spell of unemployment with some beliefs about the distribution of wage offers that they will be sampling. But they must realize that they do not really know the distribution; and they must be prepared to alter their views about it in light of experience. Statisticians would identify this as a Bayesian process: previous beliefs are modified on the basis of subsequent evidence. If a searcher obtained twenty consecutive wage offers below the average expected, they could not be entirely blamed on bad luck. The searcher might have been excessively optimistic about the distribution, even if that person could not reckon the actual probability of such a string of events at one in a million (0.5^{20}, which is $1/1,048,576$). It is hard to imagine how seriously overoptimistic misperceptions of the state of labor markets could be maintained for long. In fact, the high "dropout" rates (shifts to nonparticipation) of the unemployed can be read as evidence that searchers learn from experience; some are so disappointed in sampling the labor market that they retire from the scene.

Learning through experience thus should bring unemployment back to a normal or equilibrium fractional rate associated with the dispersion of wage offers and the cost of obtaining an offer. The model would seem to suggest that excessive pessimism, which leads to unduly low unemployment, will be corrected less rapidly than excessive optimism, which bloats unemployment. People who accept a job too quickly because they were unduly pessimistic about the distribution of wage offers may never learn of their error; because they stop searching, they may not realize that many better offers were available to them. On the other hand, those who are excessively optimistic and keep searching will be much more reliably disabused of their erroneous perceptions.

In this model cyclical fluctuations in unemployment are made to depend entirely on misperceptions based on stale information. Deviations from some equilibrium rate of frictional unemployment emerge, not because wage offers are favorable or unfavorable in some absolute sense, but rather because they are perceived as more or less favorable than they are. The level of unemployment then becomes a rising function of undue optimism (or a negative function of undue pessimism). Over a business cycle that carries unemployment above and then below its equilibrium frictional rate, the gap between the perceived and actual distribution of wage offers must grow increasingly wider as unemployment rises, as figure 2-4 illustrates. People must be most overly optimistic at the point of peak unemployment. Up to that point, the actual distribution must deteriorate more rapidly than perceptions are revised downward. During the recovery phase of the cycle when unemployment is falling but remains above normal, there must still be excessive optimism, although it must be shrinking, as indicated in the figure. Moreover, during the boom phase of the cycle, perceived offers must be less favorable than actual offers and the gap between them must be growing as long as unemployment is falling. Finally, as unemployment begins to rise but remains below normal, undue pessimism must prevail but be shrinking.

It is hard to think of any plausible set of lags in the formation of perceptions that would produce such a pattern in actual cyclical experience. After the collapse of demand late in 1974, the perception gap could have widened rapidly enough to produce a 9 percent unemployment rate in the spring of 1975. Conceivably, the Great Depression may have delivered new and increasingly unfavorable surprises to job searchers more rapidly than they could diagnose the previous state of the labor market throughout the period from 1929 to 1933. During that time, the unem-

Figure 2-4. *Misperceptions of Wage Offers and Fluctuations in Unemployment*

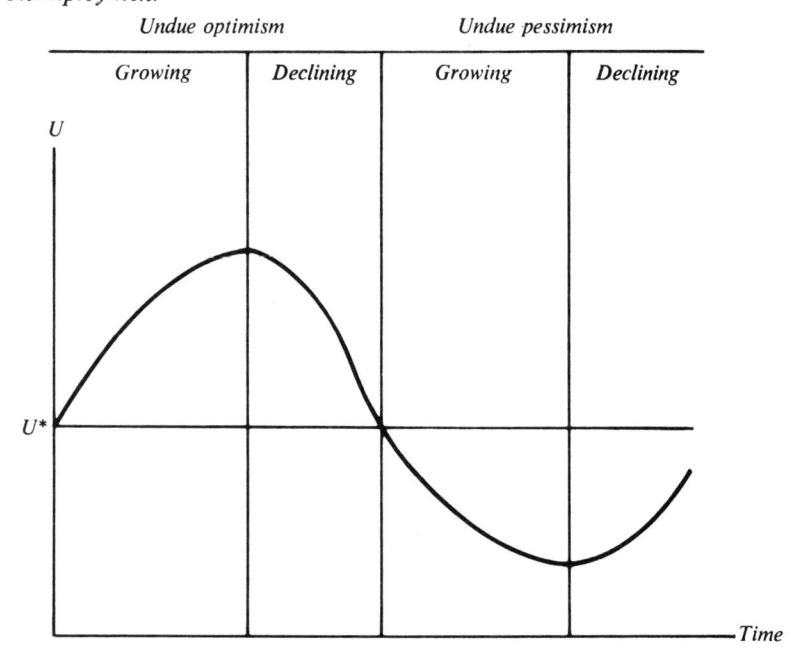

ployment rate rose 25 percent as a result of an ever-widening, overly optimistic perception gap. But to accept the model, one also has to believe that people were overly optimistic as a result of stale information in 1936 when the unemployment rate was at its lowest point in five years. People also were overly optimistic in mid-1977 when the rate was the lowest in nearly three years. Even long lags and stubborn "priors" cannot explain, through stale information, why the unemployment rate sometimes stays so high for so long during an economic recovery. To account for an unemployment rate of 17 percent in 1936 or even 7 percent in 1977, one must invoke petrified—and not merely stale—information.

An important implication of this model is that adverse shifts in wage offers that are perceived as temporary affect behavior no differently than ones that are expected to be permanent. Once fully recognized, neither type of adverse shift can lead to more unemployment. If people recognize the depressed state of wage offers and do not drop out of the labor force, they will scale down acceptance wages appropriately—whether responding to temporary or permanent shifts. In the case of a temporary shift, they will take jobs with lower pay (although not *relatively* lower pay),

partly with the reasonable expectation that those jobs will pay more when
the labor market rebounds and partly with the readiness to quit (as always) if their wage does not hold its own relative to other wages.

In this respect, the search model of the labor market is quite different
from "search" models of markets for durable assets, like that for secondhand houses, which are also subject to information costs. The seller of a
house makes a once-and-for-all decision; a current sale precludes any
future sale. If that seller recognizes the depressed state of the housing
market during a recession and views it as temporary, the best current
offer must be compared with an expected superior future offer *less* the
interest and other "storage costs" of keeping the house unsold for the
intervening period. It will be rational for the seller to set a higher "acceptance price" and thus keep the house "unemployed" longer if the
present housing market is viewed as depressed temporarily rather than
permanently.

The sellers of fresh fish do not have the same option. If the price tags
on their fish do not respond adequately to a temporary weakness in the
market, they will have rotting fish at the end of the day. Here, the storage
costs of delaying the sale approach infinity. It is reasonable to suppose
that the sellers of fresh fish may have had unusual amounts of spoilage
in 1930, but hard to believe that this would have continued into 1933,
much less 1937. Labor, of course, is even more perishable than fresh fish
(or, as others have suggested, cut flowers) rather than durable like
homes.

An Assessment

With the stale information amendment, the simple search model provides some rationale for cyclical fluctuations in unemployment. But the
information lags cannot account plausibly for the persistence of unusually high (or low) unemployment for stretches that last several years.
Because the model breaks the link between the real wage and marginal
revenue product through the monopsonistic elements described above,
it can invoke a production function with diminishing returns without
becoming locked into the incorrect Keynesian and classical prediction
that the real wage will be highest in recessions. A noncyclical real wage
can emerge from the search model—even with classical market-clearing
in the product markets—provided that the elasticity of supply of labor
to firms is somewhat higher in prosperity than it is in recession.

As a cyclical theory of unemployment, the search model with stale information is most grievously defective in ruling out discharges or lay-offs made by employers as a response to weakening demand for output. Such losses of jobs in fact account for nearly all the added unemployment in recessions. The model excludes them because the optimum strategy for an employer who wants to shrink his work force is to cut wages enough to induce the desired drop in employment through increased quits. To discharge or lay off workers in a slump irrationally sacrifices an opportunity to lower wages.

All unemployment in the search model is the result of quits initiated by workers. Not only is that palpably wrong, but so are several other predictions about the cyclical anatomy of unemployment. The model scores well in predicting that, during a cyclical upswing when unemployment is falling, the average duration of a spell of unemployment will shorten. But it supplies no reason to believe that quit rates and even the number of unemployment spells due to quitting will rise, as they do in fact. The implied wage-adjustment strategy of employers would point to a counter-cyclical pattern of quits, the opposite of the actual pattern. So would another implication of the model: a tightening of the labor market that raises wages should, because of stale information, lead existing jobholders to misinterpret their own higher wages as improved *relative* wages. Ironically, that wrong prediction about quits is the one reason the model makes the correct prediction that the total number of spells will decline in a cyclical upswing. All in all, it is reasonable to conclude that the search model has moved a step—but only a step—toward illuminating the key cyclical facts on fluctuations in unemployment.

Enriched Search Model

The ability of the simple search model to explain important real world phenomena can be enhanced by incorporating a few complications that are really logical extensions of the search paradigm. Because of the informational frictions that create the need for search, applicants may be scarce resources to employers; an "enriched" search model can incorporate the implications of the scarcity of applicants and explore the behavioral consequences of their value to the firm.

The "shadow price" associated with applicants can be seen in the framework of figure 2-3, when the firm's demand curve for output shifts.

In a competitive auction world, the firm confronted with a one-time rise in the demand for its output would make a one-time jump to a higher level of employment and production. Alternatively, in a world of static monopsony power by employers, the adjustment would require the firm to raise its wage, but it would still be a one-time move. However, in the search world, the exogenous flow of applicants makes the cost of expansion by the firm a function of the speed of that expansion. The more rapidly the firm raises employment toward an ultimate target, the greater the wage premium it must offer. To move rapidly, it needs an extremely high acceptance rate of applicants and a high "stick" rate of existing workers. On the other hand, if it is willing to add gradually to employment, it can hold down the cost of expansion: aim at more moderate acceptance and stick rates and allow its supply curve of labor to shift gradually to the right.

In effect, the firm has a long-run supply curve that is much flatter than its short-run curve depicted in the figure—indeed, the long-run curve may be completely horizontal. It can be regarded as the amount of labor that would be supplied to the firm at a given wage if the information about that wage offer were fully and instantly available to all job seekers. The gap between the two curves indicates the benefit that an expanding firm could have if it could somehow magically inform all potential applicants.[7]

The Help-Wanted Ad

The value of applicants leads firms to consider possible techniques of attracting them and leads the makers of economic models to drop the assumption of the simple search model that the flow of applicants is exogenous. For example, to the firm aiming for a major expansion of employment in response to increased demand for its output, the help-wanted ad (with specified wage offers) may become a worthwhile expenditure. The productivity of expenditures for help-wanted ads will vary among firms, depending on how favorable their wage offers are and how much their demand for incremental labor exceeds the normal flow of applicants obtainable without special efforts to disseminate information. If all firms are offered the opportunity to place help-wanted ads at the

7. The contracting firm is likely to be operating in the range where the long-run curve lies above the short-run curve, indicating that the search costs to its workers of shopping elsewhere enable it to adapt to adversity at lower cost.

same cost, some will find it worthwhile and others will not. Once that institution is introduced, workers are no longer randomly sampling the distribution of wage offers, but rather have some guidance on the location of particularly favorable wage offers. In effect, the result is less groping by applicants.

Now, if many firms simultaneously experience a strengthening of product demand and act independently to adjust to it, some will find it worthwhile to initiate help-wanted ads. Indeed, even if the improvement of wage offers is uneven among firms and actually increases the dispersion of wage offers, it can be optimal for job seekers to take the best advertised offers and end their search. Unemployment will then fall as the result of sensible decisions made by well-informed job seekers. The cyclical upswing of product demand can thus reduce unemployment—not by more fooling but by less groping.

A Stake in the Current Worker

The scarcity of applicants also introduces a special value of existing workers to the firm because they are guaranteed "applicants" for jobs. The simple search model gives employers no stake in their workers and workers no stake in their jobs: the present employer is simply one source of a wage offer that happens to be known costlessly to the employee; and the current employee is just another applicant to the firm. But if applicants are scarce and valuable, then another applicant is a matter of importance to the employer.

Suppose the firm experiences a drop in the demand for its output that it interprets as unique to itself and transitory, and expects a prompt reversal that will make it wish to restore output and employment to initial levels. The strategy that maximizes profits during its slump would hold down or reduce wages sufficiently to cut its labor supply to some lower optimal level (from N_0 to N_1). If $N_1 = \alpha_1 (N_0 + A) < N_0$, then α_1 is below the α_0 that makes $N_1 = N_0$, and must be associated with a lower wage than would α_0.

But when the slump is over and demand bounces back to its previous level, the firm would not be able simply to retrace its steps. If N_2 is to equal N_0, it takes $\alpha_2 > \alpha_0$; for $\alpha_0 (N_1 + A)$ must be less than $\alpha_0 (N_0 + A)$ because $N_1 < N_0$. The contraction of employment during the slump reduces the pool of potential workers—continuing employees and new applicants—who "apply" to the firm. To restore employment, the firm must obtain a higher acceptance rate from the reduced pool of potential workers consisting of the smaller number of ongoing employees and the unchanged flow of new applicants. To increase the acceptance rate, it must push relative wages above a path consistent with stable employment at the initial level. If it considers in advance its options over the two periods of slump and rebound, it may well conclude that it should not hold down wages sufficiently to maximize profits during the slump. The firm might choose instead to "stockpile" some workers even though their marginal wage cost exceeds their marginal revenue product during the slump. That strategy might lead to a decline in productivity during the slump. The optimum strategy might rely on reduced workweeks or even layoffs in the slump as ways of increasing the probability that the ongoing worker will continue to "apply" for the job. So the enriched search model can account for real-world institutions and phenomena that have no place in the simple search model.

Affecting the Horizon

Still another strategy available to the firm is to try to influence workers' perceptions of the "horizon," particularly when it is prepared to make a favorable wage offer to the worker.

To understand how and why firms might influence the perception of workers about the horizon, it is necessary to go back and inspect more carefully the concept of the horizon that entered into the acceptance decisions of the simple search model. The horizon that any applicant attaches to a job is a single parameter that reflects a complex assessment of how long the applicant expects the job to last and how long any wage premium (or deficiency) on that job, relative to others, is expected to last.

The first set of considerations is intended to reflect life-cycle (rather than relative wage) considerations. The student looking for a summer job or the retiree wanting work for the Christmas season cannot afford to be excessively selective—spending many days searching for a particularly good job cannot be useful when the wage premium obtained from success in that search will extend over a short period. The selectiveness of searchers should clearly depend on how long they expect to stay in the labor force with the accepted jobs. The acceptance wage of persons with short horizons will be relatively low, and those persons will tend to settle for jobs with low wages. Occasional workers with frequent entries into and exits from the labor force will have high quit rates and frequent, but short, spells of unemployment.

The second set of considerations, the persistence of the relative wage, is important to the worker thinking about long-term employment. Even for a worker making a career choice that might last forty years, the incentive for selectiveness evaporates if present wage offers give little or no indication of probable wage differentials a year hence. The applicant, in fact, must expect particularly high (or low) wages for a given type of job to regress toward the mean over time in the search labor market. In principle, applicants might distinguish among wage offers in terms of the expected duration of any premium. For example, in the distribution of figure 2-1, a current wage offer of $40 might be viewed as superior to one of $41 if the applicant had reason to expect its $2 premium over the mean to last much longer than the $3 premium of the alternative. Yet the acceptance decision in the simple search model was analyzed on the assumption that an applicant necessarily attaches the same horizon to all premiums (and deficiencies) in current wage offers. Once variability of that horizon is recognized, new dimensions open up for the employer.

If the firm offering a wage premium can convince applicants that the premium will last a long time (longer than premiums offered by other employers), it can lengthen the horizon and boost its acceptance rate. Such expectations can obviously be created through a contract that guarantees the maintenance of a wage premium. But even a nonbinding statement of intentions may influence expectations in the right direction. If a firm uses such strategies, it necessarily sacrifices its subsequent flexibility. It must fulfill the expectations that it created to hold down its quit rate and preserve the credibility needed to influence the horizon of applicants. Basically, in adopting a long-run strategy of trying to influence the horizon, the firm restricts its ability to minimize its short-run payroll costs for a given level of employment.

The self-selection of jobs by life-cycle horizons introduces a reason to distinguish the "stick" decisions of current workers from the acceptance decisions of applicants. By assumption, the applicants are a random sample of all potential workers. But ongoing workers are a nonrandom group; they have previously accepted the wage for the job, finding it above their acceptance wage (given their horizon). Thus, compared with high-paying jobs, low-paying jobs should have much lower acceptance rates by new applicants but only *slightly* higher quit rates. Workers who took low-paying jobs because they had short horizons have no reason to leave those jobs prematurely simply because the jobs continue to have low pay. More generally, various jobs should have different "steady-state" quit rates depending on the level of wages they pay. But deviations from those rates must be related to unexpected changes in the wage (disappointments or favorable surprises), rather than to its level.[8]

The firm has to recognize that its quit rate is sensitive to the wages it pays *in relation to workers' expectations*. The rate may jump as the result of the employer's making an unfavorable wage change for the worker (like a wage reduction). The impact on the stock of ongoing workers can then be large and prompt, even though the effect on acceptances by new applicants will cumulate only gradually to significant levels. The role of wage expectations in acceptance decisions and the scarcity value of applicants are enough to make wage cuts unattractive to employers. The enriched search model, unlike the simple one, can generate a Keynesian wage floor.

All in all, the enriched search model, which builds on the significance of the scarcity of applicants, has much potential. It could be developed rigorously to account for many phenomena of the real world that the simple search model cannot explain: cyclical fluctuations in unemployment that do not depend on fooling, on-the-job underemployment and the consequent recession dent in productivity, the preferred treatment of experienced workers, the importance of layoffs, and the rationale for implicit and explicit contracts. The entire breakthrough stems from the recognition of the hiring costs to employers implicit in informational frictions. An alternative way of obtaining the same results is to assume the hiring cost initially and to trace the implications of that assumption. For reasons that will become evident, I find the latter a more fruitful approach to the analysis of labor markets.

In fact, real-world employers care about retaining experienced workers for many reasons. Indeed, as will become clear below, the multitude of reasons tend to proliferate models. It is a challenge to theory to define some underlying basic value of the experienced worker in order to simplify and unify the analysis. But first I would like to show that the single, simple assumption that employers value an experienced worker changes

8. Linking quit rates to disappointments suggests that people who had recently taken their jobs would have especially low quit rates, but that pattern is reversed in actuality. The reason for that is readily understandable: in the real world, people learn many of the nonpecuniary aspects of their new jobs after they start work, and some do not like what they discover. The model has no room for that kind of disappointment.

dramatically the simple-search story presented above, and can remedy its most glaring defects.

"Toll" Model

I begin by pulling an assumption out of thin air. Suppose that a firm that puts a particular worker on its payroll for the first time must pay a substantial "toll," say, for concreteness, about the size of one quarter's wages. For the purposes at hand, that toll can be viewed as a license fee imposed by the government. In any case, the toll levied on the initial hiring of worker i by firm j is nonrecurrent—regardless of how long the worker and the firm remain together, or even if they renew their relationship after an interruption.

Decisions of Workers and Firms

As above, workers are assumed to be homogeneous (or readily gradable). In particular, the worker for whom the toll has been paid is no more productive than the new applicant. Despite their identical productivities, the applicant and the experienced worker now fit into different categories from the standpoint of the employer. Hiring the former incurs the payment of one more toll; holding on to the latter avoids a further toll.

The firm would obviously like to shift the cost of the toll to new recruits. For example, it might offer to pay them the same wage that experienced workers receive, while charging them the toll as an "initiation fee." But that is not likely to be a viable option. The payment of the toll will be worthwhile to novices only if the firm maintains jobs for them long enough at a high enough wage to amortize the intial investment. In the absence of a contractual obligation, job tenure remains within the discretion of the firm, and the very effort by the firm to collect in advance raises suspicions. A binding explicit contract, covering a fixed period of employment, wages, and the division of the costs of the toll can offer some reassurance to both parties, but only at considerable expense of negotiation and legal work, and through the sacrifice of flexibility. Moreover, when the assumption that workers have known and fixed productivity is dropped, the explicit contract raises problems of "moral hazard." The parties are more likely to develop implicit contracts—arrangements that are not legally binding but that give both sides incentives to maintain the relationship. As I indicate in some detail below, the arrangements often require a newly hired worker to accept some wage sacrifice for some period, in effect, agreeing to "installment payments" toward the toll and thus demonstrating seriousness about the job as a long-run venture. The firm still finances the toll at first, thus making an initial investment in the worker and demonstrating its earnest intention to keep that worker at least long enough to pay it off. So the novice may start a job at a lower wage than that of established workers, with some assurance that the wage sacrifice will be only temporary and, by the same token, with an incentive to remain with the firm long enough to get the reward of a full-scale wage.

Initially new workers are then paid less than their current marginal revenue product, which by assumption is the same as that of experienced workers. Subsequently wages will increase but they may always remain below marginal revenue product. The opportunity wage of an experienced worker as a novice elsewhere is held down by the liability of any other employer to pay the toll. The firm obtains a gross return from the initial toll so long as it pays a wage below marginal revenue product. The firm will earn a net return over the long run from hiring the worker if the discounted excess of the cumulative marginal revenue product over the wage during that worker's tenure of employment, y, exceeds the toll, T:

$$\sum_{i=1}^{y} \left(\frac{MRP_i - W_i}{(1 + r)^i} \right) > T,$$

where r is the interest rate applied in discounting.

The wage that the firm pays to an experienced worker cannot be determined by a marginal condition, but it can be bound by a pair of inequalities: it must be less than the current marginal revenue product, MRP, of the worker, but it must exceed the opportunity wage, OW, of the worker as a novice elsewhere: $OW < W < MRP$. Between MRP and OW lies a zone of indeterminacy—the joint surplus to the firm and worker. The sharing of that surplus is determined by the position of W in that zone. Presumably the worker and the firm recognize that the other party receives some surplus, and both know the surplus provides an incentive to maintain the job relationship. Both sides must maximize surplus over a long-term horizon. The recognition that the other party has a significant surplus that would be sacrificed in any termination of the relationship promotes "nickel and dime" strategies to capture a larger share of the surplus.

The toll attached to the establishment of an employer-employee relationship influences the calculations at the point of hiring. To the applicant, the decision posed by any wage offer is still one of accepting that offer or searching again the next day. But when an applicant receives an offer from a firm with a two-tier wage strategy, the benefits and the opportunity costs make it necessary to consider two wage rates and two time-horizons: that for novices and that for established workers. Furthermore, the established worker's wage that is important to the novice is the one that will be paid after qualifying for that status—not the current one. The initial payment of the toll by the firm reassures new workers that its hiring decision is not frivolous and helps them to estimate the horizon. But workers remain concerned about getting on the bottom rung of the right ladder. To rectify any current mistakes will require not only the sacrifice of wages for the period spent in search but also the sacrifice of income involved in a second stretch of employment at novice wages elsewhere.

In short, applicants in the toll model must judge a package that is more complex than was the case in the simple search model. In the toll variant, the choice has elements of a more serious career decision with its longer horizon. The searchers must consider their prospective "permanent" wage—much as consumers have to pay attention to permanent income.

To form expectations about the relevant dimensions of the prospective job in the absence of an explicit contract, applicants will seek information from other workers about that employer's past performance. Applicants are obliged to judge the employer, in part, by reputation; that dependence on past history for guidance about the future is one more manifestation of the "stale information" problem. If the firm has a reputation for credibility, the recruits will try to narrow the range of uncertainty by making inquiries about the firm's intentions: how long should they expect to be novices? What is likely to happen to the wage of experienced workers in the future?

Uncertainties also affect decisions by experienced workers to quit or stick because workers cannot diagnose their job options elsewhere with any confidence. To obtain the whole package of relevant information, they must (again, excluding on-the-job search) actually quit their jobs, search for others, go through a novice period, and only then learn whether they have fulfilled their hopes for higher, experienced-worker wages in steady jobs. Potentially that information could cost them a great deal.

In contrast to workers' uncertainty about alternative jobs, they know pretty well what they have in hand. Even if a quit decision is formulated in terms of a maximizing strategy, it is bound to have many of the elements of "satisficing." In some sense, workers have to decide whether their present jobs are essentially satisfactory; one criterion for that judgment may be whether a firm has lived up to the expectations that were created in workers' minds at the time they were recruited.

Emergence of a Seniority Premium

The fruitful complications that enter into the toll model arise because the toll costs of the firm, for any given average amount of employment, vary directly with the quit rate of its workers; these costs are, in turn, a function of the wage policy. In particular, that points toward a two-tier wage structure. To see how this develops, assume a world in which there is no toll. Consider a firm for which the marginal revenue product of labor per worker-year is constant at m. The supply of labor to that firm is tilted upward even when viewed over a moderately long horizon (like a year), reflecting an imperfect labor market in which it has some monopsony power. The firm's decision in the labor market is to pick a wage, accepting the supply of labor that is forthcoming at that wage.

In the absence of the toll this is a familiar and simple task of optimization, leading to a wage that equates the marginal cost of labor to its marginal revenue product:

$$m = W\left(1 + \frac{1}{e_S}\right),$$

where e_S is the elasticity of supply of labor. Because of the rising supply curve (the finite positive value of e_S) the marginal cost of a worker is higher than the wage for that worker, and the wage is held below marginal revenue product.

Now impose a toll on hiring a new worker in this world. If the toll is T and workers quit at a functional rate of q per year, the average annual cost of the toll per worker is qT. If q is exogenous (specifically, independent of the wage paid), qT simply represents an addition to the (annual) marginal cost of labor; it pushes the optimizing wage down further below m. The new condition for optimality is

$$m = W\left(1 + \frac{1}{e_S}\right) + qT.$$

The toll makes a qualitative difference only when it is realistically recognized that the quit rate will vary inversely with the wage. By offering a higher wage, the employer not only attracts more workers but also lowers the quit rate of the employees, thereby economizing on the annual toll cost per worker. Clearly, that benefit of a higher wage pushes the employer in the direction of paying somewhat more. If e_q is the elasticity of the quit rate with respect to the wage $[(dq/dW) \cdot (W/q)]$, the marginal condition is

$$m = W \left(1 + \frac{1}{e_S}\right) + qT \left(1 + \frac{e_q}{e_S}\right).$$

Because e_q is negative, the new term holds down marginal cost and pushes up the wage.[9]

The next step is the big one in this sequential analysis. The firm is likely to consider whether it can economize on its labor costs—the sum of wages and tolls—by paying a higher wage to established workers than to novices. Although all workers have the same productivity in this world, the firm is tempted to test the seriousness of recruits by asking them, in effect, to make some installment payments toward the toll in the initial period of their employment. If the firm adopted such a strategy, it would set two (or more) wage rates—one for novices, W_n, and one for experienced workers, W_x. For simplicity, suppose that the novice period must necessarily last one year and that the wages specified above are annual figures. When will the firm find it worthwhile to set the wage for established workers above that for novices, rather than simply equating the two? The answer depends on how the dual structure affects quit rates and how attractive it is to applicants.

To applicants confronted with a dual offer, W_x and W_n are two components of a compensation package that must be appropriately evaluated. The applicants presumably care about their wages both in the novice period and subsequently; they use the current value of W_x as information in predicting their future wages as experienced workers. The number of willing applicants thus rises with increases in both W_x and W_n. Suppose a particular applicant viewing a job offer with a dual wage expected to take the job and remain with the firm for y years. That applicant will then expect to spend one year earning W_n and the remaining $(y - 1)$ years earning W_x.

9. In a steady state of employment recruits, R must match quitters: $R = qN$. It follows that the elasticity of recruits with respect to the wage, e_r, must equal the sum of e_q and e_S. Since e_r is positive, $-1 < e_q/e_S < 0$; hence $qT(1 + e_q/e_S)$ is positive, but less than qT.

The effect of the dual structure on quit rates works in two ways. First, applicants who would have accepted either a flat W or the dual offer of a W_n with a W_x in prospect (such that $W_n < W < W_x$) are likely to have lower quit rates with the dual structure. They are not likely to have significantly different quit rates during their novice periods because they are looking forward to the better days of receiving the full-scale wages of experienced workers in the future. Once they are paid W_x, the additional bonus clearly discourages quitting. Second, and more important, with the dual structure the firm appeals most to those workers with large personal values of y, and they impose the lowest average annual toll costs on the firm. By offering less now and more later, the employer introduces a self-selection principle that helps to recruit those workers likely to stick with it longest. The dual structure will not only discourage the short-horizon applicant as the firm intends, but also ones who are risk-averse, suspicious, or have strong time preferences—all of whom the firm would welcome.

Indeed, given a favorable effect of the seniority premium on quit rates, the tilt of the wage structure is limited only by these elements. Consider the extreme and implausible case in which workers make no allowance for risk aversion, the chance of being discharged, and the imperfect predictive value of the current W_x for the future or for any greater time preference than that used by the firm in discounting. Under those circumstances the employer would clearly be best off, for a given expected value of total wages (pay excluding tolls) per worker, with the widest possible excess of W_x over W_n. The attraction to workers would be no different, and the saving on tolls would make such a strategy favorable on balance without limit, until it imposed the full toll cost on workers while they are novices. But applicants do not seriously take such a telescopic view. They will have risk aversion, and normally their time preference will be greater than that of the firm. They will recognize that the current value of W_x is not a perfect predictor of its future path; they will take into account the possibility that they may be laid off or discharged or even that the firm may succumb to bankruptcy. Hence, applicants will not apply a weight to W_x as large as $(y - 1)$ times the weight applied to W_n, as they would in the telescopic case (with no time preference at all). In general, applicants with expected job tenures of y_i years will weight the package using the following:

$$W_n + \theta_i(y_i - 1)W_x, \qquad 0 < \theta_i < 1.$$

Other things being equal, applicants with large (personal) y_i will trade W_n for W_x on a lower trade-off ratio than applicants with short horizons.[10] In part, θ depends on the firm's credibility to applicants in making the present seniority premium a reliable basis for predicting W_x in the future. Moreover, if the firm asks for a very large sacrifice of wages initially, that is bound to lower θ by raising suspicions that it may lay off or discharge workers in the future. If the firm wants to receive the benefits of the dual package—the potential reduction in quit rates of senior workers drawing the premium and the self-selection principle at the point of recruiting, it must develop a reputation for credibility and establish a differential that imposes a significant but "reasonable" initial sacrifice on the novice. I see no way to prove that the firm can always structure its strategy—without offering explicit contracts—in such a way as to make the dual structure worthwhile; nor can I rule out the extreme form of the dual structure that collects the full toll at the beginning. But the pull of opposing forces makes it plausible that an intermediate position of some seniority premium will often be optimal.[11]

10. Because θ is meant to incorporate the discount rate for time preference, there is a slight presumption that people with long horizons will tend to have a somewhat smaller θ_i. But pure time preference is only one of the reasons for θ being less than unity.

11. One interesting but tangential result is that a firm with rapidly growing employment is more likely to adopt the dual structure and in general to have a wider differential between novices and experienced workers. Suppose both firm A and firm B are paying a wage of $10,000 a year and are experiencing a quit rate of 10 percent a year. Both obtain 25 recruits a year at that wage offer. But firm A initially has 250 workers so its recruits merely match and replace those who quit. Firm B, on the other hand, initially has 100 workers and is able to expand employment to 115 in the following year.

Suppose both firms could obtain their 25 recruits alternatively with a tilted wage structure that offered $9,000 to novices (first-year workers) and $10,150 to experienced workers. Even before it took account of the beneficial impact of the tilted scale on the quit rate, firm B would find the tilted scale preferable because it lowered its average wage from $10,000 to $9,900. But the immediate impact of the dual structure on firm A would be a rise in the average wage to $10,035. Only by making a dent in quit rates and thus in toll costs would the institution of the seniority premium be worthwhile for firm A. The attractiveness to applicants of high wages paid to established workers gives the firm a benefit that imposes no current costs; the higher the ratio of recruits in its work force, the more incentive the firm has to tilt up the wage rate of experienced workers. The results here are reminiscent of the principle underlying a social insurance retirement system in a growing economy with an expanding labor force. It is possible for everyone to be better off by subsidizing the "older generation" so long as arrangements can be made to ensure that the next generation can and will carry on the same tradition.

Declines in the Demand for Labor: Responses by Firms

Because of the toll, the firm has an investment in its established workers and an incentive to protect that investment. The recruits that accept novice wages are making an investment in their jobs, and they capitalize on that investment as experienced workers with premium wages that generally exceed their opportunity wages elsewhere. The firm makes the investment with the expectation that workers will stick with their jobs; and workers make the investment with the expectation that the firm will stick with them.

The significance of this implicit contract becomes more evident when the firm experiences a decline in product demand that lowers the marginal revenue product of its workers. In the simple search model, the firm's response to such a situation was unambiguous: it would want to lower wages, expecting and indeed welcoming the resulting rise in quit rates and decline in acceptance rates. But the firm in the world of the toll model has a different consideration; quits by established workers will increase the toll payments the firm will need to make when and if its demand rebounds. When contemplating any trimming of W_x, the firm must consider how much that action would increase its toll costs through current increases in its quit rate, and furthermore how much the action would erode its investment in personnel by impairing its reputation for maintaining a reliable and predictable wage path—the credibility that leads applicants to attach a high θ to the firm's current W_x.

If the decline in demand is particular to the firm and not a reflection of a generally weak economy, the concern about current quit rates may be serious. Experienced workers have stuck with their jobs through some subjective evaluations of long-term satisfaction, and each has some concept of an expected wage path. Any shortfall of wages below that path can create significant disappointments that stimulate quits. Because the quit rate may jump abruptly if wages are trimmed into that range of disappointment, the employer will be discouraged from taking such action.

On the other hand, if the labor market is generally weak, the imminent threat of quits may be quite trivial. Then the longer-term consequences on the investment in personnel are likely to be the chief force inhibiting any cuts in W_x. The employer may be faced with a serious risk that, when labor markets rebound, quits will soar if that employer has disappointed workers in the interim. As a result, the Keynesian wage floor enters the toll model. This is a good reason for employers generally to operate with *lower* quit rates in a weak labor market, as they do in fact—rather than to trim wages enough to increase quit rates, as the simple search model would suggest. In the toll model, the procyclical pattern of quit rates can result from rational decisions by employers with accurate foresight. The firm may optimize by adopting a principle of keeping W_x at its "normal" level (or path) in the face of disappointments in product demand that it views as temporary.

Under those circumstances the firm may also find it optimal to keep workers on the job and keep paying them during a period of slack, even when the wage exceeds the current marginal revenue product of the workers. If the slack period is confidently expected by the firm to be very short in duration and if the goods produced by the firm are readily storable at low cost, these workers may be used to build up inventories in slack periods. But if there is considerable uncertainty about the possible duration of the slack and high costs to storage (including the impossibility of storing outputs that are services), output may be reduced. The firms may be able to assign the workers maintenance tasks like cleaning, repairing, and painting, or it may really keep them in a state of "on-the-job underemployment." I am convinced that here lies the basic explanation of the procyclical pattern of productivity with its characteristic dent during periods of recession and slack. I doubt that indivisibilities are so important and so typical that they require firms to use more than 90 percent of their initial labor input to produce 90 percent of their initial output. Indeed I suspect that most technologies create some possibility of substituting capital for labor, even in the short run. But because of cost minimization relating to the toll, many firms during slack periods will operate "off" their production function—with more workers than are technologically required to produce their output. On-the-job underemployment is therefore often optimal for the firm, and it is the source of the dent in productivity during recession and slack periods.

Other options available to the firm in responding to slack demand include cuts in the workweek and layoffs, both of which maintain the job relationship for experienced workers. These options can economize on toll costs in the longer run because the firm can increase total labor input when demand revives by using its previously hired workers and avoiding new tolls.

The rationale for layoffs and for enforced part-time schedules in response to weakened product demand is developed in detail in chapter 3. At this point, only a few comments are needed. First, part-time work and layoffs should be analyzed together because the boundary line between them is, to a degree, a statistical artifact. A firm that tells workers to stay home two days out of five is shortening the workweek, while one that orders its employees to stay home two weeks out of five is engaging in short-term layoffs. Second, the analysis of chapter 3 emphasizes the "clean hands" aspect of the layoff. The basic reason that the employer can lay off workers without creating the ill will and resulting potential explosion of quit rates associated with pay cuts is that laid-off workers know that the firm is not getting any value out of them and therefore cannot be taking advantage of them. The firm is telling them in effect: "We simply cannot use your services now and we cannot afford to keep paying you because business is poor. But we still want you and will call you back as soon as things improve." That is a much more credible statement than any explanation for a wage cut that invokes "poor business." Whenever the labor market weakens, even firms that had no intention of laying off workers might like them to accept some wage cut without ill will. Because workers know that, they will be skeptical of any plea by the firm for a concession on wages that is allegedly required to enable the firm to afford to maintain employment.

Of course, neither the short workweek nor the layoff is costless to the firm. Both will have lasting effects on the firm's reputation for providing steady, full-time employment. Both may give workers a low-cost opportunity (at the expense of leisure rather than of pay) to search elsewhere in the labor market. In reality, the majority of laid-off workers are subsequently recalled and do return to their former jobs; but the fraction that does not accept recall is much larger than the quit rate over corresponding periods for workers who are not laid off.

The circumstances that lead firms to maintain on-the-job underemployment or short workweeks or layoffs will correspondingly influence their policies on recruiting. The inhibitions that apply to holding down or cutting back the pay of established workers are not directly relevant to new recruits. The offer of a reduced W_n to a new worker does not raise problems of disappointment or breach of faith. And a weak labor market may provide a supply of willing applicants at very low levels of W_n. But the firm has to view such opportunities for bargains as strictly temporary; the wage will have to be raised if the labor market strengthens during the novice period, and the worker will have to be paid the full scale once seniority status is achieved. Weighed against the short-term bargain is the likely low level of marginal revenue product for any firm whose workers are currently in a state of on-the-job underemployment. There is no point in hiring workers just because they are cheap if they cannot add to the firm's revenue.[12] Given these considerations and a reluctance to incur toll expenses—especially during a recession—many firms choose to post no-help-wanted signs rather than to engage in bargain hiring.

Most important, among firms that have workers on layoff or short workweeks, cessation of hiring is virtually obligatory. The firm simply cannot tell its senior workers to stay home and draw no pay while it is adding recruits. Such a breach of faith would have major adverse impacts on the subsequent quit rates of established workers and acceptance rates of recruits. To say "We cannot use you now," the firm must show that it is not using some new worker instead.

Search Behavior with No-Help-Wanted Signs

Firms that are simply not hiring recruits will be common, especially in a period of slack and recession. In effect, their wage offers are zero, and that in turn greatly widens the dispersion of the distribution of wage offers depicted in figure 2-1, leading to an important qualitative change in the optimum strategy of searchers. Employers who react to weak product demand by cutting wages worsen the distribution of wage offers confronted by a searcher, but they do not necessarily increase or reduce the dispersion. Those employers who adopt a temporary policy of not hiring recruits will also worsen the distribution; but they must, at the same time, widen the dispersion by shifting to zero offers. If the group of recruits is substantial, a net widening of dispersion in the distribution of wage offers becomes likely. Any widening of the dispersion increases the optimum amount of time spent in searching by job seekers. Unemployment will rise among people who correctly perceive the distribution, quite apart from any increase resulting from stale information.

To see the impact of the no-help-wanted signs on the behavior of searchers, assume that, while all nonzero wage offers are distributed as

12. Several real-world considerations reinforce the inhibitions against bargain hunting that would create an extremely low W_n. Unusual and extreme disparities between paychecks of freshmen and sophomore workers can create morale problems. Moreover, employers may be particularly wary of recruits willing to take an especially low W_n during a recession. While in general the willingness to accept a low entry wage is interpreted favorably as evidence of a long horizon, behavior of that sort during a recession may be read by the employer as evidence of desperation by the applicant. People who are desperate in a recession may have especially high quit rates during a rebound of the labor market when their opportunities improve.

shown in figure 2-1, one-half of all firms sampled by applicants are not hiring at all. A wage of $36 will be exceeded, not by three-fourths, but only by three-eighths—that is, $(3/4) \cdot (1/2)$—of all elements in the distribution, including zero offers. Similarly, the $38 average of nonzero offers will be bettered by only one-fourth rather than one-half of all firms; and the high wage of $40 will be exceeded by only one-eighth rather than one-fourth. It now takes two days for applicants to receive as good an offer as they previously could have expected to receive in one day, since half of their days will be wasted sampling firms that are not hiring. The value of X associated with any particular dollar wage offer is unaltered by the zero offers, and it is reasonable to suppose that h is also unchanged.[13] But because π has been cut in half, the acceptance wage must fall below the value of $40 (at $\pi = 0.25$ and $X = \$1.77$) that applied when all firms were assumed to be hiring actively. If now half of them are not hiring, applicants' acceptance wage will be about $38.72, with $\pi = 0.202$ and $X = \$2.12$. Applicants are likely to spend more time searching (an average of nearly five days instead of four) and to settle for less satisfactory jobs.

A cyclical strengthening of product demand reverses the process. After recalling layoffs, restoring full-time hours, and eliminating on-the-job underemployment, firms will resume hiring. If 10 percent of firms do so (raising the figure from 50 to 60 percent), the results move closer to those obtained from the initial simple search example. The π associated with the $40 wage offer, for example, is then 0.15—that is, $(0.6) \cdot (0.25)$. Because of the improved labor market, applicants will find it optimal to set a higher acceptance wage and still to take less time searching, on average. With h constant, the acceptance wage becomes $39.08 and average search time 4.7 days. Unemployment and duration decline—without any fooling.

The changing frequency of hiring can also explain why quit rates and participation rates move in the directions actually observed during cyclical fluctuations. With fewer no-help-wanted signs, the reduction in dispersion lowers the cost of search, and tends to encourage both quits and entrance into the labor force. Just as it leads unemployed workers to become more selective—raising their acceptance wage—and to shorten their spell of unemployment, it makes experienced workers more likely to quit; they, too, can set a higher acceptance wage and expect to obtain

---

13. Because of the less efficient market, h might be marked up, but hardly enough to offset the drop in π.

it with less sacrifice of wages between jobs. Similarly, as a result of the increased fraction of firms that are hiring, persons not in the labor force who compare the value of their current activities with those of search and subsequent work will tend to enter the labor market. They now see a higher probability of meeting, within a given period of time, an acceptance wage high enough to be preferred over nonworking activities. So the cyclical movement of participation rates does not depend on a "genuinely" positive elasticity of labor supply (or, equivalently, negative elasticity of leisure demand) with respect to the real wage in the aggregate. The reduction in search costs will not drive those now in the labor force to work less, even if their supply curve is backward-bending. Nor can the fact of cyclicality in participation be invoked as evidence of a positive elasticity of aggregate labor supply, since it may well hinge on the reduction of search costs.

Improvements Made by the Toll Model

The toll model supplied a good reason for workers to have an investment in their jobs and also for a firm to have an investment in its employees. Those mutual investments can readily account for the on-the-job underemployment, part-time work, and layoffs as a rational response to a decline in product demand. In turn, those practices explain why firms may well not take on recruits even at bargain wages. Once the no-help-wanted sign (with its cyclical nature) enters the picture, it becomes evident that the mean and the dispersion of the distribution of wage offers are likely to move in opposite directions. The strengthening of product demand that raises some wage offers also makes hiring more widespread, and thus reduces dispersion. As a result, optimum search time is cut, leading to shorter spells of unemployment and hence less total unemployment. Cyclical fluctuations in unemployment no longer depend on stale information and fooling but rest on a rational foundation in a bilateral monopoly situation.

Thus far the toll model has been built on an assumption pulled out of thin air, and it has been presented only as a sketch. I develop the details subsequently; but it will always remain somewhat sketchy because its bilateral monopoly aspects preclude the determination of pinpointed equilibria and optima with respect to wages, employment, and other variables. Nonetheless, the toll model accounts for the most salient characteristics of cyclical performance in the labor market of the real world, outperforming the search model amended for stale information. In summary, the improvements include the explanation of the following phenomena: (1) layoffs and shortened workweeks and their cyclical variation; (2) no-help-wanted signs and their cyclical variation; (3) on-the-job underemployment, which offers a resolution of the cyclical productivity paradox that is consistent with traditional production theory; (4) procyclical variation of quits (high in prosperity, low in recession), consistent with rational behavior by employers and workers; (5) procyclical variation of participation in the labor force—without depending on the unknown sign of the elasticity of aggregate labor supply with respect to the real wage; (6) cyclical variations of unemployment, without reliance on a mechanism of misperception or fooling; and (7) the generally dominant role of changes in employment over changes in wage rates during both upward and downward phases of cyclical fluctuations.[14]

Interpreting the Toll

The toll can be given concrete meaning in various ways. Indeed, the potential explanations for set-up costs in the relationship between firm and worker pose an embarrassment of riches. The common and essential element in any satisfactory explanation is a departure from the assumption of homogeneity (or costless gradability) of labor. What the firm wants when it hires a worker is productive performance, which is not readily ascertainable in advance. It wishes to buy quality of work rather than merely time on the job spent by interchangeable people. The basic toll model goes a long way without incorporating such complications. It limits heterogeneity to one element—distinguishing workers previously hired by a particular firm from all other workers—and it attaches a cost of converting anyone in the latter category into the former. To bring that thin-air assumption down to earth, heterogeneity must be incorporated more realistically.

14. I suspect that the toll model could be developed fruitfully with a game-theoretic formulation. Each player is a B or an I; any B can play a game simultaneously with many I, but an I can play with only one B at a time. Anytime B_i wishes to play with an I_j for the first time, the B_i must pay the referee J dollars. A game lasts a day and has a positive value averaging Y dollars paid to the B team by the referee, but that value varies from time to time and among the B_i in a way that is not purely random. What does the B team pay the I team for the initial game? For subsequent games? What does it take to generate quits and layoffs?

In fact, it is the uncertainty and variability of productive performance that fundamentally rule out an auction market for labor. Because the relevant skills, experience, and attitudes that influence productive performance vary among jobs, the firm is unlikely to delegate to a "broker" the authority to deliver a certain number of workers with specified quality at a given wage. Any auction market operating on those principles would have high transactions costs and great difficulties in establishing meaningful categories. In perspective, the assumption of homogeneity (or costless gradability) of labor is particularly inappropriate for the search model; if that assumption were reasonably fulfilled, the labor market would approach an auction system, rendering the search mechanism unimportant.

Understandably, the personnel function is usually internalized by the firm. The firm will want to use its own judgment in appraising recruits. When it does rely on outside sources, the nature and form of the reliance helps to illustrate the significance of heterogeneity. For high-skill positions, it may use search firms—colloquially known as "headhunters"—to gather information and even make recommendations, but rarely does it authorize them to make binding decisions. When brokers are authorized to supply labor, the jobs at stake may require unskilled workers (like farm workers) or transitory workers (like office fill-ins) or involve formally graded skills (as is the case when unions certify craftsmen in construction, longshoring, and printing).

In a world of heterogeneous labor, the concern of firms about the quality of workers is reflected in various personnel practices. First, they incur expenditures for screening—attempts to use information about the applicants' backgrounds, experience, and aptitudes to forecast their productive performance and assess their quality. Second, they engage in tryouts, an empiricist technique of determining quality by putting recruits to work. Like screening, tryouts are a way of developing and using information to assess the productivity of applicants; but, unlike screening, which takes place before hiring, the tryout period comes after some tentative job relation is established. Third, a firm may train its new workers either through formal programs or through "learning-by-doing" on the job. In either case, training represents an investment in improving workers' productive performance over time. Fourth, personnel policies may develop incentives for quality performance by adopting a strategy that may be described as "rewarding." As in the case of training, the firm attempts to improve the quality of performance, in this case by offering particular rewards like promotions and merit raises. I discuss the distinguishing features of these practices below to make the payment of the toll by the employer an understandable process.

Screening with Discrete Quality

Suppose that, of all applicants for jobs with a firm, a certain fraction, z, would be "duds" with low productivity, and that they could be identified but only by an expensive screening procedure. Once searchers have agreed to accept the firm's wage offer, establishing themselves as "willing applicants," the firm assesses their probable performance by collecting information about previous records of formal education and work experience, by interviewing methods, obtaining references, or giving explicit tests before making a job commitment. Screening need not be "perfect" in filtering out the duds; and, even if it is potentially economical, pushing it to the extreme of perfection may not be efficient. But suppose the firm does find it worthwhile to screen thoroughly enough to achieve perfection, eliminating all the duds. Moreover, suppose all willing applicants who are "screened-in" are hired and are as productive, right from the start, as experienced workers. Thus homogeneity prevails among the "nonduds."

The identification of screening costs as an element of the toll leads to many of the conclusions derived above from the basic toll model. In hiring workers, the firm must expect to pay them less than their marginal revenue product during their tenure on the job in order to recover the screening costs. Indeed, it must recover the costs of screening the duds as well as the productive applicants from the latter group. An incentive emerges to charge the applicants a fee for the cost of screening. But so long as the firm relies on its subjective judgment to decide whether applicants have passed or failed the screening procedure, such an investment by applicants would be an act of faith. It is too much for the firm to expect, and so it does not try to collect. Indeed, I know of only one analogy to such a strategy in reality: the practice of some colleges of charging application fees that are not refundable even to those who are rejected for admission. It is more reasonable to limit the charge to an "initiation fee" for starting employment, and to convert that into an installment plan with a novice wage below the full-scale wage.

Such a practice has the general advantage of inducing self-selection by applicants toward those with longer expected tenure on the job. If W_n

is set below the flat wage offer available to the job seeker elsewhere, and W_x above it, applicants are asked to make an investment; and that is worthwhile only if their expected job tenure is sufficiently long. As in the basic toll model, the limitation on the optimum seniority differential stems from the workers' view of the current value of W_x as an imperfect predictor of its future value, their suspicion about the possibility of discharge, their risk aversion, and any excess of their time preference over the interest rate applied by the firm. Like the basic toll model, the screening variant provides a rationale for a seniority differential that is not necessarily linked to a productivity differential. The wage premium may turn out to be an efficient way of economizing on total compensation costs, including screening expenses as well as wages, by its influence on the self-screening by horizon and on quit rates of established workers.

The screening process could readily be incorporated into the analysis of the optimum strategy of the searcher discussed above in the framework of the basic toll model. Jobs for which the searcher would be screened out are equivalent to zero wage offers and are analogous to no-help-wanted signs. To the extent that screening rejections were randomly distributed across the distribution of wage offers, the presence of more thorough screening would lead searchers to take more time and on average settle for jobs that paid less well.

Finally, screening must influence any concept of balance or equilibrium in the labor market. The screening firm always requires more willing applicants than it has vacancies because it will screen out some of the applicants. "Full employment" in a world of widespread screening therefore cannot be defined by Lord Beveridge's famous criterion that the number of vacancies at least match the number of unemployed.

Screening with Continuous Quality

The screening model above was developed for a world consisting of duds and nonduds who can be distinguished with complete accuracy at some screening cost. Identifying the duds is the firm's sole reason for incurring screening expenses. In fact, the distribution of productivity among workers is likely to be more or less continuous; the productivity of any applicant is not perfectly predictable by any worthwhile screening procedures; and firms will try to screen out applicants whose personal characteristics suggest that they are likely to have especially high turnover as well as ones likely to have low productivity.

The screening process will yield productivity predictions that are not completely accurate and that are essentially continuous. Partly because the predictions are imperfect and subjective, the firm will not set a different wage rate for each predicted performance. The firm cannot accept two recruits for identical jobs and pay one less on the basis of the grades in the screening process. Indeed, it is likely to set a single wage rate for all novice jobs in a broad class. In the screening process the firm must then set an "acceptance quality" standard—a minimum expected productivity for new hires; and that is analogous to the acceptance wage of the applicant.

Acceptance quality and wages become joint decision variables that the firm must optimize. If the firm sets an acceptance quality as a minimum value of expected marginal revenue product, m^*, for the worker, the marginal revenue product of its average quality worker, $\bar{m}$, will clearly exceed that minimum. As always, the firm can obtain an extra worker with a small increment in the wage as determined by its elasticity of labor supply (defined over some specific period). For simplicity, suppose that the incremental worker attracted by a higher wage is one of average quality. Then, in considering a change in its wage (assuming a single wage for all workers), the firm has to meet the familiar marginal condition for an optimum:

$$\bar{m} = W\left(1 + \frac{1}{e_S}\right).$$

But now the firm has another option. At the margin, it can obtain one more worker at its present wage by lowering m^* a small amount. In that event, it pays W to obtain the extra marginal revenue product of m^*. To optimize both acceptance quality and wages, the firm must operate where the wage is equal to m^* and also equal to $\bar{m} \, [e_S/(1 + e_S)]$. It follows that the ratio of the minimum to the average marginal revenue product must equal $e_S/(1 + e_S)$.

The firm will adjust its optimizing parameters in response to shifts in its demand for labor or in the supply of labor. If the firm has an increased demand for new workers, it can obtain them without altering any dimensions of its wage scale simply by lowering its acceptance quality standard. But why would a firm that had previously optimized the trade-off between acceptance quality and wages respond to an increase in product demand (or a reduction in the supply of labor) by lowering acceptance quality? First, if surprises enter the process, changes in acceptance quality are a natural—almost an inevitable—response to them. Personnel managers who are disappointed by the number of applicants on any particular day can hire the number of novices that they had planned to recruit only by shading acceptance quality. Or if those managers are suddenly instructed to deliver more recruits at a given wage, shading acceptance quality is their only option.

Second, even after any surprise is fully recognized, the firm is likely to lower acceptance quality when its demand for labor increases if the elasticity of supply of labor in the very short run is low. In a search world in which job seekers must sample the distribution of wage offers randomly, higher wage rates can generate only a gradual growth in the firm's work force through their impact on acceptance rates of applicants and on quit rates. But it takes help-wanted advertising (or the equivalent) to generate a quantum jump of that work force. Shading acceptance quality may thus be part of any quick upward adjustments, substituting for or reinforcing the help-wanted ad.

Third, any cost of changing the novice wage can induce short-run alterations in acceptance quality. In chapter 3, I discuss the likelihood that firms and workers will adopt fixed time schedules for regular adjustments of wage rates. Under those conditions, quality (as well as quantity) adjustments are bound to occur in response to unexpected changes in supply or demand within that fixed interval. Changing acceptance quality need not be costless in order to be less costly than the initiation of wage changes outside the established schedule.

Fourth, firms may lower acceptance quality when their demand for labor jumps if their short-run marginal screening expenses are sharply rising. A firm with an increased demand for new recruits that raises wages and maintains acceptance quality must screen a larger number of willing applicants. Such a sudden step-up in the activities of the personnel department is likely to encounter rising marginal costs. Lowering acceptance quality (and maintaining wages) "flunks" fewer willing applicants and avoids the rising marginal costs of screening a larger number of willing applicants. In summary, there is a large set of plausible reasons for acceptance quality to be reduced slightly in cyclical expansion and to be nudged up in a slump.

Most significantly, the temporary cyclical adjustments in acceptance quality have *long-run* effects on the composition and size of a firm's work force. Once a firm has hired workers with slightly lower average quality during a boom, it will retain many of them when the labor market returns to normal, given the extra round of screening expenses that firings would incur. Moreover, because screening is imperfect, some novices with below-average expected quality turn out to be highly efficient workers; and some who have below-average expected horizons do nonetheless stick with their jobs.

Where cyclically variable standards of acceptance quality are widespread, they become important considerations to searchers. To any particular searcher, the relevant distribution of wage offers excludes all jobs from which that person would be screened out; those jobs represent zero wage offers. A shading of acceptance quality that increases the fraction of jobs for which the searcher would pass screening standards must improve the distribution of wage offers and also reduce its dispersion, from the viewpoint of the individual searcher. To the extent that the job seeker perceives the shading of acceptance quality, it evokes much the same reaction as the posting of additional help-wanted signs, which was discussed above in the framework of the basic toll model. It will generate a countercyclical fluctuation in the duration of unemployment, but a procyclical movement of quit rates as people are induced to play musical chairs to a greater extent. They can locate a better chair in a shorter interval of time and split the benefits of the improved opportunity between higher acceptance wages and shorter spells of unemployment. The more firms vary acceptance quality (as well as the frequency of help-wanted signs), the more changes in the job opportunities of searchers stem mainly from the availability of more and better jobs rather than from altered wage offers for the same job.

Data that cross-classify employment by industrial and demographic groups provide strong evidence of cyclical variations in acceptance quality standards. Low-productivity workers receive an especially large share of the extra jobs created during a cyclical upswing in high-paying industries like durable goods manufacturing. On the other hand, the employment of prime-age males in some low-paying industries like services is actually countercyclical. This phenomenon leaves its imprint on the cyclical pattern of real wages across industrial groups and across demographic groups. In a strong cyclical expansion, high-wage industries, by reducing their acceptance quality standards, take on a larger fraction of novices with adverse demographic characteristics. Those people quit jobs in low-wage industries that do not have the same options to shade acceptance quality and so must rely primarily on wage increases to meet their needs for labor. That is one reason why the average differential in pay between high-wage and low-wage industries narrows in an upswing. But while the novices earn less than the average pay of the industry in which they obtain jobs, they receive much better pay than they did in their previous jobs; hence the wages of the disadvantaged demographic groups show particularly strong cyclical improvement.

Tryouts as an Element of the Toll

Many of the features of screening apply as well to a process in which firms attempt to exclude duds by an on-the-job tryout. A firm pursuing a pure or extreme strategy of tryouts hires all applicants who accept its wage offer, puts them to work, and evaluates their performance during some probationary period. Those workers who turn out to be duds are dropped from the work force at the end of that period. Even if the successful novices are just as productive right from the start as are experienced workers, the firm will incur costs with the tryout strategy through the wages paid to those ultimately revealed as duds.

In choosing between screening and trying out (or adopting some combination of both), a firm must judge the relative predictive value and expense of compiling ex ante information about the performance of workers as compared to actually observing that performance. It will also be constrained by the willingness of applicants to provide performance data without compensation because screening does not involve a paycheck while trying out does. For example, theatrical auditions and athletic training camps are tests of performance in a simulated job environment, but they represent screening in the sense that they are conducted before the establishment of any employment relation and without pay to applicants.

The extent to which workers engage in a tryout strategy of their own will influence the employer's reliance on the tryout. If many novices find their work expectedly unpleasant and as a result have especially high quit rates, there is little reason for the firm to incur large screening expenses to evaluate the productivity of applicants precisely. If, in their initial months on the job, the workers are trying out the firm, the firm might as well use that opportunity to try out the workers.

However, a concern for "lemons"—that is, workers whose behavior affects the performance of other workers—rather than duds is likely to encourage the firm to screen rather than to try out workers. If the least desirable willing applicants have a substantially negative marginal product—by breaking up equipment, delaying assembly lines, or even acting as troublemakers—the firm will wish to eliminate such lemons through screening without risking a tryout.

A tryout variant will naturally feature (at least) two wage rates— a lower one for the probationary period and a higher standard wage thereafter. The optimum package of the two wage rates for the firm will depend on the various considerations discussed above in the basic toll model. Novices have more reason to discount the standard wage in the tryout model than in the screening model because they cannot know whether they will pass the probationary test. The firm may have good actuarial information on the fraction of novices who actually do flunk, and it may choose to communicate that information to applicants. But what is actuarially reliable to the firm because of risk pooling is still a high, unpooled risk to the individual. The risk of flunking is a more serious matter to applicants, even if they are no more risk-averse than is the firm. The risk element gives the firm an extra reason to pay novices more than their average marginal revenue product (which is the weighted average of the productivity of duds and nonduds). Under those circumstances, the firm makes an investment in new workers during the probationary period, and that investment generates all the familiar features of the basic toll model—the attachment between employee and employer; the bilateral monopoly element; the longer-run focus of the employment and wage decision; the emergence of cyclically variable workweeks, no-help-wanted signs, and layoffs; and the cyclical productivity pattern emerging from the stockpiling of underemployed workers in the slump.

As in the case of screening, the tryout may reveal essentially continuous productive performance rather than the two discrete groups of duds and nonduds. In that event, the firm is faced with a decision on acceptance (or retention) quality—where to peg the passing grade for adequate quality after the tryout. Acceptance quality is likely to be cyclically variable in the tryout model for the same reasons that emerged in the screening model.

The Role of Training

The training of novices represents an effort by firms to increase their future productive performance—to raise their efficiency. A formal training program for novices requires a period in which they do not contribute to the firm's output; indeed, during this period they absorb resources of the firm devoted to the program. The extent to which the firm can, in effect, charge tuition for the training is an interesting question. Gary Becker provides a neat framework for answering that question with his categories of "general" and "specific" training.[15] That analysis is worth reviewing both for its substance and for an illustration of the different implications of the auction and search paradigms.

Completely general training creates skills that are equally useful in the jobs of many firms. The incremental productivity of the worker resulting from these skills would be valued by other potential employers as highly as they are by the firm providing the training. The training should therefore increase the wage the worker could obtain elsewhere in the labor market. In a purely competitive auction market for labor the benefit obtained by workers in terms of their opportunity wages elsewhere would match the benefit obtained by the current employer through trained workers' increased productivity. Under those circumstances, apart from differences in time preference, trainees should be willing to pay full tuition for completely general training, and the firm has incentives to collect it. Once that training is provided, however, the firm must pay trained workers their fully enhanced marginal revenue product in order to retain their services.

In contrast, completely specific training improves productivity only for the job assignments of the particular firm providing that training. The opportunities for workers elsewhere in the labor market are not enhanced, and they have no reason to pay tuition for it. But, for the same reason that the training would not enhance workers' wages in other firms, the employer does not need to raise trained workers' wages commensurately with the incremental productivity for their jobs. Indeed, in the competitive auction paradigm the required pay increase is only a tiny bonus over the unchanged opportunity wage.

Once the search paradigm is brought into the analysis, however, the story changes. In that world, the full-tuition result of completely general training is an unattainable limiting case. The incremental productivity from the training provided may have undiluted value to other firms, but it will not have undiluted value to workers for two reasons: they would

15. Gary S. Becker, *Human Capital: A Theoretical and Empirical Analysis with Special Reference to Education*, General Series, 80 (National Bureau of Economic Research, 1964), pp. 8–29.

bear the costs of search to find a job in one of those firms including the cost of encountering no-help-wanted signs, and they cannot expect incremental wages to match fully their incremental marginal revenue product. Moreover, both workers and other employers would need complete and costless information to appreciate the full value of that training. Under the realistic qualifications introduced by the search paradigm, the employer is bound to do much of the initial financing even of training with broad applicability. The employer is able to collect for that training subsequently by paying wages that do not fully match the incremental productivity resulting from the training.

When completely specific training is viewed in a search world, it remains true that the firm providing the training cannot collect tuition unless workers are given some tenure at a guaranteed attractive wage. In the absence of such an explicit contract, the firm has strong incentives to provide a lower wage to trainees, in part to ensure their seriousness about staying on with the firm for the higher wage that is provided to those who complete the training courses. Whatever net costs are incurred, the firm must recapture them from the productivity of its trained workers. Their wages must be sufficiently below their marginal revenue product to amortize the firm's investment in training them. But their wages must be high enough to hold down their quit rate and thereby permit the firm to engage in that amortization. The optimization problem for the firm should be familiar by now; the solution will depend on self-selection effects, job horizons, and the confidence of workers in the implied (but not guaranteed) seniority premium.

The productivity of workers may improve from learning by doing, a by-product of carrying out their jobs, as well as from programs specifically designed to train them. Learning by doing can produce a sustained rising profile of productivity with experience; that profile would call for continuously rising seniority wage premiums. Unlike the wage differential in the basic toll, or screening, model, these seniority premiums reflect genuine differentials in productivity. The worker who has gained specific skills from either training or learning by doing is placed in a bilateral monopoly relation with the employer. The improved productivity developed from these experiences creates a surplus that is not applicable elsewhere and that becomes a likely object of bargaining. It will normally generate the standard features of the job attachment in the basic toll model.

Reward Systems

Attempts by firms to develop incentives for higher quality and more productive performance may be described as reward systems. In a sense, every job must involve certain aspects of rewarding. The firm pays the worker literally for time spent on the job, but what it really seeks is productive accomplishment on the job. That, in turn, is subject to control by workers through variations in the intensity and focus of their efforts. In these respects, labor is fundamentally different from most commodities. The seller of soybeans can be held to a precise contractual obligation to deliver a product of a certain grade to a definite place at a specified time. But the seller of labor cannot be tied down in the same way. Obviously, that seller must be present at the job for some particular period. But it is hard to specify what in particular must be done or how the seller can be compelled to deliver a certain amount of effort or output in return for pay. The firm's claim on the worker is really quite unspecific; its primary technique of making that claim effective is by rewarding workers in the form of pay increases and promotions for high-quality performance and by penalizing them through demotions or firing for failing to perform satisfactorily. Discharges "for cause" are a universal disciplinary instrument of employers.

The wage-reward system is inherently backward-looking. It explicitly pays people for their *past* productive contribution: what workers receive today depends on how well they performed yesterday. So long as the employer-employee relationship has the potential for lasting a long time, that backward-looking system provides adequate forward-looking incentives: people work today in order to improve their position tomorrow. The effectiveness of the backward-looking system depends upon a fairly frequent translation of performance into rewards or penalties. Long-term tenure contracts with wages stipulated in advance are rare because they would make the pay of workers independent of their performance for a substantial period, so long as they showed up on the job. Such insurance of wages would be subject to "moral hazard," creating inherently inefficient motivational biases. When such arrangements are made in the real world, they require formal rules and grievance procedures that can be costly.

Moreover, the difficulties of stipulating required performance in advance reduce the value to the employer of any commitment by the worker not to quit his job over a substantial future period. Athletes and entertainers provide notorious examples of the tendency for disgruntled workers bound by contracts to develop "disabilities" that impair performance. The reactions of athletes traded to another team against their wishes illustrate the difficulty of transferring to another employer the unspecific claim that any employer has over a worker.

Implicit contracts and general understandings of the link between pay and performance provide an effective mechanism for discipline and work incentives to the employee. I examine such arrangements in detail in chapter 3. Unlike machines, workers cannot be bolted down. But even if they could be bolted down by contract, they still would be different from machines because they cannot be switched on and off.

The considerations that enter into the reward system suggest that piece rates should be an efficient form of remuneration. Sales personnel typically receive commission payments that fit that model, and piece rates have their place in manufacturing. But their role is limited by many considerations. In some production processes, output is the joint product of many co-workers, and that interdependence precludes the assignment of an objective, quantitative performance rating to an individual worker. In others, remuneration geared to those measurable aspects of productive performance that can be captured in formulas would tend to create perverse incentives to sacrifice quality, caution, and even civility in the worker's conduct.[16] Moreover, technological changes embodied in new machines can lead to particularly divisive reappraisals of piece rates. Finally, to the extent that the piece-rate schedules reflect employers' notions of a norm or par-for-the-course on productivity, they may introduce a perverse incentive for workers as a group to collude in order to hold down the norm.

In general, to the extent that the reward system focuses on the performance of the worker, it deemphasizes the role of labor market conditions in altering wages. The employer's responsibility is to provide adequate rewards and penalties to enhance productive performance. A long line of applicants at the hiring gate is not a justifiable excuse for failing to honor these commitments. By the same token, while workers will respond to job opportunities elsewhere, their evaluation of their own job will depend on the general performance of the employer in responding to their productive performance. They are likely in turn to reward the em-

16. J. R. Hicks, *The Theory of Wages* (London: Macmillan, 1932), pp. 39–40.

ployer who fulfills a commitment by displaying low quit rates in the face of temporary tightness of the labor market.

When rewards take the form of movements up the rungs of a job ladder, the toll element resembles that of a generalized tryout system. Or the tryout discussed earlier may be viewed as a particular type of reward system. Even if the productivity of any particular worker is as high on the first day of the job as it will ever be (with no element of training or learning by doing), the pay structure is likely to be tilted upward by seniority in order to create appropriate incentives for self-selection by applicants and to provide bonuses that hold down the quit rates of the most productive workers.

Contributions of Alternative Models

Various models outlined in this chapter offer complementary insights into fluctuations of unemployment and wage rates. In principle, I dislike model proliferation and would prefer a single, general-purpose framework. But a single paradigm cannot serve all the purposes of cyclical analysis. Some issues can be explored with a simplified and rather abstract framework; others require a richer set of assumptions.

Despite its serious limitations, the simple search model makes an important contribution. By replacing the market-clearing mechanism with a more realistic costly and time-consuming process of making transactions, it takes the critical step in accounting for the continuing presence of unemployment, the gradual response of workers to wage differentials, and in general the dynamic nature of adjustments to shifts in supply and demand in the labor market.

The attachment between employer and employees is the key component of the toll model that was absent in the simple search model and present only with strain in the enriched search model. The basic toll model and all its specific manifestations introduce a degree of fixity into the job. But this particular kind of fixity is not just a reclassification of more payroll costs as overheads, and is not dependent upon a technological requirement for a steady and unvarying flow of labor input into the production process. Nor does it invoke any legal or contractual barrier to hiring and firing or even to changing wages. It is the initial establishment of a relationship between an employer and an employee that imposes a "set-up" cost, and that cost is generally shared by both employer and workers. As a result, the employer will have an investment in workers, and workers will have an investment in their firm. Bilateral monopoly is created, and it is made viable through the short-run sacrifice that each participant accepts in order to maintain the relationship for the long run.

When time is not of the essence—when the specific dynamic pattern of adjustment is not a crucial part of the story—it is often convenient to abstract from the search process. The toll can then be viewed as a large transactions cost in an auction market. The continuity of transactions through ongoing employer-employee relationships then becomes a way to finesse the auction market. Because the brokerage costs are large, people trade outside the exchange. The substitution of hand-to-hand for costly arm's-length transactions depends on continuous relationships and gives them a value. Thus for some issues the search paradigm is expendable; for others, it is a crucial component of the explanation.

In explaining concretely the set-up costs of the job relationship, screening, trying out, training, and rewarding all have a contribution to offer, illuminating various aspects of compensation and employment.

Even so, everyone can have a favorite among the models, and I have mine. For a general understanding of the labor market over the cycle, the continuous-quality screening model provides a reasonably neat and fairly comprehensive picture. Applicants for entry-level jobs lie on a continuum of expected performance from the point of view of personnel managers. To avoid the cost, complexity, and divisiveness of multiple entry-level wages for a single type of job, the firm sets one novice wage. It must then set some minimum acceptance quality below which it will not hire. The firm operates with a queue of willing applicants that exceeds its needs, including some who are close to the margin of acceptance quality.

When the firm's demand for labor increases (or the supply of willing applicants declines), the firm may find it optimal to downgrade the acceptance quality standard instead of, or as well as, raising its wage. People with a little less education, with adverse demographic characteristics, or with less previous experience become acceptable workers. Once the firm moves in that direction, the action has long-run consequences. Some marginal workers turn out to have unexpectedly high productivity; some who were suspected of high turnover tendencies do not quit. The relationship is established.

In the opposite direction, when the firm's demand for labor is reduced, its long-run implied commitments to experienced workers reduce the likelihood that it will curb wage rates. Again, part of the adjustment is likely to involve changing—in this case, raising—the acceptance quality standard. Beyond that, it may stop recruiting and post a no-help-wanted sign. Because of its investment in established workers, it will hold on to them even at the cost of on-the-job underemployment and depressed productivity; when it does reduce labor input, it will invoke shorter hours and layoffs in order to preserve longer-term relations. Then, when business picks up again, it takes a while before the firm has to face a choice of either raising wages or trimming quality standards.

With continuous-quality screening, the availability of jobs becomes the critical cyclical variable from the standpoint of workers. The search theorist can have the view that unemployment is "voluntary" and a rational choice—most workers could find *some* job at *some* pay. But cyclical unemployment is a serious hardship with no escape, so long as taking one job impairs the effective search for better ones (or the acceptability of the worker to employers offering better jobs). Workers are obliged to search or, more accurately, to wait for the reappearance of help-wanted signs in decent jobs for which they are normally deemed to be qualified.

What emerges is an interesting combination of quantity, quality, and wage adjustments by employers and workers to changing cyclical conditions in labor markets. That is what occurs in the cycle of the real world.

Bibliographical Notes

The two pioneering creations of search models are found in Milton Friedman, "The Role of Monetary Policy," *American Economic Review,* vol. 58 (March 1968), pp. 7–11; and Edmund S. Phelps, "Phillips Curves, Expectations of Inflation and Optimal Unemployment Over Time," *Economica,* n.s., vol. 34 (August 1967), pp. 254–81. Friedman focuses on the labor-leisure margin, which is capable of explaining cyclical changes in employment (reflecting changes in participation), but not changes in unemployment. The Phelps model explicitly trades off work against search, and does account for unemployment variations. Both rely on what I call "stale information" (sometimes characterized less accurately as "money illusion") to account for the short-run responsiveness of unemployment to higher wages. A key antecedent to the Friedman-Phelps analysis is George J. Stigler, "Information in the Labor Market," *Journal of Political Economy,* vol. 70 (October 1962), pt. 2, pp. 94–105. Actually, the essential elements of the theory were developed much earlier in William Fellner, "Demand Inflation, Cost Inflation, and Collective Bargaining," in Philip D. Bradley, ed., *The Public Stake in Union Power* (University of Virginia Press, 1959), pp. 225–54.

The formal development of the concept of the acceptance wage can be found in Meir G. Kohn and Steven Shavell, "The Theory of Search," *Journal of Economic Theory,* vol. 9 (October 1974), pp. 93–123. Other formulations of search models include Dale T. Mortensen, "Job Search, the Duration of Unemployment, and the Phillips Curve," *American Economic Review,* vol. 60 (December 1970), pp. 847–62; Edmund S. Phelps, "Money-Wage Dynamics and Labor-Market Equilibrium," *Journal of Political Economy,* vol. 76 (July–August 1968), pt. 2, pp. 678–711; and Robert E. Lucas, Jr., and Leonard A. Rapping, "Real Wages, Employment, and Inflation," in Edmund S. Phelps and others, *Microeconomic Foundations of Employment and Inflation Theory* (Norton, 1970), pp. 257–305. An excellent discussion of the search framework with some perceptive self-criticism can be found in Edmund S. Phelps, "Introduction: The New Microeconomics in Employment and Inflation Theory," in ibid., pp. 1–23. Other critiques that call attention to the inaccurate empirical implications of what I have called the "simple search" model are James Tobin, "Inflation and Unemployment," *American Economic Review,* vol. 62 (March 1972), pp. 5–9; Robert J. Gordon, "Recent Developments in the Theory of Inflation and Unemployment," *Journal of Monetary Economics,* vol. 2 (April 1976), pp. 205–07; and Steven A. Lippman and John J. McCall, "The Economics of Job Search: A Survey," *Economic Inquiry,* vol. 14 (June and September 1976), pp. 155–89 and 347–68, respectively. A wealth of evidence on cyclical patterns of duration, spells, quits, and job losses can be found in George L. Perry, "Unemployment Flows in the U.S. Labor Market," *Brookings Papers on Economic Activity, 2:1972,* pp. 245–78.

Articles that assume long lags in learning by searchers (and ignore the differences discussed in the chapter between labor and houses) include Robert E. Lucas, Jr. and Leonard A. Rapping, "Unemployment in the Great Depression: Is There a Full Explanation?" *Journal of Political Economy,* vol. 80 (January–February 1972), pp. 186–91; Thomas J. Sargent, "Rational Expectations, the Real Rate of Interest, and the Natural Rate of Unemployment," *BPEA, 2:1973,* pp. 429–72; and Michael

R. Darby, "Three-and-a-Half Million U.S. Employees Have Been Mislaid: Or, an Explanation of Unemployment, 1934–1941," *Journal of Political Economy,* vol. 84 (February 1976), pp. 1–16.

The significance of employer-employee attachments for labor market behavior has long been recognized. A distinction between "regular" and "casual" jobs is developed in some detail in J. R. Hicks, *The Theory of Wages* (London: Macmillan, 1932), pp. 63–74. An important contribution was made by Walter Y. Oi, "Labor as a Quasi-Fixed Factor," *Journal of Political Economy,* vol. 70 (December 1962), pp. 538–55. Many features of the basic toll model are found in an outstanding article by S. C. Salop, "Wage Differentials in a Dynamic Theory of the Firm," *Journal of Economic Theory,* vol. 6 (August 1973), pp. 321–44. The implications of career jobs for wage and employment fluctuations are analyzed perceptively by Donald F. Gordon, "A Neo-Classical Theory of Keynesian Unemployment," *Economic Inquiry,* vol. 12 (December 1974), pp. 442–59. That paper was written at approximately the same time that I published my first discussion of the subject; see Arthur M. Okun, "Upward Mobility in a High-pressure Economy," *BPEA, 1:1973,* pp. 207–52.

Important discussions of the way the heterogeneity of labor (and the cost of evaluating labor quality) influences employment and wage decisions can be found in Peter B. Doeringer and Michael J. Piore, *Internal Labor Markets and Manpower Analysis* (Heath, 1971), chaps. 2 through 4; Gary S. Becker, *Human Capital: A Theoretical and Empirical Analysis, with Special Reference to Education,* General Series, 80 (National Bureau of Economic Research, 1964), chaps 2 and 3; Charles C. Holt, "Job Search, Phillips' Wage Relation, and Union Influence: Theory and Evidence," in Phelps and others, *Microeconomic Foundations,* pp. 53–123; and Oliver E. Williamson, Michael L. Wachter, and Jeffrey E. Harris, "Understanding the Employment Relation: The Analysis of Idiosyncratic Exchange," *Bell Journal of Economics,* vol. 6 (Spring 1975), pp. 250–78.

Cyclical aspects of quality adjusting responses by employers are discussed by M. W. Reder, "The Theory of Occupational Wage Differentials," *American Economic Review,* vol. 45 (December 1955), pp. 833–45. Quality adjusting plays an important role in Robert E. Hall, "The Process of Inflation in the Labor Market," *BPEA, 2:1974,* pp. 347–60. Hall's interpretation, however, makes quality adjustments essentially perfect substitutes for wage adjustments, unlike the analysis I presented in the chapter. Various aspects of screening are explored by Kenneth J. Arrow, "Some Models of Racial Discrimination in the Labor Market," RM-6253-RC (Rand Corporation, February 1971); Edmund S. Phelps, "The Statistical Theory of Racism and Sexism," *American Economic Review,* vol. 62 (September 1972), pp. 659–61; Joanne Salop and Steven Salop, "Self-Selection and Turnover in the Labor Market," *Quarterly Journal of Economics,* vol. 90 (November 1976), pp. 619–27; and Michael Spence, "Job Market Signaling," *Quarterly Journal of Economics,* vol. 87 (August 1973), pp. 355–74.

Empirical evidence on the cyclical upgrading of demographic groups is presented by Wayne Vroman, "Worker Upgrading and the Business Cycle," *BPEA, 1:1977,* pp. 229–50. The "digestion" costs associated with increased rates of hiring are discussed by Robert M. Solow, "Short-run Adjustment of Employment to Output," in J. N. Wolfe, ed., *Value, Capital, and Growth: Papers in honour of Sir John Hicks* (Aldine, 1968), pp. 481–84.

III

Wages and Employment

THE WORLD of employer-worker attachments creates a complex optimization problem for the firm's personnel management. The firm is not only required to minimize the wage costs of a given employment but also to develop effective mechanisms to promote and assess productivity, and to build a reputation that will both enhance the supply of willing applicants and hold down quit rates. Job seekers, in turn, must assess the relative attractiveness of job offers that differ in many dimensions. The resulting arrangements for setting wages and adjusting employment establish the role of various determinants of wages. Most of all, they determine the way that cyclical changes in product demands are translated partly into changes in employment and partly into changes in wages. Those are the areas of inquiry in this chapter.

The Personnel Strategy

The firm must make an initial choice of a personnel strategy and deal with the toll as a decision variable. It must decide how much it wishes to emphasize low turnover and high productivity, given the costs of such an emphasis in the form of screening, trying out, training, or rewarding. Some firms adopt strategies that do not rely on attachments; they operate with a casual rather than a career work force and avoid investments in personnel. They attract workers with short horizons and any others who are not willing to make the sacrifice of taking substandard novice pay to develop the long attachment, and also workers who lack the skills to meet stringent screening requirements. When the majority of firms pursue career personnel strategies, they create a "hole" in the labor market to be filled by firms that choose the opposite, casual labor strategy.

The Casual Labor Strategy

Operation with a casual labor force will be most appealing to a firm that can simplify and routinize the tasks of its workers in ways that minimize productivity differences among individuals and particularly that permit untrained and unskilled workers to perform effectively.[1] Obviously, many jobs with such characteristics are tailored especially for teenagers. The pure case of a casual labor strategy would involve zero screening and training expenditures, so that anyone (or at least anyone having readily ascertained demographic characteristics) who accepts the firm's wage offer is hired; it would offer a single wage rate to all workers regardless of tenure with the firm; and it would maintain a perpetual tryout (or penalty) system whereby workers are fired if their performance falls below some acceptable level.

Because high pay represents a return to some differential skill or attainment on the part of workers, the unsorted casual workers are bound to be paid low wages. They are stuck with "dead-end" jobs, which are nonetheless their means of livelihood. The firm with a casual labor strategy must expect high and cyclically sensitive quit rates; its workers will have no inhibitions about quitting to obtain more favorable opportunities as they arise elsewhere in the labor market. Because there is no job attachment, layoffs have no place in such areas. Wages will be much more flexible than in career jobs because the employer may have no good alternatives to wage hikes in a strong labor market and need not have serious inhibitions about curbing wages in a weak one. But apparently the purely casual strategy is rare. Casual empiricism about the casual labor market suggests that the Keynesian wage floor nonetheless operates; the pay of car washers or stock clerks is seldom cut in a recession, even when it is well above any statutory minimum wage.

Weak employer-worker attachments also seem to apply to certain types of blue collar craftsmen who have relatively high skills and earn high pay—construction and dock workers, workers in the printing industry, and so on. These characteristics seem to arise most prominently when (1) an industry has many firms within a locality; (2) a firm has extremely variable demands for labor; (3) the worker's skill is "general" in Gary Becker's sense, that is, readily transferable across firms within the industry; and (4) the individual worker's degree of skill is categorized by conventions that develop among employers or unions or through government-sponsored occupational licensing. Carpenters thus may be classed as apprentices, journeymen, or masters; and references from one

1. A single firm may establish compensation structures that create career attachments for some jobs and appeal to casual labor for others.

employer to the next carry weight. In such cases, workers develop an attachment to a local industry rather than to an individual employer.

The Career Strategy

Firms that opt for a career labor strategy must expect to pay premium wages in order to achieve long attachments. They must confront the inherent problems of employment and wage arrangements in the toll model—an investment must be made in hiring a worker, and the worker cannot be bolted down or switched on and off. The nature of the problems can be clarified by a hypothetical toll example in which those problems would not arise. Suppose a single, self-employed worker could become a mini-firm by bearing the cost of a large toll (say, by training) without any requirements for investment in physical capital. The individual will decide to engage in this venture if the present value of marginal revenue products, M, is expected over the life of the "firm" to exceed the sum of the present value of the next best opportunity for wages or home activity elsewhere, V, and the toll, T, corrected for any differentials in risk:

$$\Sum \left[\frac{M_t}{(1 + r)^t} \right] - \Sum \left[\frac{V_t}{(1 + r)^t} \right] - T > 0.$$

Once the individual invests in the toll, the "firm" operates as long as $M > V$. If M falls below V for reasons that the firm views as temporary, it "lays the individual off" and suspends operation, but expects to resume when M exceeds V once again. If the worker's productivity depends on the effort put into the job, that individual adjusts the effort, making the contribution to M match the disutility of that harder work. This is a straightforward problem of optimization, and the individual can make efficient decisions on whether to begin the employment, how hard to work, and when to quit. If T is a decision variable, such that training can be taken in varying amounts with a continuous influence on M, the individual can in principle handle that issue as well.

Obviously, such mini-firm entrepreneurs are not typical because of the tremendous value of the division and specialization of labor and of other economies of scale in production, financing, and risk-pooling. These make relationships between the firm and its workers more efficient than single-person endeavors for most pursuits. But the toll introduces enormous complications in reaching efficient solutions within the framework of the employment relationship.

In a hypothetical world of perfect honesty and openness, the worker-firm solution would still be straightforward. Initially, workers would indicate their life-cycle work intentions; the firm would then estimate (or ask them to estimate) their quit probabilities over time and decide thereby whether the investment in the toll was worthwhile. After hiring the workers, the firm would calculate and tell each of them their M each week, and the workers would state their best estimates of V. The actual wage paid would be a weighted average of M and V. The weights determine the sharing of surplus and they would be decided by hard (but open and honest) bargaining. Clearly, if $M > V$, work continues; and if $M < V$, it ceases—just as efficient joint maximization would imply. If M was below V temporarily, workers would be voluntarily laid off. The incentive to effort could be properly geared to induce workers to generate extra productivity as long as it outweighed the disutility of the extra effort. All it would take to produce such an efficient solution is a world of completely honest and open people![2]

The decisions confronting the "mini-firm" or the thoroughly honest and open bargainers require complex and uncertain estimates over the distant future. But they are not contaminated by distrust between parties, and so are free of the crucial element that determines the arrangements under the toll model. That distrust focuses on the sharing of the bilateral monopoly surplus that emerges from a mutually advantageous relationship. Firms and workers have incentives to establish and to maintain such relationships by mechanisms that overcome distrust. If neither explicit nor implicit contracts could be developed that curbed the role of distrust, firms would be obliged to pursue the strategy of hiring casual workers; in that event, they and the whole society would forgo the productivity increments that come from screening, trying out, training, and rewarding. The development of rules and conventions for fair play becomes an essen-

2. There is an alternative solution that does not require honesty from workers (although it does from the firm) and that avoids wage differences among employees. The workers pay the toll plus a bonus to the firm in return for a tenure contract at a wage that always matches the varying value of M. In that world, however, the workers carry all the risk of changes in M, over which they have no control; or, more accurately, the risk of changes in their employer's estimate of M (which is the reason the firm's honesty must be impeccable).

A contract (transferable) whereby the workers sell themselves into slavery almost works efficiently. It has a few problems, however, in getting the proper recognition of the value of the workers' leisure and effort.

tial element in the pursuit of efficiency. In this dimension, equity and efficiency are tied together rather than traded off against each other.

At the time of a hiring decision, the assumption by the employer of major toll costs assures successful applicants that the firm seriously intends to employ them for a substantial period of time. The workers' willingness to accept a substandard novice wage gives the employer some assurance of their seriousness. To reinforce the dual assurances, willing applicants have an incentive to be reliable, steady, and immobile workers, and the firm is induced to convince those applicants that it is committed to be a first-class employer for the long run. Both sides will try to create favorable and firmly held expectations about their intentions. They can do so by assuming contractual obligations, but those have obvious costs in the loss of flexibility and the problem of motivational hazard. Alternatively, the firm in particular can attempt to influence the workers' expectations with nonbinding statements of intention and information. The workers are likely to attach some credibility to these because they recognize that the employer will be reluctant to disappoint them in the future lest they be led to quit prematurely. These considerations lead to a variety of explicit and implicit contracts, which are discussed below.

Such arrangements contain, but do not eliminate, the costs stemming from distrust. For example, for the workers in the mini-firm model, the quit decision is based on a comparison of present values of M in their current pursuits with those elsewhere, net of the toll cost of the new endeavor. Those net total returns are also the socially relevant considerations on where workers are optimally employed. To the workers in the toll model, however, the decision to quit is based on an assessment, not of total return, but of their shares of the return; what matters is the total return *less* the portion of bilateral monopoly surplus that the employer will capture. The best job for the worker thus need not be the job that is most productive insofar as the worker perceives employers as more or less "greedy." There can be "inefficient" quits in the sense that some potential bargain between the employer and the employee would make it worthwhile for both to maintain their relationship. Nonquits can be inefficient when mini-firm workers should change pursuits. Similar problems of inefficiency arise with respect to decisions on the amount of training and the number of workers on layoffs, which are explored below.

Some strategies of either party in the bilateral monopoly situation improve the joint maximization of the welfare of the employer and the worker (and presumably of society as well), while other strategies seek to enlarge the party's share of the surplus. For example, the employer may improve the joint maximization by reducing inefficient quits through methods that raise the "marginal" wage—the return from sticking with the firm an extra year—above the current wage. The marginal wage can be raised by tilting the pay scale upward with length of service (over and above any productivity differentials) and by seniority-related fringes such as vacations and retirement benefits that improve with length of service.

As an example of a strategy to influence the sharing of the surplus, experienced workers want the employer to believe that they are on the brink of quitting (a sharp contrast from their posture as willing applicants). They want to bloat the employer's perception of V to raise the wage that the latter will consider optimal. Meanwhile, the employer wants to shrink the workers' perception of M. The bluffing and guessing game that results has an interesting asymmetry. Any nonunion employer who overestimates V and thus sets a wage that is only slightly below M (higher than ideal for the employer's own interests) sacrifices profits but conserves joint surplus. But any employer who underestimates V and sets wages too low tends to destroy joint surplus through inefficient quits. Of course, this result is linked to the general rule that efficiency is promoted whenever monopolists or monopsonists fail to exploit their market power fully.

The adjustments in the toll situation are guided benevolently by a principle of Pareto optimality. If any dimension of the compensation package can be altered in a way that adds more (in value) to the welfare of the worker than it costs the employer, the employer will find it worthwhile to offer that benefit and to collect for it by shrinking other dimensions of the package. As I show below, that principle applies to explicit and implicit contracts and to tenure, promotion, and fringes as well as to wages.

Nonetheless, the basic problem of the need for trust arising from the toll and the inherent reasons for distrust is not soluble. Distrust is a pervasive fact of economic life that extends far beyond the career labor market. Enormous resource costs could be saved in a perfectly honest and open world that would permit do-it-yourself cash registers and communal lawn mowers. Just imagine how much labor and capital would be released from drawing up contracts, collecting and auditing bills, punching time cards, providing police protection and a court system, monitoring advertising and labeling, and from the whole network of safeguards against burglary and shoplifting. The need for arrangements to counter distrust in the career labor market exemplifies a general problem of human relationships in a complex interdependent society.

Explicit Contracts

In particular, because reduced risk and uncertainty about pay and tenure are valuable to the worker, the firm may find it worthwhile to assume binding obligations for a specified period of time about some components of the compensation package. Those binding obligations may be designated as explicit contracts. Under them the firm guarantees to the worker for an extended period some rate (or specified rising steps) of pay, W, or some quantity of employment, H, or both, $W \cdot H$. Inspecting the last of these first, it is clear that the simplest way to contract for both the rate of pay and the quantity of employment is to stipulate an annual salary for full-time employment. If the firm guarantees total earnings, $W \cdot H$, it assumes a large burden of both motivational and market risks. The motivational hazard arises from the principle that, once employees are guaranteed income, their incentive for productive performance is weakened. Moral hazard is a problem for sellers of all forms of insurance. Fire insurance companies know that their well-protected clients may be less careful about fire prevention, for example. The problem seems particularly serious for job-and-pay insurance (and, incidentally, least serious for life insurance).

Moral hazard, in particular, sharply reduces the value to the employer of "no-quit" contracts. If workers want to quit and are not permitted to do so, they can lay down on the job and withhold productive performance in subtle ways that cannot be prohibited by a contract. Even if workers wanted to pledge in advance to maintain peak effort and efficiency, they cannot make such a pledge credible. The firm may, of course, qualify the guarantee of employment by stipulating its unlimited right to fire workers for inadequate performance. But then moral hazard becomes a burden on the workers. If the firm is the sole judge of performance, it is more likely to render an adverse verdict if the market deteriorates, discharging workers who would otherwise be acceptable. Some neutral or bipartisan process for judging inadequate performance would seem to provide a way out of the dilemma. Collective bargaining often establishes explicit grievance procedures and makes them manageable. But no grievance procedure can make a no-quit pledge credible; what does it do with a worker who wants to be discharged in order to escape from a contract?

The $W \cdot H$ contract is therefore asymmetrical. The firm carries the risk of excessive employment at unduly high wages in the event of a sharp deterioration of markets. Although the firm should in principle be reducing its risk in the event of a sudden tightening of labor markets, it really cannot enforce the pledge of the worker not to quit.

Total earnings contracts are usually limited to short intervals and, even then, to cases in which they are expected to be renewed. The prospect of renewal provides the main incentive for performance during the period covered by the contract, reinforced by some provision permitting discharges for misbehavior. The contract is openly asymmetrical, generally specifying explicitly the worker's right to quit. The $W \cdot H$ contract is typically brief in duration because of the market risk assumed by the employer, who then cannot cut the workweek and lay off workers as escape valves in the event of weak product demand.

These considerations limit the scope of total earnings contracts and lead to explicit contracts in which the firm guarantees the hourly wage rate but not the amount of employment. Because employers retain their discretion over the number of hours of work and hence the total pay that they will provide, their pledge has a paradoxical aspect. The employer is telling the worker: "I cannot promise how much employment I will offer you, but I do promise to pay you so much per hour to the extent that I do employ you." That pledge looks empty at first glance; but it does mean something. After all, that is the basic character of the typical contractual wage arrangement under collective bargaining (and, as I discuss below, the standard practice of nonunion firms that announce a wage schedule for the coming year). In fact, employers are constraining their own behavior by such a pledge. They are promising not to hire another worker in that worker's place during the term of the contract. Such firms sacrifice the opportunity to take advantage of bargains that may arise in the labor market and, in particular, commit themselves not to initiate layoffs while still recruiting new workers. On the other hand, the workers accept a mild constraint on their behavior in return for the contractual obligation; they must refrain from strikes or slowdowns or heartrending pleas to management to raise their pay during the term of the contract.

The H contract, which guarantees the quantity of employment but not the rate of pay, is illustrated by tenure for university professors, teachers, and civil servants. The awarding of tenure does imply some obligation of the employer with respect to the pay path; in this case the employer is saying to the individual: "I will reserve a slot for you at the pay I offer to others with your qualifications." A guarantee of full-time employment is thus really a right of first refusal. As such, it is more readily applicable to individuals or selected groups of workers than to an entire work force.

Implicit Contracts

In addition to, or instead of, affecting expectations by specific binding obligations, the firm may try to influence the expectations of willing applicants and of potential quitters by various types of statements about the future that are not binding. They can have some force and some credibility by putting the firm's reputation on the line. The firm providing such implicit contracts must decide how much of an investment it is prepared to make in its personnel policy. If it makes strong statements that paint a rosy future for its recruits, it can hope to increase the supply of labor in the short run, but it then faces greater risks of excessive payroll costs to fulfill its promises or of costly disappointments by its workers that trigger higher quits and lower productivity if it fails to fulfill those promises.

Employers do, in fact, rely heavily on the "invisible handshake" as a substitute for the invisible hand that cannot operate effectively in the career labor market.[3] While nonunion firms do make commitments that are morally, and even legally, binding for a year ahead on wage rates (and, for some salaried employees, on total earnings), they generally opt for implicit rather than explicit contracts beyond that period. Apparently employers believe they can influence the long-term expectations of workers favorably with nonbinding statements that preserve much of their own flexibility. The credibility of these statements as forecasts is based on the firm's past performance, and that creates an incentive for it to build a good reputation.

The implicit contracts provided by the employer condition the expectations of workers. If those expectations are fulfilled, and if the workers do not learn of the emergence of superior opportunities elsewhere, presumably they stick with their jobs. In principle, any worker who quits to change jobs either has been disappointed about compensation (or

3. The term "invisible handshake" was first used in Arthur M. Okun, "The Invisible Handshake and the Inflationary Process," the Seidman Prize Lecture, *Challenge*, vol. 22 (January–February 1980), pp. 5–12 (Brookings Reprint 356).

other dimensions) of a job or has received some new information about more favorable alternative opportunities. It is either repulsion from the present job or attraction to other ones that makes the worker sever the relationship.

In the simple search model, repulsion and attraction are symmetrical. So long as the workers know the distribution of wage offers (even though they do not know the location of the best offers), a 2 percent increase in the mean of the distribution (with no change in percentage dispersion) exerts exactly the same pull away from a current job as a 2 percent cut in pay in that job. But in the toll world searchers must assess a complex package with uncertain future seniority premiums. They have to feel more confident about their ability to assess a current employer than other employers in the labor market.

As a result, a major asymmetry between repulsion and attraction arises because of the character of the information available to workers. They know more about the details of the package in their present job and the likely prospects with their current employer than they can know—without costly research—about the job market elsewhere. For that reason, the quit response to wage disappointment will be larger than to an equivalent improvement in other wage offers. Repulsion becomes stronger than attraction. The firm is competing, not merely with other firms, but with its own past efforts to develop favorable wage expectations. The wage it pays relative to other wages is part of the story; but that wage relative to the worker's previous expectations of that wage is another part.

To develop an effective implicit contract, the employer must try to promote favorable expectations and yet to curb the likelihood of subsequent disappointments. It can be helpful to educate workers about the criteria applied in assessing individual performance and the considerations from labor and product markets that would influence the employer's wage decisions. If workers know in advance that a bad profit year for their employer or mass layoffs by other firms in their community will curb their pay increases, the chances of major disappointments are reduced. But whatever criteria the firm highlights, it must decide how far it will go "out on the limb" with its statements about the future—offering forecasts (with varying degrees of expressed conviction), setting floors, or merely supplying facts.

FORECASTS. The firm may try to influence the expectations of entrants by stating its own expectations about improvements in compensation, without taking on a binding obligation. The forecast can be expressed as a technical best estimate, a target, or very nearly a pledge. In the short run, the firm practicing such a strategy has incentives to "puff up" future prospects and to underfulfill its previous predictions. But it knows that it will lose credibility in the long run by so doing. The incentives may lead to honesty. Or they may generate optimistic shading—accentuating the positive but maintaining sufficient accuracy to avoid antagonizing people.

The practice of scrupulous honesty is expensive and not readily demonstrable. A firm that honestly announced its own best expectations with respect to future wages as an admittedly uncertain, nonnormative forecast would overpredict half the time. Only after a great many rounds could the unbiased nature of its predictions and its actual honesty become evident to its employees; and it might take even longer for that reputation to become known, through the reports of current employees, to potential applicants. Honesty may be the best profit-maximizing policy if the firm's horizon is very long; otherwise, self-interest is likely to create a golden (or leaden) mean between honesty and dishonesty![4]

FLOORS. By pledging a wage path for the future that exceeds some minimum—in effect, stipulating some wage inequalities, the firm may provide "catastrophic insurance" to its workers, thereby eliminating their most serious concerns while retaining a large degree of flexibility for itself. Such a strategy may be an effective way of sharing risks. In its weakest form, the inequality simply pledges that the future dollar wage will not fall from its present level ($W_t \geq W_0$ for all $t \geq 0$). The attractiveness to the firm of eliminating the risk of wage cuts for its workers with only a limited sacrifice of its own flexibility can thus create the Keynesian wage floor.

The firm is likely to go beyond that pledge and promise to raise pay periodically without specifying the magnitude of the increase (that is, make the inequality strict, at least for t greater than some value). To make that pledge concrete and credible, the firm has to indicate *when*

4. The advertising manager faces the same decision problem in trying to promote a brand. There, the incentives lead more clearly to optimistic shading. It is better to have gained and then lost a customer than never to have gained one at all. That is not generally the case in the labor market, where the novice worker who quits in disappointment before the toll is recouped imposes a net loss on the firm.

wages can be expected to rise, and that encourages the establishment of a specific time schedule for increases. The firm can tell its workers: "So long as you perform satisfactorily, your wage will go up every year on July 1." Once the firm commits itself to wage increases on a definite schedule, it will be reluctant to raise wages in the interim, even in response to a sudden tightening of the labor market. Such considerations seem much more important in explaining the infrequency of wage adjustments by individual firms than do any specific bookkeeping costs of revising wage schedules. The fixed time schedule of wage increases has major consequences that will become evident below. One implication was noted in chapter 2; fixed schedules encourage the firm to shade acceptance quality in response to an unexpected tightening of its labor market encountered between scheduled dates.

FACTS. The complications of forecasting and the constraints of floors may make the firm choose merely to emphasize the facts about its past and present performance. This is an attempt to turn "stale information" into a virtue—encouraging workers implicitly to extrapolate data from the past into the future. In so doing, however, the firm is expressing an implied intention to maintain the same kinds of policies that generated its past and present track record. Indeed, it takes on an obligation to avoid discontinuities in policy toward less generous compensation and even responses to changing conditions that may *appear* to involve such a discontinuity. It sacrifices some flexibility and develops an investment in its reputation and its credibility.

Influences and Standards in Wage Setting

In this section, I abstract from changes in the tightness of labor markets and consider other factors that are likely to influence wages. I take a micro view, focusing mainly on the behavior of a nonunion employer of career workers with implicit contracts. The employer develops a system of compensation related to various criteria or determinants of wages. To the extent that workers are informed about these criteria, their expectations are conditioned and that, in turn, constrains the employer's actions to curb disappointments. The influences thereby take on a normative aspect and become standards as well. Below I identify five types of influences or standards in wage setting: norm rates of increase, other wages, product prices, profits, and consumer prices.

Norm Rates of Increase

In the career labor market workers expect improvements in their remuneration, in part because of the upward trend in the productivity of the firm and throughout the economy, and in part because of the seniority differentials that lead them to count on moving up the ladder within the firm. While the economist focuses on the movement of *average* wages from one year to the next, the individual workers are concerned with the movement of *their own wages.* In the presence of seniority differentials and in any firm engaged in some new recruiting, the wage increase experienced by the average worker who sticks with the firm for one more year will exceed the increase in the average of wages per worker that is calculated over the entire work force of the firm, including recruits.

Workers are likely to develop some notion of how fast they expect their wages to rise when they begin employment and when they decide whether or not to go shopping for other jobs. When changes in wages are announced by the employer (or newly negotiated in collective bargaining), they are assessed against the background of these expectations. The employer may find it worthwhile to encourage reliance on such a guideline, norm, or par-for-the-course on pay increases, but there are costs to such a strategy. Any subsequent slowdown below the norm must be justified and explained to experienced workers. If the employer stresses the norm, a Keynesian wage-floor phenomenon may apply to the rate of increase of wages, and not just to their level. The firm that is aware of such an attitude on the part of its workers may be reluctant to accelerate wages, lest it set a higher base or, even worse, a higher growth norm that it will be expected to maintain in the future.

Hence firms seeking to maintain their flexibility should want to avoid an overly strong attachment by their workers to a particular guideline for wage increases. Such firms cannot contract implicitly for a steady pace of increase over the long run, given the uncertainties they face about the product and labor markets. Employers should thus want to make workers aware of criteria or indicators of conditions that would call for a slowdown in wages, even though they recognize that, by such a posture, they arouse expectations of a speedup under the opposite conditions.

Even so, if the labor market is rather tranquil, inflation fairly steady, and the firm's fortune reasonably favorable over time, the employer may wind up granting wage increases that do not vary greatly from year to year. Then, even without encouragement by the employer, the practice becomes the norm and takes on inertia.

Wage-Wage Effects

The logic of the search model points to wage-wage comparisons as the central criterion for both the employer and the worker. The wage increase for experienced workers is meant to keep them from quitting—presumably by keeping their pay favorable relative to the wage offers they would obtain if they were to quit and shop the job market. The firm would like to tell its workers that they have just as much reason to stick with it this year as they had last year. By revealed preference, the experienced workers did find it worth sticking with the firm previously, and they should be persuaded by clear evidence that they have no reason to change their minds currently.

Such evidence is easiest to convey when alternative sources of employment are readily defined and workers' wages can be averaged into some kind of weighted universe. Some large nonunion employers thus hire "neutral" management consulting firms to do surveys of wages paid in comparable jobs by other employers in their community, make the results available to their employees, and adjust their wages according to the findings of the survey. The federal study of pay comparability for civil service workers is an especially formalized example of such practices.

Because it is difficult and costly to define and sample objectively a universe of such "reference wages," firms and workers may focus on a few key indicative wages as the basis for a pattern of emulation. Sometimes the pattern is not linked tightly to the logic of relevant alternative job opportunities. The keen attention that the steel industry gives to wages paid by the automobile industry is out of proportion when compared with the competitive attraction of jobs in auto firms for steel workers. Similarly, plumbers in Syracuse inspect the pay of plumbers in Seattle, although few contemplate cross-country migration. Apparently workers and firms need a standard to guide their judgments of *fairness* more than they need a precise indicator of market pressure. In other cases, the reference wage may serve another function; when nonunion employers seek to outpace union wages in their industry, their intention may be to discourage the search for a union rather than the search for another job.

Any wage-wage pattern necessarily relies on stale information. The only wage levels or wage increases that can be observed are those set previously—although presumably most weight is attached to ones determined in the recent past. Such patterning, like the reliance on a norm or guideline rate of increase, lends inertia to the rate of wage increase in the economy. If some of the reference wages were themselves influenced by emulation of previous wage decisions, the chain of lags could be very long indeed. Moreover, when wage emulation is widespread, it becomes important to find the leaders of the parade that so many people are trying to follow. Those firms or industries that set wages independently—in other words, that do not pattern on other wages—can have a large "multiplier" effect on the whole system. At the limit, a model of wage-wage emulation has to specify a prime mover.

Moreover, the operation of wage emulation depends on an unsynchronized schedule of wage adjustments for different firms and different groups of workers. If every worker received one wage adjustment each year on January 1, and the decisions on wage adjustments were made in an uncoordinated fashion by employers in nonunion firms and by decentralized collective bargainers in the union sector, emulation could not be the star of the show. To be sure, the typical employer would be considering relative wages when reckoning how much of an increase to grant as New Year's Day approached. Presumably those who felt that it would pay to bring down their quit rates or increase their flows of willing applicants would be seeking to raise wages by more than they expected other employers to do. Other employers in the opposite position would want their relative wages to drop a bit. Each employer would therefore try to guess the increase that other employers were likely to make. But they might find no good clues on which to base such guesses.

In fact, the inability of firms to assess relative wage prospects would destabilize the synchronized situation. Every employer would like to make a decision in full light of the decisions that others had made, but would also like to respond promptly. So an employer would want to move a bit behind the schedule followed by the others. As a result, some employer would decide to shift the wage adjustment date to February 1, in order to observe what all the other employers had done. Others would also want to make such a move, but obviously everyone cannot exercise the preference to bat last. The likely result of this "time-location" problem is analogous to that of some spatial location problems. It generates a tendency to spread the distribution of wage-adjustment dates around the calendar.

Suppose that such a distribution is established in a nonunion world, so that one-twelfth of all firms posts their new wage rates each month and puts them into effect for the following twelve months. In any firm, the workers know their month of wage adjustment. If September is the month for a particular group, they expect to be a little below the average wage of comparable workers in August and a little above in October. Both the firm and its workers have sacrificed some flexibility in order to obtain greater predictability and to reduce decision costs. The workers recognize that they cannot plead for wage increases during eleven months of the year, and the firm knows that it is obliged to grant increases in September. As in any futures contract, the fixed period for wage setting has the advantage of reducing some risks for the participants and the disadvantage of locking them into arrangements that may prove regrettable in retrospect. With the fixed schedule, the wage at any point in time usually deviates from a sustainable equilibrium, but in a particular and predictable form that is aimed to average out to zero during the course of the entire year. Experienced workers who take a reasonably long view of their job relationship are likely to view the disequilibrium calmly, and even new applicants need not be so myopic as to regard the wage offers of the firm as terribly unattractive in August and especially appealing in October. Tolerating the minor transitory highs and lows in the relative wage position is unlikely to be costless, but it need not be burdensome.

Suppose a typical "September firm" and every other firm are executing such a strategy. The average wage rate in August of all firms that are relevant competitors in the labor market with the September firm reflects the wage increases awarded between September of the past year and August of the current year; that reference wage is an average of wage levels newly established over the preceding twelve months. If the typical firm merely matched the reference wage when it set its new wage in September, it would expect its relative wage position to be below the average during the entire period of the next eleven months, as other firms raise their wages subsequently. The firm must sense a need to play leapfrog, to add some appropriate percentage to the reference wage at the time of its adjustment in September. How can it find—and communicate to its workers—a standard for the appropriate jump that will put its relative wage level on the high side by the right amount in September, allowing it to sag correspondingly on the low side by the following August?

Obviously the firm can explicitly forecast the growth of the reference wage over the coming year. If the predicted growth is g percent, the firm making its wage adjustment would expect to achieve an appropriate average relative wage over the coming year by jumping over the current reference wage level by $g/2$ percent. If, for example, g is 4 percent, its wage will initially be 2 percent above the reference wage; the differential will drop gradually during the year, reaching a value of -2 percent at the end of the year, assuming that its forecast is correct. But forecasting the wages of other firms is complex and costly, and communicating the validity of the forecast to workers may be equally challenging. So the firm may decide to look backward at the growth of the reference wage during the past year, and add half of that gain to the reference wage level at the time of its adjustment.

A third alternative emerges, still assuming that the firm has no intent to raise or lower its relative wage over the year ahead. It can finesse the issue of the appropriate leapfrog by raising its wages by the same percentage increase that the reference wage experienced in the intervening year. If the firm's wage was 3 percent above the reference wage last September, and then it matches the increase registered by the reference wage between last September and this September, it will be once again 3 percent above the reference wage. In effect, it is saying that it had made an appropriate leapfrog a year earlier and wants to restore it currently. In this way, the size of the jump really enters the decision whether or not it is explicitly considered.

The alternative ways of implementing a wage-wage pattern have interesting implications that will come up again later in this chapter and in chapter 6 when the strategy of firms that want to raise or lower relative wages is examined. Whatever form it takes, wage-wage emulation is bound to be an important influence and norm in wage setting. It swims with the tide of the job market; it highlights and processes relevant information. The wage-wage convention prevents disappointments in the pay of the current job by linking pay to the attraction of other jobs. Both repulsion of the status quo and attraction elsewhere are contained simultaneously. But exclusive reliance on a wage-wage pattern is not likely to satisfy firms insofar as it fails to reflect changes in their product markets that influence profitability, as well as both their demand for workers and ability to pay them.

Productivity and Product Prices

In short, wage-wage patterns are keyed to the supply side of the firm's labor, and some criterion from the demand side may be desired. The demand side of the story is contained in the marginal revenue product curve. But the marginal revenue product is not a tractable norm for wages, most significantly because it is not observable to workers. For some purposes, average revenue product can serve as a proxy, and it is in principle subject to measurement—as total revenue divided by total worker hours.

Average revenue product, in turn, reflects both average productivity and product prices. Productivity is the key to real wage gains in the economy as a whole, but the differential growth of productivity across industries or over time has only a limited effect on the wage structure, for obvious reasons. Workers in industries that, for technological reasons, have low productivity growth (like services) will quit in droves if they keep receiving pint-sized wage gains. Conversely, firms in industries with rapid productivity growth do not need to pledge or deliver more rapid wage gains than others in order to hold on to their workers. Understandably, the differential growth of productivity across industries mainly changes relative prices over time—for example, pushing up prices of services relative to those of durable goods—rather than significantly altering the pattern of relative wages. Even cyclical slowdowns and speedups in productivity are accepted as the firm's responsibility (for better or for worse) and are found empirically to affect profits far more than wages.

Product prices are the other element in average revenue product. For the microeconomic determination of wages, they receive little attention in either the literature or the lore of labor markets. Yet, for aggregate wage behavior, they get star billing in recent econometric studies (performing much more strongly than consumer prices). How can this be possible? Product price movements from one year to the next result from changes in the costs of nonlabor inputs, labor costs, and profit margins. Increases in material or capital costs to the firm should swell its wage gains only to a minor degree through the limited short-run substitution of labor for those other factors. The part of price increases that reflects previous wage increases can generate still further raises in pay only through the emulation of current wage increases on previous ones, that is, with product prices acting as a proxy for past wages. Of course, wider profit margins, which reflect a genuinely increased return from the product of labor, should swell pay advances by raising the demand for applicants and the cost of quits. I suspect that the empirical success of the product price as an explanatory variable for wages in the aggregate reflects its blending of two quite distinct influences—wage emulation and profitability.

Profits

Profitability is an important indicator of what the firm can afford to pay its workers and what it is receiving from them. Profits are one of the ways that the demand curve for labor influences the formulation of wages. But profits cannot be the basic wage norm for any firm or industry. The separation of roles between firms and workers implies the willingness and ability of the firms to take the managerial responsibility to bring in the profits, and to assign to its shareholders—not its workers—the risk of profit variability. In addition, the calculation of profits is subject to a great deal of discretion by management and its accountants, and any precise reliance on profits as a standard for wages would require workers to participate in the accounting decisions, invading an important managerial prerogative. Nonetheless, formal arrangements for some elements of profit (or loss) sharing are part of the compensation package in a small fraction of firms; the growing use of employee stock-ownership plans creates another link between profitability and labor compensation. Even when it is not formalized, the profit criterion often enters into the discussion and assessment of wages.

As a variable in aggregate wage equations, profits have had their ups and downs over time. The cycle in econometric findings seems to parallel the cycle in profits themselves. During the sixties when profits were strong, they were generally found to be an important influence on wages; during the seventies when they were weak, their econometric influence was less pronounced and subject to greater professional controversy. Their effect may actually be asymmetrical with greater upward influence from high profits than downward influence from low profits.

Consumer Prices

During the past decade of increasing concern about inflation, the influence on wages that has drawn most attention is consumer prices. "Indexing," or cost-of-living escalation, is an important and growing phenomenon. I have reserved this factor in wage setting for discussion last, not to slight it but to give it the attention it deserves. Nonetheless, the striking fact is how small—rather than how large—a role the cost of living plays as a wage determinant in the United States. Cost-of-living escalators are essentially absent in the nonunion sector and in nearly half of union contracts, and rarely, if ever, offer increases that are fully proportionate to rises in the consumer price index. Of course, indirectly and informally, consumer prices have somewhat greater effect, partly through the emulation of wages that are escalated. Still, econometric findings on aggregate wage behavior accord a less important role to consumer prices than to past wages or product prices. I believe that this limited role of consumer prices is understandable (and, as I argue in chapter 8, that it is socially desirable).

It is axiomatic that rational workers care, not about the number of dollars in their pay envelopes, but about the bundle of goods and services that it enables them to buy. Clearly, the risk-averse worker will prefer certainty about real wages to a certain path of nominal wages whose real worth has the same expected value but is subject to uncertainty. But the fact that workers care about the predictability of real wages is not sufficient to make the cost of living a major wage influence or a tractable wage norm. That will be the case only if their quit rates are raised by increases in consumer prices for a given distribution of nominal wages in the labor market; or if their concern about the cost of living enables the employer to sell them "real wage insurance" profitably. Consumer prices must be linked to wages by either quit-rate sensitivity or efficient insurance contracts.

As I have stressed repeatedly, rational workers deciding whether to quit their present jobs to search for better jobs elsewhere must focus on *relative* wages, not real wages. If these workers are fully informed about the distribution of (dollar) wage offers in relation to their present wages, the cost of living is irrelevant. Indeed, this is relevant information for any worker who is on the margin of quitting a present job in order to drop out of the labor force and engage in home activity. But this is only a trivial concern for the firm when making any realistic estimate of the elasticity of the supply of labor with respect to the real wage. The firm needs to worry about workers who quit to shop elsewhere, not those who quit to stay home.

Once the simple-search assumption about full information concerning the distribution of wage offers is dropped, however, I can envision two different rationales for an influence of consumer prices on quits to shop elsewhere. One amends the search paradigm to suggest that, in their uncertainty about the distribution of wage offers, searchers (or potential quitters) use consumer prices as one clue to the likely distribution. Because the cost of living is positively—though imperfectly—correlated with wages, it may have effects on people's expectations of wages. That would establish the link, but it seems farfetched to me (and has never been expounded, so far as I know, by anyone).

The second rationale is a satisficing argument for career jobs. Presumably one of the attractions of a career job is the prospect of a reasonably secure and rising standard of living for the long run. A sharp increase in consumer prices that curbs real wages is bound to be disappointing to workers, even if their employer did not violate any element of an implicit contract that was obviously formulated in nominal terms. Any disappointment may mark down the perceived valuation of workers' stakes in their career jobs. If they attach less value to their current jobs, workers may become more likely to quit, even without any direct evidence that their wages have deteriorated relative to alternatives elsewhere in the job market. Once the employer believes that, even holding constant the distribution of wage offers, a sharp rise in consumer prices would raise the quit rate, there is an incentive to adjust the wage of experienced workers in response to changes in consumer price inflation and, moreover, to specify that practice as part of an implicit contract. *Some* role for the cost of living as a determinant of quit rates can thus be established; and the argument is plausible if not compelling.

The insurance rationale can also be developed plausibly. If workers attach a high cost to wage uncertainty, employers may have the opportunity to redesign their compensation package, preserving its value to the worker at lower cost to themselves, by indexing wages and thus reducing (or even removing) the costly real-wage risk carried by the workers. It is not obvious, moreover, that the employer would be assuming much added risk by providing that insurance. To the extent that surprises in the movement of consumer prices are positively correlated with surprises in marginal revenue product, employers that provide real wage insurance do not add as much to their risk as they subtract from the risk of the workers. Indeed, a firm that sells as a price taker in a competitive auction market will actually reduce its profit risk from a given level of employment. It does this by supplying real wage insurance if a 1 percent surprise in the cost of living is associated, on average, with a surprise in the same direction in the price of its product of more than 0.5 percent.[5]

5. I ignore the imperfect hedge provided to any worker whose personal market basket differs from that used in the index or whose community's inflation rate deviates from the national average.

Cyclical surprises that reveal more (less) inflation and increased (reduced) strength of product markets might meet such a test. In that event, the escalated wage (compared to the nominal wage with the same expected real value) is "super-efficient," making both sides better off with no compensating adjustment. Nonetheless, for reasons that will become clear when the whole system is put together, short-run relationships between overall consumer prices and the strength of a particular product market are likely to be weak. In any case, the major risk to the firm from the wage escalator is that it may get out of step with other competitive firms in the product and labor markets. If the wages of the firm's competitors follow a nominal standard, their cost of output will move differently; and so will the prices they charge. That will give the indexing firm a competitive advantage in some circumstances and a competitive disadvantage in others, making its profit path more variable.

The same point applies to the labor market. If most firms are not indexing, when prices spurt, the firm that does index will be paying higher relative wages. Conversely, if price increases slow down surprisingly, the firm's relative wages will be lower. Its quit rate will be lower in the former case and higher in the latter as a result of being out of step. Again, a strong short-run relationship between acceleration of consumer prices and tightening of the labor market may serve as an automatic stabilizer of the firm's quit rate. But if the relationship between tightening of the labor market and acceleration of consumer prices is rather weak (or substantially lagged), the variability of that firm's quit rate is increased. In general, in holding on to experienced workers, the firm has strong incentives to stay in step with the rest of the labor market. Those workers have already displayed their willingness to stick with the firm, and the maintenance of relative wages is the key to holding onto them. Finally, if planning for capital inputs and for financial resources is conducted in nominal rather than real magnitudes, the firm with a real wage policy also takes on added risk in those dimensions by getting out of step with its banker.

The problem of getting out of step illustrates a general principle that will come up again in subsequent chapters. Because reliance on the dollar as a yardstick is deeply entrenched in the American institutional structure, attempts to develop a substitute "real" yardstick impose risks and information costs on the innovator. The dollar yardstick was adopted before the possibility of an alternative "real" yardstick had been created by technological advances in government statistics that now supply a monthly index of consumer prices on which people are willing to rely. The dollar and its conventions still prevail, imposing the cost of getting out of step; this, in my judgment, is the main deterrent to indexing and the key explanation for its limited scope.

As an alternative explanation, it is sometimes suggested that workers may not put a high value on real-wage insurance because they have other ways of dealing with the uncertainty of prices. In particular, they can offset inflation risks on their income by adjusting their balance sheet, using their holdings of real assets as leverage, and increasing their debt. In fact, the booming demand for homeownership in recent years is evidence of a balance-sheet response to inflation risk. However, as will become clear in the discussion of asset markets in chapter 5, no portfolio manager can assemble a balance sheet with a predictable response to inflation. Surely such opportunities are far more limited for most workers, who have neither the net worth nor the borrowing capacity to offset any significant real-income risk through the management of their assets and liabilities.

Moreover, collective bargaining agreements demonstrate that workers do attach a high value to real-wage certainty. Under the pressure of major unions, firms have accepted indexed wage arrangements—especially when threatened with a shift to contracts of shorter duration. It is noteworthy that agreements that even approach full cost-of-living protection have been made only through industry-wide bargaining in large industries for which the price elasticity of product demand is rather low. Through this bargaining all firms are forced into step, and their joint acceptance of escalation reduces the risks they assume individually. Industry-wide collective bargaining thus cuts the costs of indexing to the firm. Moreover, these strong indexing agreements pertain to high-wage industries in which firms probably need not worry much about adverse wage-wage comparisons (and resulting quits) in the event of a slowdown of inflation.

Nonunion firms do not ordinarily offer cost-of-living escalators in their compensation packages; their wages are often indirectly affected by consumer prices with a longer lag through emulation of union wages that have formal escalators. Furthermore, some seem to adopt annual wage increases, and even implicit contracts, that reflect consumer prices through "catching up" with last year's inflation, while avoiding forward-looking formulas. Both the extent of indexing in the union sector and of informal "catch-ups" in the nonunion sector are clearly influenced by experience and expectations about consumer-price inflation. Beyond that important influence, I am convinced that such price expectations play only a very minor role in the determination of wages. The reliance on escalators as contingent contracts demonstrates that unions and firms recognize that they do not know how to forecast changes in the inflation rate. The contracts in the union sector that are not escalated reflect an acceptance of looking backward or of placing less weight on consumer prices directly; they do not reflect agreement on an inflation forecast by labor and management. I have never heard of an econometric price forecasting exercise in a collective bargaining negotiation. Moreover, despite the emphasis that many macroeconomists place on consumer price *expectations* as a wage determinant, I have never seen an explanation of why and how a nonunion employer would apply a forecast of such prices in setting wages.

Implications of Various Wage Influences

Again, the analysis encounters an embarrassment of riches. A plausible case can be made for a variety of wage influences—norm increases, other wages, product prices, profits, and consumer prices. The wage-wage story stands out as particularly compelling, but all items on the list play a role.

The implications of alternative determinants are similar for some types of disturbances and different for others. For example, norm increases, other wages, product prices, and consumer prices all imply that a jump in wages is likely to trigger further rounds of larger wage hikes. (Profits alone do not.) In the case of general inflation in nonfarm domestic prices, product prices, consumer prices, and profits convert the higher prices into higher wages, but norm increases and other wages do not. For some types of disturbances or policy instruments, the differing verdicts are especially important. Consumer prices and product prices lead to contrasting predictions of how much oil-price hikes of the Organization of Petroleum Exporting Countries or increased state excise taxes will push up wages.

Thus in some cases the primary influence does matter a great deal, and must be carefully identified. Empirical studies of wage behavior in different industrialized nations show different degrees of emphasis on the various determinants. For example, Europeans seem to accept as fact that higher income taxes raise wages; in the United States that is evidently not the case. Yet it is inconceivable to me that any theoretical model could have "predicted" that difference in wage behavior on the two sides of the Atlantic. Wage standards are conventional and habitual. They have their logic and they take on a life of their own. They become entrenched because firms have incentives to get into step with other participants in the labor market. There may be more determinacy in the persistence of any reasonable convention than in its precise nature for any particular time or any particular country.

Adjustments to Cyclical Changes

The implicit contracts in the career labor market are intended to make continued employment of experienced workers a normal state of affairs. But affairs are not always normal. When markets become abnormally tight, the number of workers who quit increases, creating pressures for upward wage adjustments. When markets become slack, the employer is faced with the choice of maintaining "redundant workers," instituting part-time or layoffs, or cutting wages relative to the path of the implicit contract.

Consider a downward cyclical movement generated by a reduction in aggregate demand that cuts the marginal revenue product of workers. If the change occurs between the dates at which wages are normally adjusted—say around mid-year for a firm that customarily alters wages on January 1—it would have to be extremely large to dislodge the firm from an established pattern built into its management practices and communicated to its workers. The firm may have some flexibility for making "hidden pay cuts" by hiring at lower grades, slowing the rate of promotions, and the like. It may have less inhibition about cutting the novice wage than the wage of experienced workers. If it engages in continuous quality screening or trying out, it can make quality adjustments. But it may find it worthwhile to institute part-time schedules or layoffs in the interim.

The serious dilemma of trading off the downward wage adjustments against downward quantity adjustments continues until the next scheduled adjustment of wages. For the firm in the simple search model, the solution is simple because there are no inhibitions against cutting wages. The firm would not post a no-help-wanted sign; it would not lay off a productive worker; it would clearly not raise average nominal wages while experiencing an excess supply of workers at its previous wage. In the toll world, firms not constrained by explicit contracts will engage in such practices only because of their concern about economizing on toll costs. Because their quit rate in a slack labor market is likely to be below levels they normally consider optimal, it is future, not current, workers who quit and possible negative impacts on incentives for productive effort that restrain firms from trimming the wage. The restraining forces are bound to be larger in those firms for which toll costs are higher. One would expect wages for casual jobs to respond much more to cyclical weakness of the labor market than wages for career jobs.

When employers institute layoffs or part-time schedules or post no-help-wanted signs, they are testifying that their current wages exceed the marginal revenue product at their current employment. To react to that situation by cutting employment rather than cutting the wages is bound to impair profits in the short run. Such action can only reflect a conviction that the toll costs saved in the long run justify that short-run burden. If nonunion employers grant an increase in nominal wages at a time when their workers are on layoff, when there is enforced part-time, or when no-help-wanted signs are posted, they reveal an even stronger assessment of the costs of deviating from their implicit contracts. Those costs are apparently sufficiently large to make quantity variations play a dominant role in the adjustment to recession and slack.

Cutting Labor Input: The Costs and Benefits

Suppose an employer experiences an unexpected decline in product demand and decides not to trim the wage rate below the path of the implicit contract, but to operate at a level of employment at which W exceeds M. The employer must then decide whether to accept the excessive payroll costs or to cut them back by shortening the workweek, instituting layoffs, or some combination of the two. Because W exceeds M, a reduction in labor input will bolster profits immediately; but, through its impact on the employer's reputation, it will raise compensation costs for the longer run. Given the drop in product demand, the employer must ask whether the cutback in payrolls would contribute more to profits in the short run than it would subtract from them in the longer run.

The considerations that enter into these calculations are readily identified. The costs of retaining redundant workers depend on the uses that can be made of them. Any cushions under M that keep it from falling drastically when product demand falls will curb the net cost of maintaining an excess worker, which is $(W - M)$. If the demand for the firm's output is highly elastic in the short run, it may be able to maintain sales with only modest price cuts and thereby minimize the net short-run costs of excessive employment. In Japan, where the willingness of employers to keep paying unneeded workers during a slump has become legendary, the adjustment apparently stresses a compensatory expansion of volume in the export market through reductions in prices and profit margins. It becomes clear in chapter 4 that, for a firm selling in domestic customer markets, the price elasticity of demand is likely to be low in the short run—especially in slack periods.

If firms have a flexible schedule of maintenance tasks (like painting or repairing) to which regular production workers can be assigned, those tasks may provide an alternative low-cost means of holding up employment for a time in the face of adversity. Furthermore, if the firm has a readily storable product, it may do some cyclical production-smoothing, maintaining output in excess of sales and building inventories. While such smoothing is a typical business response to seasonal fluctuations, it apparently is not a response to cyclical ones. The timing of the subsequent rebound in demand seems too distant and too uncertain to justify the interest expenses of building countercyclical stocks and to motivate investment in warehouse capacity to hold them. Finally, firms that normally subcontract part of their operations may be able to implement a no-cut strategy inexpensively by suspending that practice. Indeed, that is sometimes an important incentive for subcontracting during prosperity.

On the other side of the ledger, various types of costs are associated with part-time schedules and layoffs. They arise through future increases in quit rates of experienced workers and reductions in the supply of new applicants. Most directly, workers on layoff and part-time are given a "free" opportunity to search for other jobs. The employer risks the loss of some experienced workers; in fact, the fraction of laid-off workers who do not accept subsequent recall is far higher than the quit rate of paid workers over a comparable time period. The size of this risk is influenced by the state of the labor market; it is much greater when employers are instituting layoffs in response to their own adversity at a time when the overall labor market is strong, than in a period of recession or slack. The financial consequences of increased quit rates and reduced rates of willing applicants depend on the magnitude of the toll in the employer's personnel strategy. They may also depend on the selection procedure for the cutback. If the firm lays off its least productive workers in any job category (and has a convincing way to demonstrate its objectivity), the longer-run impact of layoffs on quit rates of the best workers may be reduced (and the short-run benefits enhanced).

The less direct and more diffused, though probably more important, effect on future labor supplies of a cutback decision operates through the impairment of the employer's reputation for providing steady work. The workers observe the employer's response to adversity; and, to some degree, they extrapolate that response into the future. But it is extremely complex for the worker—or the economist—to convert the information actuarially in an expected-value calculation on long-run remuneration; and it is terribly difficult for the firm to assess the worker's response in advance. How much the cutback reduces the value of employment with that firm, as perceived by workers, depends on (1) the accuracy and extent of information about the event, (2) the expected frequency of "slumps" like the one that triggered the cutback, (3) whether the firm's response is viewed as a reliable predictor of its future behavior, (4) whether the employer behaved differently from the way that was generally expected, and (5) the current costs of the cutback to affected workers.

The last two items require further explanation. The surprise element is critical to the story. Workers must have some notion of the probable response of their employer to adversity. If the new observation is entirely consistent with those expectations, it will presumably not alter the firm's reputation for providing steady work. Indeed, a firm that adopts a no-cut decision in the face of obvious adversity must thereby enhance its reputation. In general, the firm must allow for worker responses related to their previous expectations or implicit contract with the firm. For example, if the firm stressed steady employment as one of its advantages in its previous recruiting, it is bound to be penalized more heavily for a cutback. Recognizing that, the firm is induced to fulfill its implied commitments. In that sense, the more stable its product market is, in the view of the firm, the more it will go out on a limb, implicitly contracting for steady employment; and as a result, the more it will be committed to fulfill that pledge. According to this reasoning, a serious recession following a long period of stability is likely to generate fewer (or more postponed) layoffs than one that extends an era of instability.

In another sense, the employer is obliged to treat the layoff as a regrettable response to unexpected adversity. A firm cannot hire recruits at a bargain wage in a weak labor market while it has experienced workers on layoffs or part-time. The no-help-wanted sign becomes a part of the cutback strategy and may be a cost of that strategy. Beyond that, the firm with many plants that have different pay scales will be inhibited in shifting production schedules among them to the degree it might otherwise choose, in view of the disappointment to, and resentment of, the high-wage workers on layoff. Similar inhibitions apply to subcontracting during cutback periods. According to Daniel J. B. Mitchell, such restraints are sometimes formalized in union contracts.

As noted in the fifth and final item above, employees downgrade the value of their jobs after a layoff or a stretch of part-time work to a degree that is related to the "true" costs of the experience to them. In general, the employee's true or fully adjusted costs are smaller than the loss in earnings (even after tax). First, the opportunity for free search that imposes costs on the employer must, by the same token, confer a benefit to workers. That particular benefit must be only a fraction of the workers' wages—otherwise they would have quit or taken time off to search on their own initiative. Second, workers are likely to attach *some* value to the extra home activity that is generated by the cutback in work. That issue is particularly difficult to assess. The value people attach to leisure is grossly misleading as a guide because leisure is, by its nature, voluntary and taken at the individual's initiative. It is, of course, a truism that people find something to do with nonworking time; but it is also a truism that they *must* find something to do with it. Striking anecdotes describe the family frictions that can develop when the laid-off husband of a one-earner household is around the home during the day, or when either spouse is out of work in a two-earner family. Even more significantly, sociological and psychological studies document cases of serious emotional disturbances among workers deprived of their normal productive activity.

The net economic cost of the layoff to the affected worker will be reduced by any receipt of unemployment insurance benefits. As a result, the firm can count on the adverse shift of long-run labor supply from instituting layoffs to be smaller than it would otherwise be. Clearly, if the unemployment benefits were costless to the firm, it would have an incentive to rely on layoffs more heavily, relative to either the no-cut strategy or part-time work. In fact, the typical employer is charged higher tax rates as a result of increased layoffs through an experience-rating feature of the system. Indeed, for some employers, the present value of the future marginal tax liability incurred by an extra layoff may be greater than the benefit received by the laid-off worker. But cases of more than "fully actuarial" costs are likely to be unusual. Because the tax rate has a ceiling and any increase in the rate is deferred and contingent, the typical firm tends to bear "fractionally actuarial" costs.

A mandatory, fractionally actuarial system does not necessarily create a net inducement to layoffs, however. The firm does not always receive a dollar of value for a dollar of insurance benefits paid to laid-off workers; it may receive no value from the benefits paid to those who do not accept recall. Indeed, there is evidence that firms do not value the benefits that fully. Before the enactment of the unemployment insurance system, any firm could have volunteered half-pay (for example) to its laid-off workers as part of its compensation package. Yet, to the best of my knowledge, no such practice ever developed in the private market-place, implying that the perceived benefit to employers through the expected effect on workers did not match the extra payroll costs. Hence a zero-sum system of unemployment insurance that simply mandated transfers from employers to laid-off workers would impose on employers a net disincentive for layoffs. It is not clear where the point of neutrality in a system of unemployment would lie, but it must be short of "fully actuarial" marginal costs to the employer.[6]

For a given reduction of earnings, the work force as a group would presumably find shorter hours less costly than layoffs. Part-time employment is a work-spreading device as compared to layoffs, and hence a type of catastrophe insurance on income losses. If individual workers during a recession were confronted with a choice between a one-fifth probability of a prolonged layoff and a sure prospect of a four-day week, most would opt for the latter. Yet cuts in the workweek account for a much smaller fraction of the adjustments of labor input of contracting industries in recessions than do reductions in the number of workers on the payroll.

6. The view expressed here is that society is imposing a contract on workers and firms that they would not have opted for, acting atomistically. That can be a rational social choice because of the external benefits to macroeconomic stability from automatic countercyclical transfers and because of a possible redistributive social interest in protecting those workers within firms most vulnerable to layoffs. Another possible element is that workers are more confident of the government's commitment to pay benefits than of any employer's pledge for the same liability. If the latter consideration was the only reason that barred private arrangements for unemployment insurance, a mandated fully actuarial system might be neutral. (These further thoughts were generated by a comment by Walter S. Salant during the preparation of this chapter.)

Technological considerations apparently limit the attractiveness of shorter hours to the firm. If the firm maintains its total number of business hours, cutting the hours of individual workers requires a recasting of work schedules into a proper fit, and that may be costly and awkward to implement. If, on the other hand, a firm reduces its total number of business hours, closing a plant for a substantial stretch of several weeks or cutting out a full shift may be less costly than converting to a four-day week or a six-hour shift. Moreover, "free" search time of a day per week for all its employees may be more costly than full-time free search for one-fifth of the workers.

Finally, the selection procedures adopted by firms to decide which workers to lay off may hold down the costs of layoffs relative to part-time employment. If firms can "weed out" the least productive workers in each job category, that helps. Even if that is too divisive (or banned by union contract), workers may receive some benefit from a "pecking order" related to seniority, in which novices are normally laid off first. Inverse-seniority layoffs represent another means of tilting the wage structure in favor of workers with longer tenure, as well as reducing their risks. The toll model provides good reasons to offer such advantages to workers with longer tenure (even with uniform productivity), and can make inverse-seniority layoff arrangements efficient and optimal. As long as novices know that they will receive the greater layoff protection if they stay with the firm, the model has an appropriate incentive effect and all the essential components of fairness.[7]

Efficiency of Layoffs

The discussion above can be summarized in a simple algebraic framework. When the employer institutes a cutback through layoffs or part-time employment, the hourly cost to the worker may be designated as $(W - V)$, where V represents the offsetting value to the worker resulting from search opportunity, home activity, and government transfer and tax cushions such as unemployment insurance benefits. Except in patho-

---

7. Martin Baily argues persuasively that the political power of senior workers may be an important source of the inverse seniority system. See Martin Neil Baily, "Contract Theory and the Moderation of Inflation by Recession and by Controls," *Brookings Papers on Economic Activity, 3:1976*, pp. 606–11. Unlike Baily, however, I find the system plausibly efficient even in the absence of that consideration. In taking issue with him on this point, I want to stress that my basic treatment of layoffs and efficient arrangements draws heavily on Baily's work.

logical cases, V will be positive and less than W. So the loss to the worker is less than W.

The net saving per hour of cutback to the employer, as compared to the no-cut strategy, can be designated as $(W - M - Z)$, where Z represents the sum of cutback costs to the employer, including the search opportunity provided to the worker, the adverse future supply response from deteriorated reputation, any increased tax liability for unemployment insurance, and the commitment to avoid recruiting new workers. The cutback will be made so long as $W > (M + Z)$.

In the example of the individual entrepreneur discussed at the beginning of this chapter, Z did not get into the act. There were no distinct *employer* costs and no complications from unemployment insurance. The entire surplus in prosperity from the current activity accrued to the worker and the value of search time for other pursuits had to be smaller than when the employer shares the surplus. The workers essentially laid themselves off when V exceeded M, but V had a somewhat different meaning. In an employer-worker relationship, Z is important and is related to V in complex ways. The more valuable the search opportunity is to the worker, the more costly it will be to the employer. On the other hand, the more valuable home activity or a stopgap job (so long as it is clearly inferior to a regular job) is to the workers, the less costly the layoff will be to the firm; under those conditions, workers will be less concerned about subsequent layoffs and their future quit rate will be increased to a smaller degree. Unemployment insurance will raise both V and Z for layoffs (but not for part-time employment) and is likely to add more to V than to Z.

Consider a particular layoff (versus no-cut) decision of a firm in which the opportunity for free search (and hence the chance of a subsequent rejection of recall) is the only element of Z. The layoff saves the employer more than it costs the worker so long as $V > (M + Z)$. What workers receive away from the job exceeds the sum of what they can provide on the job to the employer, given the depressed state of demand and the costs to the firm of the layoff. In that situation, the layoff may be regarded as "efficient." But layoffs will be made at the employer's discretion whenever $W > (M + Z)$. Layoffs that cannot be regarded as efficient will take place under conditions in which $(M + Z)$ is between V and W; I call them "regrettable" because "inefficient" would be too strong, for reasons soon to be explored. Figure 3-1 divides the spectrum of possible values of M, for given values of V, W, and Z, into ranges of

Figure 3-1. *The Layoff Decision as a Function of Marginal Revenue Product*

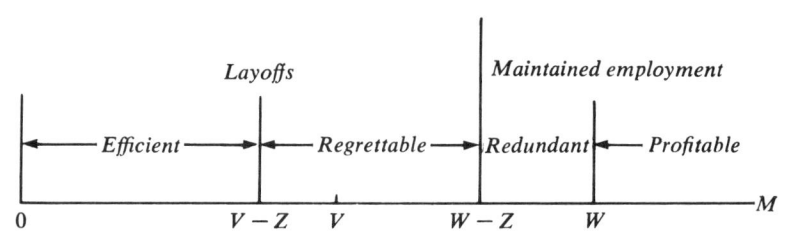

efficient layoffs, regrettable layoffs, and maintained employment. The zone of maintained employment to the right of $(W - Z)$ is divided into two parts: the portion in which M lies between $(W - Z)$ and W is currently unprofitable employment (redundant labor that is kept on the payroll), and that to the right of W, which is currently profitable.

Suppose M lies in the upper part of the range of regrettable layoffs. In principle, if a temporarily depressed wage of W' lying between V and $(W - Z)$ were set and the employer adopted a no-cut strategy, both the employer and the laid-off worker would be better off. In the absence of explicit contracts, the employer obviously has the power to do precisely that—to announce that wages are temporarily cut from W to W' and that no cutbacks in employment will be instituted. In fact, V is not necessarily a floor on W'. If workers believe that the pay cut is temporary and therefore attach value to their jobs, the employer may be able to evoke work even when the pay is below the value of other pursuits to the worker. That asymmetry arises because only the employer can initiate a layoff with the option of subsequent recall. When a firm decides on a layoff rather than a temporary pay cut, it reveals a conviction that some other set of costs, Z', associated with the cut in the wage to W' would make this an inferior option: $(W' + Z') > (M + Z)$. The costs involved in Z' are the adverse long-term effects on labor supply associated with making a wage cut. These may be magnified particularly if employees suspect that the firm is merely taking advantage of a weak labor market to enlarge its share of the bilateral surplus; in particular they may suspect that, in the absence of the wage cut, the firm would be in the zone of maintained employment and would absorb the excess payroll costs. In effect, the behavior of firms that engage in layoffs implies that the perceived adverse reactions of future labor supply from wage cuts exceed those from layoffs. In the latter case, the employer's cutback is undertaken demonstrably only in response to genuine distress, when M is clearly below $(W - Z)$. The employer is obviously not squeezing any surplus out of the laid-off worker. The "clean hands" of the employer ameliorate the unfavorable consequences for future labor supply.

In short, temporary downward adjustments of wage rates to avoid employment cutbacks may be viable only if they can be agreed upon jointly by the firm and its workers. That requires a "political process" within the firm, which would impose set-up costs and involve specific negotiation costs for each decision. In collective bargaining, the organization for such a bipartisan verdict is set up, but the costs of specific negotiations can still be large. According to a study by Peter Henle, temporary downward deviations from explicit contracts are confined to extreme cases in which the firm has an obvious emergency that poses a clear prospect of a drastic and prolonged cut in employment in the absence of a wage reduction. It would take an eminent and sagacious neutral arbiter a la King Solomon (or at least John T. Dunlop) to eliminate the regrettable layoff, and his consulting fees may be so high that in the last analysis it becomes efficient to live with the regrettable layoff.

Adjustments during Economic Expansion

During the recovery phase of economic expansions, the adjustments in labor markets take the form of unwinding the cutbacks made during recessions. Laid-off workers are recalled. Because employers recognize that the improvement of labor markets increases the probability that their laid-off workers will find a superior career job, firms that lag behind in the recovery may nonetheless wish to recall them and shift to a no-cut strategy with redundant employment. Help-wanted signs are hung out once again at the personnel offices. The workweek is restored, and as output and employment move up, overtime hours become more widespread. Empirically, the frequency and magnitude of overtime are good indicators of the disappearance of on-the-job underemployment. In the aggregate, the level of overtime is highly correlated with the growth of productivity. One should not infer that those additional hours yield unusual increments of output, but rather that reliance on overtime reveals the elimination of unproductive hours spent in underemployment. Shading of acceptance quality also becomes increasingly important as labor markets strengthen.

As firms find their quit rates rising and flows of willing applicants falling, they are forced to consider raising wages above the path of the implicit contract. The longer-run considerations about granting extra wages in expansion are not merely the mirror image of the concerns about trimming pay during periods of slack and recession. Obviously workers enjoy cyclical "bonuses" in pay, and consequently may become more attached to the firm for the long run and perhaps more willing to accept the costs of part-time work and layoffs in subsequent recessions. On the other hand, they may tend to apply a norm rate of wage increase to their cyclical peak wages and be disappointed if the firm merely trims wages back down to the path that was previously regarded as normal.

The career attachment has one consistent effect in periods of slack and tightness: it operates to make the supply of labor less elastic over any given time-horizon. Even when other firms are eagerly recruiting with favorable wage offers, the typical firm in a high-wage industry has only a small fraction of its experienced workers on the margin of quitting. The toll costs confronting their potential new employers hold down the wage offers they can hope to obtain and thus make it optimal for the majority to stick with their old jobs. Under those circumstances, extra wages above the normal path reward many workers who are not on the margin of quitting in order to influence the minority who are close to that margin. Because the supply of novices is likely to be more elastic, the firm has incentives to raise its novice wage relative to its wage for experienced workers during periods of particularly tight labor markets; indeed, that differential does narrow in the aggregate. But the potential disappointment and resentment of experienced workers inhibit the firm from changing the wage structure very much in favor of novices.

Cyclical Variations in the Wage Path

All things considered, it is understandable that quantity variations dominate wage variations in the short run. Econometric studies of U.S. aggregate data since the Korean War suggest that a rise in nominal aggregate demand that adds $10 billion to nominal payrolls in a particular year will on average add between $8 billion and $9 billion to labor input (hours and employment) and only between $1 billion and $2 billion in higher wage rates. Moreover, the increment associated with higher wage rates will be concentrated in areas of casual jobs. In the career labor market, some wage variations reflect the role of relative wages, profits, or consumer prices in the implicit contract, and some represent small upward adjustments from the path implied by that contract in light of higher quit rates and smaller flows of willing applicants. Firms opt for implicit rather than explicit contracts because they want flexibility. When markets deviate from the norm, that flexibility will be used to vary the rate of increase of wages cyclically in light of the state of the labor market, which is reasonably summarized by the unemployment rate.

Effect of Demand Increase

The dynamics of wage inflation in such a world can be illustrated with a particular example. Suppose wage rates have been rising by 4 percent a year for some time and suppose that all wage periods are annual with one-fourth of all firms adjusting in each quarter. The typical firm that makes its wage adjustments in the summer quarter will grant a 4 percent increase by deciding either to match the percentage increase in the reference wage over the past year, to maintain a norm rate of 4 percent, or to go above the level of the reference wage by a standard jump of 2 percent for that quarter. All three rules produce the same behavior.

Now suppose that this stable situation is disturbed by a general increase of demand in product markets that impinges on the economy late in the spring. (Nothing important about this example makes it depend on an upward rather than downward shift; either would do.) Assume further, for simplicity, that by posting help-wanted signs, engaging in help-wanted advertising, and shaving acceptance quality, firms are all able to increase employment in June. As the summer quarter begins, they have no extraordinary unfilled demand for labor, but they experience significantly reduced flows of willing applicants as a result of the decline in unemployment and the tightening of the labor market. As a result, the typical firm making its wage decision in the summer quarter may well raise its wages by 5 percent, adjusting its norm upward 1 percentage point, thereby moving the relative wage level of its workers 1 percentage point higher than it had been last summer.

The story so far is summarized in the first seven rows of table 3-1. The reference wage for "summer firms" is the average of newly set wages in the preceding fall, winter, and spring quarters. In year zero, that reference wage for the summer (third quarter) is taken as the benchmark for an index and is thus 100.0. Until the jump in demand, the reference wage and newly set wage both rise smoothly at an annual rate of 4 percent;

Table 3-1. *Hypothetical Adjustments to Wages in Response to a Tightening Labor Market*[a]

Quarterly wage indexes

Year	Quarter	Reference wage	Newly set wage	Aggregate average wage
Zero	1	98.0	100.0	98.5
	2	99.0	101.0	99.5
	3	100.0	102.0	100.5
	4	101.0	103.0	101.5
One	1	102.0	104.0	102.5
	2	103.0	105.1	103.5
	3	104.0	107.1	104.8
	4	105.4	108.6	106.2
Two	1	106.9	110.1	107.7
	2	108.6	111.9	109.4
	3	110.2	113.5	111.0
	4	111.8	115.2	112.6
Three	1	113.5	116.9	114.3
	2	115.2	118.7	116.1
	3	116.9	120.4	117.8
	4	118.7	122.2	119.6

a. The reference wage, R, is the arithmetic average of the newly set wages, NW, of the three preceding quarters: $R = (1/3) (NW_{-1} + NW_{-2} + NW_{-3})$. The newly set wage is $(1 + g)$ times R, where $g = 0.02$ through the second quarter of year one; and $g = 0.03$ thereafter. The aggregate average wage is $0.75R + 0.25NW$. Figures are rounded.

the third quarter of year one, however, displays a double-sized jump over the preceding quarter in the newly set wage. That extra point adds an extra 0.3 point to the reference wage index for "fall firms." To restore the relative wage position that these firms had a year earlier or to follow the standard rule of leapfrogging the reference wage by 2.0 percent, they must increase wages by 4.4 percent. Moreover, like the summer firms, they experience reduced flows of applicants as they consider their wage adjustment. They may wish to raise their relative wage position by an extra point; and, in that event, they will post wage increases of 5.4 percent over their 103.0 level of a year earlier, yielding an index of 108.6.

The advance of the reference wage for the first quarter of year two from the first quarter of year one is then 4.8 percent; and, if winter firms follow the same reasoning, their newly set wages will be 5.9 percent above a year earlier. By the third quarter the reference wage for the summer firms that initially started the process will have risen about 6.0 percent over their level a year earlier (110.2 over 104.0). The wage of the summer firms before their move will be 2.8 percent below the reference wage. That relative wage is nearly a percentage point *lower* than it was at the same point in the preceding year—in contrast to the intended position 2 percentage points higher than the reference wage. Now the summer firms must grant a wage increase of nearly 5 percent merely to achieve this standard leapfrog jump above the reference wage. But if their labor market is still tight, as I continue to assume, they are likely to award an extra bonus much as they did the preceding summer. Suppose they decide to leapfrog the reference wage by 3 percent in the summer of year two, as they did a year earlier. Then they must raise their wages nearly 6 percent (from 107.1 to 113.5), matching the increase of the reference wage over the past year.

If all firms reason and act similarly, the rates of increase of the reference wage, newly set wages, and average aggregate wage all converge to about 6 percent—an increment of 2 percentage points due to the tightening. Under those ultimate circumstances, each firm making a wage adjustment will grant 3 percent to match the reference wage and another 3 percent to go ahead of it.

Algebraically, the process can be described by a linear difference equation incorporating four terms or three lags with the coefficients summing to unity. The distributed time schedule of wage adjustments causes a minor stretching out of the response of wage inflation to changes in the unemployment rate. But in this example the lag is short—the average aggregate wage is rising at a 6 percent rate early in year two. There is prompt convergence to a steady higher rate of inflation, accompanying the maintained lower rate of unemployment. What emerges is a Phillips curve world with modest lags—a given reduction of unemployment is "bought" with a particular and ultimately stable increment in the inflation rate.

Possibilities for Acceleration

The key step in developing the Phillips curve result in the above example can be traced to the summer of year two, when the firms that started the acceleration of wages came to bat for their next inning. They had jumped over the reference wage level by 3 percent in the preceding year in order to raise their relative wage position; in fact, however, it deteriorated. Presumably, they were disappointed in the quantity (or quality) of applicants they attracted with the wage they set in the summer of year one. In the example, those firms in the summer of year two chose to exceed the wage increase they had made the previous year. To that extent, they responded to the surprisingly rapid increase in the reference wage during the intervening year. But they were not ready to extrapolate that increase of the reference wage into the coming year; they saw it as a cyclical phenomenon, which experience had taught them to distinguish from changes in secular trends. So they expected that, with an "unusually large" rise in their wage (nearly 6 percent) and equivalently an "unusually" big leapfrog (3 percent) over the reference wage, they would strengthen their relative wage position over the year ahead.

The tightening could well have been one of those cyclical occurrences, and the firms would have been right, and the story would have shifted to the adjustments to rising unemployment. But the more interesting question is what happens if the tighter markets endure. That is the way table 3-1 is constructed. Even for a second or a third year, firms may view the situation as an unusually long boom. But if a tight labor market were actually maintained indefinitely, the pattern of firm behavior and attitudes would change. Acting individually, some firms will conclude sooner or later that they must raise wages by more than 6 percent if they seriously intend to increase their relative wages on average over the year ahead. In effect, they come to view as obsolete the 2 percent leapfrog that was appropriate for a 4 percent wage inflation. Firms may conduct this agonizing reappraisal of personnel policy by looking either backward or forward. They may simply conclude that the world is now typified by 6 percent wage inflation, which requires a 3 percent leapfrog; or they may explicitly forecast the reference wage over the year ahead and reach the same verdict.

If some firms then step up wage increases to 7 percent, the whole process is pulled in an upward direction. It may reach another plateau with 7 or 8 percent wage inflation. Subsequently, the recognition of that figure as a new annual norm may dislodge the process once again. If one stays with it long enough, the indefinitely increasing inflation predicted by the accelerationist model can emerge.

There is a second important reason why the Phillips result cannot be viable for an indefinitely maintained very tight (or very loose) labor market. It implies that wage differentials prevailing in any month will be wider ultimately than they were initially; in fact, the wider differentials are likely to affect the behavior of workers in a way that upsets the result. With wages rising by 6 percent a year, the pay of the typical firm ranges from 3 percentage points above the reference wage at the time of its wage adjustment to 3 percentage points below at the end of its wage year, while initially that range was only 2 percentage points in each direction. As noted above, the very existence of a time schedule of wage adjustments around the calendar indicates that workers are not highly sensitive to the differential at any particular time so long as it can be expected to average out over the year. But to suppose that workers will not be influenced at all seems extreme. The searchers in the fall know that the summer firms are well ahead of the pack, but they do not have adequate information to know whether the winter firms are about to leapfrog by an amount that is fully compensating. Moreover, some workers may have especially high time-preferences.

Firms may experience a distinct seasonal pattern in their flows of willing applicants—or even in their quit rates. And the effect of such seasonality is not symmetrical: they suffer more from the deficiency of applicants encountered in some months than they gain from surplus applicants in other months. If the widened transitory wage differentials have such disturbing effects, firms are likely to respond by shortening the time interval of wage adjustments. Such a shift would push wages still higher. For example, firms that moved in the summer may introduce an interim further adjustment in the winter when they normally would not have altered wages. By doing that, they push up the reference wage relevant to firms that bat during the spring; and the resulting actions of those firms will raise the reference wage they encounter next time around. In effect, a new leapfrog emerges on top of the old one. At the extreme, such a process could generate an indefinitely increasing rate of wage inflation in response to a given reduction of unemployment, conforming with the accelerationist rather than the Phillips curve model.

These forces that disturb the Phillips result are rather subtle, but they are likely to be insistent over the long run. If one seriously imagined a major one-time reduction in the unemployment rate to an unusually low level that was maintained indefinitely, this result would be unstable and would give way to an accelerationist trend. Both the agonizing reappraisals of firms about relative wage optimization and the uncertainties of workers about wage differentials would contribute to that upward displacement of the Phillips curve.

On the other hand, variations in the unemployment rate and the rate of wage inflation that are interpreted by firms and workers as standard cyclical phenomena are likely to generate Phillips rather than accelerationist responses. Under those circumstances, firms and workers will adjust their behavior to reflect tightness or looseness in the labor market, but not in a manner that widens the leapfrog, shortens the schedule of wage setting, or otherwise pulls the Phillips curve off its moorings. Cyclical experience teaches firms not to extrapolate every surprise in reference wages into the future.

Such a contrast between transitory cyclical results and adaptations to an assumed (though historically unprecedented) permanent shift in utilization rates is not confined to wage setting. In the event of a "permanent boom," the cyclically elevated shares of corporate profits, consumer purchases of automobiles, and business spending on fixed capital could not persist indefinitely. Yet it is instructive to identify these cyclically sensitive components and similarly to identify the rate of increase of wages as cyclically sensitive.

In the cycles of the fifties and sixties, the Phillips curve result predicted effectively. The personnel policy of a firm that offers career jobs is a system and a strategy that must be communicated to experienced workers and recruits. If successful, the policy reduces the firm's dependence on point-estimate predictions of the state of the labor market. The policy is not scrapped every time the economy moves from one phase of the business cycle to the next, any more than the standard workweek is revised as the number of daylight hours changes with the season. But if the labor market defies the patterns of previous experience for a long time, adaptations will be made, and old rules and traditions will be discarded. When that happens, a breakdown is observed of entrenched patterns of behavior rather than gradual fine tuning in response to changes in forecasts. People live with the older patterns of behavior even after they conclude that the environment of the past is unlikely to return. Change is costly; getting out of step is risky for the first firms that shift schedules, institute escalators, or the like.

Prolonged experience with what was initially regarded as a cyclically high rate of wage increase or a cyclically tight labor market leads to adaptations that lift the Phillips curve off its moorings. Some combination of duration and intensity of the departure from experience of the past ultimately breaks the Phillips pattern. The direct cause is not an unemployment rate below some critical value but rather an inflation rate far different from that in the history that generated current institutions like the wage norm and the time schedule. Such a sketch can explain the absence of significant accelerationist tendencies in 1950–51, 1956–57, and 1966–68, and their emergence at the beginning of the decade of the seventies.

Threshold effects of an analogous type have been posited by Otto Eckstein and Roger Brinner and by George Perry. The Eckstein-Brinner model linked the threshold effect to a prolonged high rate of price (rather than of wage) inflation, but it is equally applicable to both. Indeed, as I emphasize in chapter 6, only the behavior of auction markets (and in particular of supply shocks in that sector) distinguishes the implications of a price-wage and wage-wage model. Perry's interpretation of European wage experience at the end of the decade of the sixties as an "explosion" is linked mainly to the behavior of factor shares. The emergence of a division of income among factors that proved unacceptable to workers could reflect the operation of a wage system that kept squeezing wages over a prolonged period. I return to this area of inquiry in chapter 6, discussing its relevance to product markets as well as labor markets and to their interaction.

The Role of Unions

Unions and collective bargaining arrangements have kept creeping into the script, but I have not put them on the center of the stage thus far. Their institutional role is easier to comprehend after the discussion of arrangements that would be expected to develop in a career labor market without them. The preservation and allocation of joint surplus enter into any set of arrangements between firms and workers. Every career wage is, in a sense, a "bargain," even if it is set unilaterally by the employer. The implicit contract is the general case; the shift to explicit contracts with unions creates the special case. The objective of unions is to shift the allocation of the surplus in favor of the worker, and they are constrained by the problem of preserving the joint surplus. Many of the activities of unions can be viewed as formalizing and institutionalizing the conventions of the nonunion career labor market—not only in determining the wage structure but also in developing understandings about hiring, layoffs, promotions, firing, and the environment of the work place. Because of the very presence of a union, applicants to an organized firm may feel less uncertainty about the prospective package that they will obtain in the future. Confidence in the effectiveness of the union can allay worries resulting from lack of confidence in the reliability of the employer. Those functions of the union may well enlarge the joint surplus. Thus collective bargaining can raise efficiency.

Unions may enhance efficiency in other ways as well. First and most generally, they may reduce the effective degree of monopsony of firms in the career labor market. By extracting a wage at which more than an ample supply of recruits is forthcoming, the union closes the gap between the marginal cost of labor and the wage, preventing the exploitation of monopsonistic power. Also, through the bargaining power of the union, firms may be forced into a high wage structure that entails low quit rates; they are then likely to adjust to the high pay in part by making additional investments in trying out, screening, and training. And that adjustment is likely to raise efficiency because it offsets some of the tendencies toward underinvestment in training and the like that result from the inherent market imperfections discussed in chapter 2.

Cyclical Sensitivity

In general, the union influence tends to create strong and broad career relationships; firms are deprived of the option of pursuing a casual jobs strategy with low wages and high turnover. Deeply entrenched career arrangements, in turn, make union wages particularly insensitive to the state of the labor market. And these are reinforced by other considerations.

In particular, the unionized firm must be concerned about the unique quit phenomenon associated with a strike, when concerted and mass quits are reinforced, through picket lines, by a constraint on hiring to replace the quits. Activating the strike weapon may be more costly to the workers than to the firm, but the option and the initiative to use it are in their hands. The lockout is not an equally powerful weapon for the employer: in a world in which wages are expected to rise every time a contract is renegotiated, the employer is generally happy with the status quo and willing to continue operating under the terms of the old contract.

Because of the strike threat, the union is generally able to extract from the employer a higher wage than the latter would offer in the absence of that threat. It is always in the interest of the union to extract some increment, even recognizing that a higher wage implies a greater likelihood of part-time employment and layoffs. Because of the firm's incentives to use its monopsony power in the absence of the strike threat, the wage that is optimal for the firm is too low to be optimal for the union. At the same time, the wage will generally lie below the ceiling that the union would choose if it were certain that the employer would meet its wage demand without a strike.

Assume that a firm and a union are operating with a pay structure substantially higher than the firm would offer in a nonunion situation. A contract is about to expire, and at that time the labor market weakens significantly, but the strength of the firm's product market is unchanged. The weakening in the labor market is likely to have only a limited effect on the new contract. The firm could not draw on the queue of willing applicants to replace strikers; nor is it much influenced otherwise by their appearance, since it is already paying a wage that provides an abundant labor supply. That queue of willing applicants is not recognized by either the firm or the union as a rationale for holding wages down. So long as the firm's product market is unchanged, the cost of a strike is not any lower for the firm; and, for the union, prospective employment is no lower for any given wage in the new contract. Indeed, the principal way in which the weakening of the labor market affects the cost-benefit calculation of the union is by reducing the opportunities of strikers to pick up casual stopgap jobs during the work stoppage.

A deterioration in the firm's product market may have a somewhat greater influence on the negotiation. That would reduce the cost of a strike to the firm, in part by lowering the profitability of the output of labor and in part by enabling any firm producing storable goods to catch up with demand more easily after a strike. Moreover, with weak product demand, any given negotiated wage would entail more unemployment for union members—although to a degree limited by the elasticity of demand for the firm's product and the importance of labor costs in the total marginal cost of output.

All in all, the insensitivity of union wages to the current state of the labor market stands out in empirical research. In his statistical analysis of union contracts, Daniel Mitchell found no significant influence of the rate of unemployment prevailing at the time of the negotiation on the magnitude of wage increases over entire three-year contracts, although the effect on the first-year wage increment was significant. Interestingly, Mitchell found that insensitivity of wages to unemployment was characteristic not only of the union sector but also of nonunion industries that have key features associated with career relationships: high fringe benefits, high values of capital per worker, a high ratio of adult males in their work force, and high average pay. The result is consistent with the interpretation of union arrangements as particular types of long-term personnel relations.

Longer-Term Explicit Contracts

Collective bargaining has another important influence on wage determination in the United States by creating long explicit contracts. The negotiation and decision costs of setting wages in collective bargaining are far higher than in the nonunion situation. In addition, the threat of a strike arises each time a contract is negotiated. Union wage decisions are therefore less frequent than nonunion ones. The strike threat and extra decision costs tilt the schedule away from the point that nonunion employers would choose on their own, weighing their loss of flexibility against the benefits of greater certainty about the path of wages on the behavior of workers.

During the period of rapid and volatile inflation in the 1970s, unions began to view lengthy contracts with a fixed path of nominal wages as particularly risky. Employers begrudgingly accepted cost-of-living escalators as a way to maintain the three-year contract. Those indexing provisions remain an institution of collective bargaining that has not spread to the nonunion sector. Even beyond the formal indexing of wages to movements of consumer prices in the contracts, union wages seem to be more strongly influenced by recent changes in the cost of living than are nonunion wages, according to Mitchell's findings.

Quite apart from the escalator, the three-year intervals of major collective bargaining settlements can create important patterns of lags and jumps in the labor market. Once a contract is signed in any industry, subsequent developments cannot influence wages (except through special contingent provisions like the escalator) for three years. In the case of responses to changes in labor market conditions, the zero effect after the signing of the contract is not much smaller than the insignificant influence at the time of the settlement. If the ultimate effect is negligible, the existence of a long lag before the effect takes place is of little consequence. For wage emulation and consumer price influences, however, the three-year interval can be important. The particular sequence of the largest collective bargaining negotiations in the United States creates the concept of a bargaining round. Because two years that contain many major negotiations are followed by one year of light bargaining, it is natural to think of the resumption of major bargaining after the light year as a new bargaining round. (One way to remember the timing of the three-year sequence is that the year divisible by three is in the middle.) Patterns of settlements emerging early in that round may influence contracts during the remainder of the round. As a result, major new developments that occur in the middle or late phase of one bargaining round—like an acceleration of nonunion wages or of consumer prices—may exert a large discrete influence on the pattern of the next wage round.

That may be part of the story of the adverse overall wage response to recession in 1970–71. Because nonunion wages responded more sensitively than union wages to tight labor markets in the late sixties, because escalator clauses in union contracts at that time were rare and weak, and perhaps because government jawboning had influenced collective bargaining, union wages suffered a sizable loss relative to nonunion wages in the period from 1965 to 1969. Strong militancy to catch up and determination to obtain escalator clauses for future protection characterized the bargaining round that began in 1970.

Union and Nonunion Wages

Union and nonunion wages can interact in a number of ways. Because relative wages influence implicit contracts in the nonunion sector and explicit contracts under collective bargaining, the interactions will reflect two-way causation. A rapid rise in nonunion wages that narrows differentials will put pressures on union leaders to restore the premiums that their members have come to expect as a return for their dues. Empirical findings by Robert J. Flanagan underline the strong chain of causation running from nonunion to union wages.

In the opposite direction, the visibility of union settlements, which are widely (although not always accurately) reported and quantified in the press, makes them obvious candidates for the prime mover in a process of wage-wage emulation. To some nonunion employers, the pay of the union sector may be most important as an indicator of the strength of temptations for their workers to organize collectively. Because union wages are especially responsive to rises in the cost of living, their influence on nonunion wages enlarges and strengthens the overall impact of consumer prices on wages. Any acceleration of consumer prices that stems from food and oil supply shocks (or anything except accelerating wages) will widen the differential between union and nonunion wages in a way that may have distorting effects on the allocation of labor resources and haphazard effects on income distribution.

Because nonunion wages are less insulated from the state of the labor market, the differential between union and nonunion wages has a marked countercyclical pattern, which is widest when the unemployment rate is at its peak and is narrowest at its low point in the cycle. In addition, the industries whose product demands are most cyclically sensitive—especially durable goods manufacturing—are highly unionized. Quite apart from any effects from shifts in relative wages, employment tends to be weakest in the union sector relative to the nonunion sector at a time when the wage differential makes union jobs attractive. From an allocative point of view, that pattern must be perverse. The wider dispersion during recession raises optimal search unemployment: it becomes worthwhile to search (or wait) longer for union jobs, given the wider differential. On the other hand, the prevalence of no-help-wanted signs in the union sector during a recession makes nonunion jobs attractive. The actually observed increase in the flow of willing applicants and reduction in quit rates in the nonunion sector during recession makes it clear that the changing frequency of help-wanted signs is the more powerful magnet. The net attraction of union jobs to nonunion workers was larger in 1968–69 when the wage differential was smaller but firms were actively hiring. Paradoxically, nonunion firms have the least need to protect their labor supplies from the attraction of the union sector when the wage differential is largest; and that is why they can let the differential widen in weak labor markets. Even so, the extent to which the nonunion employers could lower their rates of pay increases in 1975–77 was probably limited by the awareness of their workers that major unions were gaining three-year increments of 30 percent or more.

Inflationary Bias

The bargaining power of unions is likely to lead to higher wages for the organized sector; but that power, once exercised, should not create a more rapid rise of wages indefinitely. Yet the labor market may be subject to an inflationary bias, and unions are suspect as contributors to such a bias.

In a dynamic view of the uses of union bargaining power, the possibilities for creation of an inflationary bias become evident. In fact, in a newly organized industry, the union may "feel its way" to the full exercise of its bilateral monopoly power in a number of ways. First, if the willingness of the firm to accept a strike depends on the size of the demanded *increase* in wages, newly organized workers cannot immediately get the full gain that their power will ultimately permit. Second, once the union pushes the wage scale upward, the firm's own adjustments may make it vulnerable to further pushes. Suppose that in its first collective bargaining contract the firm pays a premium over what it would have offered in the nonunion situation in order to avert (or to terminate) a strike. When the next contract comes up, the firm is paying a higher wage than it would if it had not been organized. The wage that it would then offer optimally with no threat of a strike becomes higher because of its history; at a given wage, it would anticipate a higher quit rate of workers who have geared their wage expectations to the new situation. Then the union can extract another strike-avoidance premium. That possibility is enhanced if the firm responds to the high wage by improving the quality of its work force through intensified screening and training. The allegedly "one-time" jump in relative wages resulting from collective bargaining may be repeated, to a degree, for many wage rounds.

Furthermore, unions have to keep justifying the dues collected from members and the salaries paid to executives. That creates bureaucratic incentives to keep pushing wage differentials upward, especially when such a widening can benefit the majority of members even if it imposes large costs of job losses on a minority.

Finally, unions may have reasons of broad strategy to resist holding down wages in weak labor and product markets. In the case of a weak labor market, the power of the union may be exercised precisely for the purpose of insulating experienced workers from downward wage pressures resulting from a long queue of willing applicants. The union may wish, and may be able to, repeal the Marxist law that the "reserve army of unemployed" acts as a disciplinary, wage-restricting force. That leads the union to rule out explicitly the state of the labor market as a relevant standard in negotiations.

Under conditions when product markets weaken, the union wants the firm to regard the costs of layoffs as large in relation to the costs of maintained employment. In particular, it does not want the firm to believe that the presence of layoffs will help to hold down the negotiated wage. The union may resist holding down wages specifically in any bargaining when many members are on layoff. A satisficing attitude by workers may reinforce that determination. They may feel that layoffs are bad enough and, if anything, are reasons why they should get *higher* wages when they are employed.

Unions may formulate a game strategy against the government's stabilization policies for similar reasons and in similar ways that they seek to counter the employer's layoff policies. The union wants the government to believe that a weakening of aggregate demand will be a poor and ineffective means of curbing inflation. If it can credibly make its wage demands immune to (or even perverse to) the strength of the labor market, that helps to teach the government the proper lesson. (The government's side of the game will be examined in detail in chapter 7.)

Some potential sources of inflationary bias in labor markets are not linked to collective bargaining. One points to the asymmetry of upward and downward deviations from a previously announced wage. Even after a firm has, in effect, offered an explicit wage contract for a year ahead, it still retains the option of overfulfilling its pledge. It will not do so lightly, but it may find such action worthwhile if its labor market should tighten dramatically or if its product market and hence its demand for labor strengthen unexpectedly. Decisions are made to award extra wage increases or unusual Christmas bonuses. But underfulfilling is not a symmetrical option. Realistically, the firm cannot institute negative Christmas bonuses!

Presumably, nonunion firms recognize this asymmetry in their subsequent options at the time they make their wage offers and reduce them a little in light of the possibility of overfulfilling. Nonetheless, by its effect on consumer prices and other wages, any upward wage drift from overfulfilling tends to create not merely a temporary bulge but a longer-term addition to the level of wages. The asymmetry between overfulfilling and underfulfilling thus can generate an inflationary bias.[8]

In chapters 2 and 3, I have developed the labor-market portion of the analysis. I offered answers to some of the key questions about wage and employment movements over the cycle. I also discussed the considerations affecting some questions I could not answer. But some issues about

8. Any verdict on asymmetry in the wage response to an equal upward and downward change in labor market tightness depends on the units in which tightness is measured. The usual econometric scaling by the reciprocal of the unemployment rate implies that an extra point of unemployment will depress wages less than a reduction of a point will raise them. That in itself is a degree of inflationary bias.

labor markets depend on the way product markets behave; and these issues must be shelved until those markets are examined and discussed —the task to which I now turn.

Bibliographical Notes

The distinction between casual and career labor markets is related to (although not identical to) the "dual labor market" approach developed in, among others, Peter B. Doeringer and Michael J. Piore, *Internal Labor Markets and Manpower Analysis* (Heath, 1971, pp. 163–83); Lester C. Thurow, *Poverty and Discrimination* (Brookings Institution, 1969), pp. 46–138. An incisive critique of that approach is in Michael L. Wachter, "Primary and Secondary Labor Markets: A Critique of the Dual Approach," *Brookings Papers on Economic Activity, 3:1974,* pp. 637–80.

My analysis of distrust, obligation, and communication problems follows the spirit of Thomas C. Schelling, "An Essay on Bargaining," *American Economic Review,* vol. 46 (June 1956), pp. 281–306. In the analysis of explicit and implicit contracts and of layoffs, I lean heavily on the work of Martin Neil Baily, "Wages and Employment under Uncertain Demand," *Review of Economic Studies,* vol. 41 (January 1974), pp. 37–50, and "Contract Theory and the Moderation of Inflation by Recession and by Controls," *BPEA, 3:1976,* pp. 585–622; Herschel I. Grossman, "Risk Shifting, Layoffs, and Seniority," *Journal of Monetary Economics,* vol. 4 (November 1978), pp. 661–86; Costas Azariadis, "Implicit Contracts and Underemployment Equilibria," *Journal of Political Economy,* vol. 83 (December 1975), pp. 1183–1202; and Donald F. Gordon, "A Neo-Classical Theory of Keynesian Unemployment," *Economic Inquiry,* vol. 12 (December 1974), pp. 431–59; I also draw from my "Upward Mobility in a High-pressure Economy," *BPEA, 1:1973,* pp. 235–52, and "Inflation: Its Mechanics and Welfare Costs," *BPEA, 2:1975,* pp. 366–73. I also benefited from Oliver E. Williamson, Michael L. Wachter, and Jeffrey E. Harris, "Understanding the Employment Relation: The Analysis of Idiosyncratic Exchange," *Bell Journal of Economics,* vol. 6 (Spring 1975), pp. 250–78, who offer a particularly interesting discussion of a variety of aspects of the long-attachment employment relationship. Martin Feldstein analyzes layoffs in his "Temporary Layoffs in the Theory of Unemployment," *Journal of Political Economy,* vol. 84 (October 1976), pp. 937–57. Robert J. Gordon offers another model of contracting in his "Aspects of the Theory of Involuntary Unemployment—A Comment," in Karl Brunner and Allan H. Meltzer, eds., *The Phillips Curve and Labor Markets,* Carnegie-Rochester Conference Series on Public Policy, vol. 1 (Amsterdam: North-Holland, 1976), pp. 98–119, and summarizes the literature in this area in his "Recent Developments in the Theory of Inflation and Unemployment," *Journal of Monetary Economics,* vol. 2 (April 1976), pp. 207–10. Peter Henle documents the scope of concessions to maintain employment in his "Reverse Collective Bargaining? A Look at Some Union Concession Situations," *Industrial and Labor Relations Review,* vol. 26 (April 1973), pp. 956–68.

My own product differentiation stresses the various limitations on explicit and implicit contracts stemming from unobservable or unenforceable criteria. These make layoffs a "clean hands" solution relative to temporary cuts in pay. They also require continuing incentives for productive performance, since that is subject to the worker's own control and cannot be nailed down by any contract.

A persuasive case for wage-wage emulation as the dominant pay standard is made by Robert E. Hall, "The Process of Inflation in the Labor Market," *BPEA, 2:1974,* pp. 343–93. Much of the collective bargaining literature focuses on standards of wage comparison: see John T. Dunlop, *Wage Determination under Trade Unions* (Macmillan, 1944), pp. 45–73; Arthur M. Ross, "The Dynamics of Wage Determination under Collective Bargaining," *American Economic Review,* vol. 37 (December 1947), pp. 793–822; and Albert Rees, *The Economics of Trade Unions* (University of Chicago Press, 1962), pp. 48–68. Patterns involving nonunion firms are discussed by Lloyd G. Reynolds, *The Structure of Labor Markets: Wages and Labor Mobility in Theory and Practice* (Harper, 1951), pp. 230–35.

Among the econometric studies that identify profits as a determinant of wages are Richard G. Lipsey and M. D. Steuer, "The Relation between Profits and Wage Rates," *Economica,* n.s., vol. 28 (May 1961), pp. 137–55; Otto Eckstein and Thomas A. Wilson, "The Determination of Money Wages in American Industry," *Quarterly Journal of Economics,* vol. 76 (August 1962), pp. 388–401; and George L. Perry, *Unemployment, Money Wage Rates, and Inflation* (M.I.T. Press, 1966), pp. 27–30, 48–52. While most recent wage studies have omitted profits as a determinant, they are stressed in Laurence S. Seidman, "The Return of the Profit Rate to the Wage Equation," forthcoming in *Review of Economic Studies.*

Analysis of the private costs of unemployment include: E. Wight

Bakke, *Citizens without Work: A Study of the Effects of Unemployment upon the Workers' Social Relations and Practices* (Yale University Press, 1940); Robert J. Gordon, "The Welfare Cost of Higher Unemployment," *BPEA, 1:1973,* pp. 133–95; and Harvey Brenner, "Estimating the Social Costs of National Economic Policy: Implications for Mental and Physical Health and Criminal Aggression," in Joint Economic Committee, *Achieving the Goals of the Employment Act of 1946—Thirtieth Anniversary Review,* vol. 1: *Employment,* Paper 5, 94 Cong. 2 sess. (Government Printing Office, 1976).

Alan S. Blinder discusses the analytical reasons to believe that wage-indexing will be widespread and then suggests that asset adjustments substitute for them; see his "Indexing the Economy through Financial Intermediation," in Karl Brunner and Allan H. Meltzer, eds., *Stabilization of the Domestic and International Economy,* Carnegie-Rochester Conference Series on Public Policy, vol. 5 (Amsterdam: North-Holland, 1977), pp. 69–105. The particular issue of direct taxes and wages is analyzed in Alan S. Blinder, "Can Income Tax Increases Be Inflationary? An Expository Note," *National Tax Journal,* vol. 26 (June 1973), pp. 295–301; and Thomas F. Dernburg, "The Macroeconomic Implications of Wage Retaliation against Higher Taxation," *International Monetary Fund Staff Papers,* vol. 21 (November 1974), pp. 758–88. The effect of this variable for the United States is reported in Robert J. Gordon, "Can the Inflation of the 1970s be Explained?" *BPEA, 1:1977,* pp. 264–72.

The statistical performance of product prices (measured by the nonfarm deflator), consumer prices, and past wages are discussed in ibid.; and in George L. Perry, "Slowing the Wage-Price Spiral: The Macroeconomic View," *BPEA, 2:1978,* pp. 270–79, for the United States, and "Determinants of Wage Inflation around the World," *BPEA, 2:1975,* pp. 403–35, for other countries. In addition to Perry's inferences from statistical results about differences in wage standards across nations, Lloyd Ulman and Robert J. Flanagan present a wealth of institutional information and insights in their *Wage Restraint: A Study of Incomes Policies in Western Europe* (University of California Press, 1971). Otto Eckstein and Roger Brinner examine the role of intense and persistent price inflation in their *The Inflation Process in the United States,* prepared for the Joint Economic Committee, 92 Cong. 2 sess. (GPO, 1972), pp. 3–4, 7–19.

There is a vast literature on trade unions and their behavior, including the books by Dunlop, Rees, and Reynolds cited above. Two other key references are S. Rosen, "Trade Union Power, Threat Effects and the

Extent of Organization," *Review of Economic Studies,* vol. 36 (April 1969), pp. 185–96; and M. W. Reder, "The Theory of Union Wage Policy," *Review of Economics and Statistics,* vol. 34 (February 1952), pp. 34–45. Daniel J. B. Mitchell contributed to this literature analytically in his "Union Wage Policies: The Ross-Dunlop Debate Reopened," *Industrial Relations,* vol. 11 (February 1972), pp. 46–61, and empirically in his "Union Wage Determination: Policy Implications and Outlook," *BPEA, 3:1978,* pp. 537–82, and in *Unions, Wages, and Inflation* (Brookings, 1980). Empirical studies that find influences of union wages on other wages include H. G. Lewis, *Unionism and Relative Wages in the United States: An Empirical Inquiry* (University of Chicago Press, 1963); and O. C. Ashenfelter, G. E. Johnson, and J. H. Pencavel, "Trade Unions and the Rate of Change of Money Wages in United States Manufacturing Industry," *Review of Economic Studies,* vol. 39 (January 1972), pp. 27–54. The view of unions as followers is illustrated by Robert J. Flanagan, "Wage Interdependence in Unionized Labor Markets," *BPEA, 3:1976,* pp. 635–73.

Discussions of inflationary bias include James Tobin, "Inflation and Unemployment," *American Economic Review,* vol. 62 (March 1972), pp. 9–18; Costas Azariadis, "Asymmetric Wage Behavior," in Oldřich Kýn and Walfram Schrettl, eds., *On the Stability of Contemporary Economic Systems: Proceedings of the Third Reisenburg Symposium* (Göttingen: Vandenhoeck and Ruprecht, 1979), pp. 51–68; and Gordon, "Recent Developments," p. 210.

IV

Product Markets

MOST TRANSACTIONS in product markets involve price tags and shopping, and they bear strong resemblances to those in the labor market made through wage offers and search, which were analyzed in the last two chapters. But, unlike the behavior observed in any labor market, some products are priced in a way that fits the classical paradigm of continuous market-clearing achieved by an auctioneer. I begin with a brief analysis of auction markets, but that poses no serious problems because, for two centuries, economic analysis of these markets has been ongoing. Most of the work that lies ahead concerns the vast nonauction area, which is the focus of this chapter.

Auction Markets

The financial pages of the daily newspaper depict the scope of active auction markets. The products traded include selected financial assets, especially stocks and bonds; agricultural commodities, mainly foods but also certain nonfood items like cotton, lumber, and rubber; and some primary metals. In addition to the standard auction markets, the auction method is frequently used for the sale of nonreproducible tangible assets like antiques and art objects; finally, some nonstorable products like fresh fruits, vegetables, and fish are marketed on exchanges that have many of the characteristics of auctions.

Prices, Inventories, and the Cycle

The auction markets of most concern here are those for the agricultural and mining products that are part of the gross national product. Those commodities traded on auction markets have a large number of producers and of potential buyers; they are homogeneous or readily gradable; and typically they are storable at relatively low cost. For some

134

purposes it is useful to classify the participants in the marketplace into three categories: producers generating a supply of new output; users demanding the product for processing and ultimate resale for consumption; and traders holding stocks and engaging in business activities that may place them on either the buying or the selling side of the market. Obviously producers and users can also hold stocks and vary them in response to current and expected prices, but the activities of the traders are sufficiently distinct to warrant special treatment.

Stockholding plays a clear role in the case of crops whose output is subject both to a distinct seasonal pattern and to large stochastic variations from year to year as a result of changing weather conditions. The seasonality of output creates a predictable pattern in prices during the course of the year that allows the holders of stocks to earn a return from their activity. Beyond that, a positive return also becomes available for carrying over supplies from years of unusually bountiful harvests to ones of lower output. Inventories introduce an intertemporal link for prices and end-use quantities of a product. The holder of stocks will improve the allocation of resources by "transporting" wheat, for example, through time from periods when it is plentiful to ones when it is scarce. Traders build up their inventories when they judge that prices are abnormally low and likely to rise sufficiently to cover the cost of storage (including interest); conversely, they liquidate stocks when they judge that prices are relatively high.

The traders affect the going price with these judgments. If their judgments are correct on balance, they will reduce the variance of the price around its trend and simultaneously smooth end-use consumption around its trend. If the price rises significantly in one crop year, the holders of stocks have to make complex judgments in order to decide whether or not to carry their inventories over to the next crop year. How much will producers respond to the higher price with an increase in output? To what extent can the recent price increase be attributed to a lasting change in underlying demand or in the supply price of producers that may continue and even intensify? To what extent will other holders of inventory liquidate their stocks?

In cases in which there are active futures markets in the commodity, the trader can read the consensus verdict of the marketplace about the outlook for prices in the year ahead. In any case, there is room for differences of opinion among traders. Indeed, if there were not, all traders who experienced similar storage and interest costs would dump their stocks in unison when the price crossed a particular threshold. At least some traders will be mistaken at any point in time. If many are mistaken, stocks can be built up in a period of rising prices and liquidated in disappointment at low prices. Under those circumstances speculation will add to the volatility of prices rather than providing the desirable intertemporal smoothing.

Understandably, weather-related shifts in supply dominate the price movements of crops. Nonetheless, fluctuations in aggregate demand are evident in the time-series of prices—remarkably so, given the extremely low income-elasticity of demand for food. With the exception of 1958, U.S. wholesale prices of domestically produced food crops fell (absolutely) in every recession year since World War II.

In the case of metals, the role of cyclical fluctuations in demand is more pronounced for obvious reasons. The basic users of metals are the highly cyclical industries of durable goods manufacturing. Although strikes and political upheavals in foreign countries can produce erratic fluctuations in supply, these are not typically as important as are weather variations for crops. Nor is there the seasonal discontinuity of supply experienced in crops; and, as a result, supply is more responsive to price variations in the short run. Since mining is the paragon of an industry operating subject to rising short-run marginal costs (or diminishing returns), a decline in price should lead reliably to a cutback in output by a price-taking producer.

Traders in metals should perform their function by varying stocks countercyclically. To the extent that they have a fairly well-defined notion of medium-term equilibrium price and inelastic expectations about current price variations, they should build stocks in response to the price declines of a recession and liquidate stocks in response to price increases of major proportions during a boom. The expected cyclical pattern of metals prices is readily confirmed; for example, Richard Cooper and Robert Lawrence estimate that an increase in world industrial production (relative to trend) of 1 percent adds between 3 and 6 percent to the price of nonferrous metals.[1]

On the other hand, the predicted countercyclical pattern of inventories is not generally evident in the data. In part this may reflect the extremely deficient quality of data on stocks; and in part it may be that increased "speculative" inventories in periods of recession are offset by

1. Richard N. Cooper and Robert Z. Lawrence, "The 1972–75 Commodity Boom," *Brookings Papers on Economic Activity, 3:1975*, p. 691.

lower "transactions" stocks of metals that are in the process of fabrication.

The Cycle and Efficient Markets

The observed cyclical pattern of prices for auction commodities and of production for mineral products is fully consistent with the efficiency of the markets in which they are traded. The "efficient market" theory developed by John F. Muth is an important recent development in macroeconomics. It implies that auction markets will not clear so long as unexploited profit opportunities remain that offer a distinct expected gain to any trader who could take a long- or short-term position with the intention of liquidating that position at some time in the future. For example, if soybean traders can expect to make a clear profit by buying beans at today's price, holding them for a month, and selling them, their actions to build stocks will push up today's price enough to eliminate that opportunity. It takes only a fringe of speculators and arbitrageurs among the participants in the marketplace to ensure that result.

An unexploited profit opportunity exists whenever buyers and holders of stocks can expect an appreciation in the price that will exceed their total holding costs, which include storage, interest, and transactions costs, and any risk premium required to induce them into that activity. If traders expect the price in one period hence to be E_t^{t+1} and their total holding cost per unit is C, they do not sell currently at a spot price, P_t, below the expected price in the future by more than that total holding cost. Or, to put it in reverse, they sell only if $P_t > E_t^{t+1} - C$. Similarly, if there is an organized futures market in the commodity with the price F_t^{t+1} for delivery next period, the trader can earn a risk-free return by arbitraging (rather than speculating) and holding stocks and selling futures if $F_t^{t+1} - P_t > C$. In that case, C need not include a risk premium.

Total holding costs can be substantial and can drive a considerable wedge between the current price and the consensus expectation of the price in the future, even in a thoroughly efficient market. Traders could believe firmly that the current price in a recession was well below normal and was bound to rise again without finding it worthwhile to build extra stocks unless they had confidence that the rebound was imminent.

On the bearish side of the spectrum of expectations, no trader should hold stocks (except for transactions purposes) when prices are expected to fall or even to rise at a rate less than C. But the zero floor on the pos-

sible holdings of stocks creates an asymmetry. That is especially important in futures markets, where no conceivable shortfall of the futures
price below the spot price can create arbitrage opportunities. Once
speculative stocks are depleted, the efficiency of the market sets no absolute upper limit on the expected rate of price decline.

If all changes of prices for storable auction commodities were merely
random walks in response to new information and previously unfore-
seen developments, the process of stock responses by traders and output
responses by producers would be abysmally inefficient. Wherever stocks
and output respond rationally to the signals of price in the marketplace,
price movements must have some systematic component. A price that is
high enough to attract a major flow of capital and labor into an industry
is a price that is bound to fall, at least in relative terms. A price at which
traders disgorge their inventories must be one that most of them expect
to decline. Conversely, an unusually large buildup of stocks reflects a
verdict that the current price is unsustainably low.

Still, with all the appropriate qualifications, the efficient-market
theorem stipulates that the predictable component of price movements
in auction markets for storable commodities be limited. That theorem
has an important negative message as well. When the price movement of
any product is readily predictable over a fairly sizable range and for a
broad class of circumstances, when it displays lags with respect to shifts
in costs and in demand, when it exhibits strong inertial tendencies, and
when it leaves large backlogs and surpluses, the transactions in that
product cannot be effectively approximated by the auction-market
paradigm. Rational traders and a skilled auctioneer would not let such
phenomena prevail.

Customer Markets

The hallmark of auction markets is the absence of price tags; sellers
are price takers and not price makers. In fact, most products are sold
with price tags set by the seller and through a process of shopping by the
buyer. As long as there are costs associated with shopping and limited
information about the location of the lowest price in the marketplace,
buyers do not find it worthwhile to incur all the costs required to find
the seller offering the lowest price. Rather, they adopt a strategy analogous to the acceptance wage of a searcher in the labor market—being

ready to settle for some price at which the additional cost of more shopping outweighs its benefits.

The Shopping Process

In modeling the shopping process, I put to use some of the tools developed in chapter 2 for the simple search model of the labor market. Suppose that shoppers have distinct convictions about the distribution of prices in the marketplace but no information about the location of the lowest ones. In particular, shoppers for shoes believe that the prices are distributed in the same way as the daily wage was distributed in figure 2-1, forming a normal distribution with a mean of $38. Suppose that a shopper found a pair of shoes with a price of $36. One-fourth of all prices lie below $36 (just as one-fourth of all wages exceeded $40 in the example used in chapter 2). Further, the average of all those lower prices below $36 is $34.23 (the same difference of $1.77 that applied in the wage example). If the buyer shopped at one more store, the probability is three-fourths that an inferior, higher offer would be found; and the probability is one-fourth that there would be a superior, lower offer, preferable by an average amount of $1.77. The expected benefit from shopping at one more store is $0.44. If the cost to this particular buyer of shopping at one more store exceeds this amount, the $36 pair of shoes will be purchased; if it is below it, the buyer continues shopping. If the purchaser's cost is $0.44, the $36 price will be the "acceptance price," the lowest price at which that purchaser would stop shopping. Clearly, for any specific cost of shopping at one more store, the optimizing acceptance price of a shopper can be determined from the price distribution.

This example omits any concept analogous to the "horizon" introduced in the selection of a job. It is as though the person is shopping for something that will be bought once in a lifetime, like a wedding gown (at least by tradition). Or it may be a pair of shoes bought in an emergency on an unusual journey. In any case, the buyer is assumed to obtain no future benefit by locating a low-priced seller who might be a supplier in the future.

Shopping costs give the sellers some monopoly power even when a large number of them offer a similar product. Moreover, if the purchase is of the type purchased once in a lifetime and information does not spread, there is no force to make prices converge to a single price, even if the process continues indefinitely with no change in costs or demand.

Sellers charging high prices will have a lower "acceptance rate" among shoppers, but they will also earn a higher margin of profit per sale. The balance of these forces can lead to multiple equilibria; different prices are viewed as optimal by various sellers and the prices are not competed into uniformity. Indeed, some sellers will cater to customers who have particularly high shopping costs. Anybody who has had to buy suntan lotion in a resort hotel knows that the prices are at the top of the distribution. But those sellers are not trying to develop a clientele; rather they are catering to demands that are nonrecurrent for any single individual but sufficiently recurrent for a broad group of potential customers to keep the sellers in business.

Recurrent purchases are different from the once-in-a-lifetime or emergency purchase insofar as consumers believe that the experience of their last shopping expedition conveys relevant information for their next one. If they had no reason to believe that the store offering a favorable price last time is still a low-priced seller, they would shop randomly, like the purchaser of a wedding gown. In fact, people do extrapolate experience from one shopping trip to another. If they have a favorable assessment of the terms of their last supplier, and if they believe that the information obtained from the last purchase is still relevant—that is, that the supplier is still offering essentially the same terms—they are likely to return to that supplier as customers or at least as shoppers. Presumably the buyers made their last purchases with satisfaction (at least ex ante) about the price and other dimensions of the offer; unless they were subsequently disappointed, they can be expected to repeat the decision.

Once customers establish a relationship with a particular supplier, then, on each shopping trip, they essentially make a quit-or-stick decision analogous to that of the worker who has a job. Insofar as buyers think they know the distribution of prices but not the location of the lowest ones, they have incentives to behave in a manner analogous to the selfselection by horizon in the labor market. The person who needs an expensive prescription filled every week has good reason to be selective and to shop intensively to find a pharmacist with a particularly low price. On the other hand, the person who needs a nonrefillable prescription or who expects to be in a large city only briefly may knowingly patronize a pharmacist who charges above-average prices. For this reason, a highpriced store will tend to have a lower rate of repeat business—like the higher quit rate of employees experienced by a low-wage firm.

The differential in repeat business will lead to some dynamic shifting of market shares, in contrast to the example of the wedding gown. Suppose that, of many stores in the city, a new store A is a high-priced seller while a new store B charges particularly low prices. Assume that they have an equal number of first-time shoppers, but the "acceptance rate" at store A is only half that of store B. Obviously, as new businesses, B's sales volume would be twice that of A. But those who settled for A's offer are likely to be infrequent purchasers. Suppose the customers of store A buy only half as often as those of store B; in that case, the ratio of B's volume to A's ultimately approaches four to one, never quite reaching it, so long as new shoppers flow into the system. Although this change in market shares may put pressure on A to price more competitively, it does not ensure convergence to a single price for the two stores even if the process continues with a static set of demands and costs. Store A might find that its higher profit per unit offsets its lower volume.[2]

Incentive to Continuity

Customers are valuable to sellers because of their potential for repeat business. That process of repetition makes the current level of demand experienced by a firm depend positively upon its volume of sales in the past. The extent to which firms are likely to enjoy repeat patronage depends both on the satisfaction of customers with previous purchases and their confidence that the supplier will maintain good performance.

The firm comes to recognize its ability to discourage customers from shopping elsewhere by convincing them of the continuity of the firm's policy on pricing, services, and the like. It knows that its customers have indicated by their previous purchases that they regarded the firm's offers as satisfactory. It can encourage them to return to buy, or at least to shop, by pledging continuity of that offer, ensuring them that past experience will be a reliable guide to present and future offerings. The firm wants to promote a reliance on intertemporal comparison shopping. It wants the patron to rely on past information—and insists that the information be fresh and not stale.

Customers are attracted by continuity because it helps to minimize shopping costs. They know the terms of the previous supplier's offer

---

2. Frequency of purchase is only one consideration in the intensity of shopping. For example, wealthy people and two-earner families may value time especially and view their shopping costs as high. They may therefore tend to settle for higher-priced offers.

without shopping if they can count on its continuance; but they must shop to determine the offers of unfamiliar sellers. That information is available, but it can be obtained only at a cost. Given that cost, maximizing behavior for the customer resembles satisficing behavior. If the status quo is satisfactory, the expected value of the information about alternatives is low. In these respects as well as others, customer markets share the characteristics of career labor markets. Both feature search costs, information costs, and bilateral-monopoly surpluses associated with established relations. Customers avoid shopping costs by sticking with their supplier much as workers avoid search costs by sticking with their employer. The customer product market even has some arrangements analogous to the seniority rules and privileges of labor markets that are designed to enhance the marginal benefits from extending relations. These may include special facilities for credit, provisions allowing regular customers to refund unsatisfactory purchases, and bargain sales that are announced only to regular customers.

Contrasting Arrangements in Product and Labor Markets

There are some differences between arrangements in product markets and those in labor markets. The essential feature of the toll model of the labor market is the initial investment made by the employer in the worker, which means the firm is vulnerable to a net loss if that relation is terminated quickly. Examples of similar set-up costs in product-market relations can be found: some manufacturers must invest in special tools to make components for another firm; some savings banks offer free toasters to new depositors. However, these seem to be exceptions rather than the rule in the product market. Even in these exceptions, the size of the initial investment is typically far smaller than those in the labor market, which can involve painstaking screening or lengthy training. Typically customers who buy once and are lost still leave the seller better off than if they had never bought at all.

Similarly, the supplier who, after an initial sale, closes doors or stops offering the product does not impose a serious cost on the buyer. Consequently, in the customer market the buyer and the seller do not need to probe each other's seriousness at the point of initiating a relation as the firm and worker do in the toll model of the labor market. Because there is little initial sacrifice to be shared on the two sides, arrangements like the reduced novice wage are not frequent in product markets. In these respects, the customer market resembles the enriched search model of the labor market more closely than the toll model. Customers, like job applicants, are often scarce and consequently have value. In particular, the firm finds it is worth incurring some expenditures to inform them by advertising; it is worth making expenditures or sacrificing revenues to preserve the relations once they have been developed. To the buyer in the product market, even when there is no scarcity of suppliers offering to sell a product, the withdrawal of the existing supplier from the market does impose shopping costs. Even if the relation is developed without an explicit investment, its termination can involve an opportunity cost.

There is a particularly interesting contrast between the career labor market and the customer market in who sets the price tags. That assignment is held by the buyer in nonunion labor markets but by the seller in product markets. The worker or the customer then engages in, and incurs the expenses for, the search or shopping activities. The seller in the product market and the buyer in the labor market must be the price makers in order to display equitable treatment of the people with whom they deal. Both in selling products and hiring labor, the firm typically makes many similar transactions. Wage discrimination among similar employees of the same firm or price discrimination among its customers would be destructive to long-term relations.

The Hotel Example

Some features of these product-market arrangements may be seen more vividly with a specific example. Suppose that many similar small hotels are operating in a large city. The marginal cost to these firms of renting an additional room (rather than leaving it idle) will be assumed to be negligible. Furthermore, I assume that the total demand for hotel rooms is always large enough to achieve full occupancy of the entire local industry at a positive price. Finally, I ignore the possibility of informing potential customers by advertising or the like.

AUCTION MARKET. First, consider how the hotel industry might operate if all potential customers went through a central exchange with an auctioneer or broker. The auctioneer is instructed to achieve competitive equilibrium, with the objective of keeping occupancy essentially full and stable by varying the price. Every hotel has to be a price taker, agreeing to abide by the market-clearing price. It faces a perfectly elastic demand for its rooms at that price. By assumption, the auctioneer ignores the possibility of exploiting any cartel power that could be used to improve the profitability of the hotels through higher prices and some unoccupied rooms. The equilibrium established by the auctioneer might be at a point at which the price elasticity of total demand for the local industry is less than unity (in absolute value), even though in such a case a higher price and less than full occupancy would clearly make the industry more profitable. So the auctioneer produces continuous "full employment" of rooms, and translates any shifts in demand promptly in price variations.

RANDOM SHOPPING. Next, dispense with the auctioneer and assume that firms must be price makers; in response to any inquiries, they state the price at which they are offering a room for any given day. Meanwhile, suppose that anyone interested in a hotel room engages in a random shopping process among the hotels, with an estimate of the distribution of prices and hence an acceptance price in mind. The absence of the auctioneer imposes shopping costs on the buyers. It also introduces a degree of monopoly into the industry in the sense that each firm's demand curve is tilted downward on any day. Obviously prices among hotels offering the same quality of service may be different on any particular day, in contrast to the uniformity imposed by the auction-market process. But if shopping makes the price elasticity of demand for each firm exceed unity throughout the relevant range, the firm will in fact maximize profits whenever it determines the room charge that precisely achieves full occupancy with no excess demand. If customers have no inherent preferences among hotels, any differences in room charges tend to create underoccupancy in some hotels and excess demand in others. Such a situation induces the price makers to adjust prices in the direction of greater uniformity. Full uniformity would be attained at the same price at which the auctioneer would have established the equilibrium. In effect, the hotels would really be jiggling the price in such a way as to act as do-it-yourself auctioneers.

The auctioneer will be missed particularly when demand shifts suddenly and unexpectedly. For that auctioneer would have promptly adjusted the price in that event, maintaining full occupancy. In contrast, the price-making hotels translate demand surprises initially into underoccupancy or excess demand. But the hotels adjust their prices in response to such surprises—unless they view the shift in demand as entirely transitory. A new process of groping for the market-clearing price follows a shift in demand, but firms striving to act as do-it-yourself auctioneers should be able to execute that task without a long delay. It may take a while to diagnose the situation and then to establish the new price schedule. But there should be no prolonged periods of under-occupancy or excess demand, accompanied by only slight changes in room charges. Prices still do most of the adjusting, and quantity varia-tions are rather minor.

The random shopping result will be different, however, if the daily demand curve perceived by the individual firm is price-inelastic at full occupancy. In that case, the firm finds it worthwhile to exploit the "monopoly power" stemming from the shopping costs of the customers, opting for a higher price and underoccupancy and thereby obtaining larger total revenues (and, by the assumption of no marginal cost, a larger total profit). Under those conditions, demand shifts typically will change equilibrium quantities. But demand for an individual firm in a large industry will be price-inelastic only if the shopping costs of potential customers are very large.

SHOPPING BASED ON EXPERIENCE. Now consider an arrangement in which firms are price makers and shopping is not random, but rather guided by past experience. All the people who previously stayed at hotels in the large city and who were satisfied with that experience are assumed to inquire first about the price and availability of a room in the hotel of their previous supplier. If the price is no higher than they paid previously, they become buyers; if it is somewhat higher, they may or may not decide to shop further. The elasticity of demand of these repeaters to an individ-ual firm is likely to be discontinuous. It is bound to be low with respect to price reductions because presumably the repeat callers were ready to rent a room for the same price that they paid the last time. But the elas-ticity may be substantial at higher prices because the repeaters are re-sponsive to price levels that exceed what they experienced previously or reasonably expected when they made their inquiries. Those potential customers who never stayed previously in a hotel in that city or who were dissatisfied with their previous hotel are essentially random shop-pers, and as a group their demand curve is likely to be elastic and con-tinuous. The combined demand curve of repeaters and random shoppers would then have a discontinuous marginal revenue curve, as illustrated in figure 4-1.

Suppose that the demand curve had intersected the full-occupancy Q_f with positive marginal revenue at that point and the firm had been operat-

Figure 4-1. *Hypothetical Demand Curves of Random and Repeat Shoppers*

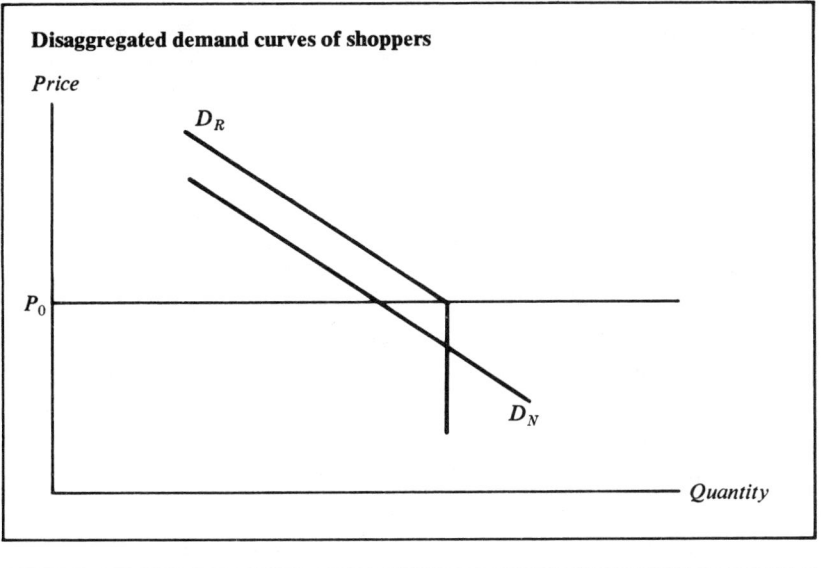

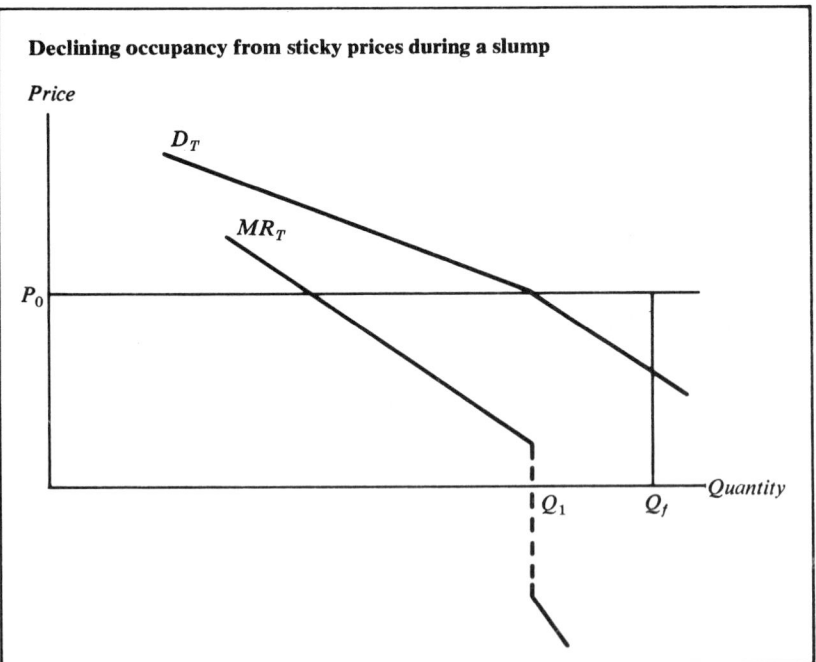

Notes: D_R = demand of repeat shoppers; D_N = demand of new (random) shoppers; D_T = total demand; MR_T = marginal revenue; P_0 = previous price; and Q_f = full occupancy.

ing for a considerable period with full occupancy achieved at a price P_0. Now, the economy experiences a slump, and both components of demand shift to the left in a manner that maintains the elasticity at each price, except for the fact that the angle in the demand curve of the repeaters remains at P_0, the price that had become customary to them. The demand curve and the discontinuous marginal revenue curve of the slump are illustrated in the figure. The firm would then maximize short-run profits when a decline in demand occurred by accepting a reduction in occupancy and holding its price at P_0. The firm cannot attract additional business from repeaters with a lower price, and that creates an asymmetry and an "inflationary bias" because any isoelastic shift upward in demand will raise the short-run profit-maximizing price. Unless the elasticity of demand from the random shoppers is large enough and their component of total demand sufficiently great that the weighted overall elasticity of demand exceeds unity at full occupancy, the short-run profit-maximizing price in the slump will be sticky and the quantity will decline.

This reasoning takes a myopic view of the firm's profit maximization. It ignores the interdependence introduced by the customer relations between today's occupancy and tomorrow's level of demand. In broader perspective, the value of obtaining random shoppers as customers includes not merely the proceeds from their current purchases but also an additional benefit associated with the likelihood that they will return to patronize the hotel in the future. When that long-run consideration is incorporated into the story, how much does the result change? Clearly, the short-term value of marginal revenue shown in the figure understates the long-term contribution from the occupancy of an additional room. The appropriately corrected marginal revenue curve would be less likely to lie in negative territory and therefore more likely to call for a price cut to maintain full occupancy. The firm may find it worthwhile to "underprice" for the short run, setting a price below the one that maximizes current profits in order to maximize its discounted stream of profits over the long run. But that incentive tends to be limited by "bargain-hunting bias." If the firm cuts prices during the slump, it attracts as additional patrons only those random shoppers who would refuse to pay a price as high as P_0. Those particular patrons may not be worth much as customers when demand revives and the firm raises its price back to P_0. There is not much point in attracting bargain hunters as customers unless the firm is prepared to supply the bargain consistently. Even an appropriately corrected marginal revenue curve may still contain a substantial discontinuity, which would produce sticky prices and falling occupancy rates in a slump.[3]

THE RELIABILITY OF PAST EXPERIENCE. As a final variant of the hotel example, assume now that not all satisfied customers necessarily inquire first at the hotel they previously patronized. At times, for example, they may be able to obtain the offer of another hotel at an especially low cost of shopping. The probability that they do check with their previous supplier will then depend in part on their confidence that the former offer is still available. If they believe that the previously satisfactory hotel has an extremely variable policy with respect to price (or any other dimension of its offer), they are less likely to bear any additional shopping costs to check there rather than elsewhere. If, on the other hand, they are confident that a room is there at the same price, they are more likely to go back. Once the hotel recognizes that behavior on the part of its patrons, it has an incentive to try to convince them by word and deed that it is committed to the continuity of its pricing and service policies. The more fully the firm can convince the patrons to expect the same offer next time around, the more likely they are to use past experience as a guide to current offerings and return to inquire about a room. Once the firm makes that commitment, it has an additional reason to stabilize prices, thereby necessarily accepting greater variations in quantity.

Insensitivity of Customer Prices to Shifts in Demand

The lessons from the tour of the hotel industry can be summarized and stated in more general terms. As contrasted with the auction mechanism, the process of random shopping introduces two sources of lagged responses of prices to shifts in demand. One lag represents the time required by firms to diagnose the shifts; the second stems from policies of firms to maintain their price lists for certain intervals of time. Such practices reflect the managerial costs of reviewing prices and the various costs

3. "Special introductory offers" are not made to attract bargain hunters, in the sense described here, and do not provide contrary evidence. Rather they are efforts by firms to convince shoppers that a price that seems high really is moderate in view of the superior quality of the product. In effect, the firm gives shoppers an opportunity to assess the quality of an unfamiliar product at a low price in order to convince them that it is worthwhile paying the higher price subsequently. If the hotel believes that it offers superior quality, it may be encouraged to discriminate (subtly) against regular patrons in a slump with such special offers to new customers. The benefits and costs are analogous to the employer's temptation to raise the wage of novices relative to that of experienced workers in a tight labor market.

of implementing changes in them. But these lags cannot account for any prolonged downward inflexibility of prices to weakening demand. They are simply not an adequate explanation of the extent and persistence of quantity adjustments and price insensitivity to cyclical fluctuations in demand.

When the customer shopping model is introduced, an added reason for price insensitivity emerges from the asymmetrical price elasticity of repeat customers. The firm does not need to lower its previous price to keep its business; but it may need to avoid raising prices. In a slump, the value for the longer run of attracting new customers encourages some price response. But that consideration does not necessarily reduce the optimizing price when demand shifts down. Bargain-hunting bias limits the effect. The firm can attract only bargain hunters by cutting its price; and that may be a poor investment in future demand if it expects to raise its price again and thus disappoint the bargain hunters.

A further important rationale for demand-insensitive prices stems from the recognition by sellers that they can influence the shopping behavior of customers by pledging continuity of an offer. Once sellers commit themselves to maintain an offer, they promote reliance on intertemporal comparison shopping by buyers. Yesterday's offer has a strong influence on today's demand.

Sellers who have adopted that strategy are inhibited from exploiting increases in demand by raising the price. Unlike the effect from the customers' asymmetrical price elasticity, the sellers' commitment to continuity introduces upward as well as downward stickiness of prices. Sellers may even find it worthwhile to leave unsatisfied excess demand, if it appears that customers are less antagonized by back orders than by jumps in the price. Conversely, when demand is temporarily weak, because sellers cannot pledge continuity of a bargain price, they are less likely to adopt one. The maintained strategy of continuity influences the pattern of demand; because prices vary less widely and less frequently, repeat shoppers are more common, and clientele relations dominate markets.

The insensitivity of prices is reinforced by another set of considerations. Whenever the firm allows for the future value of customers in maximizing its discounted stream of profits and thereby holds down its price and sacrifices some profits in the near term, it forgoes a reasonably predictable immediate gain in favor of a much more uncertain gain in the future. Whenever it underprices for the short run with an eye toward the crucial long-run price elasticities of demand, the firm makes a quantitative judgment on which it cannot have confidence. In such a situation, a rational firm is unlikely to "fine-tune" prices to fluctuations of demand because it cannot have conviction that such actions would enhance long-run profitability. It may opt instead to invest more heavily in building its future market when current conditions are favorable than when they are adverse. It will do that automatically if it forgoes opportunities to raise prices (and current profits) in response to cyclical upswings in demand. Conversely, during a temporary weakening of demand, it will sacrifice less of its current profits and do less to promote future profits, if it does not lower prices. As William Fellner has described such a decision process, the firm is "slanting" the probabilities away from the higher risk and more uncertain outcome for the long run and doing so incrementally in response to adversity. The same tendency may take a bureaucratic form insofar as managers prefer to report to shareholders a record of profits that is less volatile over the cycle. Even so, the preference of managers and shareholders alike for such a result may go beyond cosmetic concern for the income statement and reflect a genuine desire to underprice most competitors—and invest heavily in future demand—in particularly good times.

Scope of Customer Relations

Customer relations are extremely broad in scope. They are very important to any firm whose demand curve is higher than would be the case if it were offering its product for sale for the first time with no clientele, reputation, or record of performance. That must be true of virtually every firm that is a price maker. Firms find it desirable to cement these relations by many methods. They may appeal to customers on the basis of quality, transportation arrangements, credit terms, and speed and reliability of delivery.

The model of customer-supplier attachments applies most obviously to suppliers of services that are not easily evaluated by shopping. The resulting list is long and important in terms of the consumer's budget, including medical practitioners like the physician, dentist, and veterinarian; personal services like those of the barber, beautician, and dry cleaner; repair services of the automobile mechanic, house painter, plumber, and electrician; financial service suppliers like the lawyer, accountant, insurance agent, and branch banker. The considerations extend to goods as well as services, with only a fuzzy boundary line: the consumer wants a reliable optician, pharmacist, antique dealer, butcher, and clothier.

These are all sellers of differentiated items, and the price tag offers only limited information to prospective buyers. The potential bilateral monopoly surplus in these relations is large, although it can be destroyed or disrupted if suppliers raise prices in a way that antagonizes customers. Suppliers must beware of rocking the boat with their price actions.

It is more surprising to witness the importance of dependability and reliability to *professional* buyers, even to those procuring physically *homogeneous* products. But they clearly do prefer continuing relationships with suppliers and are often willing to pay premiums for dependability. It is remarkable that, in a weak steel market, imported steel may be priced 10 percent or more below the physically identical domestic product. Conversely, in a strong market, reliable customers of domestic firms are assured of supplies in amounts geared to their past purchases at prices far below those of imports. The copper industry has established a rather unusual two-price, two-market system; one market displays relatively little price variation over the cycle and rests on its continuing relations and assurances of supplies in periods of peak demand; the other is an auction-like market for arm's-length transactions, which tends to have lower prices in a slump and higher ones in a boom.

In the case of "big-ticket" items that are bought infrequently by consumers, like automobiles and household appliances, repair services are a means of maintaining relationships. More generally, firms seek to establish brand-name reliability in a way that counts on reputation (a flow of information from one consumer to the next) to substitute for repetition of experience by the same consumer.

Price Standards

Continuity and reliability are vital to all these arrangements. But because firms are subject to cost increases that they cannot control, they cannot maintain and realistically pledge constancy of price over an indefinite horizon. They can nonetheless establish some practices designed to build the confidence of their customers in their dependability and reliability. The supplier conditions the expectations of customers with pricing standards that are analogous to the wage standards discussed in chapter 3.

FIXED-TIME SCHEDULING. The firm can obtain and provide some benefits to its customers by specifying a period during which it expects to hold prices constant. It may establish a practice of limiting its price adjustments to an annual (or otherwise periodic) reconsideration at the time of release of new models, a new catalogue, or the like. As noted earlier, such a practice could develop in a world of purely random shopping because of the costs to firms of making decisions and providing information about price changes. But actually observed intervals of price adjustment extend far beyond these considerations, reflecting the desirability of commitments to customers to offer an unchanged deal.

PRENOTIFICATION. Some firms that will not commit themselves to price stability for any specific period may establish a practice of notifying customers in advance of any price increase and giving them an opportunity to place a last round of orders at the old price. Prenotification could not emerge in an auction market nor could it be the strategy of any profit-maximizing, price-making firm that attached no value to customers. Once such a firm determined that its profit-maximizing price had increased, it would want to put the change into effect as soon as possible and with a minimum amount of anticipatory buying by its customers. Prenotification makes sense as a strategy only because it provides valued customers with greater continuity of the firm's offer.

MEETING COMPETITION. When firms buy and resell or process items subject to major changes in price, they may find it too risky to engage in either fixed scheduling or prenotification. Supermarkets and discount houses cannot promise customers that they will hold their prices constant or notify them in advance of increases. But they can promise to meet competition. In effect, they create a price-price pattern; it is somewhat analogous to the wage-wage pattern in the labor market, although price comparisons operate with much shorter lags than does wage emulation. Meeting the price of competitors is obviously what any maximizing monopolistic competitor would be expected to do, quite apart from its customer relations. But in the customer-market world the announced strategy or pledge to meet competition serves to assure the customer that shopping would not be worthwhile and thereby to encourage repeat business. The firm that is likely to meet competition on a case-by-case basis can benefit by proclaiming such action to its patrons as a consistent strategy. If customers can be convinced that "nobody but nobody undersells Gimbels," they are more likely to continue shopping at Gimbels. Like the wage-wage model, the price-price standard needs a prime mover; here, it is a price leader. To unleash a wave of price cutting, some competitors must be eagerly trying to increase their market share.

COST-ORIENTED PRICING. The setting of prices by marking up costs is a good first approximation to actually observed behavior in most areas of industry, trade, and transportation. Firms not only behave that way, but also condition their customers to expect them to behave that way. It is easy for anyone to understand that cost increases can force the firm to break the continuity of its offer. Higher costs are an accepted rationale for raising prices. In many industries, when firms raise their prices, they routinely issue announcements to their customers, insisting that higher costs have compelled them to do so. No price announcement has ever explained to customers that the supplier has moved into a new position to capture a larger share of the surplus in the relation as a result of a stronger market. Price increases that are based on cost increases are "fair," while those based on demand increases often are viewed as unfair. In fact, there is overwhelming evidence that firms in most industries adjust prices more promptly and more reliably in response to changes in costs than in response to changes in demand. Prices in the recession of the mid-seventies were not inflexible or even especially sluggish; they responded fully to rising costs, although only slightly to falling demand.

The fairness of marking up costs is explicitly recognized in a number of types of institutional arrangements. For example, it is the accepted pricing formula for brokerage: the broker receives a specified fraction of the total value of the transaction. In a sense, many supplying firms represent themselves to their customers as procurement agencies operating under a brokerage arrangement. They expect to obtain, and ask the customer to pay, a specified fraction of the value of the items they supply as compensation for their contribution.

The rules of public utility regulation similarly link "fair returns" to costs. For some highly concentrated unregulated industries—like automobiles—pricing behavior seems to follow closely a model of self-regulated public utility standards. During wartime price controls and the Phase II standards, cost increases were the key justification for price increases. John Kenneth Galbraith's analysis suggests that the federal government administered the price controls program of World War II successfully by replicating (and then constraining) the cost-oriented rules for pricing that actually operated in uncontrolled customer markets. Consumer attitudes toward their suppliers also reflect the cost-based standard of fairness—for example, in the wave of antagonism to the re-marking of grocery products that were already on the shelf during the 1973 explosion of food prices.

The Logic of Cost-Oriented Pricing

It is much easier to document empirically the widespread nature of cost-oriented pricing practices and their acceptance as inherently fair than it is to provide an analytical foundation for those practices and attitudes. Indeed, in one respect, cost-oriented pricing is a deficient price standard because its operation is not readily observable by buyers. They cannot monitor the firm's diligence in carrying out an implicit contract that links prices to costs. Cost-oriented pricing shares that defect with the wage standard linked to marginal revenue product; in chapter 3 the rarity of reliance on that wage standard was noted; that seemed plausibly related to the fact that it could not be monitored effectively by the employee.

The cost standard has the merit of sanctioning price increases that are inevitable; and, in the eyes of some, of ruling out objectionable price increases that stem from greater demand. The antagonism toward price increases based on rising demand as "gouging" or "exploitation" is understandable as a micro phenomenon. If the firm raises its prices relative to those of its competitors, it is bound to create suspicions that it is starting to depreciate its investment (or "good will") in customer loyalty. Once the firm draws a clientele with attractive implicit contracts, any deviation unfavorable to customers is seen as a violation of these contracts. If customers believe that their share of the surplus associated with the relation is being trimmed, they are bound to react adversely. In a cyclical economy, customers may in fact be as well off by relying on a supplier that systematically widens margins in booms and narrows them in slumps. But customers would find it difficult to diagnose the firm's intentions or to establish that the more variable pricing policies in fact average out over the cycle. The firm would have grave uncertainties in assessing the probable reactions of customers. So the firm leans on a cost standard for pricing—using customer ignorance about costs to lift its prices above the standard without creating waves of antagonism. In that way, the customer-supplier relation is made viable.

These customer-supplier relations can be efficient arrangements that economize on a variety of information and transaction costs. They emerge because the auction market has severe limitations. In a world of universal auction markets, contracts would be encumbered with detailed specifications of heterogeneous, complex goods and services and with detailed arrangements for delivery, repair, and the like. Because the resulting transactions costs would be enormous, the world is dominated by price making. If all shopping were random, the transactions costs would still be large. The customer-market attachments save a huge volume of resources that consumers would otherwise devote to shopping (and trying out) products with every transaction. To firms, an established clientele increases the predictability of sales, permitting important savings in inventory costs and in production scheduling.

The costs of establishing new relations with the suppliers encountered when one moves into a new community illustrate the benefits of the established relations. Consider a mental exercise. Ask yourself how much you would have to be paid to take a pledge never again to engage in any economic transaction with anyone with whom you have ever chosen (among alternative suppliers) to do business as a buyer. That sum is your part of the bilateral monopoly surpluses shared with your suppliers.

On the other side of the ledger, prices rarely, if ever, equal marginal costs in a customer market and generally exceed them by a significant margin that varies among firms and products and over time. That creates an inefficiency from the point of view of society and of the participants in any bilateral relation. The typical supplier can provide an extra unit of output at an additional cost that is less than the value of that output to some customer. That unit should be produced but it is not. Mutually beneficial contracts could be devised to correct that inefficiency if buyers and sellers were thoroughly open and honest and always kept their word. (These possibilities were explored in chapter 3 for analogous situations in the career labor market; the application to customer product markets is straightforward.) But in the real world of mere mortals, such agreements cannot be negotiated because both sides would have incentives to misstate their positions and attempt to fool each other.

The Nature of the Cost Standard

Cost-oriented pricing must rest on a well-developed conceptual framework for defining and measuring costs within the price-making firm. A price-taking firm is also concerned with the measurement of costs—both as a guide to controlling costs and to selecting its level of output. But for price-taking firms with customer relations, costs take on particular significance.

The measurement and definition of costs need to be routinized and systematized within the firm so that parts of the operation can be delegated to clerical workers and so that the estimate of any second-level manager can be subjected to audit. The test of reproducibility or objectivity provides a basis for managerial control. Once the system of cost accounting is established, the firm's decision variable is the markup to be applied to unit cost in setting the price of output. The markup decision is the focus for considerations about elasticity of demand and investment in clientele.

Historical Costs

The need for objective and systematic measurement forces the cost standard to be backward-looking—or at least sideward- rather than forward-looking. Firms know what they paid for inputs at the time they acquired them; they do not know what they will pay when they place the next order, and they often do not know the current price, because they are not in the market for all of their inputs at any time. In addition, the most recent acquisition costs of inputs may reflect the orders or contracts placed much earlier, with a fixed price quoted by the seller. Any attempt to forecast input costs or to put them on a current replacement basis, which necessarily entails a forecast, would add to expenses, introduce a subjective element into cost calculations, and complicate the task of managerial control. Bygones cannot be mere bygones if they are the sole sources of systematic information.

The reliance of firms on historical costs is evident in many empirical studies of price-cost relations. The wage terms in price equations exhibit mean lags of a few quarters. The timing patterns observed among wholesale prices according to the stage of fabrication and from wholesale prices to consumer prices confirm the historical elements in costing. Those lags emerge because fabricators and retailers are relying on actual, recent prices of inputs in determining their selling prices. It is reasonably predictable that today's changes in cattle prices will show up on the supermarket counter only after a lag; the butcher does not keep changing price tags in pace with changes in some putative replacement cost.

The exceptions that occur to me arise when processed raw materials are sold on auction markets, as in the case of flour or soybean meal. In those cases, the processed products promptly reflect changes in the (auction-market) prices of the primary products; the processors must assume risky long positions in the raw product during the period of fabrication unless they hedge these positions by selling futures. Indeed, the miller is the protagonist in a favorite textbook example of the possibility for hedging (that is, reducing risk) by short selling.

The same considerations that lead to pricing on the basis of historical costs also account for the general preference of firms (and their accountants) to measure profits on that basis. From an economist's point of view, the concept of opportunity cost calls for valuing inputs on a replacement cost basis. If a retail firm currently sells a sweater at $20 for which it paid $19 sometime earlier but has to replace for $22, the sale generates a loss of $2 relative to replacement cost, rather than a $1 profit relative to historical cost. The firm did not recover enough from the sale of that sweater to replace it and thereby maintain its capital intact. Nonetheless, implementing consistently a reckoning of opportunity costs is not a straightforward matter, either conceptually or practically. Suppose that the initial shipment of sweaters was received on October 1, and the retailer sells them during October and November. On October 15, the manufacturer raises the price from $19 to $22; the retailer receives notification of that price increase on October 19. On November 1, the retailer places a fixed-price order with the manufacturer for additional sweaters at $22. The new merchandise is received on November 15, and it is placed on sale as the old shipment is sold out on December 1. When did the firm's cost rise from $19 to $22, and how can the accounting system incorporate that increase at the proper time? The puristic concept of replacement cost would argue that, whether or not the firm was aware of it, sweaters in fact cost $22 as of October 15; and therefore the cost of all subsequent sales of sweaters should be reckoned at that new, higher price. At the other extreme, traditional inventory accounting, following the convention of FIFO (first in, first out), applies historical cost and values the original shipment of sweaters at $19 apiece —regardless of how long that shipment remains on the shelf or what the replacement cost of it might become.

The contrasting convention of LIFO (last in, first out) is a compromise that moves in the direction of replacement cost. Indeed, it goes as far as possible in that direction, while still relying on actual billings to the firm. Under LIFO, the cost of the sweaters would shift from $19 to $22 on November 15, thus lagging behind replacement cost between October 15 and that date, but catching up with it subsequently. To shift sooner than that, the accountant would have to rely on price lists that the firm might or might not have received or that might or might not reflect accurately what the firm would have had to pay for its next purchase. LIFO continues to build the accounting system on actual rather than hypothetical transactions.

LIFO does, however, require firms to classify inputs, so as to decide the conditions under which a shipment is sufficiently similar to the preceding one to be viewed as its replacement. The concept of homogeneity may be manageable in the case of providers of crude oil or soybeans, but it may create severe problems for suppliers of sweaters or toasters. Does a new model or new style represent a new product? If so, the cost of items in the previous shipment is unchanged. If not—that is, if it is sufficiently close to the old version—then the remaining items in the old shipment take on the higher cost of the new shipment.

The difficulty of constructing rules for such decisions as part of an accounting system is an important deterrent to the adoption of the LIFO method. A second deterrent is that the LIFO method may present a misleading indication of performance from period to period for a firm that is in fact a "FIFO price maker." To avoid costs of changing price tags on products, to maintain a commitment when a product price is advertised to customers, or to facilitate centralized price setting, retailers may rationally adopt a policy of setting prices firmly at the time of receipt of shipments. Similar policies may be pursued by manufacturers and processors who find it important to accept orders from their customers for delivery at guaranteed prices.

Suppose the retail firm selling sweaters is a FIFO price maker that consistently marks up the manufacturer's price by $1; it sells one hundred sweaters each month that were received during the previous month. As indicated in table 4-1, the manufacturer's price sometimes varies from month to month; but according to the FIFO method, the firm earns $100 each month—a constant flow of nominal income, albeit a declining flow of real income if the general price level and the price of sweaters advance. LIFO accounting, however, records sharp fluctuations in income. If the firm holds the conviction that it can sell its sweaters to a steady clientele with a net return of $1 over the cost it paid last month, it believes the FIFO scorecard. It is not better off when the manufacturer's price is constant or falls, or worse off when that price rises.

In the national accounts the measure of inventory investment for

Table 4-1. *Comparison of FIFO and LIFO*

	Price		Retail	Total cost		Profits	
Month	Factory	Retail	revenues	FIFO	LIFO	FIFO	LIFO
0	19	...	...	...	...	...	...
1	19	20	2,000	1,900	1,900	100	100
2	21	20	2,000	1,900	2,100	100	−100
3	22	22	2,200	2,100	2,200	100	0
4	21	23	2,300	2,200	2,100	100	200
5	22	22	2,200	2,100	2,200	100	0

society must reflect the current period's production; it must be the value of the increase in stocks, rather than the increase in the value of stocks. The retail firm that replaced $19 sweaters with $22 sweaters experienced an increase in the value of its stocks but no increase in them. That fact shows up appropriately in the national accounts when inventories are reckoned on a LIFO basis. But no correction for such "capital gains" is needed at the firm level if the gain is, in effect, passed on to the customer. In that event, the gain need not be taken from profits because it never enters them.

Until the inflationary explosion of 1973–74, FIFO was overwhelmingly preferred by American business firms. It was estimated that only about 15 percent of all stocks were valued along LIFO lines in the early 1970s. That followed nearly a generation of an upward trend in the wholesale price index, with an obvious tax incentive in favor of LIFO accounting. (Unlike the case of depreciation practices, corporations must do their inventory accounting for tax purposes on the same basis that they report to their shareholders.) The majority of firms, who were FIFO price makers, were willing to forgo that tax benefit when it was fairly small in order to obtain the greater simplicity and accuracy of that accounting. (Indeed, at that time, a significant portion of the inventories based on LIFO fitted the flour-wheat example cited above.) The actual prevalence of FIFO pricing is reflected in empirical findings by William Nordhaus—that price-cost relations for the nonfinancial corporate sector fit better when the costs are defined on a historical basis (excluding the inventory valuation adjustment and consistent with FIFO) than on a replacement basis. I have obtained similar results using data extending into 1978.

The revealed preference of firms, showing continued reluctance to adopt LIFO, suggests that these FIFO pricing practices have not disappeared. After more than a decade of intense inflation, fewer than half of all inventories are valued on a LIFO basis. LIFO has a major tax advantage, but it remains misleading for FIFO price makers. An alternative interpretation has been suggested—that firms retain FIFO because they do not want to report the lower profits associated with LIFO. I find that conjecture implausible: it is inconsistent with other aspects of corporate accounting that lean on the conservative side; it implies an incredible willingness of managers to pay nearly one genuine dollar to the U.S. Treasury to report an extra dollar to shareholders; and it is totally unable to explain the survival of FIFO among unincorporated enterprises.

The detailed discussion of the valuation of inventories illustrates the difficulties and conceptual problems posed by any general conversion of nominal-unit accounting to an "inflation-adjusted" system. The concept of replacement cost for fixed capital is far more elusive than that for inventories because firms cannot know what it would cost today to build their current plant and because most would build quite a different plant if they had to make the decision anew. Interest payments and receipts pose vexing problems. In an inflation-adjusted system, some portion should be viewed as a restoration of the real capital of the debtor and not as genuine income. But alternative views on the appropriate adjustment are reasonable and defensible. In general, accounting systems rest on various conventions, especially on ones that define the boundary between income and capital gains (or losses). The logic of these conventions does not translate from nominal to real units in an obvious way. Professional discussions of inflation-adjusted accounting have foundered on legitimate controversy in the face of enormous complexity. After generations of keeping score in terms of the dollar, society cannot shift smoothly to a new system denominated in real units.

Standard Volume

Many industrial firms apparently use a concept of standard volume in formulating prices. Using standard volume as a reference for the unit cost that is incorporated into prices prevents the cyclical changes in average costs due to output variations from entering prices. Because, for given wage rates and prices of materials, most firms experience higher average costs (direct and total) at a lower volume of output than at a higher one, the standard volume or "normal" cost yardstick avoids cyclical perversity. Reliance on unadjusted unit costs would raise prices in a slump and lower them in prosperity. Econometrically, the standard-volume practice is reflected in price equations that show more influence of *trend* productivity growth than of actual productivity growth in short-run price determination. The bonus of above-average productivity gains generally obtained during a cyclical recovery (and the burden of reduced productivity performance in a dying expansion and early recession) tends mainly to raise (lower) profits rather than to hold down (push up) prices.

In effect, a concept of normal (cyclically average) unit costs guides the pricing decision. To implement such a concept, managers may follow one of two methods. First, they may develop measures of normal costs by correcting currently experienced costs for any inefficiencies (such as on-the-job underemployment) associated with low output or special economies associated with particularly high ones. Alternatively, they may calculate normal costs from current wages and other input prices and an estimated normal productivity (without measuring the actual level of productivity). In either case, they must select some operating rate as the "standard volume" and decide when to modify it. Apparently their choice of standard volume is influenced by actual experience of capacity operation. For example, Charles Schultze obtained good results in an analysis of prices and profits by assuming that the operating rate viewed by a firm as "standard" was based on its actual operating rates of the previous five years. Under those circumstances, by lowering the five-year moving average of operating rates, prolonged slack would actually tend to have a delayed inflationary effect.

Full and Direct Costs

For forty years the literature of economics has carried a running debate on whether "full" or direct costs are the basis for price making by most firms. The debate began in the late thirties when R. L. Hall and C. J. Hitch advanced the full-cost thesis on the basis of interviews with corporate executives, while Michal Kalecki analyzed factor shares as the result of marking up direct costs. Rationalizing full-cost pricing is a difficult assignment for any theorist, much more difficult than to identify and invoke practical considerations that can shift the focus from marginal costs to average variable or direct costs. William Fellner offered an intriguing theoretical rationale for full-cost pricing; he suggested that the sensible entrepreneurs who are strongly averse to losses might allow for fixed as well as variable costs in their pricing decisions.

The differences in the cyclical variation of direct costs and full costs are not so large if both are calculated at *standard* volume than if they are reckoned at actual output. Indeed, in the former case those differences may be subtle and therefore may be difficult to detect statistically. At any time, markup applied to direct costs is equivalent to some smaller markup applied to total costs. If the firm consistently applies a standard volume concept, that equivalence will not be disturbed by variations in output even though such variations will change the actual ratio of average total cost to average variable cost. If the average direct cost at standard volume is $6 and average total cost is $8, the firm arrives at the same price of $10 by marking up either direct costs by two-thirds or total costs by one-fourth.

The results of the alternative markup rules diverge, however, when the ratio of unit total cost to unit direct cost changes *at standard volume.* That ratio is likely to be disturbed by accelerating inflation. The largest component of fixed cost is depreciation on fixed capital (measured by historical costs), while the largest element of variable costs is labor compensation. Suppose that initially prices of capital goods and unit labor costs were stable (say, with wages and productivity both rising by 3 percent a year), but that inflation develops with prices of capital goods and unit labor costs rising at an annual rate of 5 percent. Although the relative price of capital and labor does not change, in fact, the reliance on historical cost depreciation will hold down the calculated rise of average total cost because inflation in capital goods will be reflected only gradually as new goods enter the capital stock. Unit fixed costs (at standard volume) will then rise much less than 5 percent in the initial year of the inflation, while unit direct costs will fully reflect the inflation rate of 5 percent. Full-cost pricing (at a constant markup) will delay the transmission of inflation by the firm, as compared with direct cost pricing. In the latter case the firm's prices rise by the full 5 percent, and nominal accounting profits rise by more than that percentage.

Interest payments on long-term borrowing are the second largest component of average fixed costs. Like depreciation, under present accounting systems they will lag behind a rise in the inflation rate because interest on existing bonds and mortgages is unchanged. But, unlike depreciation, interest will rise more than in proportion to the price level once it is affected. Inflation of 5 percent is likely to raise interest rates by far more than 5 percent of the initial rate; indeed, on the favorite first approximation the inflation, if expected to be permanent, would raise them by 5 *percentage points*. If the initial rate were 4 percent, interest payments on newly issued debt would then more than double. Under those circumstances, average fixed costs may rise even more rapidly than average direct costs for firms with large issuance of new debt; in such cases, full-cost pricing (at the initial markup) would amplify the inflation. Typically, however, a full-cost markup that is equivalent to a direct-cost one under conditions of price stability will yield a lower price in a world of inflation, damping down the acceleration of labor and material costs.

The coefficient on wages in a price equation probably provides the most decisive empirical test to distinguish full-cost from direct-cost pricing. When the price level of the nonfarm private economy is fitted to wages (and other input costs and, possibly, demand variables) in logarithmic form, the pricing models imply different values of the wage coefficient. According to the full-cost view, that coefficient should be approximately 0.7, matching the ratio of labor compensation to the total value of output. But according to the direct-cost view, the coefficient should approach unity, falling short of it only by the proportion of imports and agricultural materials in the value of product. The results of this test point to direct-cost pricing as the predominant practice. In price equations for private nonfarm business or the nonfinancial corporate sector, the coefficient on wages tends to be well above 0.7 and indeed does approach unity (although with a distributed lag of several quarters).

Direct costs and historical full costs may rise at quite different rates during an era of intensifying inflation and create serious behavioral distortions and cognitive problems. One illustration may be the widespread complaint of top executives of major corporations that, at today's product prices, they cannot operate profitably using new capital facilities, although they are earning gratifying profits on output from plants acquired in the 1950s and 1960s. That nostalgia for the previous costs on the old plants could be the result solely of the reflection in the accounting system of original-cost depreciation and fixed interest payments on existing bonds and mortgages. If prices are set by marking up direct costs, and fixed costs tend to rise less than proportionately, profit margins widen. Current income statements are bloated by the gains on the capital goods bought and the bonds sold in the "good old days." By the same token, the adverse assessment of profitability on projected new facilities may also reflect the interaction of nominal-based accounting and inflation. If in fact inflation continues at its recent pace and direct costs keep marching up, the application of a constant markup over direct costs during the life of a new plant will keep widening the margin of reported profits because average fixed costs are likely to lag behind. As a result, the profit rate in the later years of the new plant will be higher than it is initially.

These scorekeeping problems may be compounded by more substantive developments. If the unit costs associated with new capital have substantially outpaced unit direct costs in the recent inflationary era, new facilities really might have a low profitability. Or if the firms actually set prices allowing fixed costs (on the historical cost basis) as well as direct costs to have an influence, a profit squeeze on new facilities would be understandable. Margins over direct costs would be narrowed, as some of the gains on the old bonds and the old capital goods would be currently passed along to customers. Whatever the source of the complaint, its consequence has been to make firms feel the need for widening markups in order to establish a price structure that can justify new investments in terms of prospective profitability.

A Special Role for Material Costs?

Some views of marking up direct costs distinguish increases in the costs of purchased materials from increases in standard unit labor costs, implying that the former are likely to be passed through to customers essentially on a dollars-and-cents basis, while the latter are passed through with a percentage markup. Because many of the materials bought by manufacturing corporations are auction items with cyclically responsive prices, the treatment of increases in material costs by price makers may significantly influence the overall pattern of inflationary behavior. The percentage markup of material costs would make the price level more volatile cyclically than would a dollars-and-cents pass-through. This issue has been studied particularly carefully for the processing and distribution of food products; my impression is that the consensus of the empirical work suggests the truth lies somewhere in the middle. When raw sugar prices double, say rising from 10 cents to 20 cents a pound, the resulting price increase at retail tends to be larger in absolute terms (more than 10 cents), but smaller in percentage terms (less than 100 percent).

Actually, in a classical model that assumes positively sloped supply curves for processors and distributors, the predicted increase in retail prices in this example would be less than 10 cents. In that model the price responsiveness of demand would shift some of the increased cost of the raw material back onto the processor and distributor, forcing them to lower absolute as well as percentage margins. I am not aware of empirical evidence of such cost-absorption (except as a transitory phenomenon).

Upward and Downward Symmetry?

As noted in chapter 3, the economic system may have an inflationary bias in the sense that increases in demand or in costs raise prices or wages more promptly and more substantially than corresponding decreases in demand or in costs lower them. Studies of pricing behavior, however, do not generally provide evidence of such an asymmetry, as James Tobin has observed in summarizing their findings. Yet case studies and anecdotal evidence suggest asymmetrical price responses. In the early sixties, some claimed to detect a downward rigidity of prices that was analogous to the Keynesian wage floor. For example, in the 1965 Economic Report of the President, a comparison of price and productivity trends for nineteen manufacturing industries led the Council of Economic Advisers to suggest that "in some instances, industries with large productivity gains made only token reductions in prices, or even raised them. Except where these movements reflect divergent movements in nonlabor costs, such cases give an upward bias to the overall price level" (p. 57).

At this point, there is no general evidence to indict pricing behavior for the crime of inflationary bias, but neither can it be exonerated from all suspicion.

Price Responses over the Cycle

The empirical evidence for the United States suggests that cost-oriented pricing is the dominant mode of behavior. Econometrically, demand is found to have little, if any, influence on prices outside the auction market for raw materials. As Phillip Cagan summarizes the findings: "Empirical studies have long found that short-run shifts in demand have small and often insignificant effects [on prices], and that, instead, costs play a dominant role."[4] Similarly, William Nordhaus reports: "Considerable evidence has accumulated that industrial firms tend to set prices as a markup on *normal* average costs. . . . Faced with temporary changes in demand, firms generally alter production and employment rather than price."[5]

The generally negative verdict on the role of demand is a balance of results—in some industries, capacity utilization, backlogs, or some other demand indicator has a detectable positive influence on markups over standard costs; in many, the effects are negligible or absent; and in a few industries such as automobiles and public utilities a perverse influence emerges whereby high volume is associated with a low markup even over standard direct costs. The picture that emerges is that non-auction customer markets are mainly a transmission belt in the inflationary process. They are not a source of inflation; they do not magnify it, nor do they damp it down. Rises in wages and increases in input prices that stem from the auction sector of materials and imports are reflected in prices rather fully and more or less promptly, depending on the precise nature of the cost standards applied in pricing. But by acting as a transmission belt for inflation, these sectors accentuate quantity variations over the cycle, enlarging the output losses of a slump and the output gains of a rebound. The entire burden of price responsiveness is shifted to labor markets and the auction sector of product markets.

Actual price behavior provides a sharp contrast to the competitive Cobb-Douglas model, which, as was noted in chapter 1, implies that a 1 percent change in output relative to capacity should be associated with a change in product prices (given input prices) of one-third to one-half of a percentage point. The behavior of customer market prices also contrasts sharply with auction prices that move very rapidly and widely in response to the cycle. The prices of industrial, nonfood raw materials, excluding fuel, fell by 14 percent from their peak in April 1974 to a trough in March 1975. Over that same eleven-month interval, producers' prices of nonfood finished consumer goods *rose* by 12 percent while those of producer finished goods soared by 21 percent. By the same token, this category of auction prices turned up as soon as recovery began after March 1975. Although demand was so weak that unemployment

4. Phillip Cagan, *The Hydra-Headed Monster: The Problem of Inflation in the United States,* Domestic Affairs Study 26 (American Enterprise Institute, 1974), p. 22.

5. William D. Nordhaus, "The Falling Share of Profits," *BPEA, 1:1974,* p. 183.

rates and operating rates both remained near records for the era since World War II, the *strengthening* of demand was enough to raise market-clearing prices. In contrast, the prices of finished products lagged behind during the recession, slowing down during the first year of recovery. They then rose at a fairly moderate rate during the next two years, and did not display a clear acceleration until 1978.

The contrasting cyclical profiles are inconsistent with the popular explanation of stagflation in terms of "inflationary expectations." To suggest that copper prices fell in 1974–75 because of deflationary expectations while steel prices rose because of inflationary expectations is "bootstrap" theorizing. The auction markets that clear every day provide definite readings of the expectations of traders; any bolstering effect on prices during the recession from longer-run inflationary expectations was strongly outweighed by the collapse in demand for end use. The rising trend of prices outside the auction markets did not provide much information about expectations of future prices; it reflected experience of recent changes in costs. The nature of price making and of cost making (particularly through the labor market) kept prices rising throughout customer markets even during the severe recession.

Relative prices among products traded in customer markets vary markedly with a distinct cyclical pattern, reflecting both the volatility and timing of changes in input prices and the workings of the transmission belts in different industries. Prices of finished goods that have a high content of materials costs stemming from auction markets display significant cyclical responses. Prices of products for which the wages of casual labor loom large in costs reflect the responsiveness of that underlying cost component. Prices of products whose costs are dominated by the compensation of career workers exhibit little cyclicality. Many of those products are the outputs of durable goods manufacturing and experience especially large cyclical sensitivity of demand. Hence some of the products with the greatest fluctuations in output over the cycle may show only a slight impact of the cycle on their prices.

Prices of different products also display varying sensitivities in response to acceleration or deceleration of the overall inflation rate. The economy-wide inflation rate of the current year, $\bar{p}$, as compared with the average of the preceding three years $(1/3)(\bar{p}_{-1} + \bar{p}_{-2} + \bar{p}_{-3})$ may be taken as a rough measure of the "surprise," s, or "innovation" in inflation. If that is used to explain the deviation for a particular commodity group of the inflation rate in the current year, p^i, from its preceding three-year average,

$(1/3)(p_{-1}^i + p_{-2}^i + p_{-3}^i)$, a clear pattern emerges. The time-series regressions of the s^i variables on s display slope coefficients above unity for crude materials (the auction market items) and less than unity for most finished manufactured goods, and particularly small values for automobiles and household durable goods. Clearly, relative prices are systematically influenced by changes in both real activity and inflation.

As noted above, some aspects of cyclical price patterns emerge because the transmission belt from costs to price operates with different speeds for different types of customer products. Price increases generally lag behind cost increases, with an average lag of a few quarters, but longer in some industries and shorter in others. Industries vary in their consistency in marking up historical costs and in the lag between the purchase of labor and materials and their embodiment in output. The lag in each industry will depend on whether firms take orders at fixed prices, and, if so, how long a period elapses between order and delivery. Finally, the lag will be longer in those industries in which prices are reviewed only periodically by management, and cost increases accumulate for some time before they are reflected in increased prices.

The timing patterns in the transmission of cost increases into price increases reflect practices of looking backward that, as I have emphasized, can often be efficient and economical for business. How much firms rely on such practices depends on their confidence in the stability or predictability of their costs. If those costs are sufficiently predictable, firms can make commitments to deliver at fixed prices well into the future; they can adopt model-year conventions for price setting, and they can pursue a FIFO pricing strategy. The degree of reliance on such practices that is appropriate during an era of relatively stable costs becomes excessive during an inflationary era that generates rapid and erratic increases in costs. For example, a firm that reviews its pricing decisions only once a year would experience a squeeze in profits during an inflationary era if it maintained its previous percentage markup and applied that to standard unit costs as currently estimated at the time of its annual review. In that case, the price that was appropriate at that instant would be too low subsequently as costs rose.

Ultimately, firms are likely to adapt to the change in the economic environment. They can do so by one of several alternatives: (1) shift from annual to quarterly (or irregular or ad hoc) reviews of pricing, (2) raise the percentage markup they apply to make room for some rate of increase in costs during the coming year, or (3) explicitly forecast costs and apply the established percentage markup to the average of predicted costs. The first alternative has been implemented in recent years by many industries, notably the automobile manufacturers and some catalog retailers. In many respects the second route is like the third, but it rests on an implicit forecast or simple extrapolation rather than on a formal predictive procedure. Moreover, its consequences may be different: decisions to alter the percentage markup may take on the character of conventions and be longer lasting, showing less responsiveness to subsequent slowdowns (or further speedups) in cost inflation. My subjective guess is that far more firms have traveled the second route than the third, generally changing the tactics of their backward-looking strategy rather than shifting explicitly to a forward-looking one. The particular form of the adaptation is of limited significance, nonetheless, because all these forms speed the transmission through the customer-market sector of inflationary forces stemming from elsewhere. They all bear out a story with the same moral—prolonged experience with unusually rapid inflation intensifies the inflation.

Pricing, Information, and Competition

The analysis of this chapter stresses that the vast majority of sellers are price makers. They must develop a procedure for putting price tags on their products. In principle, they could execute that task by mimicking the auctioneer in an effort to "clear markets." Indeed, sellers would introduce modifications to exploit market power and to incorporate short lags and modest thresholds in pricing that reflect the time and trouble of revising the price list. But, in practice, observed pricing behavior is a vast distance from such do-it-yourself auctioneering, even after allowing for such modifications. The rationale I emphasize for that striking contrast is that the seller learns that the short-run price elasticity of demand of established customers is low because of shopping costs and can be made even lower by a pledge of continuity of the seller's offer. That is an adequate explanation for infrequent and limited changes in price tags. But some additional factor must be invoked to explain why prices are much more responsive to changes in costs than to shifts in demand. What needs to be explained is not rigid or sticky prices, but rather the flexibility of prices in following costs even when demand is pulling in the opposite direction.

I suggest that the asymmetry stems, in part, from implicit contracts or conventions that introduce a concept of fairness in the relations between suppliers and customers whereby price increases based on cost increases are generally accepted as fair, but many that might be based on demand increases are ruled out as unfair. That analysis leaves many specific questions unanswered. Some forms of peak-load pricing by utilities or transport firms are accepted (even by regulators) as fair; some hotels in college towns charge especially high rates on football weekends. On the other hand, firms in the sports and entertainment industries offer their customers tickets at standard prices for events that clearly generate excess demand. Popular new models of automobiles may have waiting lists that extend for months. Similarly, manufacturers in a number of industries operate with large backlogs in booms and allocate shipments when they obviously could raise prices and reduce the queue.

The customer market model does not explain when and how firms establish concepts like standard volume, how they choose the cost definition that they mark up, or how they determine the particular magnitude of the markup. Those who are setting prices must organize information in some systematic fashion within the firm, reach decisions, and then distribute information outside the firm. Because information about prices (in all their dimensions) is costly for buyers to obtain, firms have incentives to adopt strategies that make established customers unwilling to incur the time, trouble, and expense of collecting that information from other suppliers. The information system extends far beyond the relations between suppliers and customers to embrace relations within the firm. Many aspects of the tactics of pricing seem to be guided by the need for managerial principles that can be monitored and enforced by top executives and taught and delegated to subordinates.

The view of pricing as the product of an information system helps to illuminate the distinctions between the customer-market view and two contrasting paradigms of pricing—the "rational expectations" model and the administered price thesis.

Prices and Rational Expectations

For the product market, the paradigm presented by the rational expectations view resembles the misperception explanation of changing cyclical unemployment that was discussed in the analysis of the labor market in chapter 2. Sellers of products are assumed to have only limited or stale information about the general price level but to observe promptly the prices that they receive for their products. When a major upswing in economic activity bestows on them unexpectedly high prices, they interpret those prices, not merely as high absolutely, but as high relative to other prices. That misperception encourages sellers to expand output; if the increased prices of their output were correctly interpreted as part of a general rise in prices, they would not expand. It appears that imperfect information creates fluctuations in output, while perfect information leads to a prompt equilibration of markets with unchanged output and increased prices.

Imperfect information is a reason for cyclical fluctuations in output and employment to take place even in a world in which all markets are continually cleared. The traditional classical model discussed in chapter 1 ruled out shifts in aggregate demand as a source of fluctuations in real activity; the rational expectations variant restores that possibility, resting its case on the misinformation that leads sellers to send to market more or less output than they would if they had full information about all the elements relevant to their supply curves. The rational expectations theorists wish to demonstrate that the business cycle is not a "mere" product of the transactional mechanism but rather is more "fundamental" and would emerge even in a regime of universal auction markets with no transactions costs. But they must throw some sand on the frictionless classical machinery to deviate from its conclusion, and that takes the form of information costs about other prices.

The exponents of the view depict as the critical experiment a hypothetical disturbance to the demand side that is "correctly" and uniformly perceived by all private agents. Suppose that the money supply is increased enough to raise nominal GNP by 1 percent. If buyers, sellers, and auctioneers are aware of that disturbance and its implications, presumably the market clears with all prices 1 percent higher, and with no changes in quantities. Although the critical experiment is formulated as an unexpected change in the money stock, it would be equally applicable to anything else that altered nominal GNP in a clearly and uniformly perceived way—a money-economizing innovation, fiscal policy, or changes in spending (relative to money holding) by consumers, investors, or foreigners.

As it applies to a universal auction world, the prediction of this model that the response to fully recognized shifts in aggregate demand will be purely a price adjustment seems basically unassailable. Conceivably, income effects on debtors and creditors might change the mix of demand and relative prices. But that cannot be a serious qualification. In the framework of that auction world, the theory explains adequately why disturbances that are not subject to misinformation lead to the standard classical result sketched in chapter 1.

The theory is weak, however, in explaining why any demand disturbances in that world should be so poorly perceived for so long that they create pronounced cycles in real activity. No evidence is offered that sellers are unaware of movements in other prices. In the absence of such evidence, one wonders why the recognition of general price movements by sellers would be more delayed than the publication of the monthly consumer and producer price indexes; and, indeed, for those factor prices that enter into their direct costs, why the recognition of movements would be subject to even that long a lag. To put it another way, if misinformation or missing information accounts for decisionmaking errors and fluctuations in real activity, what information would be required to prevent the errors and eliminate the fluctuations? Is there a case for at least one dimension of government stabilization policy, namely, the subsidization or direct provision of that missing information? In short, what would the U.S. Bureau of Labor Statistics have to do to eliminate the cycle?

The theory is formulated for a world of auction markets, and it decays rapidly when it is applied to a world of price making. Consider the impact of the demand disturbance that adds 1 percent to nominal GNP in a price-making world. The key conclusion of a pure price adjustment will hold only if every seller acts as a do-it-yourself auctioneer, presumably acting on the assumption that all other sellers adopt that same strategy. But in a price-making world in which the costs that transactions would have in auction markets preclude reliance on that transactional mechanism for most products, do-it-yourself auctioneering would be irrational behavior. Shopping necessarily creates tilted demand curves for the short run, and they, in turn, discourage transitory price adjustments. Moreover, economic agents find efficient ways to economize on transactions costs by developing explicit and implicit contracts, investing to establish a clientele with a pledge of continuity, and creating employer-worker and customer-supplier relations. These institutions further reduce the benefits and raise the costs of price (and wage) adjustments. The key points were illustrated in the hotel example earlier in this chapter. Once the absence of the auctioneer tilts the demand curve, rational behavior requires the firm to recognize the information costs on the part of potential occupants and to reject do-it-yourself auctioneering as an inefficient strategy. The cycle in real activity stems from transactions costs that lead to customer markets, rather than from information costs about other prices in a hypothetical world of universal auction markets.

Many cyclical features actually observed in product markets are critically related to price making. The patterns of inventory behavior are a prime example. Surprises in inventories are unique to price-making firms. Indeed, inventory liquidation—the hallmark of U.S. recessions— must be linked to the behavior of price-making firms. As indicated at the outset of the chapter, sellers in auction markets have complete control over their inventories and should be expected to increase them deliberately when their markets are unusually and temporarily weak. The observed cyclical pattern of order backlogs is equally inexplicable in an auction model and is, in fact, not observed in any auction market. In the price-taking world of rational expectations, an inflation surprise must occur to change output; in fact, reversals in the path of output often precede changes in the rate of inflation. The systematic variations in relative prices experienced during the course of cycles (and during eras of chronic inflation as well) are not susceptible to explanation in terms of an auction model. In short, economists need a theory of cycles grounded in the realities of how motor vehicles, machinery, and metal products are sold in the marketplace. The market does not have much use for a theory that stresses the possibility of a cycle in an economy consisting exclusively of wheat, silver, and hide markets.

Administered Prices

A more substantial challenge to the customer-market view is the thesis of administered prices that has been expounded for decades by Adolf Berle, Gardiner Means, and John Blair. In that view of the world, prices are seen as information communicated to competitors. The insensitivity of prices to shifts in demand is taken as the result of an informational system among oligopolists that permits them to engage in tacit collusion.

Like customer markets, administered prices supply an explanation for prices changing so little cyclically, or equivalently for changes in quantities dominating cyclical adjustments. The unresponsiveness of prices to demand is basically a manifestation of market power. Oligopolists seek viable rules of competitive behavior that will realize the potential joint surplus of their concentrated industry. They want to maintain a large monopoly rent that they can share, and to avoid approaching the purely competitive result of normal profitability. In pursuing those goals, managements of rival firms implicitly agree not to chase shifts in demand with price changes upward or downward. Such price flexibility is ruled out as unfair—but as unfair to competitors rather than to customers.

Furthermore, according to the administered-price model, the likelihood that such implicit agreements are maintained depends on the extent of industrial concentration. The more numerous the sellers, the greater the likelihood that some maverick will upset the oligopolistic applecart. Hence antitrust policies come to the fore. Breaking up concentration would help to increase price flexibility. So might legal standards of pricing performance; using some criterion of the expected degree of price flexibility under competition, they might force firms to reduce or conceivably cease their tacitly collusive behavior, even in concentrated industries.

Empirically, the thesis is buttressed by an impressive display of the contrasts in the pricing patterns of highly concentrated and atomistic industries over the cycle. In concentrated industries, price declines are rare; changes in prices are less frequent; prices decelerate by a smaller amount during periods of recession; and, as a mirror image, accelerations of prices are smaller and generally more sluggish during periods of extremely strong economic activity.

The implications of the thesis do not necessarily depend on an asymmetry of prices in the upward and downward direction. To the extent that price flexibility would reduce fluctuations in output and employment and enhance macroeconomic stability, the inflexibility of prices associated with oligopoly is viewed as socially undesirable even if it is symmetrical in response to excess demand and excess supply. But additional evidence and extended theorizing is sometimes offered to suggest an asymmetry whereby the net effect over the entire cycle involves some inflationary bias.

Unlike the analysis developed in this chapter, the administered-price view does not stress any differential responses of prices to changes in costs and changes in demand. The empirical evidence is generally structured to demonstrate the inflexibility of prices rather than that of margins or markups. Studies that do focus on markup variation tend to find reduced, but still noticeable, effects of industrial concentration. Oligopolies may experience less cyclical sensitivity of costs than do competitive industries. The dominance of collective bargaining and nonunion career labor arrangements may make the wage costs of highly concentrated industries less cyclically sensitive. Only a few oligopolies have a major component of costs from raw materials with cyclically sensitive auction prices—in contrast to some atomistic industries like food processing and textiles. Even so, less flexibility of costs is not the entire explanation for less flexibility of prices in oligopoly.

At a theoretical level, it is easy to imagine how a system of tacit collusion could provide for greater flexibility of prices in response to changes in costs than to shifts in demand. Price changes in response to cost changes might be less disruptive and more acceptable as fair play among competitors, partly because changes in input prices (including wages) are likely to be experienced and perceived rather uniformly by the various firms in the industry. Consequently, the focus of administered prices could be shifted to markup rigidity by oligopolists. Oligopoly is clearly not a sufficient condition for markup inflexibility. The exponents of administered prices have frequently had to explain away the flexibility of prices in some highly concentrated industries. They have sometimes invoked special factors like the importance of international competition or of peculiar structures of marketing. In cases such as nonferrous metals and lumber, which are concentrated industries with prices that respond significantly to demand shifts, the key explanation, in my view, seems to be weaker attachments between suppliers and customers. Why they are weaker cannot be neatly explained by the customer-market view either. But that model allows for various causal factors to determine the pricing behavior of an industry, while the administered-prices view focuses on the single explanation of industrial concentration.

It is understandable that efforts to build a clientele will be characteristic of many highly concentrated industries. Because unbridled price competition can destroy the joint surplus (as the administered-prices thesis emphasizes), oligopolistic firms will seek to compete in nonprice dimensions. Those methods include the provision of special services to customers and the emphasis on reliability of quality, prompt deliveries, financing arrangements, and the like. When such industries exhibit markup inflexibility, the basic explanation lies in the strength of customer attachments rather than the degree of concentration, even though the latter may have contributed to the former.

Markup rigidity seems to me simply too pervasive across the U.S.

economy to be attributable to oligopoly. The aggregate evidence on pricing in private nonfarm business accords closely with the markup model. Markup rigidity is not limited to automobiles, computers, aluminum, and the handful of other important durable-goods manufacturing industries in which concentration ratios would make an oligopoly pricing model plausible. To my knowledge, retail trade displays no significant markup responsiveness to shifts in demand, and surely the structure of that industry is as atomistic as any avid trustbuster could wish. If markup rigidity stems from tacit collusion, the opportunities for that collusion must extend over a sufficiently wide range of industrial structures to defy any conceivable antitrust crusade. Customer attachments in atomistic industries create low short-run price elasticities and pricing patterns resembling that of an oligopoly. The local jewelry shop has a low price elasticity of demand in the short run, but that does not justify the conclusion that the jeweler is an oligopolist. The elasticity is low because the shop has established a clientele and so have its competitors.

In my view, the kinked demand curve, which is the classic explanation for rigid prices under oligopoly, really is a feature of a clientele relationship rather than of oligopoly. As that model has been expounded, oligopolists know that any reduction in their prices will compel their competitors to follow them downward. They cannot gain market shares from price reductions and can increase sales only by moving, with all their competitors, down an industry demand curve with a rather low price elasticity. On the other hand, when they contemplate increasing prices, they recognize that their competitors may not follow; in that event, they would lose their market share and move up along a highly elastic demand curve. That situation is illustrated in figure 4-2; the perception by rivals of asymmetric responses to reductions and increases in price generates, for any individual firm, a kink at the existing price and a corresponding discontinuity in the marginal revenue curve. If the industry demand curve then shifts from D to D', the kink may remain at the existing price, P_E, and the price will not be altered unless the elasticity of demand changes enormously at that price. Often, after a shift in the marginal revenue curve, the vertical portion of the new curve will intersect the marginal cost curve, calling for an unchanged price (and a change in quantity from Q to Q'), as illustrated in the figure.

The serious defect of that analysis is that it offers no explanation of why any firm that would like a higher industry price should be reluctant to initiate a price increase on an experimental basis to determine whether

Figure 4-2. *Oligopolistic Response to a Shift in Demand*

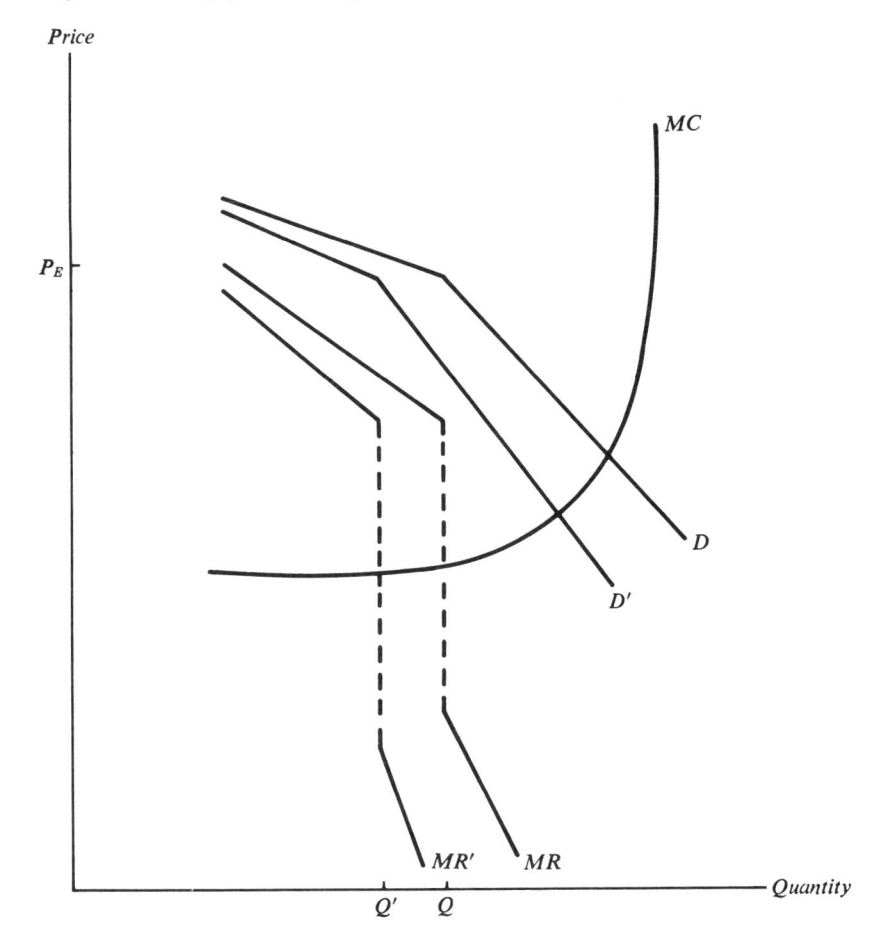

its competitors would follow. It identifies no significant cost of acting as a would-be price leader in an upward direction. If competitors do not follow, the leader retreats after losing only a few sales for a brief period. When customer attachments are invoked, however, it becomes clear why that strategy is not attractive. A firm that tries to lead prices upward in the industry toward the joint monopoly price takes the risk of losing customers during the interim. While it maintains a price higher than that of its competitors and waits to see whether they will follow, its rivals obtain an opportunity to exploit the price differential by "stealing" its customers. The major loss lies, not in the sales sacrificed during that brief period, but in the possible destruction of customer relations for the long run—the kink that enters figure 4-1 rather than that usually associated with oligopoly. The serious inhibitions to raising prices in response to demand shifts comes from customer attachments rather than from high concentration.

The theories of customer markets and of administered prices imply vastly different welfare consequences of markup rigidity. The customer-market view does not regard the inflexibility of prices as necessarily an adverse consequence of oligopoly. On the contrary, it accepts the attachment between buyer and seller as an inherently desirable institutional arrangement that economizes on the expenses of shopping, trying out products, and otherwise engaging in transactions. This view suggests that many firms that have established a clientele have done so by placing a value on customers who regard them as reliable and fair. Indeed, the pricing behavior of the customer markets creates a persistent excess of price over marginal cost, which detracts from social welfare. Society pays the costs of monopoly elements and collects the benefits of genuine economies of transactions. It is not clear whether the benefits exceed, or fall short of, the costs. That diagnosis does not point to antitrust measures as a likely remedy for chronic inflation or macroeconomic instability.

In summary, I do not claim to have demolished the thesis of administered prices. At the very least, it deserves credit for giving an early and emphatic recognition to the gap between the real world of pricing and the implications of short-run profit maximization. But I do claim that the observed rigidity of markups throughout the private business sector requires a customer-market (rather than an oligopoly) view of product markets—a recognition of the benefits of customer attachments.

Bibliographical Notes

The relations among movements in inventories, prices, and production in auction markets discussed in the text are entirely consistent with the analysis presented by John F. Muth in his classic article, "Rational Expectations and the Theory of Price Movements," *Econometrica,* vol. 29 (July 1961), pp. 315–35, especially pp. 322–30. The omnipresent assumption of a random walk on prices in the literature on efficient markets was introduced by Muth's followers; it is not a hallmark of the original piece, which drew most of its analytical examples from commodity markets. For example, Muth concludes the discussion of one model (p. 327) as follows: "If inventories are an important factor in short-run price determination, . . . the time series of prices has a high positive serial correlation." In an interesting book on the behavior of commodity markets, Walter C. Labys and C. W. J. Granger note the greater empirical validity of the random walk model for stock market prices than for commodity market prices. See their *Speculation, Hedging and Commodity Price Forecasts* (D. C. Heath, 1970), p. 65. John Maynard Keynes spelled out several reasons that explain why inventories are not varied countercyclically in such a way as to act as an important automatic stabilizer of production in his *A Treatise on Money,* vol. 2: The Applied Theory of Money (Harcourt, Brace, 1930), pp. 130–47.

The shopping model presented in the text to describe the process in markets that lack a clearing mechanism follows Edmund S. Phelps and Sidney G. Winter, Jr., "Optimal Price Policy under Atomistic Competition," in Phelps and others, *Microeconomic Foundations of Employment and Inflation Theory* (Norton, 1970), pp. 309–37. Two aspects of the discussion in this chapter were not incorporated in their model: the buyer's incentive to engage in intertemporal comparison shopping, and the recognition by the supplier that he can influence the shopping behavior of the buyer by a commitment to continuity. An interesting recent model of price dispersion in shopping processes is presented in Steven Salop and Joseph Stiglitz, "Bargains and Ripoffs: A Model of Monopolistically Competitive Price Dispersion," *Review of Economic Studies,* vol. 44 (October 1977), pp. 493–510. William Fellner's discussion of "slanting the probabilities" is presented in his *Probability and Profit: A Study of Economic Behavior along Bayesian Lines* (Irwin, 1965), pp. 173–80; it is specifically offered as a rationale for average-cost pricing.

Discussion of the empirical validity of cost-oriented pricing can be found in Phillip Cagan, *The Hydra-Headed Monster: The Problem of Inflation in the United States,* Domestic Affairs Study 26 (American Enterprise Institute, 1974), pp. 21–34; William D. Nordhaus, "Recent Developments in Price Dynamics," in Otto Eckstein, ed., *The Econometrics of Price Determination,* a conference sponsored by the Board of Governors of the Federal Reserve System and Social Science Research Center (The Board, 1972), pp. 16–49, and "The Falling Share of Profits," *Brookings Papers on Economic Activity, 1:1974,* pp. 169–208; and Otto Eckstein, "A Theory of the Wage-Price Process in Modern Industry," *Review of Economic Studies,* vol. 31 (October 1964), pp. 267–86. One study that finds a significant effect of demand on prices is Robert J. Gordon, "The Impact of Aggregate Demand on Prices," *BPEA, 3:1975,* pp. 632–38. The effect, however, is limited and related to changes in demand. A rationale for fixed time scheduling of price movements is presented in Stephen A. Ross and Michael L. Wachter, "Pricing and Timing Decisions in Oligopoly Industries," *Quarterly Journal of Economics,* vol. 89 (February 1975), pp. 115–37. John Kenneth Galbraith presented his insights on the relation between cost-oriented pricing and techniques of price control in his *A Theory of Price Control* (Harvard University Press, 1952).

Discussions of the transmission of various costs into prices include Robert J. Gordon, "Can the Inflation of the 1970s be Explained?" *BPEA, 1:1977,* pp. 257–64, and "Impact of Aggregate Demand on Prices," pp. 613–62; and Joel Popkin, "Consumer and Wholesale Prices in a Model of Price Behavior by Stage of Processing," *Review of Economics and Statistics,* vol. 56 (November 1974), pp. 486–501.

Full-cost pricing was advanced as a pattern of business behavior in R. L. Hall and C. J. Hitch, "Price Theory and Business Behaviour," *Oxford Economic Papers,* no. 2 (May 1939), pp. 12–45. The cyclical behavior of income shares was explained by Michal Kalecki on the basis of an assumed model of pricing in which direct costs were marked up. See his *Essays in the Theory of Economic Fluctuations* (London: Allen and Unwin, 1939), pp. 13–41. Among the important contributions to the discussion of direct-cost versus full-cost pricing are Richard B. Heflebower, "Full Costs, Cost Changes, and Prices," and Richard Ruggles, "The Nature of Price Flexibility and the Determinants of Relative Price Changes in the Economy," in National Bureau of Economic Research, *Business Concentration and Price Policy,* Special Conference Series, 5 (Princeton University Press, 1955), pp. 361–92 and pp. 441–95, respectively; and Committee on Price Determination, *Cost Behavior and Price Policy,* Price Studies, 4 (National Bureau of Economic Research, 1943). The use of the standard volume concept is discussed in Joel Dean, *Managerial Economics* (Prentice-Hall, 1951), pp. 444–54. The adaptive concept of standard volume is advanced in Charles L. Schultze, "Falling Profits, Rising Profit Margins, and the Full-Employment Profit Rate," *BPEA, 2:1975,* pp. 449–69.

The rational expectations view for product markets is developed in Robert E. Lucas, Jr., "Some International Evidence on Output-Inflation Tradeoffs," *American Economic Review,* vol. 63 (June 1973), pp. 326–

34; and Thomas J. Sargent, "Rational Expectations, the Real Rate of Interest, and the Natural Rate of Unemployment," *BPEA, 2:1973,* pp. 429–72.

The concept of administered prices was introduced by Gardiner C. Means in *Industrial Prices and their Relative Inflexibility,* S. Doc. 13, 74 Cong. 1 sess. (Government Printing Office, 1935). Another study of the role of administered prices in price inflexibility during the Great Depression is National Resources Committee, *The Structure of the American Economy,* pt. 1: *Basic Characteristics,* a report prepared by the Industrial Section under the direction of Gardiner C. Means (GPO, 1939), pp. 126–45. Studies that focus on the relation between administered prices and inflation include Leonard W. Weiss, "Business Pricing Policies and Inflation Reconsidered," *Journal of Political Economy,* vol. 74 (April 1966), pp. 177–87; George J. Stigler, "Administered Prices and Oligopolistic Inflation," *Journal of Business,* vol. 35 (January 1962), pp. 1–13; John M. Blair, "Market Power and Inflation: A Short-Run Target Return Model," *Journal of Economic Issues,* vol. 8 (June 1974), pp. 453–78; and Gardiner C. Means, "Simultaneous Inflation and Unemployment: A Challenge to Theory and Policy," *Challenge,* vol. 18 (September–October 1975), pp. 6–20. An excellent discussion of the administered pricing controversy, with additional citations, appears in F. M. Scherer, *Industrial Market Structure and Economic Performance* (Rand McNally, 1970), pp. 284–303.

For the theory of kinked demand curves in oligopoly, see Hall and Hitch, "Price Theory and Business Behaviour," pp. 21–25; Paul M. Sweezy, "Demand under Conditions of Oligopoly," *Journal of Political Economy,* vol. 47 (August 1939), pp. 568–73; and George J. Stigler, "The Literature of Economics: The Case of the Kinked Oligopoly Demand Curve," *Economic Inquiry,* vol. 16 (April 1978), pp. 185–204. A basic source on the effects of the large corporation on private property, workers, and consumers of the goods and services offered by corporations appears in Adolf A. Berle, Jr., and Gardiner C. Means, *The Modern Corporation and Private Property* (Commerce Clearing House, 1932).

V

Asset Markets

MUCH of contemporary monetary theory rests on the foundation of a general equilibrium system of perfect auction markets for goods, services, and securities. In that world, every item can be either bought or sold at its market-clearing price with no costs of shopping or otherwise acquiring information, or of carrying out transactions.

That theory often has misleading implications for a world that does not have perfect auction markets. It misses the significant consequences of transactions costs for the sphere of trading that does take place in auction markets. The theory also misses the implications for asset markets of product and labor markets that are geared to price making rather than market clearing. In addition, it cannot cope with the important nonmarket-clearing or price-tag aspects of the asset markets themselves.

The linkages between asset markets and product markets in a world of price tags are different from those in a Walrasian world, and those differences are important in the analysis both of cyclical fluctuations in real activity and of inflation. The purpose of this chapter is to outline the major amendments to general equilibrium monetary theory that are required to apply it to slack and inflation in a world of universal transactions costs and generally prevailing price tags. It is not designed to develop a full-blown theory of money and assets; in most respects I can rest on previous analysis, particularly the analytical framework created by James Tobin.

The first part of this chapter reviews the nation's balance sheet, particularly the ways in which transactions costs, information costs, and other customer-market phenomena enter into the demands, supplies, and yields of various types of assets. I emphasize the assumption that asset markets resemble auction markets usually made in the literature and, in contrast, the aspects of behavior that can be understood only by incorporating the nonauction thinking applied to labor and product markets in preceding chapters. The last part of the chapter considers a theorem of Irving Fisher that implies anticipated inflation is neutral in its consequences for portfolios and capital markets. Unlike the Fisher theorem, my analysis indicates that inflation has pervasive real effects for portfolios and saving.

Money in a Price-Tag Economy

Money and liquidity are important in a world of price tags. Indeed, the Walrasian world cannot explain the need for money, because no frictions exist in product and labor markets and every asset is perfectly liquid.

Liquidity and Transactions Costs

That limitation of the Walrasian world has been expressed succinctly by others. Leijonhufvud states: "All transactors face perfectly elastic demand functions; the full value of any good can be instantly realized. Money has no special status."[1] Similarly, Brunner and Meltzer explain: "With costs of executing transactions zero and information a free good, there are no costs of shopping . . . and no benefits from reducing the resource cost of executing transactions and eliminating cross-hauling of commodities. Any asset is just as usable as any other for executing transactions and discharging obligations."[2]

In such a world, the auctioneer in the cheese market need not care whether buyers execute transactions by paying him with peanuts, gold, or tobacco. Nor do sellers care how the buyers pay them. So long as anyone can exchange peanuts for other products costlessly, peanuts are a perfectly acceptable medium of exchange.

A modest role of some "money" as a numeraire or unit of account is likely to emerge. Even the most dedicated Walrasian might find it cumbersome to operate with a long price list giving the cost of cheese in terms of every other commodity. Indeed, that might even threaten to pollute this immaculate world with a transactions cost. To prevent that, a numeraire can be selected in which prices of cheese, peanuts, and all other products are quoted; then the exchange rate between cheese and

1. Axel Leijonhufvud, *On Keynesian Economics and the Economics of Keynes: A Study in Monetary Theory* (Oxford University Press, 1968), p. 79.

2. Karl Brunner and Allan H. Meltzer, "The Uses of Money: Money in the Theory of an Exchange Economy," *American Economic Review*, vol. 61 (December 1971), p. 804.

peanuts can be easily established by dividing their two prices as stated in terms of the numeraire. But no problem arises that would require a money to serve as a means of payment. Barter is thoroughly satisfactory and is not impeded by any need for a double coincidence of wants. As long as A has something to sell that B wants, it is irrelevant whether B has anything to sell that A wants. For A can convert anything that B will part with into something that A does want. The number of transactions that participants must make to obtain an item they want (to consume or to use as an input) is irrelevant: ten costless transactions are still costless.

Even in a Walrasian world, people who are risk-averse will have distinct preferences about the composition of their assets. All assets cannot serve equally well as stores of value even though they are equally satisfactory as media of exchange. Because the relative price of any particular commodity is subject to change, people who hold products they do not plan to consume in the foreseeable future take on undesirable purchasing-power risk. They can avoid that risk by buying futures contracts on the items for a consumption market basket, or by holding diversified bundles of commodities whose average price is likely to track the price of that market basket, which is discussed below. But those considerations do not lead to the creation of money.

Unlike the Walrasian model, the auction markets of the real world do not feature free information, free transactions, free transportation, and free storage. That set of transactions costs is important enough in practice to require significant changes in the theory, pointing it toward the development of money as a means of payment and a store of value. If the cheese auctioneer is offered one numeraire's worth of various goods, it is readily understandable that a nod will be given to the bidder who offers to pay with a product that the auctioneer wants to use; so the double coincidence of wants enters the picture. If it is to be resold, the auctioneer will prefer an item with low costs of storage and transportation, or one of homogeneous quality and neat divisibility. Thus some commodities are inherently well qualified to serve as money. Once a commodity is adopted as money, that success reinforces itself: information and transactions costs are bound to be low because the good is bought and sold so widely. But no commodity money will pass all the tests. Ultimately, commodity money is supplanted by a more convenient version of fiat money backed by the government.

Products sold by means of price tags often have inherently high transactions costs that make them inappropriate for the workings of an auction market. Those same characteristics initially make them unlikely candidates for money. Once a product such as soap is marketed through price tags, there is no known value that the cheese auctioneer can be sure to realize by accepting soap in exchange for the cheese. The soap seller earns income by serving as a reliable supplier of soap and adds something to the buying price for soap in forming the selling price and thus obtaining that income. If the cheese auctioneer were to accept soap, that auctioneer would have to divert efforts to find the buying prices of soap sellers. Information on the price of a price-tag product is not a free good obtainable from the morning paper but rather an important piece of private property that is acquired and used by specialized traders. Setting prices is one of the many specializations facilitated by a monetary economy.

Once any asset is established as the means of payment, some stock of it will be demanded to execute transactions. The required stock will be smaller to the extent that sellers take "future money" by accepting credit cards, extending trade credit to customers, or tolerating interest-bearing promises to pay. But for reasons discussed below, the IOUs of individuals are bound to have limited acceptability. To deal with sellers who demand "spot money" (that is, cash assets) in payment, the potential buyer must hold some amount of that money.

People needing more spot money than their initial stock to make a purchase must engage in a separate transaction at some cost to convert some asset into money or to incur a debt. For example, they may have to contact their banks to shift funds from a savings to a checking account and perhaps pay a fee for that shift if a bank has previously agreed to make such a transfer automatically. So even though money provides no explicit income, it is held because it saves transactions costs.

Money has been at times defined as the asset whose full value can be instantaneously realized with no transactions costs. Since the notion of "full value" is cash value, that definition is tricky. It is no more remarkable that the full money-value of money can be instantaneously and costlessly realized than that the full peanut-value of peanuts can be. The definition does not promise that the full peanut-value of money can be realized costlessly (without shopping or brokerage) any more than can the full cash value of peanuts. But the cash value is especially important because money is usable as a purchasing power over all other items; it is the asset traded in all markets. First, the conversion between peanuts and money is not symmetrical in a price-tag world; the special knowledge required of a peanut seller far exceeds that of a peanut buyer. Second and more important, the conversion from peanuts to cheese takes two steps—from peanuts to money and from money to cheese. For money, no intermediate costly transactions are required; holding money ensures minimum transactions costs. The real world creates one asset that has properties somewhat akin to the frictionless properties that all assets have in the hypothetical Walrasian world.

Unlike productive real assets and securities, money has (at least conventionally) a zero interest yield. The opportunity cost of holding money is the sacrifice of income potentially available from other assets. The demand for money by a person with a known future stream of unsynchronized receipts and payments is determined by balancing at the margin the transactions costs avoided and the interest yield sacrificed by holding more cash, as has been elegantly set forth in the Tobin-Baumol model of the transactions demand for money.

Near-Money

From another vantage point, the costs of transactions in earning assets can be viewed as analogues to the tolls in the model of the labor market developed in chapter 2. Because of the toll in the financial market, the investor who holds a security for only a day or two is likely to incur a net loss, as is the firm that retains a novice for only a brief period. Just as the toll in the labor market has a number of possible dimensions, so in the asset market a toll may extend beyond the transactions costs at time of purchase to include an allowance for the capital-value risk and any additional "brokerage cost" of selling the asset prematurely. Any earning asset has a "break-even horizon"—a minimum period over which it must be held to produce a net gain as contrasted with holding money. For example, suppose that the interest rate on a Treasury bill is 8 percent a year, and that it costs 1 percent of face value to acquire it and another 1 percent to sell it. Then it would take three months to generate enough interest income to cover the in-and-out transactions costs.

The shorter the break-even horizon for an asset, the greater its "moneyness." Consider an alternative asset whose interest yield is only 4 percent a year, but for which the brokerage costs are one-sixth of 1 percent for acquiring and selling. For that asset, the break-even period is only one month. Clearly there will be a place for the second asset in some portfolios despite its lower interest return. Indeed, to put it more strongly, if the second asset with the lower transactions costs had as large an expected interest return as the first, it would entirely dominate the first asset and drive it out of the portfolios of risk-neutral investors. For assets of different liquidity, rational investors in efficient markets will act, not to equate their expected interest returns, but to ensure a differential that reflects their relative "moneyness" and their relative supplies. A model that ignores the required differential commits the egregious sin of Walrasian illusion—the treatment of asset markets as though they were perfectly frictionless.

The passbook savings deposit in a commercial bank or a thrift institution is a prime example of near-money, readily convertible to cash at low transactions costs and with no capital-value risk. Treasury bills and other short-term securities issued by borrowers whose risk of default is trivial also impose relatively low transactions costs; although they have some risk of fluctuating capital value, that risk is limited by their short maturity and they also qualify as close substitutes for money.

As compared with long-term bonds that have much higher capital-value risk, near-money has yielded a lower interest rate historically. Of course, such a pattern of the maturity yield structure can be consistent with equality of expected returns if there are general expectations of rising long-term yields that would generate expected capital losses on bonds. But the historical evidence is inconsistent with the supposition of equal expected returns. Since the 1920s, the yield of Treasury securities with very short maturities (three to six months) has exceeded those with long maturities (more than three years) in only a few years—for example, 1973, 1974, 1979, and early 1980. Obviously, just as people hold demand deposits at zero yield in efforts to achieve perfect liquidity, they will rationally sacrifice some interest yield to achieve partial liquidity. Indeed, the balance sheet of the household sector suggests that the average American family values liquidity highly and pays heavily to get it. Of $2.9 trillion of total holdings of deposits and securities in the household sector at the end of 1979, $1.6 trillion was in currency, demand deposits, savings accounts, and U.S. short-term and savings bond obligations; those are assets with yields below that of top-quality bonds and with considerably greater liquidity.[3]

3. These data were provided by the Flow of Funds Section of the Board of Governors of the Federal Reserve System. Of the remaining $1.3 trillion of total holdings, $894 billion was in corporate equities and $416 billion was in other U.S. government securities, mortgages, state and local obligations, corporate and foreign bonds, and open-market paper.

In a world in which the acquisition and disposal of assets in general are subject to substantial and differing transactions costs, the size of those costs apparently is an important attribute of alternative assets. The minimum transactions costs associated with money and the relatively low ones of near-money must command a price in a rational world of non-Walrasian markets that are imperfect and have frictions.

Customer Market for Loans

The demand for money and near-money by individuals and firms is influenced by the interest and transactions costs and availability of loans they might obtain if they need to make payments that exceed their income receipts. At the extreme, one could imagine a "credit-card world" in which futures money is the means of payment but spot money is not held in portfolios. That would require the universal acceptability of such credit cards, universal access to credit "vending machines," or a much greater and more elastic use of trade credit ("free" loans from suppliers to customers).

Although opportunities to borrow to meet contingencies do in fact reduce reliance on holdings of money and liquid assets, they play a limited role and do not drive cash out of portfolios. Understandably, no one faces a perfectly elastic supply curve of loans. The quality of an IOU depends on various characteristics of the signer: holdings of assets, income experience and prospects, and also the number of IOUs already issued. So borrowers must expect to pay a higher interest rate than they can obtain on default-free claims and a rate that increases with the amount they borrow. Also, they must find lenders who are able to appraise the quality of their signatures. Suppliers of loans to individuals and small businesses essentially specialize in compiling and applying such information. This is true for both financial intermediaries and firms supplying trade credit. Of necessity, the loan market to households and most firms fit the customer relations model rather than the auction market model.

The use of collateral on loans supplements the signature of the borrower with the value of a particular asset as a way of reducing risks of default. Real estate loans and mortgages rest heavily on collateral, but the collateral is meant to support and augment the signature and to add a threat that helps collections rather than to substitute for the signature. Mortgage lenders want assurance that the borrower can meet the payments; the income statement and balance sheet of the home buyer are appraised as carefully as is the parcel of real estate. It is interesting that some assets, like automobiles and household appliances, are much easier to collateralize at the time they are bought than subsequently. The transaction with the dealer provides the lender with an independent costless appraisal of the value of the asset.

Saving and Household Portfolios

The difference between the interest rate of the lender and that of the borrower has important implications for the theory of household saving. That rate differential is substantial; for example, during 1979 the average interest rate paid by households exceeded 10 percent on home mortgages and approximated 14 percent on consumer installment debt, while the average yield on all interest-bearing assets held by households was about 7 percent. Because the marginal cost of borrowing far exceeds its average cost (while the marginal and average return on lending are essentially equal), the more meaningful gap between the marginal cost of borrowing and the marginal return to lending would be larger than the average gap by a wide margin. For many would-be borrowers, the marginal cost of debt is the rate charged by loan sharks, and for some it is essentially infinite. Household savers who add to their nominal assets at a time when they have outstanding debt, rather than reducing that debt, are sacrificing net interest income in the conviction that the *marginal* cost of debt (compounded by the probability of needing debt) is sufficiently larger than the average cost to justify that sacrifice. A similar revealed preference is also expressed by anyone who incurs debt while holding liquid assets; in fact, people often seize opportunities to borrow at 14 percent at the time of purchase of a new appliance and hold on to their savings account that yields 5 percent.

The gap between the borrowing and lending rates accounts for important observed deviations of consumption behavior from that implied by simple life-cycle models that assume a single interest rate for borrowing and lending. In those models, people with an average degree of time preference would be expected to plan for a stable and trendless standard of living during their lives. For medical students, for example, such a lifetime plan might require two decades of negative net worth. Obviously, loans on such a scale are unavailable or at least prohibitive in cost, and so the doctors of tomorrow maintain standards of living today that are far below even the most conservative expectation of a lifetime average. Farmers and small businessmen can shift the supply curve of loans in their favor by increasing their own net worth; understandably they save much more than families with similar incomes in other occupations, thereby using their holdings of productive assets as leverage. In recessions unemployed workers (and even those threatened by unemployment) tighten their belts far more than the life-cycle model implies because of the high cost of borrowing and the accompanying high value of a cushion of liquid assets. Econometric short-run consumption functions appear to have much larger responses to cyclical fluctuations in aggregate real disposable income than would be implied by life-cycle or long-horizon, permanent income models.

The same considerations have important implications for portfolio choices. Because of the gap between the lender's and the borrower's interest rates, nominal assets with short-term maturities, like savings accounts and bills, are more attractive than long-term bonds. Consider a world that, at any time, had a single interest rate for all maturities and for all lenders and borrowers. Suppose the interest rate varies over time but the inflation rate does not. Then, life-cycle planners who are accumulating wealth to finance retirement and bequests would minimize their exposure to risk from future variations in the interest rate simply by buying an annuity and a life insurance policy. That long-term portfolio is extremely safe. If the course of income receipts and consumption payments follows the expectations of these planners, they are totally immune to any risk of fluctuating interest rates. Surprises in income or consumption requirements will lead them to expand their savings (that is, to buy an additional annuity) or to borrow at interest rates that are initially unpredictable, but those risks are unavoidable and essentially symmetrical for favorable and unfavorable surprises. The possibility of surprises in receipts and payments does not shorten the very long maturity of the optimal portfolio.

A gap between the lending rate and the borrowing rate, however, alters the verdict on the optimum maturity. An unfavorable surprise in income or consumption needs requires borrowing at a high interest rate, while a favorable surprise permits extra lending at a lower rate. Recognizing that, the household wants some assets that can be readily resold to finance periods of negative saving without reliance on borrowing. The annuity fails miserably by providing no opportunity for resale. A long-term bond is salable, but its market value is subject to large uncertainty, because it is especially sensitive to a change in the interest rate. The household is pushed toward some holdings of short-term assets.

Once the maturity of the portfolio is shorter than the retirement annuity, the welfare of consumers is no longer immune to changes in the interest rate. Along their expected path of receipts and payments, they will "roll over" some assets at the going lender's interest rate when they reach maturity. So long as they remain positive savers, they are clearly in a better position if there is a rise in the interest rate and in a worse position if there is a decline. The higher market value of holdings associated with a lower interest rate is worth something as a contingency; it moves consumers farther away from the brink at which they would have to incur costly debt. But if their lifetime plans call for holding assets to maturity (at least), as long as they remain net buyers of securities over the horizon, they must be sorry to see the price rise. For such a saver, a fall in interest rates raises the market value of wealth, but generally reduces welfare— cutting the expected maintainable stream of consumption available to a household over its lifetime.

A household with a portfolio of claim securities of varying maturity would be totally misled by tracking its "Haig-Simons" income, which adds changes in the market value of wealth to current earnings from work and property. The changes in wealth stemming from changing interest rates would give the wrong signals.

Increases in the market value of assets that reflect increases in their expected future earnings do represent increases in welfare, that is, a higher maintainable lifetime consumption standard. But for no asset—land or common stocks or anything else—is it possible in practice to keep accounts that make a strict separation of the two sources of changes in wealth (the variations in the numerator of prospective returns and the variations in the denominator of the discount rate). The inability to carry out that exercise is an important reason that income and wealth are often thought about as separate and distinct items. In effect, people are pushed toward the maintenance-of-capital concept of income, in which the portfolio of assets is regarded as an entity in itself that must be preserved to maintain the activities of the firm or household. That approach draws a sharp distinction between the capital account and the current account, limiting the measurement of income (and presumably the considerations affecting spending decisions) to flows on current account.

I suspect that the commitment of accountants and widows alike to that reckoning reflects not merely a conceptual preference for maintenance of capital, but also a recognition that changes in wealth due to changes in interest rates can be misleading indicators of welfare. They recognize that capital gains due to lower interest rates cannot in general be consumed without reducing the planned menu for the future. They act rationally with respect to those gains, but in the process postpone the opportunities for consuming capital gains associated with higher prospective property incomes until those prospects actually materialize.

Financial Institutions

The loan market is divided into a customer market, served largely by commercial banks and thrift institutions, and an auction market that deals in bonds and commercial paper. The auction portion provides large borrowers with very low (or zero) default risk and with a scale of transactions that justifies costly efforts to compile information on their creditworthiness. Bondholders benefit from information compiled and disseminated by bond-rating services both directly and indirectly by guiding other investors and enhancing the marketability of securities.

Banks

No one in the bond market is willing to monitor the default risk of a small business that is likely to be a small borrower. Such an effort is worthwhile only for an institution that can expect to do a major share of the limited business of the small firm. So commercial banks become the main source of financing for small businesses and households. They establish customer relations; the firm agrees to provide information regularly; because the bank and the business typically operate in the same locality, news of any major development affecting the default risk of the firm is likely to reach the banker.

That kind of implicit contract leads to markup pricing for loans as it does for products. The bank charges the borrower an interest rate that marks up its costs of funds. In turn, the bank takes on an implicit contract to meet a borrower's needs for financing throughout the cycle within limits set by the borrower's default risk. Once the bank promises an umbrella to the borrower in the event of a rainy day, it must honor that obligation. The borrower is most likely to encounter the rainy days when credit is tight, and demands larger loans from the bank. To maintain customer relations, the bank tends to meet those demands, even though interest rate differentials would often point to a shift away from customer loans in tight credit periods.

The loan portfolio of the banker will range from loans to "prime" borrowers with virtually no default risk to ones with a moderate default risk covered by charging an extra 2 or perhaps 3 percentage points above the rate on prime loans. But rarely will it include loans with interest rates 10 (or even 5) percentage points above prime, although presumably some of these transactions could be profitable and indeed are made by other types of lenders. Loans with high risk are regarded as not "bankable." Government regulators reinforce that convention, but the convention preceded the regulations. Why do banks specialize in loans of limited risk? In a sense, the expertise required to assess modest to moderate risk of default may be quite different from that needed to sort risks of 5, 10, and 15 percentage points. This is analogous to the personnel policy of a firm that sets high screening standards under which the unskilled worker is simply rejected rather than offered a job at especially low pay. In part, banks that operate locally may view the risks among high-risk borrowers as highly correlated, and very sensitive to the general health of the community's economy.

Probably the most important reason for excluding high-risk loans from the bank's portfolio is similar to the considerations that underlie laws and conventions about usury. It is genuinely hard to distinguish high interest rates that invoke the monopoly power of a lender to "take advantage" of someone with an urgent temporary need (or extremely poor information) from those that are actually justified by high risk. Loans with unusually high interest rates would expose the banker to criticism as a grasping monopolist. It can therefore be prudent for a bank, which depends heavily on its reputation in the community, simply to avoid such loans. The bank's rejection may then be criticized as heartless, but it clearly is not taking advantage of the rejected applicant. The high-risk applicant gets shunted to the personal finance company, and the very-high-risk borrower turns to the loan shark and the pawnbroker.

The customer relations in the lending operations of local banks tend to dampen the cyclical volatility of interest rates on loans, especially those to small businesses. The markup practices seem to be influenced by average costs, and do not fully reflect the swings in the marginal cost of funds to banks, as indicated by yields of short-term securities traded in auction markets. In recent years, however, the major money-center banks have explicitly announced formulas that link the prime loan rates they charge to trading yields on commercial paper or other short-term assets. As a result, pricing in the customer market has moved closer to the auction paradigm. The futures price on borrowers' use of the umbrella provided by their banks now is less certain. But the umbrella option retains its significance. Strikingly, banks often close their loan windows to potential new customers during periods of tight money. Established customers must be allowed to exercise their option. The bank cannot afford to contaminate its general reputation for customer relations by engaging in evident price discrimination. Just as a firm will not hire a new worker at a wage far below that paid to recent novices, so the banker cannot charge new customers a much higher interest rate than that paid by established customers. Nonprice quantity responses to the cycle play a significant role in the loan market as well as in the labor market.

Thrift Institutions

For the past twenty years the slowdowns in real growth in the late phases of U.S. expansions that have led the way into inventory recessions have been dominated by major declines in home building. Those declines in turn have stemmed from the disintermediation phenomenon that interrupts the supply of home mortgage financing from thrift institutions. Those financial intermediaries have played a dominant role in the business cycle, and yet have been accorded a negligible role in economic modeling. Their behavior cannot be readily captured in the kind of models that economists like to build because they operate in a complex framework of customer markets.

The majority of U.S. home mortgages are issued by savings and loan associations and mutual savings banks; and home mortgages were the dominant asset held by this industry with more than $500 billion of total assets at the end of 1979. Like any financial intermediary, the thrift institution is strongly constrained by government regulations and policies. It can lend very long on mortgages while it borrows short on passbook or certificate deposits because of the establishment of a powerful lender of last resort, the Federal Home Loan Bank Board. The thrift institution concentrates heavily on mortgages because of government restrictions on the composition of its assets. Finally, the interest rates it pays to its depositors change very sluggishly over the cycle because of government ceilings on those interest rates.

Those government regulatory policies are intended to make the institutions serve society by channeling funds toward the financing of owner-occupied homes. The structure established for this industry is one of many methods, ranging from tax preferences to mortgage guarantees, by which the government pursues its housing policies. In the absence of any intervention by public policy, interest rates on home mortgages would undoubtedly far exceed those on corporate bonds, reflecting the greater default risk of individual signatures and the high information costs of evaluating real estate collateral.

In fact, society seems consciously to view owner-occupied housing as the source of a beneficial economic and social externality because it gives people greater stability, closer ties to the community, more of a stake in law and order, and the like. There is a case not just for righting the balance to equalize the private financing costs on homes with that on business capital, but for tilting the balance in favor of homes.

The government provides one subsidy with no explicit budgetary costs by offering the services of a powerful and generous lender of last resort to financial intermediaries that are willing to concentrate their lending on home mortgages and otherwise conform to regulations. That lender enables the intermediaries to lend long while borrowing short.

By supplying depositors with assets that are types of near-money (no capital-value risk and low transactions costs of conversion), the thrift institution may also correct another bias of a laissez-faire marketplace—one in favor of short-term lending and short-lived capital assets. Because fewer individual lenders willing to go long-term are needed to finance homes, the supply of funds for industrial plants and turbine generators is indirectly enhanced. That tends to narrow the equilibrating differential in rates of return on assets of different life spans, which could be substantial in the laissez-faire world but which would reflect costs and risks that are essentially irrelevant to society. By borrowing short and lending long, the thrift institution provides savers with preferred near-money, and at the same time increases the flow of loans for long-lived capital goods.

These important potential benefits of the thrift institutions must be balanced against significant distortions that are by-products of their operation. Because mortgages are such long-lived assets, the average interest yield earned by thrift institutions on their assets changes very slowly through time, in line with a weighted moving average of past mortgage interest rates that goes back for years. As a result, the average return on a dollar of deposits held by the institutions can be different from the marginal return from an extra dollar. The marginal return reflects the current interest rate on *new* mortgages, which can diverge sharply from the weighted average of past mortgages. Under competitive conditions, the institutions would be strongly influenced by the marginal return in determining the yields offered to depositors. If the interest rates paid to depositors tracked new mortgage interest rates, the institutions would experience enormous profits in years when mortgage interest rates were below those of the recent past, and enormous losses in years when mortgage interest rates went to new highs. In some of these cases, if portfolios were capitalized by the new mortgage rates, the institutions could be deemed insolvent. The extreme volatility would be further complicated by an asymmetrical response of competition from new entrants, who could offer depositors the marginal value of funds in a period of unusually high interest rates without incurring losses on a portfolio inherited from the past. Under those circumstances, the lender of last resort would have an impossible job, not merely to provide ultimate liquidity but to counter insolvency.

The rate ceilings that suppress price competition are not bureaucratic conspiracy to cartelize the industry, but perhaps an inevitable concomitant of the institutions' portfolio structures. The particular interest rate ceilings now in effect have glaring inefficiencies and inequities that have properly drawn the fire of many economists. The variety of interest ceilings applicable to passbook accounts and certificates of various denominations and maturities introduces a peculiar form of price discrimination. That pricing policy favors investors who are most alert to the changing schedules, most willing to accept a penalty on premature withdrawal of their funds, and, particularly unfairly, most able to meet substantial minimum requirements (as high as $10,000) for savings.

The complex menu deliberately increases costs of information and shopping for the small saver to facilitate price discrimination. Yet the institution appeals to small savers by telling them that they will obtain a reasonable deal over the cycle by holding their savings passively and drawing a steady and predictable interest rate. In fact, in periods of low interest rates, small savers earn more on their passbook account than the business firm can receive on Treasury bills (which is why businesses cannot be given unrestricted access to the thrift institutions).

It is not hard to visualize the ideal contract between thrift institutions and their depositors that would make the whole system viable. Depositors would pledge to maintain a regular pattern of saving throughout the cycle, except in the face of personal needs for meeting income shortfalls or unusual consumption requirements. In particular, they would have to refrain from making withdrawals (or making deposits) in order to take advantage of unusually high interest rates on alternative assets at the peak of the cycle. In return, the institution would pledge a steady, healthy yield geared to the average return on past mortgages. Moreover, it would promise to return funds to depositors at no penalty whenever required for their personal needs. If nobody is greedy, everybody can be better off. Like the hypothetical ideal contracts to improve labor allocation discussed in chapter 3, however, such a contract cannot be enforced and hence cannot be written.

The discriminatory "special deals" actually used help to contain the outflow of funds when interest rates on auction markets soar. The discrimination protects the institution by inhibiting increased interest payments to the majority of depositors who are not sensitive to rate differentials and who use their account as a savings vehicle throughout the cycle. But that discrimination still permits wide swings in the net inflow of deposits, which is the base for new mortgage lending. So the supply of mortgage financing does fluctuate wildly.

Curtailments in the supply generally lead to credit rationing—closed windows for mortgage applications—as well as to higher interest rates on mortgages. The "average-return pricing" on the interest rates paid to depositors inhibits the institution from making large increases in the mortgage interest rate it charges to borrowers. That would be palpable "gouging" and would impair the institution's reputation as a fair supplier of housing financing to the community. The resulting combined process of credit rationing and rate rationing is a major source of the extreme cyclicality of home building, which is costly to the society. The sensitivity of mortgage financing to movements of short-term interest rates above a trigger-point of disintermediation makes monetary policy a blunt instrument. Increases in auction-market interest rates within a range that does not generate thrift outflows may have only a modestly depressing effect on real activity, while increases that trigger disintermediation may have massive impacts on home building after a considerable lag.

There has to be a better way! But that improvement cannot be obtained merely by the elimination of ceilings on interest rates paid to depositors while the industry continues to lend long at fixed rates and to borrow short. Variable rate mortgages deserve serious consideration as a possible solution; they raise some interesting issues about the adaptation of financing to an inflationary economy. Under a variable rate system, interest rates on existing home mortgages would fluctuate according to some contractually established formula geared to the yields on newly issued mortgages or corporate bonds. The interest yield of the whole portfolio of a thrift institution would rise and fall in line with auction-market interest rates. The thrift institutions could then safely vary the interest rates paid to depositors so as to stabilize the attractiveness of thrift accounts relative to marketable securities. Paradoxically, the institution would reduce its risk by accepting a more variable income stream because that stream would be closely correlated with the income from competitive assets. On the other hand, the saver and mortgage borrower would forgo some of the predictability of their interest receipts and payments, respectively.

Proponents of variable rate mortgages contend that this variation does not necessarily increase risk and may actually reduce it. If changes in interest rates stem mainly from changes in inflation rates, and if the nominal income of mortgage borrowers and the value of their homes keep pace with the price level, the real cost and burden of the mortgage are more predictable with the variable rate. Those assumptions are easier to state than to validate in a world characterized by variations in long-term interest rates resulting from sources other than inflation, inflation rates that can be dominated by oil and food shocks, and nominal incomes of individual households that do not track the price level. Even if the value of the home keeps pace with the price level, any requirement for larger monthly payments in the event of increased interest rates can confront the homeowner with a problem; cash flow is a genuine constraint in a customer-loan market. Some of the California voters who rebelled against property taxes in 1978 clearly stated that they saw higher property tax bills as an increased burden, even when the higher taxes did not exceed the growth in the value of their homes. The recognition of the concern about cash flow leads to a modified version of variable rate mortgages in which changing interest rates alter the maturity date of the mortgage without affecting the monthly payment. A rise in interest rates forces borrowers to pay for a longer period at the end of their mortgages rather than increasing the current cash payments. In effect, they are charged more but receive an automatic added loan to finance extra charges with no transactions costs. But even the loss of predictability on the end-date of mortgage payments may be viewed as a cost by the borrower. Thus far, although variable rate mortgages have been offered as an alternative to home buyers in some states, they have received only limited consumer acceptance.

Real Assets

Cash, savings and thrift deposits, loans, Treasury bills, and bonds are all nominal assets, denominated in dollars and representing commitments to pay a specified amount of money either on demand or upon some stated date of maturity. Most of the nation's balance sheet consists of real assets. Consumer inventories are a convenient component to discuss here briefly as a transition from the monetary to the real sectors; the discussion is followed by a longer and more complicated analysis of the problems posed by fixed productive capital assets.

Consumer Stocks

Economizing on transactions costs also motivates the holdings of a wide variety of stocks by consumers. Even automobile ownership can be interpreted as a phenomenon associated with transactions costs that makes permanent reliance on rental car services unattractive for many consumers.

Consumer stocks provide an interesting set of similarities and contrasts with the holding of money. Like money, they save on transactions costs and sacrifice earnings. The saving on transactions costs from holding money and consumer stocks comes in both cases from the costs of acquiring them (even though money is costless and consumer stocks costly to "resell"). Trips to the supermarket—like those to the savings bank—entail costs; stocks of both cash and canned soup result from periodic shopping. But the holding of consumer stocks avoids a purchasing-power risk associated with holding money. Holding canned soup stocks obviously achieves certainty about changes in the price of soup. If the price of soup is expected to track the general price level, soup becomes more attractive relative to money (and indeed all nominal assets) if the expected speed of (and degree of uncertainty about) inflation increases, accentuating the purchasing-power losses (and risks) on money. I return to this important issue later in the chapter.

On the other hand, given the illiquidity of canned soup, holders are exposed to a "demand-shift" risk—they will incur a loss if their demands shift away from the consumption of soup, as they might because of changes in tastes or in the prices of substitute or complementary products.

The avoidance of purchasing-power risk and the acceptance of demand-shift risk is an inevitable paired consequence of any futures purchase of a consumption good. The buyers of automobiles in effect enter into a futures contract on the services of the car—they cannot be charged any more for them if the price goes up, but they will be sorry if they change their minds about the kind of car they want. The uncertainty of consumers about their future wants and needs is an important consideration that favors cash over specific consumption items as a store of value.

Because holdings of consumer stocks and cash alike sacrifice interest income, both of these nonearning assets are made less attractive by increased yields of earning assets, so long as expected inflation rates are unchanged. Higher interest rates then generate more trips to the supermarket and the savings bank. But because higher rates of inflation do not affect holdings of consumer goods adversely, higher interest rates associated with higher inflation will not increase trips to the supermarket and may even reduce them, as will become clear below.

Business Fixed Capital

Fixed productive capital—plant and equipment, which is the largest entry on the balance sheet of the business sector—is, in general, not readily resalable. That disadvantage has vital consequences, which are missed in any Walrasian view of the economy. As compared with bonds of equal expected return, capital goods are inferior because of both the poor resalability and the greater uncertainty of the returns over time. The expected return on a capital good must be larger than that on bonds to satisfy its holders. The historical record shows that the holders of real capital have received higher average returns (as well as much more variable returns) than bondholders; they have been rewarded for the risks they have taken.

The poor salability of existing capital goods tends to dampen the cyclical fluctuations in the production of new capital goods. Imagine a world in which plant and equipment were much less specialized, and subject to only small installation and transportation costs, so that they were traded in reasonably efficient auction resale markets. In those circumstances, it would be rare for some firms to be buying computers while others had computers of the same model lying idle. The absence of a good resale market accounts for an asymmetry; firms with excess demands for capital goods must invest, while those with excess supply must merely wait, either for some capital goods to wear out or for the demand for their product to bounce up again. By eliminating that asymmetry, the resale auction market would tend to intensify the response of investment to recession. Firms that need more equipment when others have too much would turn to the market for secondhand goods. Greater efficiency in shifting unwanted existing capital goods to potential buyers of new ones would, other things being equal, worsen the cycle—an exception to the general proposition that the failure of prices to adjust leads to more adjustment of quantities. In this case, the failure of prices to reallocate the supplies of used capital goods prevents an effective substitution of old goods for new ones, and thereby raises the demand for new capital goods in the slump.

A related consequence of poor resalability is the creation of a nonlinear investment accelerator. Suppose that for a given set of prices and interest rates each firm i has a demand for some desired stock of j types of capital goods. Its demand for new investment of each type is desired stock, K_{ij}^*, minus actual stock, K_{ij}. With perfect resale opportunities, firms would be disinvestors for some types of capital goods if any K_{ij} exceeded K_{ij}^*. But at the other extreme of no resale opportunity, investment by each firm in every type of capital is bounded at zero, and total investment is

$$\sum_{j=1}^{m} \sum_{i=1}^{n} \max \left\{ (K_{ij}^* - K_{ij}), 0 \right\}.$$

With perfect resale, any unwanted holdings of machine j by some firms will be acquired by other firms that want to add to their stocks. Gross investment in machine j takes place only when

$$\sum_{i=1}^{n} (K_{ij}^* - K_{ij}) > 0.$$

In a closed economy, gross fixed investment cannot be negative, so there is a lower bound of zero that can become operative for any type of capital good. Total investment is

$$\sum_{j=1}^{m} \max \left\{ \sum_{i=1}^{n} (K_{ij}^* - K_{ij}), 0 \right\}.$$

It is reasonable to suppose that the current level of output influences expected future output linearly (although much less than proportionately). Then the desired demand for all capital goods will be linearly related to current output: $K_{ij}^* = k_{ij}^* Y + d_{ij}$. Even with perfect resale, investment would not be a linear function of output so long as a varying number of types of machines were in aggregate excess supply. But with no resale of

Figure 5-1. *Alternative Relations between Investment and Output*[a]

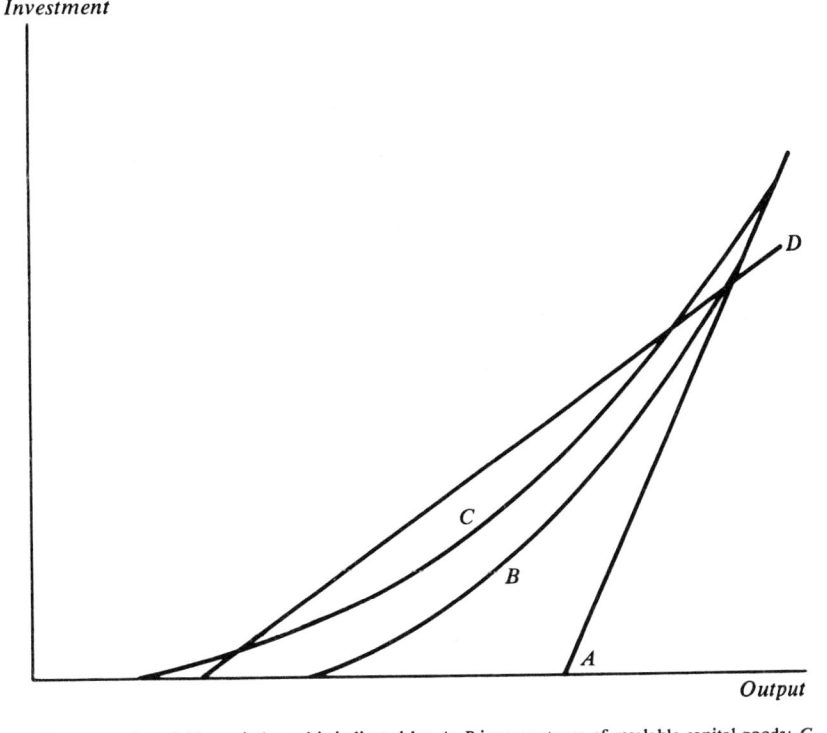

Investment

Output

a. One type of resalable capital good is indicated by *A*; *B* is many types of resalable capital goods; *C*, many types of capital goods that are not resalable; and *D* is a linear fitted function to *C*.

capital, the nonlinearity is much stronger because excess supplies at the level of the *firm* put zeros into the function. The marginal effect of output growth on investment is held down by the extra zeros in the relation above. The maximum potential effect occurs only when all the zeros disappear— that is, when *all* types of capital goods have incremental demands from *all* firms that use them. The more *ij* cells that are less than zero, the stronger the accelerator effect. If this nonlinear relation of investment demand to output is fitted econometrically as though it were linear, the resulting statistical function will underestimate investment demand in booms, as illustrated by a comparison of curves *C* and *D* in figure 5-1. In fact, most econometric models adopt linear forms of investment functions and most do tend to underestimate investment in periods of strong real activity.

Some interesting macroeconomic information might be compiled from a systematic empirical analysis of the prices and the trades for those few types of capital goods that have reasonably good resale markets (like trucks, airplanes, and retail stores and office buildings). Movements of those prices should indicate the changing state of expectations about output and future prices, as well as supply evidence on the extent to which resale opportunities do actually reduce the amount of idle capital and enhance the substitution of old for new capital.

Purchasing-power Risk

I have emphasized above that bonds are preferable to capital goods at equal expected returns because of their generally greater resalability and predictability of income. But the vulnerability of bonds (and all nominal assets) to purchasing-power risk may push in the opposite direction. The command over consumer goods and services provided by the fixed nominal returns on bonds varies inversely with the rate of inflation. Clearly, the prospective flow of real purchasing power derived from the coupons and the maturity value of the bond will be lower the higher the expected inflation rate. Moreover, the uncertainty about those real returns will be greater the more the uncertainty about the inflation rate over the life of the bond. For points in time up to maturity, even the uncertainty about the *nominal* market value of the bond is intensified by uncertainty about inflation because surprises in the inflation rate are likely to push interest rates upward and the market value of bonds downward.

The only asset that is basically free of purchasing-power risk is an appropriately weighted market basket of consumer goods and services (or, equivalently, a contract linked by formula to the consumer price index). For any particular real asset, the extent of this risk depends on two factors: the extent to which a surprise in the overall price level can be expected to generate a more or less than proportionate change in its price, and the magnitude of the variation in its price that is uncorrelated with movements of the overall price level. For example, the price of real asset $i(P_i)$ at some particular future time can be linked to the overall price level ($\bar{P}$) by the following: $P_i = f_i \bar{P} + l_i + u_i$, where the current levels of both P_i and $\bar{P}$ are arbitrarily taken to be unity.[4]

4. An alternative but more cumbersome formulation relates the *surprise* in P_i to the surprise in $\bar{P}$. Suppose that, with the horizon fixed at t, the expected price of i is P_i^e and the expected price level is $\bar{P}^e$. Then ($\ln P_i - \ln P_i^e$), which may be denoted S_i, is the proportionate surprise in P_i. Similarly, $\bar{S} = \ln \bar{P} - \ln \bar{P}^e$. The relation may then be written $S_i = f_i \bar{S} + l_i + u_i$. (The constant l_i must be zero if S_i is to be zero when the proportionate surprise in the price level is zero.)

In that relationship, the slope coefficient f reflects the sensitivity to inflation, and the error term u reflects the independent variation. For the ideal inflation hedge, f_i would be unity, and there would be no independent variation (the standard deviation of u_i, σ_{u_i}, would be zero); any change in inflation would create a proportionate change in the price of that asset, and there would be no other source of uncertainty about the price of the asset. In general, if the standard deviation of $\bar{P}$ is $\sigma_{\bar{P}}$, the purchasing-power risk of asset i (a measure of the variation of P_i in relation to $\bar{P}$) is[5]

$$\sigma^2_{P_i - \bar{P}} = \sigma^2_{\bar{P}}(f_i - 1)^2 + \sigma^2_{u_i}.$$

Obviously, good hedges might be constructed with diversified portfolios of real assets, with some f_i greater than unity and others less than unity, and with uncorrelated (or better yet, negatively correlated) independent variations among the assets.

What can be said about assets that are not resalable but whose buying price P_i tracks $\bar{P}$ with unit slope and low σ_u? The consumer market basket is a good inflation hedge even if it is not resalable because it is usable and a substitute for buying a new basket in the future at the $\bar{P}$ then prevailing. But whether an unsalable and unconsumable asset like a specialized machine is an effective inflation hedge has to be judged somewhat differently. The decision about buying that machine now or buying it later should be influenced by the expected course, and uncertainty about, the price of that machine. But that really does not pose an issue of hedging the overall price level. A long position in any asset is a hedge, in a trivial sense, against surprises in the subsequent buying price of that asset. Whether the machine is a good inflation hedge depends on whether the stream of receipts from its output tracks the price level with a slope close to unity and a small independent variation. A machine that could produce baskets of consumer goods without using variable inputs would be as perfect an inflation hedge as the market basket itself. On the other hand, one that produced dollar bills would be no better an inflation hedge than money itself. Here, the *outputs* must be resalable at their stated prices (or fully substitutable for consumer goods the asset holder would otherwise buy). If, for example, shoe prices track the price level very well but are sold in a customer market with cyclically sensitive demands, the price series is a misleading indicator of the prospective returns from the shoe-

5. This expression is the variance of the difference between P_i and $\bar{P}$. For the formulation relating the surprise in P_i to the surprise in $\bar{P}$, an analogous expression may be derived for the variance of the difference between S_i and $\bar{S}$.

making machine. In that case, the machine will not be a good inflation hedge.

Resalable assets with especially high values of f (say, 1.5 or even 2.0) offer a good *speculation* on inflation but not a good hedge against it. Moreover, some auction-market commodities subject to supply variations are likely to have high values of σ_u as well as high values of f over, say, a one-year horizon. A one-year Treasury note surely has less risk in real terms than a bushel of soybeans for that period. That note has $\sigma_u = 0$ because its price at maturity in nominal terms is certain; and $f = 0$ because that price is unaffected by surprises in the price level. It has full price-level risk but no independent variation risk. Its overall purchasing-power risk is simply $\sigma_{\bar{p}}$; most commodities (and even groups of them) have $\sigma_u > \sigma_{\bar{p}}$ and have greater purchasing-power risk for a year ahead, even if their f is unity. For minimizing purchasing-power risk (abstracting from expected returns) over a time horizon up to a year, it may be difficult to beat a short-term security.

The time horizon is obviously crucial in the relative purchasing-power risk of future money and real assets. Over one month, the savings deposit or one-month bill is virtually certain to be superior; over a generation, many real assets are likely to beat the twenty-five-year bond. As the horizon lengthens, the cumulative uncertainty about the overall price level is likely to increase more than the cumulative uncertainty about independent price variations for commodities or real assets. Inflation tends to drift over time, displaying positive serial correlation. I might be willing to place an even-money bet that I can estimate the increase in the consumer price index over the next twelve months within a range of ± 1 percentage point; but to make that bet over a ten-year horizon, I would require a range of perhaps 25 percentage points, certainly more than 1 point per year. On the other hand, I would refuse to bet that I could predict the *relative* price of retail clothing over the next year within a range of ± 1 percentage point; but with a range of less than 25 percentage points, I would take an even bet on estimating the price of clothing as a function of the general price level a decade hence. Some of the independent variation in a single year reflects erratic variations that are likely to average out in the longer run.

There is likely to be a break-even horizon for any real asset at which it surpasses future money in terms of greater purchasing-power certainty. The perception of the extent of price-level uncertainty influences that horizon. The higher the overall price-level risk, the shorter that horizon becomes, assuming realistically that the independent variation on any particular asset is not pulled up commensurately. When inflation uncertainty becomes strong, long-term bonds become particularly less attractive relative to resalable fixed assets, given the expected returns on the two types of assets. In a period of marked uncertainty about inflation, the movement away from money will start with distant future money.

The impact of inflation on the prices of various assets depends on the source of the change in the expected path of the price level. As an analytical exercise, it is legitimate to pull an increase in expected inflation out of thin air, without explaining its source. But the source and nature of the disturbance that alter the prospects for inflation are important in determining how the prospective course of output is altered. If inflation estimates are revised upward because private demand is stronger or monetary and fiscal policy are more stimulative, for example, projections of output growth would also point higher—at least for a while. On the other hand, if the new information revealed that wages and prices are likely to escalate more rapidly at any given level of output and employment, the outlook for production and employment would be weaker. Unless fiscal and monetary policy engage in a thoroughgoing effort to accommodate all of the higher inflation, bad news about beef prices or wage settlements must be bad news about real activity. Moreover, any information on a forthcoming worsening of the inflation-unemployment relation must derive from prospective changes in some relative prices of goods and factors, whether the villain is beef prices or wage settlements. Such changes in prospects for relative prices will often change the value of f and σ_u for particular commodities.

Any operational use of the f, σ_u formulation rests on an implicit concept of a probabilistic universe of all the contingent events that could produce inflation surprises. Any statistical estimation of these parameters from time-series data supposes that history has provided a representative sample of rising and falling inflation rates from whatever source derived. Over a one-year horizon in the United States, the estimates show a systematic pattern of some commodities deviating from the unity value of f— crude materials (the auction-market commodities) on the high side, and finished manufactured goods on the low side. The data confirm that a long futures position in a diversified bundle of traded commodities like copper, cotton, and soybeans is a good *speculation* on accelerating inflation; they indicate that prices of automobiles and household appliances have especially low sensitivity to overall inflation surprises. All this is understandable in light of the discussion of pricing and marketing in chapter 4.

The data also confirm the high σ_u of crude materials that are auction commodities. The risk averter looks for assets that do not have such major uncertainties about their independent variation, and recognizes the key role of supply variations and inelasticities of supply and demand in making prices of raw materials so erratic. Those supply uncertainties can be avoided by holding nondepreciating assets when the total outstanding stock is large relative to the new flow created by current production. In the case of land, paintings of the old masters, or Chippendale furniture, there is no new output and no vulnerability to supply disturbances. In the case of homes or precious gems, the supply variation of any year alters the total available stock by only a few percentage points. Variations on the demand side can be contained by holding items for which there is stability of tastes and of technology with respect to substitutes. Gems, no doubt, benefit from their venerable record as objects in great demand. Assets with these properties develop a premium during periods of inflation because of their attractiveness as ways of dealing with inflation uncertainty.

Such assets as land, homes, paintings, and gems have lived up to their reputations and turned in stellar performances as portfolio assets during the inflationary era in the United States.[6] In sharp contrast, common stock has been a dismal failure. Most of the inflation surprises, particularly in the seventies, have brought adverse news on the short-term Phillips curve, implying higher inflation at given levels of real economic activity. Through the response of policy, that meant lower growth of output and real profitability. Most of the worries about future inflation seem to focus on such possibilities rather than on the expectation of excess demand. Compared with investors a decade ago, investors today seem to expect lower average operating rates in industry for the longer run and greater variability of them from year to year; those expectations are obviously unfavorable to the stock market.

Although that is the dominant factor, in my judgment, two other possible contributors to the recent woes of the equity market might be mentioned. There is growing evidence that profits—at least inflation-adjusted,

6. The tax system influences the performance of various assets as inflation hedges. But taxes alone cannot explain this observed behavior. Long before the establishment of the income tax, for example, assets such as land and homes were viewed as preferred inflation hedges.

after-tax profits—have been unusually low, even given utilization rates. The practice of marking up historical costs described in the last chapter as the dominant pricing method in industry could readily account for a profit squeeze in a period of generally accelerating inflation. If the equity market paid more attention to inflation-adjusted profits than managers do in setting prices, stock market investors would be unhappy with the profit record.

Finally, the actuarial procedures of many large institutional investors, especially pension funds, tend to make portfolio managers satisficers in terms of nominal yields rather than maximizers. When bond yields are 8 or 9 percent, a bond portfolio offers adequate protection for fulfilling the actuarial assumptions underlying the fiduciary arrangements of the funds. Managers who fall short of the target range of nominal yields embodied in the actuarial assumptions are penalized more heavily than those who exceed the target are rewarded. As a result, bonds are favored and stocks are shunned.

The Fisher Theorem

Much of the analysis of this chapter concerns the needed qualification to Irving Fisher's theorem that an increase in the rate of expected inflation adds commensurately to the rate of interest. As Fisher saw it, an extra 1 percentage point of expected inflation raises the nominal expected rate of return on real capital assets by 1 percentage point and induces a parallel increase of 1 percentage point in bond and bill yields to keep expected returns in balance.

The Fisher theorem is important because it implies that anticipated inflation is neutral in its impact on portfolios and capital markets. It recognizes that a sudden change in the expected inflation rate bestows positive outcomes on debtors and imposes negative ones on lenders. But it holds that, once expectations change and the marketplace establishes a new set of asset prices and yields, people have no incentive to change their portfolios or their flow of new investment or saving. The economy just continues to operate at the new expected inflation rate, much as it did at the old one. All the adjustments occur in prices and none in quantities.

The Fisher theorem applies to a world that has no taxes on property income. The departures from neutrality created by the presence of taxes in the real world have been thoroughly analyzed in the literature. The tax system tends to receive the blame for distortions of saving and investment behavior associated with inflation.

Much less has been said, and much more needs to be said, about the various other sources of nonneutrality. The tax system is not the only way —and may not even be the most important way—that the realities of the contemporary American economy differ from the assumptions underlying the Fisher theorem. For that theorem to hold, all yields must be set in auction markets; the costs of transactions (and of illiquidity) must be zero; risk aversion must be either absent or marginally inoperative so that changes in all expected returns can be equated with no change in any risk premium; and the change in the expected inflation rate must be unaccompanied by any change in expectations about relative prices. The analysis of this chapter points to the importance of the complications that emerge when these restrictive assumptions are dropped. I focus in what follows on the necessary major amendments, without summarizing the vast body of literature in this area and without incorporating the role of taxes, because that is the one job economists have done quite thoroughly.

For convenience, throughout this section I assume that all economic actors have previously expected an inflation rate of zero, and that they suddenly obtain information that makes them expect an inflation rate of 1 percent a year for the indefinite future. The key amendments to the Fisher theorem arise because of the fixity of some interest rates, the likely change in the degree of uncertainty about the inflation rate, and the likely change in expected relative prices. The fixity of the zero rate of interest on money and trade credit forces quantity adjustments, for example. Furthermore, if the increase in the expected inflation rate is associated with an increase in uncertainty about future inflation rates, assets with low purchasing-power risk (and ready resalability) will attract greater demand and may be subject to quantity adjustments. If the increase in expected inflation alters expected relative prices (as it must if it has any implications for aggregate output and employment), portfolio shifts will be induced by differential changes in expected returns. Quite apart from taxes, major departures from neutrality are likely.

Fixity of Interest Rates

When markets open after the rise in the expected inflation rate, the interest rate on money and trade credits remains at zero; and at least for the short run, there is no change in interest rates in various customer-market segments of the financial sector, including those on savings pass-books and certificates, bank loans to households and small businesses, and home mortgages.

The zero interest rate on money is the one source of departure from neutrality other than taxes that is recognized in the standard theoretical approach to inflation. It leads to the single welfare cost generally attributed to anticipated inflation, namely, the resources used in more trips to the banks. People economize on their cash balances as a result of the higher yield on interest-bearing securities. If an extra yield of 1 percentage point is offered on all interest-bearing claims, the result will be an excess demand for securities, particularly for those securities that are near-money, with low capital-value risk and low transactions costs of conversion. But the interest rate on passbook savings deposits, which to households represents the closest substitute for money, is constrained by a ceiling. These assets cannot benefit from the substitution away from cash balances; quite the contrary, the portfolio shift operates against them as well as against cash. People make more trips from the thrift institution to the Treasury bill dealer—and those are more costly trips, as the normal preference for deposit-type assets suggests. The government and other top-quality borrowers are induced to reduce the maturity of their borrowing in response to the shifts in relative costs. If elasticities are finite, the quantity of short-term bills will increase and their yield will reach equilibrium with a smaller increase than that in long-term bonds.

The free loan provided by trade credit becomes more attractive as a result of higher interest rates, and bill payers delay their check writing. That increases the needs of business for the financing of accounts receivables, which, in turn, raises the demand for bank loans. Meanwhile, households (and many small businesses) further expand holdings of short-term marketable assets. Over the longer term, the terms on which the free loan of trade credit is extended are likely to be altered; and that imposes real costs, both transitionally through the costs of changing the rules, and permanently through the need for more frequent check writing.

Some of the substitution away from money and reallocation of the float on trade credit enlarges consumer stocks and business inventories, which become more attractive holdings relative to cash because they protect the holder against the next round of price increases. These types of transactions balances economize on trips to the supermarket and supplier, and offset some of the social costs of more trips to the bank. Once the differential storage costs and acquisition costs of different products are recognized, it becomes clear that demands for various goods (and their relative prices) must be affected by the rise in expected inflation.

Purchasing-Power Risk

When the risk aversion of investors is appropriately recognized, it becomes important to know whether the increase in the expected inflation rate is associated with any change in the degree of uncertainty about that rate. Conceivably, the expected inflation rate may be viewed as a random walk from the current rate. In that event, the expectation of greater future inflation could result from a surprisingly high current rate with no change in the view of the stochastic process by which the inflation rate moves over time; then the perceived uncertainty about the future would not be altered. But the stochastic process is not normally viewed that way; a rise in this year's inflation rate leads to a higher expected inflation rate for next year, but not point for point. To raise expected inflation for the indefinite future by a point a year, the new information must imply a change in the character of the underlying stochastic process. If people learn that they misunderstood the nature of that process previously, they are likely to doubt that they now fully comprehend the true nature of the process. In that event, people might be more uncertain about the future of inflation rates, whether they had revised their expectations upward or downward. Alternatively, people might be aware of evidence based on past experience and international comparisons that a higher average rate of inflation is also empirically correlated with greater year-to-year variability in inflation. In that case, they would tend to revise their estimate of the uncertainty of inflation in the same direction that they revised their expected inflation rate.

Whatever its source, a revised estimate of the variance of expected inflation has important effects on the portfolio choices of risk-averse investors. Any upward revision in perceived price-level risks makes nominal assets less attractive relative to real ones for equal expected returns. As discussed above, those nominal assets with the longest maturities are most adversely affected. Both issuers and holders of long-term bonds have to assume greater risks if the increase in the expected intensity of inflation is also associated with an increase in uncertainty about that inflation. Fixed real assets are the beneficiaries of the portfolio shift away from nominal assets. Given the assumption that the increase in expected inflation applies uniformly to all commodities, all marketable fixed real assets must become more attractive. But then their prices, expected returns, and the equilibrium stocks of them must be altered. The market equilibrium solution cannot be neutral.

Variations in Relative Prices

Although the assumption of uniform incremental inflation rates among all goods and services is an extremely convenient and tempting analytical device, it is particularly restrictive and unrealistic. Any information that leads to an expectation of accelerated inflation must also lead a rational observer of markets to expect some changes in relative prices. The exact profile of that likely change depends on the source of the accelerated inflation, as noted above. But whatever the source, once relative prices are expected to change, it is no longer true that holders of real assets simply add 1 percentage point to their expected nominal yield and can afford to pay lenders an extra percentage point of interest. Nor will those with diversified holdings of nominal and various real assets find their own portfolios still optimal with an extra percentage point of yield on their nominal assets.

Analysis of the effect of expected inflation on the demand and supply of loans and of goods requires careful disaggregation once changes in relative prices are incorporated. That disaggregation is vital because the weights of various commodities in the output basket that determines the price level are very different from their weights in determining the net demand for loans. Given a set of interest rates ruling in the marketplace, a rise in the expected price of a commodity at some future date increases the demand for loans and reduces the demand for nominal assets through three basic routes. First, intertemporal substitution may raise the current consumption demand for that commodity, reflecting the expectation that consuming it today is relatively less expensive than consuming it in the future. Second, consumer and producer demands for inventories of the commodity may be increased. Third, there may be a rise in the demand for capital goods to produce the commodity if the rise in expected price is associated with an expected increase in profitability.

Clearly, the opportunities and incentives to engage in intertemporal shifts of consumption, to build up inventories, and to enlarge stocks of productive capital varies enormously among products. As an extreme example, suppose that the expected overall inflation rate rises by 1 percentage point for next year solely from an expected acceleration of 10 percent in health care costs. That surely would generate *some* limited intertemporal substitution, such as greater demands for elective surgery to beat the increases in price. Those extra operations would mean *some* increase in consumer borrowing and *some* decrease in the holdings of securities and savings accounts by the impatient patients. Perhaps even expanded investment by hospitals and physicians might come into the picture. But surely the overall net shifts in demands and supplies for financial assets would not be expected to add anything close to a full percentage point to interest rates.

More realistic examples of the nature and sources of an expected acceleration in inflation still raise the same difficult questions. The plot thickens once the unrealistic assumption of relative price constancy is dropped, unless it is replaced by the even more unrealistic assumption that people can costlessly carry a diversified market basket through time. Are the products that lead the inflation parade ones that are particularly easy to substitute, easy to store, and intensive of specialized plant and equipment? Or are they the reverse? Are they subject to first in, first out (FIFO) pricing? Do their suppliers engage in prenotification of price increases or acceptance of fixed price orders for substantial time periods? Do loans for these products impinge most on customer or auction segments of the financial markets?

In the case of inflation that accompanies a cyclical upswing in aggregate demand, stocks of raw materials traded in auction markets are likely to play a key role in pushing up short-term interest rates. Because raw materials are subjected to fabrication and distribution, and because readily storable commodities are those most likely to be traded in auction markets, the direct and indirect weight of these commodities in stocks is likely to be much larger than their weight in the market basket used for calculating the overall price level. Because their inflation sensitivity is large (in terms of the earlier analysis, $f > 1$), they are attractive to rational speculators in a period of expected acceleration in inflation. But because the independent variation in the prices of those auction products is extremely large, demands for them are limited by risk aversion, on the part of either the traders themselves or those who finance the traders. Demands for auction products are also influenced by the cost of holding incremental stocks.

An equilibrium price in an auction market can be attained at a time when an informed professional observer would bet that the price will outpace the general price level over the year ahead. In fact, the relative price of auction products has been systematically cyclical in the past, and presumably the markets were kept in equilibrium by changing risk perceptions and changing storage costs that offset changes in their expected returns. The manufacturer of cotton goods, for example, has an incentive to build up stocks during a period of expected acceleration in inflation (or to acquire a futures position in cotton, which gives someone else an incentive to hold stocks). On the other hand, the manufacturer of dacron goods has much less incentive. That individual buys dacron in a price-tag market and may well be able to place orders for future delivery at fixed prices or to count on prenotification of price increases from a supplier; the manufacturer knows from experience that the price is not very sensitive in the short run to the overall inflation rate. Perceptions of systematic changes in relative prices thus have real effects. When interest rates adjust to some average influence, the dacron manufacturer cuts inventories in real terms while the cotton manufacturer enlarges inventories. There are changes in the frequency of "trips" to all suppliers—not just to the banks. The entire network of stock-flow relations is altered in the process, even if the change in the inflation rate is accurately anticipated.

Booksellers may provide the extreme example of merchants whose stocks are indistinguishable from nominal assets in relevant ways. The price charged by publishers for a volume becomes the basis for the price charged by booksellers, whether they sell it at list price or at discount. Booksellers are pure FIFO pricers and realize no gain from inflation by increasing holdings of inventories. The public utilities sector—about 10 percent of private GNP—provides an equally clear and more important example as a result of regulatory rules enforcing historical cost pricing.

Many real assets are effectively "nominalized" at the time of acquisition; their price-level sensitivity is negligible. Others have a high degree of price-level sensitivity and offer a good speculation on inflation. But it is no accident that they also tend to have large independent variation and so are not a good hedge against inflation or anything else. The few assets with properties that make them good candidates as inflation hedges, such as land and homes, command a premium for that reason during periods in which inflation risk looms particularly large.

The task of keeping wealth rising in pace with expected inflation, particularly when the rate of inflation is uncertain, is a serious challenge. There is no obvious portfolio whose selling price rises in step with expected inflation. In principle, those who can cope best with the challenge are investors who can afford to sacrifice liquidity and whose scale of operations is large enough to hold down the transactions costs of entering commodity and real estate markets. It is particularly trying for the average household that needs liquidity because of the costliness of borrowing.

One asset that has fared particularly well in the inflationary environment of the seventies has been the single-family home, which looms largest in the balance-sheet of middle-income households. But the home is not a ready source of liquidity; it is not a suitable vehicle for gradual incremental saving; and it offers opportunities to different families that vary arbitrarily depending on their demographic characteristics. For perhaps the majority of families, the preferred medium of discretionary saving has been the savings account; its yield averaging about 6 percent barely matches the inflation rate. But it protects households from the 15 or 20 percent cliff of interest rates on borrowing. It has liquidity, as no higher yielding asset has.

Income Expectations

Any set of forces that raises expected inflation can also create divergent expectations and altered uncertainties about the relative prices, and the employment, of factors of production. In general, an acceleration of expected inflation creates greater uncertainty for households about their real incomes. Some households have reasonably full, formal escalator clauses or other indexing provisions that raise their money incomes by nearly as much as the inflation rate; the slope coefficient relating their incomes to inflation (analogous to f in the earlier analysis) is near unity. The money incomes of farmers and some other households must have extremely large slope coefficients on the inflation rate. But the slope coefficient for the typical family over a time horizon of a year or two must be quite small. I submit that one could expect to make a distinctly smaller percentage error in predicting the *nominal* incomes of most households for next year than in predicting their real incomes (nominal income deflated by the consumer price index). That implies that the inflation-sensitivity of the typical household's money income (its value of f) is less than 0.5 over a one-year horizon.

Over the near-term horizon, therefore, increased uncertainty about the price level translates almost fully into greater uncertainty about individual real incomes. The greater uncertainties about the prospects for real income enlarge uncertainties about the amount of their payments relative to income receipts, which increases the value of the liquidity premium on near-money. For the typical household that has access to borrowing only at penalty interest rates, doubts about the ability to buy customary Christmas gifts out of income receipts provide rational incentives to spend less on consumption and to acquire more liquid assets during the summer and fall.

Given the gap between the borrower's and the lender's interest rate, increased uncertainty about real income prospects unambiguously induces greater saving and stronger liquidity preference. The chain from higher inflation to greater uncertainty of real income to greater saving was stressed by George Katona throughout the postwar era. His thesis, which was generally viewed skeptically by most economists, has been taken more seriously during the seventies.

The Katona effect is one way in which expected inflation increases personal saving—a nonneutral effect excluded from the Fisher model. Previously in modifying the simple Fisher world to allow for the fixity of interest rates on money and savings accounts, I noted a reason why inflation reduces saving (as measured in the national income and product accounts). That reduction occurred because of a substitution of larger consumer stocks for cash and an intertemporal substitution of current for future consumption, both intended to beat the next round of price increases. These types of intertemporal substitution were long recognized, but the theoretical underpinning for the optimization of consumer stocks was first developed by Robert Clower.

In addition to the Katona effect and the Clower effect, there are two other routes by which a step-up in expected inflation may influence personal saving. One is the Pigou effect. Because the government is a net debtor through its issuance of both currency and interest-bearing obligations, the private sector typically is a net creditor. The direct holdings of assets and liabilities by U.S. households at the end of 1979, for example, included nominal assets totaling $2.0 trillion and debts amounting to $1.4 trillion. The real value of net nominal assets—here, the $600 billion difference between gross assets and debt—is reduced by accelerating inflation. As a result of the decline in real wealth, any household with a finite horizon or a discount rate greater than the government bond rate is induced to consume less at a given real income, saving more in an effort to restore its wealth position.

Finally, as Martin Feldstein and others have emphasized, some features of the U.S. tax system probably operate to reduce saving in an era of more rapid inflation. Because all interest receipts are included in taxable income and because depreciation accounting must be geared to historical costs for tax purposes, inflation interacts with the tax system to impose the equivalent of a capital levy on income-producing wealth. The after-tax return from saving is lower when inflation rates are higher. That produces a substitution effect of current consumption for saving. An income effect pushes saving in the opposite direction: the lower return on wealth means savers cannot afford to consume as much. If the substitution effect outweighs the income effect, which seems likely although far from certain, the tax effect of inflation on saving is negative.

The impacts of these various effects have not thus far been empirically isolated and quantified. Personal saving as a percent of disposable personal income in the seventies averaged 0.5 percentage point *higher* than it did during the sixties. The recent historical record therefore creates a presumption, although a rebuttable one, that higher inflation has provided a net stimulus to saving, which implies the Katona and Pigou effects have outweighed the Clower and Feldstein effects. That added saving should not be viewed as a favorable consequence of inflation; quite the contrary, the Katona effect in particular reflects higher risk perceptions that unambiguously detract from welfare. Against this background, it is hard to understand the widespread professional support for changes in the tax treatment of depreciation and interest in order to adapt them to an inflationary world. Such a "tax reform" would be likely to exacerbate what now appears to be a net distortion in favor of saving as a result of inflation. When inflation affects saving in different ways, fixing any one part of the problem can easily enlarge the distortion.

Inflation in a Monetary Economy

The heroic role played by money in an industrialized economy stems from its contribution to economizing on transactions costs. Because many analytical models of economic behavior tend to ignore transactions costs, that contribution is often overlooked. But economizing on transactions costs is really the way that the economic system has been freed of the shackles of barter and allowed to develop complex and efficient specialization and effective exploitation of economies of scale. Under the burden of barter, industrial history would have evolved with less scope for innovation and accumulation, and the world would now be generations behind in economic development. The transactions costs that are ignored in Walrasian models are a major part of economic life. Indeed, in a broad sense, they represent about one-fifth of the total gross national product. Retail and wholesale trade, the distribution functions of manufacturing, and much of transportation are activities that "merely" facilitate transactions by transporting physically unchanged products from the end of the assembly line to the consumer.

But money is a villain as well as a hero. It is the pipeline through which imbalances in aggregate demand can travel through the system. In a barter economy the supply of one good must be a demand for another good and adherence to Say's Law is ensured. In a monetary economy, any supply of goods is in the first instance a demand for money; in the second instance it may be a demand for near-money or some other distant substitute for newly produced output.

Any imbalance in product or labor markets produces the opposite imbalance in financial markets. In that sense, it is the possibility of imbalances in the financial markets that permits the emergence of imbalances in the product and labor markets. When a decline in the demand for output creates excess supply in the labor market, the two-way pathology is concretely manifested. As shown in earlier chapters, a decline in the demand for goods brought about by customer pricing leads to a reduction in the employment of labor even though the real marginal product of labor is unaltered. If firms could pay workers in the form of the output they produce, they could afford to keep their labor force employed and their flow of output undiminished. But the workers do not accept the output they produce in their pay envelopes; they are working for money. So the employing firm finds that the work force is too large at the existing money-wage rate, and it translates the drop in the demand for its product into a reduction of employment.

The workers want money as a means to purchase goods and services, not as an end in itself. It is the only acceptable means to that end, and it takes on a key and indispensable role. Money focuses attention on wages and prices in ways that are entirely rational, and are not symptoms of illusion. The crime of barter illusion is revealed in formulations that ignore the key role of money.

The functions of money as a means of payment, unit of account, and store of value become strongly intertwined in the monetary-exchange economy. The means of payment necessarily becomes a convenient unit of account. In that capacity, money serves not merely to develop exchange rates among commodities, but to keep score, express legal obligations, denominate implicit contracts, provide a vehicle for planning, and establish futures prices as well as spot prices. The scope of those valuable functions of money is inevitably limited by the extent of fluctuations in the price level. That determines the length of the horizon over which planning in nominal terms is reasonable and interdependent relations can be established. People who pledge to buy or sell at more or less fixed prices in the future must take, in effect, short or long positions on money. They can afford to do that only during periods for which the risk entailed seems relatively limited, that is, periods during which money is regarded as a reasonable store of value.

Some characteristics of a properly functioning monetary economy are most vivid by contrast with a hyperinflationary situation in which money loses its usefulness. During hyperinflation the purchasing-power risk of nominal assets explodes, and the demand for those assets collapses. In particular, savings accounts and other assets with interest rates that move sluggishly disappear from portfolios. Sellers may prefer to hold on to goods rather than to market them. The German hyperinflation following World War I produced starving children in the cities, while the farmers amassed stocks that they would not sell for meaningless cash.[7] The clock was turned back to the age of barter, but the institutional arrangements that permitted barter could not be instantaneously resurrected.

The recurring trips to the savings bank and to the broker are only a small part of the story of hyperinflation. More serious are the hasty repeated trips to the supermarket and the helter-skelter conversions of nominal assets into real ones. Costly efforts are expended in negotiating bilateral barter trades, and price tags become meaningless. Indeed, in a sense, the more frequent trips to the bank are a misleading part of the story. The problem is not that people need to go there so often but that they need to work hard to find substitutes for the role the banks customarily play.

The flight from money associated with hyperinflation has obvious costs for an economic system. However, subtle and qualitatively similar—although quantitatively far smaller—costs are associated with the crawl away from money in times of moderate inflation. Indeed, every sustained step-up in inflation brings a touch of the hyperinflation disease. Again it is reflected over a broad spectrum of economic behavior. The trips to the

7. Adam Fergusson, *When Money Dies: The Nightmare of the Weimar Collapse* (London: Kimber, 1975), pp. 78, 150, 177–80.

broker and the savings bank are again a small part of a large story. As discussed in earlier chapters, a variety of pricing and wage-making institutions contribute to the stability of future prices and future wages. Fixed price orders, leases and other explicit long-term contracts, fixed time schedules for price changes, prenotification of price changes, and the broad general commitment to continuity of offers by suppliers are important ways of aiding and abetting forward planning. Uncertainty about the price level shortens the horizons of these practices, in effect destroying some futures markets and thus imposing a welfare loss on society.

The modern economy responds not by barter, but by indexing—a kind of computerized quasi-barter that attempts to invoke a new unit of account as a substitute for money. In chapter 7 a more careful analysis is made of indexation and its long-run potentiality as a framework for new institutions that could remove some of the concern about the effects of inflation on nominal assets. So far the process of substituting for money has been costly; whether it can become costless remains to be seen.

Bibliographical Notes

The overall approach to the analysis of asset markets embodied in this chapter reflects the portfolio balance concepts developed by James Tobin in "Money, Capital, and Other Stores of Value," *American Economic Review,* vol. 51 (May 1961, *Papers and Proceedings, 1960*), pp. 26–37, and "A General Equilibrium Approach to Monetary Theory," *Journal of Money, Credit and Banking,* vol. 1 (February 1969), pp. 15–29. The foundation underlying Tobin's work, in turn, includes John Maynard Keynes, *The General Theory of Employment, Interest, and Money* (Harcourt, Brace, 1936), chap. 17, and J. R. Hicks, *Value and Capital* (2d ed., London: Oxford University Press, 1946), chaps. 11–13.

The defects of the Walrasian model as a foundation for monetary theory are clearly expounded by Axel Leijonhufvud, *On Keynesian Economics and the Economics of Keynes: A Study in Monetary Theory* (Oxford University Press, 1968), pp. 224–30, 376, 394–99; and by Karl Brunner and Allan H. Meltzer, "The Uses of Money: Money in the Theory of an Exchange Economy," *American Economic Review,* vol. 61 (December 1971), pp. 784–805.

The transactions cost model was developed by William J. Baumol, "The Transactions Demand for Cash: An Inventory Theoretic Approach," *Quarterly Journal of Economics,* vol. 66 (November 1952), pp. 545–56, and James Tobin, "The Interest-Elasticity of Transactions Demand for Cash," *Review of Economics and Statistics,* vol. 38 (August 1956), pp. 241–47.

James Tobin and Walter Dolde discuss a life-cycle model in which there are liquidity constraints so that borrowing and lending are not symmetrical in "Wealth, Liquidity and Consumption," in *Consumer Spending and Monetary Policy: The Linkages,* Proceedings of a Monetary Conference (Federal Reserve Bank of Boston, 1971), pp. 99–146. Life-cycle and permanent income models often fail even to point out the importance of the assumption of a single interest rate for borrowing and lending. The high cost of formulating a lifetime plan is another important qualification of those models in my judgment, but that issue was not central to the concerns of this chapter. The implications of the life-cycle model for maturity preferences are also widely ignored and so are the elementary points made in the text about the illusion of capital gains from lower interest rates. As one example of a recognition of this issue, Barry P. Bosworth stresses the distinction between changes in common stock values associated with changing earnings expectations and those associated with changing interest rates in his "The Stock Market and the Economy," *Brookings Papers on Economic Activity, 2:1975,* p. 278. The Haig-Simons definition of income can be found in Robert Murray Haig, "The Concept of Income-Economic and Legal Aspects," in Haig, ed., *The Federal Income Tax* (Columbia University Press, 1921), pp. 1–28, and Henry C. Simons, *Personal Income Taxation* (University of Chicago Press, 1938), pp. 49–50.

The concept of maintenance of capital was developed in A. C. Pigou, "Maintaining Capital Intact," *Economica,* n.s., vol. 8 (August 1941), pp. 271–75. The maintainable consumption concept that I regard as best is developed by Hicks in *Value and Capital,* chap. 14.

The treatment of the transactions demands for consumer stocks and the analogies and contrasts to demands for money has been developed by Robert Clower in several articles, most recently in Robert W. Clower and Peter W. Howitt, "The Transactions Theory of the Demand for Money: A Reconsideration," *Journal of Political Economy,* vol. 86 (June 1978), pp. 449–66.

The nature of the returns and risks on holdings of real capital are discussed by Tobin in "Money, Capital, and Other Stores of Value," and in "Economic Growth as an Objective of Government Policy," *American*

Economic Review, vol. 54 (May 1964, *Papers and Proceedings, 1963*), pp. 13–15, in which he distinguishes between private and social risks. The attraction of real estate to protect against inflation is part of an old literature; in the postwar era, most examples with which I am familiar have applied it to developing countries with secular inflation. For example, see E. M. Bernstein, "Financing Economic Growth in Underdeveloped Economies," in Walter W. Heller, Francis M. Boddy, and Carl L. Nelson, eds., *Savings in the Modern Economy* (University of Minnesota Press, 1953), p. 291.

Thrift institutions have become respectable in the literature only recently. See Phoebus J. Dhrymes and Paul J. Taubman, "An Empirical Analysis of the Savings and Loan Industry," and Stephen M. Goldfeld, "Savings and Loan Associations and the Market for Savings: Aspects of Allocational Efficiency," in Irwin Friend, dir., *Study of the Savings and Loan Industry,* Submitted to the Federal Home Loan Bank Board (Government Printing Office, 1970), vol. 1, pp. 67–182 and vol. 2, pp. 569–658, respectively; and Board of Governors of the Federal Reserve System, *Federal Reserve Staff Study: Ways to Moderate Fluctuations in Housing Construction* (Federal Reserve, 1972).

Fisher's theorem is set forth in Irving Fisher, "Appreciation and Interest," *Publications of the American Economic Association,* vol. 11 (Macmillan, 1896), pp. 331–442. Martin Feldstein's discussion of the modification of the Fisher theorem required by income taxes can be found in his "Inflation, Income Taxes, and the Rate of Interest: A Theoretical Analysis," *American Economic Review,* vol. 66 (December 1976), pp. 809–20, and in Martin Feldstein and Lawrence Summers, "Inflation, Tax Rules, and the Long-Term Interest Rate," *BPEA, 1:1978,* pp. 61–99. A number of views and issues surrounding this appear in Henry J. Aaron, ed., *Inflation and the Income Tax* (Brookings Institution, 1976).

The Katona effect is developed in *The Powerful Consumer: Psychological Studies of the American Economy* (McGraw-Hill, 1960), pp. 192–211. See also F. Thomas Juster and Paul Wachtel, "Inflation and the Consumer," *BPEA, 1:1972,* pp. 71–114, and "Anticipatory and Objective Models of Durable Goods Demand," *American Economic Review,* vol. 62 (September 1972), pp. 564–79.

VI

The Inflationary Process

THE TIME has come to assemble the parts and analyze the macro pattern of the various price-wage responses and output-employment responses to fluctuations in aggregate demand that were developed in chapters 3 and 4. The way in which changes in the rate of growth of nominal GNP that are associated with shifts in aggregate demand affect prices and quantities reflects the supply side and the transactional mechanisms of both product and labor markets. It is the central theme of this analysis that most prices and wages are not set to clear markets in the short run, but rather are strongly conditioned by longer-term considerations involving customer-supplier and employer-worker relations. These factors insulate wages and prices to a significant degree from the impact of shifts in demand so that the adjustment must be made in employment and output.

Features of the System

The preceding analysis emphasized the distinction between casual and career jobs in labor markets and between auction and customer components of product markets. The resulting system can be summarized by the following set of relations:

1. Wage rates for career jobs, W_1, are principally a function of lagged W_1; the norm rate of increase, g; and consumer prices, a weighted average of auction prices, P_A, and customer prices, P_C.

2. Wage rates for casual jobs, W_2, depend on lagged W_2; the unemployment rate, U; and W_1.

3. Auction prices, P_A, are a function of the output of auction products, Q_A, and nominal GNP, Y.

4. Customer prices, P_C, depend on lagged W_1 and W_2 and the markup over standard costs, b.

5. The unemployment rate depends on the output of customer prod-

ucts, Q_C, with the population, capital stock, and technology taken as given for the relevant time-horizon.

6. The equation $Y = P_A Q_A + P_C Q_C$ is an accounting identity.

7. Exogenous specifications are $Q_A = \bar{Q}_A$ and $Y = \bar{Y}$.

8. Adaptive parameters are, for the short run, $g = \bar{g}$ (g adapts if it is substantially different from the change in W_1 for a prolonged period), and $b = \bar{b}$ (b adapts if the ratio of P_C to W, the weighted average of W_1 and W_2, is unusually high or low for a prolonged period).

This set of relations incorporates a number of simplifications. The omission of the unemployment rate as a principal determinant of career wages is meant to highlight the weaker effect of unemployment on wages in that sector—not to deny that it has some role. In this respect, the wages of novices in career jobs may be classified with those of casual jobs rather than those of experienced workers in career jobs. Similarly, the omission of consumer prices as a key determinant of casual wages is designed to underline the relatively weak linkage there. But an important indirect effect of consumer prices is conveyed to casual wage rates through the influence of career wages.

The impact of nominal GNP on auction prices is the direct link between aggregate demand and prices in product markets. Goods in auction markets are viewed as not having a significant component of wage costs. In contrast, all costs of goods in customer markets are taken to be labor costs. By ignoring the significant material inputs that flow from the auction sector to the customer sector, the model, in effect, focuses on the *value-added* prices of the customer sector, rather than the retail prices of its gross product. No demand variable is shown as a direct influence on customer prices, consistent with the "transmission-belt" view of the sector developed in chapter 4. Of course, the transmission belt carries the impact of unemployment to customer prices through wages.

The linkage between the unemployment rate and real output is a reduced form that combines several relations: a production function that links employment to output, an allowance for on-the-job underemployment and enforced part-time schedules that incorporates the operation of firms when they are off the production function in slack periods, and an expression of labor force participation that allows for the impact of the state of the labor market on the size of the active labor force in relation to population.

The exogeneity of Y simply reflects the focus of this book on the supply side of macroeconomics; the demand side is exogenous—not to the whole economic system but to the scope of the analysis. Similarly, the output of goods in auction markets is taken as exogenous to limit the scope of the analysis.

For the short run, when both b and g are taken as given, the specified relations determine the set of behavioral variables: W_1, W_2, P_A, P_C, Q_C, and U.[1]

The Business Cycle

It is instructive to trace the cyclical patterns that would be expected to emerge from such a system during a prototype business cycle. Assume there is a cycle that is not marked by supply shocks and that does not disturb the values of b or g. Suppose the cycle lasts four years: it begins with a one-year recession, which is marked by sharply rising unemployment; that is followed by two years of recovery with steady declines in unemployment; and the cycle concludes with a final year during which unemployment remains stable at some low level. That pattern of unemployment is shown in figure 6-1, as are illustrative time series of the rates of increase of both career and casual wages and both auction and customer market prices. Of the two series that measure wage inflation, casual wage rates, W_2, display a much more pronounced procyclical pattern, which reflects their responsiveness to unemployment. The inflation rate for career wages, W_1, varies less, which indicates the constancy of the norm rate; it shows some procyclical pattern because of the influence of consumer price inflation. Career wages rise more rapidly than casual wages during the recession and the early stages of recovery; their inflation curves cross at some unemployment rate, and thereafter the percentage differential of the two wage *levels* (which are not shown) declines.

The rate of price change in the auction market, p_A, is assumed to be extremely volatile and conforms closely to the cycle. The bad news of recession is assumed to surprise traders at least to some degree; as a result, the inflation rate slows down and then becomes negative. The inflation rate for prices of customer goods, p_C, is a weighted and lagged average of inflation rates in the two sectors of the labor market, corrected downward for trend productivity growth, which generally permits wage inflation to exceed price inflation.

1. Lowercase letters are used to denote the rate of change of these variables over time.

226

Figure 6-1. *Rates of Increase of Wages and Prices in a Typical Business Cycle*[a]

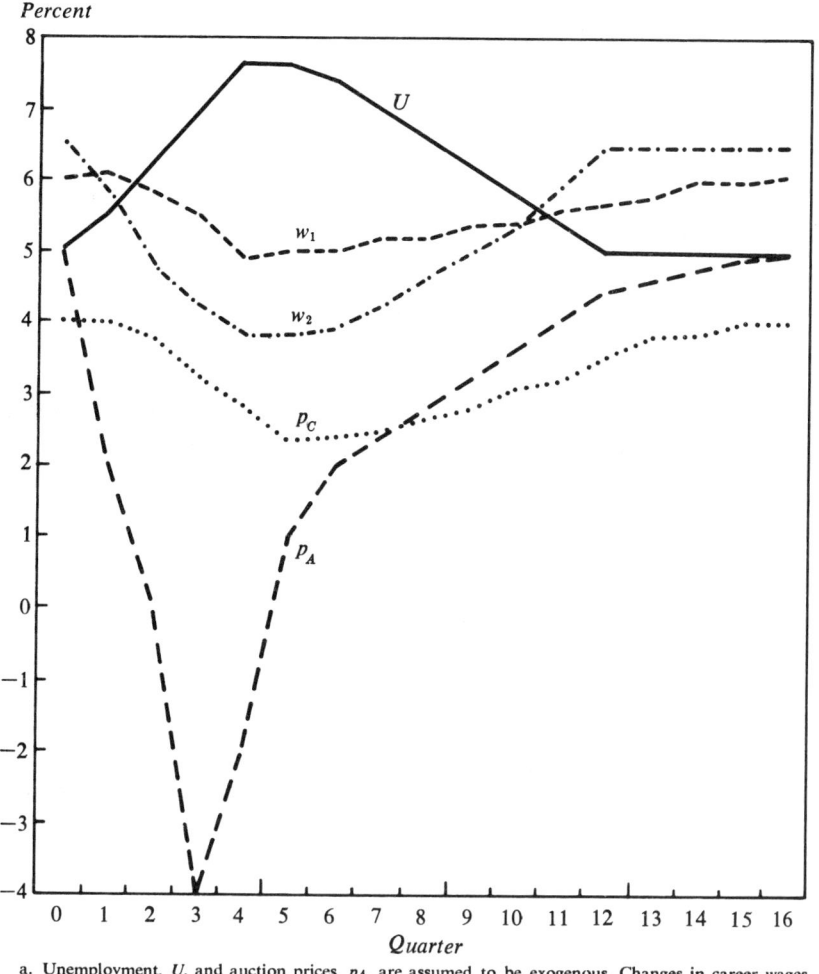

Percent

Quarter

a. Unemployment, U, and auction prices, p_A, are assumed to be exogenous. Changes in career wages and casual wages, w_1 and w_2, respectively, are derived from simulations according to the following equations: $w_1 = 4.0 + 0.4p_{C_{-1}} + 0.1p_{A_{-1}}$; $w_2 = -1.5 + 40\,(1/U)$; $p_C = \frac{1}{2}w_{1_{-1}} + \frac{1}{2}w_{2_{-1}} - 2.2$.

All lags in the figure are assumed to last only a few quarters, and that is consistent with the experience of cycles in the fifties and sixties. By the time the recession reaches a trough, inflation in all sectors is slower than it was at the peak of the cycle. But the slowdown in inflation lasts for only a small part of the recovery. These illustrative time series are consistent with the general experience that the inflation rate hits bottom early in the recovery. Even while markets are still slack by any absolute standard, the reduction in slack leads to rising auction prices. Similarly, shortly after unemployment starts to fall, casual wages end their slowdown. The upturn in auction prices and the acceleration in casual wages act, through the customer price influence, to end the slowdown in career wages.

During the period of recovery, equal successive declines in the unemployment rate have a growing proportionate impact on the pool of willing applicants for casual jobs. The growing frequency of help-wanted signs and of reductions of acceptance quality in the career labor market produces upward pressure on wage rates in the casual labor market. Wage inflation responds in a nonlinear fashion to falling unemployment. But once unemployment stops falling, the inflation rate tends to level off.

Because customer price inflation is simply lagged wage inflation in this illustrative cycle, the ratio of wages to these prices varies only a little over the cycle. The short lag in the pass-through of labor costs into customer prices has a slight procyclical effect on real wages. Measured in terms of these prices and relative to trend, real wages rise as nominal wages accelerate and fall as nominal wages decelerate. But measured in terms of their purchasing power for auction goods, real wages display a markedly countercyclical pattern, that is, highest (relative to trend) close to the trough and lowest near the peak. The real wages that are measured in terms of all prices therefore reflect a mildly procyclical movement in relation to customer prices and a strongly countercyclical pattern in relation to auction prices. The overall relationship may display no distinct cyclical pattern. The procyclical pattern of productivity in turn converts such a noncyclical pattern of real wages into a strongly countercyclical movement of labor's share (or procyclical movement of capital's share) of the national income.

The behavior of employment, unemployment, labor force participation, and productivity in such a cycle can also be described in light of the analysis of previous chapters. The sharp rise in unemployment during recession is the joint product of an increasing number of spells of joblessness and longer duration for the average spell. Because of layoffs and discharges, a larger fraction of the unemployed are "job losers" (rather than quitters or entrants into the labor force). The increased frequency of no-help-wanted signs and the widening of the wage differential between high-wage career jobs and low-wage casual jobs increase the dispersion of wage offers and the duration of unemployment consistent with the pursuit of an optimal search strategy by the job seeker. The same increases in costs of search discourage participation in the labor force and enlarge "hidden unemployment."

The reduced participation in the labor force, in addition to the shortened workweek and depressed productivity stemming from on-the-job underemployment, cushions the rise in unemployment associated with any decline in output. As a result, percentage variations of real GNP around its trend are much larger than percentage-point fluctuations in the unemployment rate. Nearly twenty years ago, I found in the data of the fifties an approximate rule of thumb that an increase of one percentage point in unemployment was associated with a decrement of about three percentage points in real GNP. The rule of thumb held up so well over the next decade that some of my professional colleagues named it "Okun's Law." During the late seventies, the three-to-one ratio no longer approximated reality. Because of the marked slowdown in the trend of productivity growth, it is very difficult to disentangle the cyclical and secular factors in recent productivity performance. However, a quantitative relation between unemployment and real output must depend on the duration and severity of the typical cycle and on the size of tolls in the labor market. Those forces jointly determine the willingness of employers to tolerate on-the-job underemployment during periods of recession and slack. If employers encounter an unusually deep recession and expect the subsequent period of slack to be especially long-lasting, they are likely to cut back employment more nearly in proportion to the decline in output. That may be related to the breakdown of the three-to-one approximation during and after the 1973–75 recession.

Typical and Unfamiliar Fluctuations

The cycle that I outlined is intended to represent a typical or normal fluctuation. It has the amplitude and timing that firms, households, and government policymakers have come to expect. They are unable to predict its turning points, and they are generally somewhat surprised when the recession strikes and when it is supplanted by the recovery. But the observations of fluctuations in demand during the cycle are viewed as a more or less familiar dynamic process—as drawings out of a lottery that decisionmakers understand. The inflation-unemployment points generated by that typical cycle fit the Phillips curve. Inflation rates rise (and fall) with only modest lags in response to declines (and increases) in the unemployment rate. Although some unemployment rate would be associated with a zero rate of inflation, it has no optimal and indeed no special properties. Moreover, no particular unemployment rate can be viewed as the equilibrium.

As the analysis of previous chapters has made clear, the Phillips result is likely to be disturbed if fluctuations change in a way that leads decision-makers to believe that the old urn of the lottery has been replaced by a new one. The summary of the system at the outset of this chapter stressed two particular ways in which such disturbances might be incorporated into the inflationary process—through a change in the norm rate of wage increase and a change in the standard markup. The norm rate of wage increase is the rate of wage inflation that on balance produces neither favorable nor unfavorable surprises for workers. It is a par for the course that just fulfills implicit contracts, with no net upward or downward shading. If wage increases keep exceeding the norm for so long that the disparity cannot be interpreted as a merely cyclical phenomenon, the notion of par for the course will change. If $w_1 > g$ for a long period, the value of g will begin to adjust upward. By the same token, a prolonged period of slack will begin to push g downward.

Similarly, the markup over historical costs must allow for a return to firms that covers any typical upward crawl in costs whereby replacement costs normally exceed historical costs. The pricing formulas based on historical costs that are appropriate for some typical rate of increase in costs will squeeze profits (at least in real terms) if costs accelerate and rise for a prolonged period at a more rapid rate than was previously viewed as normal. One way that firms can adjust simply, as was noted in chapter 4, is by enlarging their markup.

If a strong expansion lasted atypically for six or nine years instead of the typical three years, the values of b and g would be likely to start moving upward. Such a process of adaptation shifts the original Phillips curve upward, producing a higher inflation rate at a given unemployment rate than the system would have generated previously. Once such accelerating forces are set in motion, they are not necessarily halted by a downturn of the economy. If, during a recession, the par for the course or perceived secular average rates of wage and price inflation are viewed as higher than they were initially, the Phillips curve keeps shifting upward even as the recession produces a movement along the curve to the right. As illustrated in figure 6-2, the economy then exhibits a set of inflation-unemployment points that lie on successively higher Phillips curves, producing a disappointing, slight reduction of inflation during and after the recession.

Figure 6-2. *A Worsening Trade-off between Inflation and Unemployment*

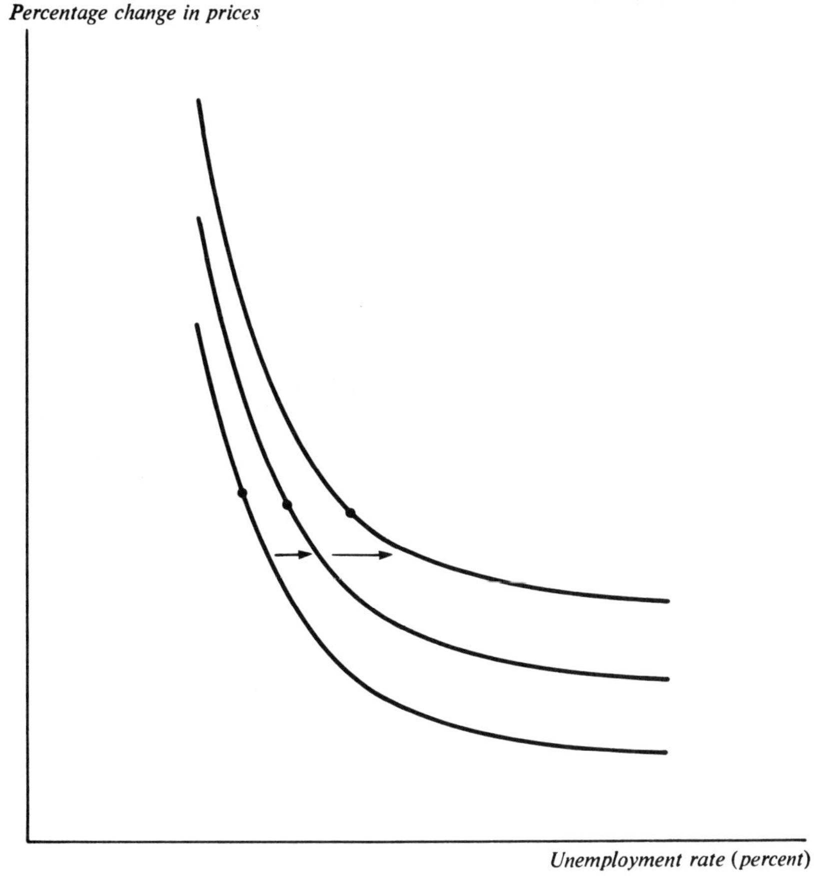

Percentage change in prices

Unemployment rate (percent)

• = Inflation-unemployment points during and after recession.

Those disappointments are bound to intensify suspicions and indeed convictions of decisionmakers that the secular inflation rate has increased. When economic agents are convinced that the normal inflation rate has increased, they will change behavior in a way that reinforces that result.

The norm rate of wage increase and the markup are key parameters that illustrate the process of adaptive acceleration. They are not alone; other features of this system are also likely to participate in the process. A cyclical experience that changes the notion of the typical cycle is likely to alter the length of the pass-through lags from costs to prices, the schedule of wage setting, the strength of the consumer price effect on wages (both through formal and informal cost-of-living escalation), and other modes of behavior that provide "futures contracts" to participants based on backward-looking formulas.

The choices between casual and career personnel strategies and between customer and auction marketing strategies also depend on the notion of the typical amplitude and duration of cycles. Incentives to invest in tolls in the labor market depend on the perceived ability to use the human capital created by the tolls rather steadily over a long period. In a world of extreme volatility and cycles of great amplitude, investments in career job attachments would be relatively small. The construction industry, which displays particularly severe fluctuations, displays a "fly-by-night" syndrome marked by high turnover of firms and low confidence of customers. If the entire economy were marked by similarly severe alternations between boom and bust, more fly-by-night operations would develop for both work forces and firms. The incentives to rely on subcontracting and on employment services supplying "temporaries" for work would be strengthened. Similarly, in the planning of industrial capacity, greater value would be attached to standby peak-load capacity for booms and also to flexibility in cutting back output at large cost savings. Wherever opportunities emerge to reduce average total costs at full capacity by assuming greater fixed costs (whether by training programs or by a large-scale automated plant), that trade-off becomes less attractive in an economy of greater variance. With greater volatility of aggregate demand, there would be more interindustry turnover of workers; more firms would be operating in clear "disequilibrium" situations in the labor market—at times with no recruiting and many layoffs, at other times with marked overtime. The retreat from career and customer strategies would be likely to steepen the Phillips curve, but the steepening would probably not be symmetrical. The inflation rate associated with the cycle-average unemployment rate would be likely to increase.

In summary, the level and shape of the Phillips curve depend on the average rate of both inflation and unemployment over the cycle and on their variation. A change in the characteristics of cyclical fluctuations that alters the perceived (or expected) secular inflation rate or cycle-average unemployment rate or the variance around them shifts the curve. Current institutions at any time are adjusted to some conception of typical fluctuations. New developments that make people suspect that the urns have been switched lead to a change in expectations. But economic agents are bound to recognize that they are unfamiliar with the contents of the new urn. They rightly feel a greater sense of uncertainty and act in ways designed to guard themselves against that uncertainty.

A Comparison with Other Views of Price-Quantity Adjustments

The view of the cycle and of chronic inflation that emerges from this analysis draws heavily from previous theoretical formulations and yet contrasts in important ways with all of them. In this section I explore the key similarities and contrasts between my analysis and three other views: those of the "vintage" Keynesian model, the Phillips curve approach, and the accelerationist theory.

Vintage Keynesian Model

As I stressed in chapter 1, the basic Keynesian model departs from the classical view of the supply mechanism mainly through the assumed floor on nominal wage rates. That produces two sharply distinguished possible states of the labor market: with less than full employment, the money-wage rate remains constant and all variations in the demand for labor are reflected in changes in employment; at full employment, however, increases in the demand for labor affect only the wage rate and leave employment unaltered. The view of the inflationary process that I have developed has room for the nominal wage floor and, indeed, embeds it in a broader mechanism of implicit contracts that explains the insensitive response of wages, and the sensitive response of employment, to variations in demand at low rates of utilization. Without invoking the sharp either-or distinction of the simple Keynesian model, this view offers a reasonable understanding of why wage and price variations should absorb a larger fraction of fluctuations in nominal GNP at high utilization rates. Moreover, it provides a linkage, which is absent from the vintage Keynesian model, whereby inflation can become chronic and thus persist in the face of excess supply.

In the vintage Keynesian model, inflation persists as long as an ex-ante inflationary gap characterizes the economy. There could be an inflationary process with maintained full employment. But the dynamics reflect continued and persistent expansionary disturbances of demand, rather than any built-in supply mechanism that keeps inflation churning. In that model the price level rises when aggregate demand in nominal terms, Y, exceeds the dollar value of full-employment output, $\bar{Q}_F$, measured at the preexisting price level P_{-1} or $Y > \bar{Q}_F P_{-1}$. The difference between these two nominal GNP values is defined as the "inflationary gap" and the jump in the price level resulting from any gap is simply that required to reduce real demands for goods and services to the level of full-employment output: $P/P_{-1} = Y/\bar{Q}_F$.

An increase in the price level with constant output necessarily raises the nominal value of factor incomes in parallel. The vintage Keynesian model has to explain why the higher price level reduces real demands and restores a market-clearing equilibrium. The theory does so by invoking one or both of two lags in private behavior: one of spending behind income, and the other of wages behind prices. In the former, consumers and businessmen are assumed to formulate dollar budgets for some time ahead and to maintain those nominal spending plans for that period. A rise in the price level curbs the real volume of spending during that period; the predetermined level of nominal spending fetches a smaller market basket. In the latter variant—the wage lag—higher prices squeeze real disposable income and depress real consumer demand even if nominal spending does not lag behind nominal income.

Wages can lag behind prices only if firms operate, at least for a while, in positions "off" their demand curves for labor. The wage lag thus departs from full market-clearing even at full employment. Nonetheless, it serves as a stabilizer of demand, rather than of costs, in this world. The wage lag makes the price level dynamically determinate by limiting the immediate response of nominal demand to inflation. While it also limits the rise of costs, that is irrelevant, because prices are not cost-determined in this inflationary world.

The market-clearing price level that emerges with either the budgeting lag or the wage lag is a dynamic solution that, in general, does not remain stationary. Once prices jump, nominal budgets are reformulated for the next period in light of the higher levels of incomes; and nominal aggregate demand shifts upward, requiring another jump of prices in the next period.

Under the conditions of World War II when the inflationary gap analysis was in vogue, there was a "nonstabilizing" benchmark for fiscal-monetary policy, with real budgetary demands of the government large and steady and monetary policy acting in an accommodative role to keep interest rates low and steady. Under those assumptions, the inflationary gap tended to remain constant in real terms, requiring repeated jumps in the price level (as either budgeting or wages caught up with the last jump). That meant a steady rate of inflation, reflecting the dynamics of demand —not of price setting or of wage setting—as it affected supply or costs.

In principle, inflation could be stopped in its tracks. If increases in tax rates (for example) drained enough private income out of the system to hold nominal aggregate demand for the current period to the level experienced last period, the inflationary gap would be eliminated. The price level of the last period would then clear markets in the current period. At most, supply considerations prevented any rollback in the price level because the inflationary experience established a new and higher floor on the level of nominal wages.

This potentially happy ending does not emerge from the customer-career market view of the inflationary process. Auction prices can be stabilized and even rolled back by restraint on aggregate demand. But career wages and customer prices pose a different set of problems for policy-makers. At any point in a period of inflation there is a backlog of further escalations of price tags, reflecting the lags in the pass-through of costs into prices and in the effect of consumer prices on wages. Those elements raise the supply price of next period above that of the current one. Any demand-management policy that stabilizes the price level absolutely will entail a substantial cutback of output and employment. Moreover, if the economy has experienced inflation as a normal state of affairs, the level of utilization that promptly eliminates inflation is likely to be very low and to have no normative significance for social welfare. Finally, if the economy has recently suffered a lengthy bout of rapid inflation, a process of adaptive acceleration may be encountered, adding further to the output losses entailed in stabilizing the price level. The dynamics of inflation are embedded in the process of wage and price determination and cannot be eliminated solely by fiscal and monetary measures without incurring great losses of output and employment. The trade-off is a pervasive fact of life and a limitation on the powers of demand management.

Phillips Curve Approach

In all these respects, except adaptive acceleration, the customer-career view agrees with the Phillips curve approach. But the reasoning that admits chronic inflationary tendencies in the absence of excess demand is quite different. The theoretical underpinning of the Phillips curve relation that was examined in chapter 1 is James Tobin's ingenious combination of the rounded corner amendment, a disaggregation of the wage floor, and stochastic variations in demand across industries. As long as resources are not completely mobile in the short run, and as long as industries experience different rates of growth of demands, bottlenecks can emerge while most industries are operating on flat (or even falling) portions of their marginal cost curves. If separate wage floors apply to particular industries and occupations, wages do not fall in the slack sectors and will rise in the bottleneck sectors.

In principle, the aggregate wage level may rise whenever even a single community or a single firm encounters a bottleneck. Clearly it may rise more rapidly than the productivity trend even if the aggregate of excess supplies of labor in the slack industries exceeds that of excess demands in the bottleneck industries. Under those conditions, all slack industries, regions, and occupations would be constrained by the wage floor and register no change in money wages. The economy would display two patterns of wage behavior—constancy in the slack sectors and increases in the bottleneck sectors. Then the aggregate rate of wage inflation could be a continuous negative function of unemployment because the number of tight areas should be larger the more nearly overall full employment is approached.

These disaggregated implications of that model do not accord with experience. Since World War II, U.S. wage rates have risen in virtually every industry during every year. They have risen in industries and among firms that have neither explicit contracts requiring increases nor excess demand. Wages have gone up among firms with workers on layoffs and enforced part-time schedules, with no-help-wanted signs, and with no unions. The departure of observed behavior from the market-clearing model goes well beyond the operation of any kind of a floor on the money wage. The recipe consisting of the disaggregated wage floor, the rounded corner, and relative demand shifts can explain why the aggregate wage level rises during periods like 1958–63 and 1975–77, but it cannot explain why wages rise in virtually all industries during such periods of slack.

In a sense, the analytical framework of implicit contracts can be viewed as reformulating the wage floor hypothesis into a resistance to declines of *relative*—and not just absolute nominal—wage rates. Indeed, the stickiness of relative wages emerges as the fundamental pattern of behavior that generates especially strong resistance to absolute declines in the money wage. That was indeed one line of the argument that Keynes developed: because cuts in money-wage rates "are seldom or never of an all-round character, . . . any individual or group of individuals, who consent to a reduction . . . will suffer a *relative* reduction."[2]

Given the influence of relative wages, the money-wage rate in any industry not only must maintain the level it achieved in the past but also must keep pace with the levels achieved elsewhere. When wages rise in response to excess demand in some sectors, they tend to be pulled up elsewhere. That pull is a relative wage pull, not just a contraction of labor supply in the slack industries that lose workers to the bottleneck sectors. Implicit contracts convert a rise in wages in selected sectors into a general pattern of rising wages.

Under those conditions, the aggregate wage level cannot be frozen at a given unemployment rate that has been associated with rising wage rates. Other workers have to catch up, and so wage inflation is likely to be a continuing process even far from overall full employment. The nominal wage floor keeps crawling upward, and the fact that it has been crawling upward makes it continue to do so.

The stickiness in relative wages emerged as a feature of the analysis of chapters 2 and 3. It arises in a labor market with no auctioneer in which firms set wages and jobs are allocated by decisions of existing workers to quit or stick and by acceptance decisions of searchers. Implicit contracts between firms and career workers develop and they produce a stickiness that acts as a stabilizer: it tends to hold wages down (that is, to slow their rise) in tight markets and to bolster them (acting more or less as a floor) in weak markets. Whether the implicit contract focuses on wage-wage patterning, on norm rates of wage increase, or on prices, it generates a Phillips curve and provides a rather satisfactory foundation for that relation. During a typical cyclical process when decisionmakers do not perceive a change in long-term forces that calls for an adaptation of institutions, the implications of the customer-career model accord with those of the Phillips curve approach.

The price level is driven by a dynamic process on the supply side. Because at any time some wages are "out of kilter" with other wages or because prices and wages are out of balance, further movements of the aggregate wage and price level must take place. They generate a Phillips curve world; the price level that is high enough to evoke the output of the current period (and an associated rate of unemployment) must keep rising

2. John Maynard Keynes, *The General Theory of Employment, Interest, and Money* (Harcourt, Brace, 1936), p. 14.

at essentially a constant rate to keep evoking output associated with the same rate of unemployment in subsequent periods. A disturbance in aggregate demand works through these supply dynamics; as a result of them, any change in nominal GNP is split between a real and a price component. The mechanics of this inflationary process are supply-dominated, in contrast with the vintage Keynesian model in which the dynamics on the demand side prevail.

The Phillips curve approach provided a satisfactory description of U.S. inflation-unemployment behavior during the period between the end of the Korean War and the late 1960s. As shown in figure 6-3, a scatter diagram of price inflation rates and unemployment rates for the years 1954–69 forms a hyperbola. The fit is good, and the hyperbolic function suggests that the reciprocal of the unemployment rate served as a reasonable measure of demand pressure. A comparable diagram with wage (rather than price) inflation would show a somewhat looser but still acceptable fit. The scatter diagram allows for no lag in the response of prices to unemployment; the introduction of a short lag improves the fit. Strikingly, the terms of the trade-off indicated by the years 1965–69 are consistent with those of 1955–57. The result is especially noteworthy because the demographic composition of the labor force shifted during the intervening period in a way that was unfavorable to the trade-off.

As the scatter diagram suggests, a positive rate of inflation was a normal feature of the economy. Absolute stability of the price level might have required a 10 percent rate of unemployment—beyond any plausible point of balance in labor and product markets. The customer-career paradigm attributes such a secular inflationary tendency to wage norms and markup standards that essentially anticipated an upward creep in the price level and made that the normal state of affairs. With that feature, the Phillips curve approach captured the essential features of the cyclical process of inflation and unemployment and provided a reasonable framework for prediction and explanation.

The Accelerationist Theory

Milton Friedman and Edmund Phelps independently attacked the logic of the Phillips curve at a time when that approach was scoring empirical successes. Basically their message was a pessimistic forecast—not an interpretation or explanation of experience—that inflation would accelerate if the unusually low unemployment rates of the mid-sixties were main-

Figure 6-3. *The Phillips Trade-off, 1954–69*

Implicit GNP price deflator (percentage change)[a]

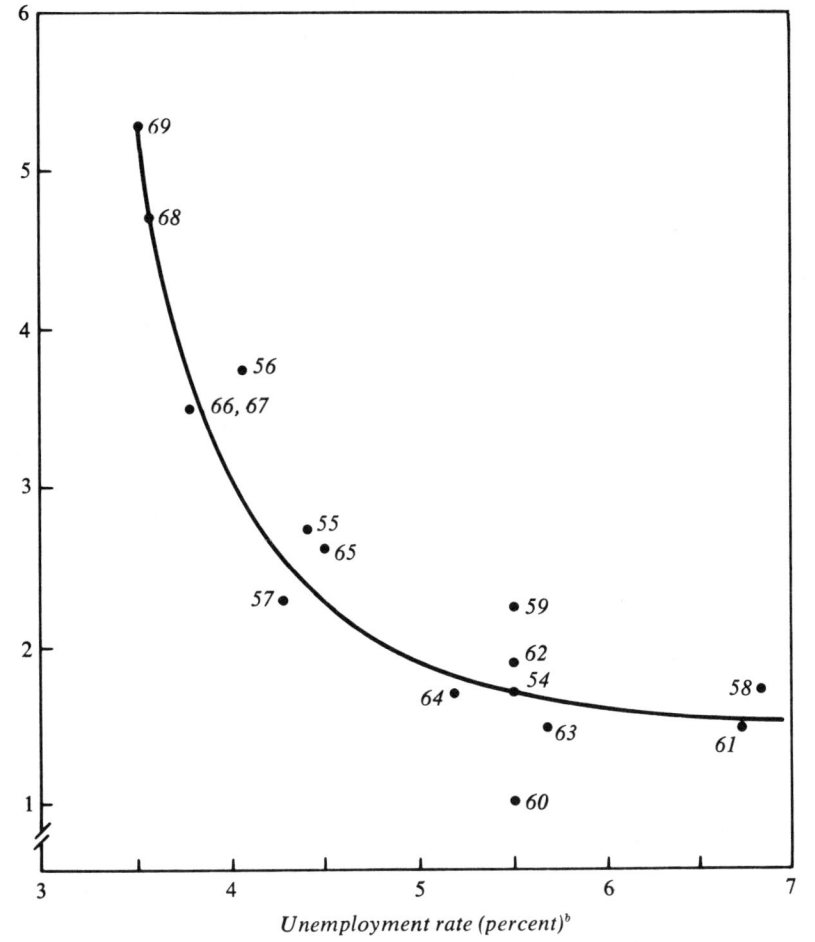

Unemployment rate (percent)[b]

Sources: *National Income and Product Accounts*, table 7.1; *Economic Report of the President, January 1980*, p. 237.
a. Change during the year calculated from end-of-year deflators (derived by averaging the fourth quarter of a given year and the first quarter of the subsequent year).
b. Average for the year.

tained. In their view, the short-run Phillips curve was unstable and would shift upward in response to the persistence of tight markets. Unlike the Phillips model, which implies that maintained low unemployment entails high but stable inflation, the accelerationist model warns that it leads to *accelerating* inflation.

Although the accelerationist theory is defective in many ways, the prophetic accuracy of its pessimism must be admired. As figure 6-4 indicates, the unemployment-inflation experience of the 1970s reveals a much more unfavorable trade-off than that of 1954–69. In the sense that all economists must recognize that adverse shift of the short-term Phillips curve, they have all become accelerationists now (to reverse Friedman's celebrated concession to Keynes).

The behavioral assumptions underlying the accelerationist conclusions about labor markets were discussed in chapter 2. In one formulation, a rise in money-wage rates associated with tight labor markets induces people to take jobs in the mistaken belief that they are being offered a bonus in real wages. As they learn that prices are moving up with equal rapidity, the inducement for that extra work vanishes unless wages keep rising at an ever-accelerating rate. I emphasized above that the hypothesized mechanism is a theory solely of cyclical movements in labor force *participation,* not a theory of unemployment. Even as a theory of participation, its premises are shaky. Because the elasticity of the supply of labor is exceedingly low in relation to increases in the real wage, why should one assume an elastic response to *misperceived* increases in the real wage? Moreover, why should information about the acceleration of money wages be perceived more rapidly and more accurately by households than information about rising prices?

A formulation stressed by Phelps posits a misperception of *relative* (rather than real) wages and of the optimal margin between work and search (rather than leisure). Because of stale information about the distribution of wage offers, searchers tend to accept a job offer with a higher money wage than they had expected, even when that offer does not provide a particularly good relative wage because the whole distribution has improved.

In chapter 2, I noted the serious deficiencies of that theory in explaining the observed cyclical swings in unemployment. Years and years of maintained slack or tightness can occur only through an incredibly (and irrationally) slow learning process by job seekers. The model does not explain the cyclical pattern of the quit rate and of the number of spells (as well as the duration) of unemployment, the phenomenon of layoffs, the existence of no-help-wanted signs and help-wanted ads, and the upgrading process.

The customer-career framework offers a more satisfactory account of movements along the short-run Phillips curve and, at the same time,

Figure 6-4. *Changes in Prices and Unemployment Rates, 1954–79*

Implicit GNP price deflator (percentage change)[a]

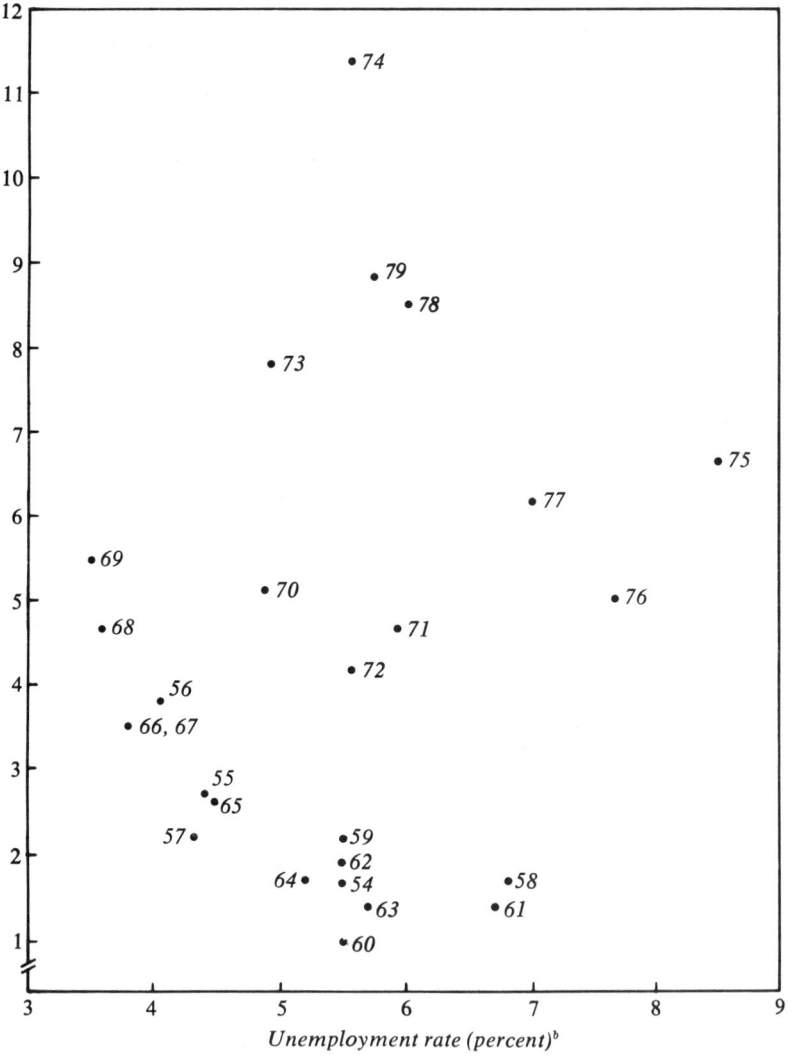

Sources: Same as figure 6-3.
a. See figure 6-3, note a.
b. See figure 6-3, note b.

builds on the underlying logic of the accelerationist model in explaining shifts in that short-run Phillips curve. It will be shifted adversely by persistent operation of the economy at utilization rates and inflation rates that depart greatly from the average of historical experience. In the customer-career paradigm, the dynamic character of the inflationary process is grounded in the establishment of time schedules for price adjustment and wage adjustment, in patterns of emulation and cost-of-living adjustment for wages, in the application of markup in setting prices, and in other features of implicit and explicit contracts. These modes of behavior are not explicitly geared to forecasts, but are predicated on some assumptions or underlying conception of the longer-run stability of real activity and prices.

The arrangements that become established in any economy must depend on the perceived or expected stability of its price level. They cannot be the same for countries like Brazil and Germany. If there are major and prolonged departures from the accustomed degree of stability, and if they are interpreted as likely to persist, behavior patterns will change. When American citizens begin to believe that their economy is behaving more like that of Brazil (and less like that of Germany), the institutional arrangements also become more Brazilian. The resulting shortening of lags and increases in the magnitude of response coefficients generate upward shifts in the short-run Phillips curve. They confirm the basic prediction of the accelerationist model that the maintenance of a tight economy imposes not only rapid inflation but also accelerating inflation.

Even so, the process of adaptive acceleration outlined in this book leads to predictions, explanations, and prescriptions that differ from the standard accelerationist model in several ways. First, it is the prolonged experience of unusually high inflation—rather than of unusually low unemployment—that triggers and maintains the upward shift of the Phillips curve. Once practices have begun to adapt to a higher secular rate of inflation, a cyclical episode of above-normal unemployment is unlikely to halt the adaptation. The 1975 experience in which inflation rates remained unusually high even during the deepest recession since the thirties may well have reinforced the conviction that the secular rate of inflation had accelerated.

Second, the adaptive process is consistent with the inflation rate reaching its low point early during periods of cyclical recovery and accelerating thereafter as the unemployment rate *falls,* even while unemployment remains high by any standard. The outline of the prototype cycle earlier in this chapter illustrates that point. Indeed, the standard accelerationist prediction that inflation decelerates during recovery until unemployment crosses a particular boundary line has been contrary to fact throughout modern times. Qualitatively, the Phillips model predicts correctly the rising prices of 1934–37, the renewed price declines during the 1938 recession (when unemployment nonetheless remained below its 1934–35 rate), the absence of any progressive deceleration of prices from 1959 to 1963, and the stepped-up inflation in 1977–78. History makes clear that the inflation rate is raised, after a short lag, by a decline in unemployment, not merely by very low levels of unemployment.

Third, although the standard accelerationist model suggests that the Phillips curve starts shifting up once markets become tight and keeps moving up gradually, the customer-career paradigm—and the facts—point to more discrete and discontinuous shifts.[3] An estimate of expected inflation inferred from bond yields or commodity prices began to register gradual increases in 1966. Yet the price and wage performance of the economy relative to the unemployment rate continued to track the old Phillips curve for some years thereafter. People changed their minds about the near-term outlook for inflation much sooner than they did about the secular outlook. Even when the perceived secular outlook changed, habits and conventions did not change at once in a significant way. In part, the discontinuity reflects the costs of deviating from prevailing practices and getting out of step with others in the marketplace. The first major retailer that removes a fixed price list from its seasonal catalogue encounters more customer resentment than the competitors that follow its lead. When firms in an industry have been taking orders at guaranteed delivery prices for decades, abandoning that practice is a risky step for the innovator. The first union that seeks nearly full cost-of-living protection with an escalator has to fight a major battle; its success eases the task of those that follow it. In general, changing one's behavior to adapt to rapid inflation is different

3. While algebraic formulations of accelerationist models generally imply continuous shifting, Milton Friedman expresses a different view, with which I fully agree: "Stated in terms of the rate of change of nominal wages, the Phillips Curve can be expected to be reasonably stable and well defined for any period for which the *average* rate of change of prices, and hence the anticipated rate, has been relatively stable. . . . Curves computed for different periods or different countries for each of which this condition has been satisfied will differ in level, the level of the curve depending on what the average rate of price change was. . . . For periods or countries for which the rate of change of prices varies considerably, the Phillips Curve will not be well defined." Milton Friedman, "The Role of Monetary Policy," *American Economic Review*, vol. 58 (March 1968), p. 9, note 5.

from and more difficult than changing one's mind about the secular rate of inflation.

Fourth, the customer-career paradigm does not invoke (nor does it deny) a vertical long-run trade-off between inflation and unemployment. The question of whether the trade-off vanishes over an indefinitely long horizon is of distinctly limited interest, as long as the lags are long enough to make a trade-off relevant over any reasonable horizon of policymaking. Far more fundamentally, the hypothetical experiment needed to answer the question requires the elimination of *fluctuations* in unemployment that are themselves a vital influence on price making, wage making, and the entire character and scope of contracts and institutions. To explore seriously the implications of freezing the unemployment rate indefinitely at 3 percent or at 8 percent, it would be necessary to identify the consequences of eliminating the variability of unemployment as well as those of making it especially low or high. I noted in the previous section some features of the economy that depend on cyclical variability, but that was a brief and impressionistic set of remarks; to do justice to those complex issues might require another book about as long as this one!

Fifth, for the same reasons that the vanishing (or nonvanishing) trade-off is not a part of this analysis, neither is the "natural" unemployment rate. In the short run, with typical cycles that do not generate adaptive acceleration (or deceleration), a wide range of unemployment rates can represent equilibria consistent with different inflation rates, as the Phillips curve approach implies. But for the long run, because the elimination of variation in unemployment would transform the behavior of product and labor markets, any unemployment rate maintained indefinitely would shift even the long-run Phillips curve inherited from a cyclical world. I suspect that some narrow range—and perhaps even particular value—of the cyclical average unemployment rate would result in a constant cyclical average of inflation over the long run, provided that the shape of the cycle, supply shocks, technology, the stock of physical and human capital, taxation, and government regulation are all taken as ceteris paribus. But then that cyclical average unemployment rate can hardly be called natural.

Finally, the adaptive acceleration sketched here puts more emphasis on looking backward or sideward and less on looking forward than the standard accelerationist model. This is a matter of degree; any behavioral adjustment to a new era is predicated on some implicit forecast that the old days are not returning tomorrow. Yet it is a central theme of this book that the arrangements between firms and workers and those between customers and suppliers are intended to finesse the costly formulation of and reliance on point-estimate forecasts as a basis for decisionmaking. By the same token, changes in these relations are adaptations that result from experience rather than from prediction or forecasting. As I see it, after experiencing surprisingly rapid inflation, union workers demand an escalator clause in their next contract just as a homeowner who has experienced a serious fire opts for particularly comprehensive fire insurance on the next home. Similarly, after an unusually snowy winter more people buy and mount snow tires the next autumn. Surely they are not acting as amateur meteorologists raising their point-estimates of the probable snowfall during the coming winter. Any behavioral scientist who chooses to regard such decisions as the product of forecasts made by extrapolating the past is introducing an unnecessary and cumbersome link in the chain of reasoning. To some degree, the issues are semantic and methodological, but they have some importance in the design of anti-inflationary policy, as will become clear in chapter 8.

A Simplified Algebraic Representation

A simple algebraic model that truncates the system outlined at the beginning of this chapter can describe some features of the price-quantity adjustments in response to short-run disturbances. For convenience, I focus on the auction-customer dichotomy in product markets but ignore the heterogeneity of jobs and workers to characterize a one-sector labor market. Furthermore, I assume that

1. Customer prices are set by a markup over costs with a one-period lag, while auction prices clear markets.

2. All the costs of customer goods and none of the costs of auction items are wages.

3. The supply of auction-priced items is completely inelastic (over some unspecified but significant period), while the output of customer items can be expanded at constant real cost.

4. Technology, human capital, and stocks of goods are unchanged throughout.

5. Income and price elasticities of demand are unity for both types of goods, so that each captures a fixed share of total expenditures.

6. Nominal income is determined by a separate set of demand relations that include (but are not limited to) fiscal and monetary variables.

The Model[4]

The behavior of prices and output in the two sectors can be summarized by the following three equations:

(1) $$P_A \bar{Q}_A = a\bar{Y}$$

(2) $$P_C Q_C = \bar{Y} - P_A \bar{Q}_A$$

(3) $$P_C = bW_{-1},$$

where P and Q refer to prices and output, respectively; the subscripts A and C refer to auction and customer items, respectively; Y is nominal income; and the bar over Y and Q_A denotes that they are taken as exogenous.

Completing the model requires a wage equation. Before introducing that, however, I point out a few features of the model by assuming, unrealistically, that the level of wages is unvarying: $W = \bar{W}$. Suppose that income rises at an annual rate of m (some small fraction, like 0.05), reflecting stimulation from monetary and fiscal policies. Then P_A must also rise at a rate m because Q_A is fixed. With wages constant, P_C will also be constant while Q_C expands at a steady rate m. Real wages measured in units of customer items are unchanged (because both W and P_C are constant); but real wage rates measured in terms of the market basket of the consumer must decline because the latter includes some auction goods whose prices rise. In this world, the supply curve of the auction sector is vertical; but the customer sector has a "quasi-supply" function that is horizontal. Economic expansion is marked by increases in the output of customer goods and in the prices of auction goods. This represents an extreme form of the general proposition that, with different supply responses among sectors, the growth of nominal income must affect relative prices and the mix of output. In addition to illustrating that important departure from neutrality, this bare-bones model highlights (in a negative way) the fact that wages are the transmitter of inflation into the customer sector.

Next the model can be completed with a more realistic wage equation:

(4) $$w = g + S(X).$$

Here g represents the norm or "descriptive guideline" for wage increases; the $S(X)$ term links the rate of wage increase to the tightness of the economy—S is a behavioral response function and X is a measure of tightness.

4. The derivation of this model is given in the appendix to this chapter.

In particular, X is taken as the ratio of actual Q_C to that value denoted as Q_C^* at which w equals g. This is merely a way of defining the "utilization rate" of the customer sector so that it is unity when upward and downward shading of wage increases from the norm balance out. When Q_C is Q_C^*, X is 1 and $S(1)$ is 0. For Q_C greater than Q_C^*, X is greater than 1 and $S(X)$ is positive; while for Q_C less than Q_C^*, $S(X)$ is negative. The first derivative of S (which will be denoted by s) is positive; and the second derivative is also positive, indicating that equal successive increments of customer output add progressively larger increments to the rate of increase of wages.

Menu for Fiscal-Monetary Policymakers

In the world of this model, policymakers are confronted with a trade-off between inflation and unemployment characterized by a traditional Phillips curve. Price stability requires lower output, and high levels of output and employment entail inflation. Society can achieve more output if, but only if, it is prepared to accept a higher rate of inflation. The menu of choices is shown in figure 6-5. The figure focuses on the rate of wage inflation, which can alternatively be viewed as the rate of inflation of customer prices in the subsequent period. By their influence on the level and growth of nominal income, the fiscal-monetary authorities determine the inflation rate. In that sense, inflation is always a monetary (or, more accurately, a monetary-fiscal) phenomenon. The growth of nominal income also determines the output of customer goods, and so output and employment are equally monetary phenomena.

Fiscal-monetary policy influences output and prices in this world through the impact of the instruments—taxes, public expenditures, money growth, and interest rates—on the course of nominal income. Responses in private wage setting and price setting split the growth of nominal income into price and output components. Suppose that the instruments of demand management are set to achieve a steady growth of nominal income at a rate m. Then, ultimately, steady inflation will be experienced at a rate m for auction prices, wages, and customer prices. The output of customer goods will also be constant at a utilization rate X_0 such that $S(X_0) = m - g$, because that is the one output level at which w will equal m. Clearly the higher the value of m that is chosen, the higher will be X_0 and hence Q_{c_0}.

Suppose the growth of nominal income has been steady at a rate m for a sufficient time to achieve constant utilization at X_0. Now assume that,

Figure 6-5. *Choices for Fiscal-Monetary Policymakers*

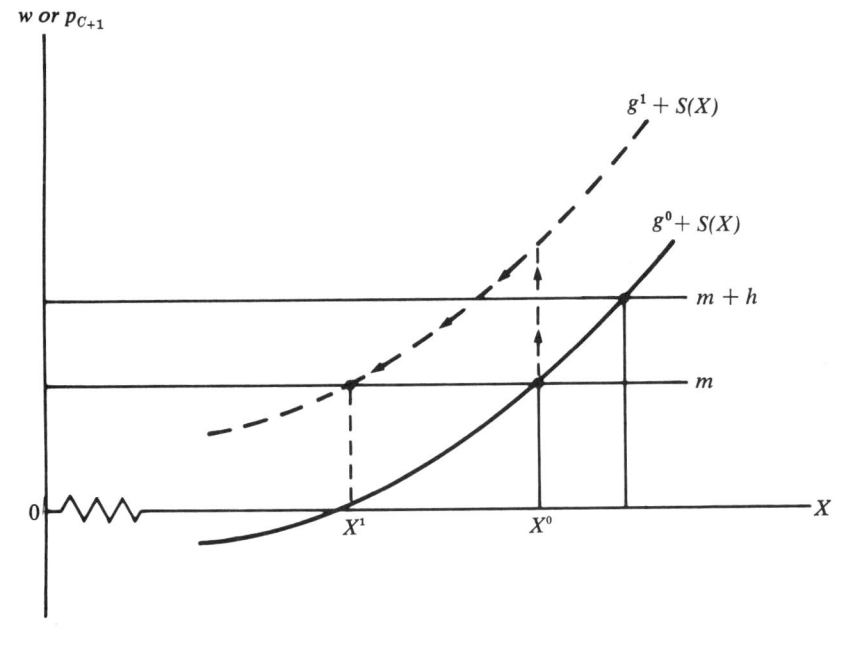

for any reason, it accelerates to a rate $(m + h)$, and remains at that higher rate. Immediately prices of auction goods exhibit a higher inflation rate equal to $m + h$. But in the initial period the prices of customer goods still rise at the rate m, while their output increases by a proportion h. In that period the rate of wage increase rises from m to $m + sh$. Reflecting that acceleration of wages, prices of customer goods accelerate in the next period and keep rising at an increasingly rapid rate that ultimately reaches $m + h$, eventually matching the inflation rate of auction items. At that point, however, the output of customer goods has risen by a proportion h/s over its initial level. (It is assumed that h is small enough that S can be treated as linear in the relevant range.)

The stimulative monetary-fiscal strategy therefore adds h to the inflation rate and a proportion h/s to the output of customer goods. The increment to overall real GNP is $(1 - a)$ (h/s), reflecting the weight of customer goods in overall output. The terms of the trade-off are critically influenced by the size of s. In effect, the reciprocal of s is the "output multiplier" of the inflation rate. The larger the size of s, the more closely the system resembles a neoclassical world of auction labor markets; more of the stimulus to aggregate demand raises wage inflation, and less serves to expand output and employment. As interpreted by the career model, a low value of s reflects a strong influence of implicit and explicit contracts and of conventions that insulate wages from tightness and slack in the labor market. Empirical research on U.S. wage responsiveness to unemployment and output suggests that the value of s on an annual basis is approximately 0.1 (and surely below 0.2) at an unemployment rate of 6 percent. Under those circumstances, the split of any incremental growth of nominal income is dominated by extra output.

As long as the parameters of this Phillips curve system are unchanging, a large bonus of extra output and only a small burden of incremental inflation result from any adoption of more stimulative policies. But if policymakers follow such a course and are successful in maintaining reduced unemployment rates (along with somewhat higher inflation rates) for a prolonged period, they encounter adaptive acceleration. The Phillips curve shifts upward, raising the burden of extra inflation relative to the bonus of extra output.

The choice of fiscal-monetary strategies will also influence relative prices and the composition of output. In the example in which the proportionate growth of nominal income is increased by h, the mix of output shifts in the direction of customer goods, and relative prices of auction goods rise. Because the output of customer goods rises by a proportion h/s over its initial level, and because the fraction of total expenditures on those goods is unchanged, their price relative to auction goods must fall below its initial value by that same proportion h/s.

Similarly, real wages relative to prices of customer goods are driven up, while profit margins on those goods are pushed below their initial level. The ratio W/P_C must be higher than it was initially by a proportion h, reflecting the wider differential between the wage level of the current period and that of the previous period which determines the customer prices of the current period. On the other hand, because P_C/P_A is lowered by a proportion h/s, W/P_A will be reduced by $[(h/s) - h]$. Wages fare well relative to customer prices and poorly relative to auction prices. If the weights of the two types of items in the consumer market basket are $(1 - a)$ and a, respectively (corresponding to their shares in Y), real cost-of-living wage rates rise if $(1 - a) h$ is greater than $a [(h/s) - h]$. Simplification makes it clear that the inequality holds if s is greater than a (and is reversed in the opposite case). If s is large, much of the effect of nominal income expansion serves to accelerate wages and customer prices (rather than to raise output), which keeps the differential between W and P_A and bolsters real wage rates (rather than stimulating employment). If the auction weight (a) is large, that pulls real cost-of-living wages down. The uncertainty in the real world about the cyclicality of real cost-of-living wage rates is preserved in this simple model.

Although the examples assume that monetary and fiscal policies stabilize the rate of growth of nominal income, the cyclicality of economic activity reflects the fact that they do not. When the growth of Y varies, the observed inflation-unemployment combinations are traced by movements along a Phillips curve like that of figure 6-3. The wage observations all lie on the curve in the context of this simplified model because the cyclical impact of real activity on wage inflation is taken to be unlagged. The one lag in the system is that of prices behind wages, which reflects the markup practices of firms producing customer goods. That makes the rate of price inflation lag modestly behind the level of real activity. The model misses the empirically relevant considerations, namely, that a tightening of labor markets takes some time to exert its full impact on the rate of wage inflation, even if the norm is unchanged and customer prices do not influence wages. Nonetheless, the nearly coincident timing of inflation measures at cyclical turning points as well as econometric estimates for the U.S. economy in the fifties and sixties generally support this simplification. To capture the spirit of a real world in which the Phillips curve is not shifting dramatically, lags should be kept short and simple rather than long and complex.

The Role of Productivity

At the cost of a modest complication in the model, its realism can be enhanced by allowing for trend growth of productivity (that is, output per hour worked) at a rate r in the customer sector. The price equation for customer goods must then be revised in dynamic form to show that unit labor costs rise less rapidly than wages by r:

$$p_C = w_{-1} - r.$$

The output proxy (X) for labor market tightness may still be regarded as Q_C/Q_C^*, but Q_C^* must grow at a rate r to hold employment constant. In other words, the growth of output tightens markets only when it proceeds at a rate exceeding r.

If Y grows consistently at a rate m, auction prices and (ultimately) wages rise at that rate, while customer prices increase at the rate $(m - r)$. Output of customer goods reaches "equilibrium" when X is such that $m - g = S(X)$; it rises at a rate r thereafter.

If the trend growth of productivity should accelerate (while m is unchanged), wage and auction-price inflation will not be altered; but customer price inflation will slow down, and output of customer goods will grow more rapidly. The model suggests that productivity growth can slow inflation as well as speed progress. In fact, it is the trend growth of productivity that permits a positive wage norm to prevail without necessarily enforcing a rising trend in the prices of customer products. That was the lesson that the Kennedy-Johnson guideposts sought to convey in defining the noninflationary rate of wage increase.

Cyclical variations in productivity around its growth trend have somewhat different implications. As long as customer prices are geared mainly to the trend growth of productivity rather than to actual cyclical experience (as was suggested in chapter 4), the cyclical variations affect principally the distribution of income between workers and property owners. In particular, they accentuate the cyclical volatility of profits. During a period of strong expansion, the cyclical bonus in productivity swells the realized profit margins of customer firms, reinforcing the effect of spreading nonwage overhead costs and countering the effect of the lag of customer prices behind wages.

Shifts in the Wage Norm

An autonomous rise in the wage norm alters unfavorably the menu of choices facing fiscal-monetary policymakers. If g jumps from one level (g^0) to a higher one (g^1) while m and the other parameters of the system are unchanged, the rate of wage inflation is immediately increased (see the dashed line in figure 6-5). In the next period, the prices of customer goods will be commensurately higher and the output of those goods reduced. Over time, X and Q_c will slide until the value of $S(X)$ falls sufficiently to offset the increase in g. At the ultimate position (denoted by the superscript 1), $-s \cdot (X^1 - X^0) = g^1 - g^0$. The shift in g has a negative multiplier on customer output; it equals $-(1/s)$. At that point, wage rates and prices of both customer and auction goods will rise at the rate m, just as they were before the jump in g.

At the time of the disturbance, real wages in terms of both auction and customer prices are raised by the full proportion of the change in g. As wage increases slow down toward m, customer prices catch up gradually and ultimately restore their initial relationship to wage rates. On the other hand, auction prices, which rise at a constant rate m throughout, never catch up and remain lower relative to both wages and customer prices. Even in the ultimate equilibrium, real wage rates measured in terms of overall consumer prices gain as a result of the higher value of the ratio W/P_A. Nonetheless, in appraising the long-run consequences for workers, the gain in real wage rates must be balanced against the reduction in employment. Indeed, aggregate real wage income must be lower in the new situation than on its initial path, because the path of nominal wage income (like that of overall Y) is unaltered while customer and auction prices are higher. If m is unaltered, the ultimate result of the jump in g is a contraction of customer output and employment and a higher price level, but not a permanently higher inflation rate.

The fiscal-monetary authorities can prevent the loss of output and employment, but only by raising the value of m in parallel with the jump in g, ratifying and validating a permanently higher inflation rate as well as the shift of real income to workers. To the extent that g is subject to influence by labor through a concerted bargaining effort by trade unions or through lobbying in the political process, the fiscal-monetary authorities face the problem of formulating their bargaining strategy. If they are not expected to accommodate any autonomous rise in g, labor is less likely to strive for one because the prospective loss of employment and erosion of the incremental wage will loom as important disadvantages of the higher norm. But if, even so, labor strives for and achieves a higher norm, any hard-line nonaccommodative policy will cut the real incomes of property owners and of workers who were not the cause of the problem. I return to this issue in chapter 7.

Linkage from Customer Prices to Wages

In equation 4, the focus of wage setting is summarized in terms of the norm rate of wage increase, a type of wage-wage relation. The wage-wage linkage deserves the chief emphasis because of its primary importance empirically for the United States. The linkage from customer prices to wages is also significant and must be incorporated into the analysis.

Results that are analytically interesting, though empirically farfetched, emerge when wages are assumed to move proportionately to the cost of living but to be unaffected by the state of the labor market. In that case the wage equation explaining the annual percentage rate of wage increase, w, becomes a function of the annual rates of price increase, p_A and p_C:

(5) $$w = ap_A + (1 - a)p_C.$$

The weight of auction goods in the cost of living is taken as a, which is their weight in Y. With this form of wage determination, inflation enters the customer sector only through a feedback of auction prices to wages. In the earlier variant, when nominal income accelerated, the fractional impact raising wage rates was given by s; here, it is given by a. Most of the results of the earlier model are left intact with the mere substitution of a for s. One qualitatively different result emerges: real wage rates measured as purchasing power over the consumer market basket become determinately constant in the cost-of-living variant.

A less extreme and more realistic way of incorporating cost-of-living effects into the wage equation would make the norm depend, in part, on price inflation (p, a weighted average of p_C and p_A), while maintaining a wage response to unemployment. In effect, the norm becomes a compromise of nominal wage increases (with weight $1 - k$) and real wage increases (with weight k). That mode of behavior could be described by

(6) $$w = (1 - k)g + kp + S(X).$$

Under these circumstances, economic expansion creates inflation in the customer sector along two routes: a pull on wages from the tightening of labor markets, and a push on wages from the acceleration of consumer prices. If s is as large in equation 6 as it is in 4, the extra channel clearly augments the inflationary impact of nominal income expansion and correspondingly reduces the impact on unemployment and output. The trade-off is steepened and, in effect, the system is made more "auction-like" in its response to changes in the growth of nominal income. Nonetheless, the system retains its essential qualitative features as long as the response to the cost of living is fractional ($0 < k < 1$) rather than fully proportional. In the case of a unity coefficient on the cost of living, however, the system loses its Phillips curve identity and becomes strictly accelerationist. Steady inflation can be attained at only one possible utilization rate.

Moreover, the price-wage link introduces a further lag into the system. Even if wages are assumed to respond to the cost of living instantaneously, they are in effect responding to last period's wages, which are the determinant of customer prices in the current period. With that additional lag, the simple model can no longer be summarized by a first-order difference equation system. Instead, it becomes a second-order system similar to the familiar one used to describe multiplier-accelerator interactions. The algebra is presented in the appendix to this chapter.

Intuitively, some of the results of such a system should be evident in the case in which the growth of nominal income is maintained at a steady rate m. Then the output of customer goods, Q_C, and the utilization rate, X, will achieve constancy only when P_C is rising at the rate m. That can happen only when wages are rising at the same rate m. When w and p are set equal to m in equation 6, it becomes clear that under those circumstances $(1 - k) \ (m - g) = S(X)$. If different values of m are considered, $(1 - k) \ \Delta m = s \Delta X$. The output multiplier associated with a small change in the steady growth of nominal income is therefore $(1 - k) \ (1/s)$; it was $(1/s)$ in equation 4 when k was taken to be zero. In that respect, a stronger influence of prices on wages is equivalent to a stronger influence of unemployment on wages; that illustrates the sense in which the system is made more "auction-like" by the cost-of-living linkage. A different verdict on that linkage emerges, however, when disturbances take the form of supply shocks rather than changes in aggregate demand.

Supply Shocks

Under the restrictive assumptions of the model consisting of equations 1 through 4, an exogenous shift in the supply of auction goods, Q_A, has limited effects on the system. In the event of, say, a crop failure that reduces Q_A, P_A experiences a one-time increase that is the reverse of the percentage reduction in Q_A. If m is unchanged, the customer sector and the labor market are fully insulated from the supply shock. The higher level of auction prices cuts real wage rates measured in terms of the consumer market basket, but it does not alter nominal wage rates or customer prices, output of customer goods, or employment. In particular, though the price of food is higher, no downward pressure is exerted on other prices.

That insulation is critically dependent on the assumption of a unitary price and income elasticity of demand for auction goods. Because they absorb the same dollar volume of expenditures, these goods cannot alter nominal aggregate demand for customer goods in the model. But, in fact, farm crops (and, indeed, most major categories of auction products) have notoriously low price elasticities of demand—in the short run, closer to 0.1 than to 1.0. If that price inelasticity is incorporated into the model, the results of a supply shock are altered significantly. Equation 1 must be rewritten $P_A Q_A^{1/e} = aY$, where e is the absolute value of the price-elasticity and is considered to be less than unity. Then, the reduction in Q_A increases P_A more than proportionately, and this raises the expenditure on auction goods out of a given Y. Hence the nominal expenditure for customer goods is compressed when Y is unchanged. As a result, both output and prices in the customer sector are pulled down—just as they would be by a one-time reduction in Y. With the drop in Q_A, the overall price level would necessarily be higher; the decrement in P_C would offset the rise in P_A partially but not fully, so that some compression of nominal expenditures for customer goods would be reflected in lower output and employment. In this situation, a monetary-fiscal action that adds to nominal demand exactly the amount that is absorbed by the higher price of auction goods will restore the insulation that occurred automatically when the price elasticity of demand was taken to be unity. That "accommodation" of the shock permits the overall price level to be raised by the increase associated with P_A but it simply preserves the initial path of prices of customer products and of wages.

The plot thickens considerably when equation 6 is substituted for 4, thereby incorporating the effect of consumer prices on wages. Indeed, a significant cost-of-living influence changes the economy most importantly by altering the response to supply shocks or other "real" disturbances. In that event, higher auction prices push up wages through the cost-of-living effect, given the level of customer output and employment. Even with the assumption of unitary price elasticity, the constant nominal expenditures on customer goods must be spent on less output at a higher price. In that situation, the effect of the supply shock is unambiguously downward on customer output and upward on customer prices. The higher price level in the auction sector is contagious and spreads to prices in the customer sector.

When the low (less than unitary) price elasticity of demand for auction products is recognized, the profile of the bad news changes to some degree. Then, for given nominal GNP, total expenditure for customer goods is lowered by the reduction in Q_A, so output is contracted even more. Indeed the output effect may be sufficiently strong to offset the cost-push inflationary effect on P_C, and P_C may decline if Q_C is sufficiently depressed. The overall price level is still raised, but less dramatically in this case.

Regardless of the strength of the effect of prices on wages or the size of price elasticity of demand, the output effects on the customer sector stemming from the supply shock in the auction sector can be neutralized by a sufficiently "accommodating" monetary-fiscal action. That would require raising nominal GNP enough to maintain the real aggregate demand in the customer sector. Such accommodation requires the acceptance of a higher level of wages and customer prices as well as auction prices. In view of the empirical importance of supply shocks in the history of the seventies, I return to the policy issue in chapter 8.

Responses to International Disturbances

The example of the crop failure above was discussed as though domestic output and domestic consumption of the goods were equal and no international trade was involved. If fixed exchange rates are assumed, only a minor modification of that analysis is in order. To the extent that a good is exported, its weight in GNP will exceed its weight in consumer prices; to the extent that it is imported, the reverse will be true. That difference will influence the magnitude of the upward push on wages (and customer prices) that works through the consumer price influence on wages.

In the case of exported or imported goods (as in some of the domestic disturbances discussed above), changes in fiscal-monetary policies would probably be required to maintain the path of nominal GNP. Because the demand of foreigners for U.S. grain is price-inelastic, a partial crop failure will raise export proceeds and shift the Hicksian *IS* curve upward. Conversely, a crop failure in coffee would drain U.S. purchasing power and push the *IS* curve downward. Moreover, insofar as imports as well as domestic production generate some transactions demand for cash, the rise in the price of coffee would increase the demand for money at a given level of nominal GNP.

If, in fact, the policy dials are turned to maintain the path of nominal GNP, rising dollar prices for any imports or any exported goods that appear in the U.S. consumer's market basket exert upward pressure on domestic wages through the cost-of-living effect. Whether the effects on the terms of trade are favorable (as in the grain example) or unfavorable (as in coffee), the shift of the Phillips curve is unfavorable given the level of employment and customer output. That result contrasts with the case of a rise in productivity, which reduces inflation at given employment while it increases real income. In contrast, a jump in wheat prices (even one that resulted from increased foreign demand rather than from a partial crop failure) adds to inflationary pressure at a given level of employment, even though it affects favorably the potential real income of the nation.

The introduction of flexible exchange rates complicates—or, some might say, enriches—the analysis. The complications concern the impact of the real disturbances on the exchange rate. The effects flowing out of the exchange markets themselves are reasonably straightforward. A purely exogenous appreciation of the dollar (for example, based on a change in expectations) lowers the dollar price of imported goods and thus tends to reduce wage inflation through the cost-of-living influence. It is also likely to affect aggregate demand. To the extent that the appreciation pushes the balance in the current account toward deficit, it shifts the *IS* curve downward. With fixed settings of the fiscal and monetary dials, nominal GNP would then tend to be lower.

The controversial and unsettled issue concerns how much the real disturbances that change the trade balance alter the exchange rate of the dollar. Some economists would count on the news of a Soviet crop failure, for example, to strengthen the dollar substantially; they would stress that, in the auction exchange markets (as in the auction grain markets) the strengthening would precede any flow of higher revenues from grain exports or any acceleration of retail consumer prices. Others point to the asset markets as the arena in which exchange rates arc determined and suggest that the crop news seems to point to a minor and indirect effect. In all candor, I have nothing to contribute to this dialogue. Whatever appreciation—trivial or large—does result from the expected rise in proceeds from grain exports pushes down on the cost of living and on wages and customer prices. That induced exchange-rate effect reduces the effect of the higher price of grains in the domestic market basket. The exchange-rate effect should thus partially offset the domestic price effect. It might even dominate the domestic effect, especially if the real disturbance is expected to be long-lasting (a blight rather than a freeze, for example) or if it involved a commodity of which the major portion of U.S. output was exported and only a small part consumed at home (as is the case for rice). In any case, the flexibility of exchange rates does not ensure the elimination of the paradox cited above—that, while a high price of an exported product should raise U.S. consumption possibilities, it can have an important destabilizing effect.

In all examples of the responses to real disturbances, the cost-of-living influence on wages makes the economy behave less like the auction model. In the auction world a rise in the demand for commodities that are not produced by labor would be equilibrated through lower nominal wages and lower prices of labor-intensive products. These results are relevant to the consequences of indexing as a means of coping with inflation, and I return to them in the next chapter.

The Accelerationist Variant

The bare-bones algebraic formulation can readily be converted into a simple accelerationist model. As a pedagogical device, the mechanics of acceleration are most readily described in terms of the adaptation of the norm rate of wage increase to actual and expected experience with wage inflation. Starting with the wage-setting described by equation 4, the accelerationist outcome can be derived along the following lines. People develop a notion of the secular rate of wage inflation (w^*). It is based on experience of the past several years, and may be modified by any firmly held expectations of different behavior in the future. When w^* diverges far enough and long enough from g, then g changes, moving toward w^*.

That suggests another equation specifying g as a monotonic function of current and lagged values of $(w^* - g)$. As a matter of conviction, I resist the temptation to summarize "long enough" and "far enough" in quantitative terms. What needs to be underlined, in the current state of knowledge, is the uncertainty about what is required to produce the shift. Neither the rapid inflation following the termination of wartime controls in 1947–48 nor the Korean War boom of 1950–51 left an accelerationist heritage. Neither did the renewed inflationary experience of 1956–57. On the other hand, after the pronounced inflation of 1966–69 lasted four years—longer than had ever been experienced without controls and without a full wartime mobilization—the Phillips curve did become unhinged. Similarly, after two or three years of the Great Depression, even the Keynesian wage floor collapsed; by 1932, wage declines were prevalent in the United States. These episodes of history provide clues, but not definitive answers.

No matter how g responds to the magnetic attraction of w^*, an accelerationist theorem of some sort will emerge. Consider an experiment in which a particular rate of utilization was maintained for decades and in which every parameter of the system other than g was kept unchanged. Then, if the w generated by that X was much larger or much smaller than the initial value of g, wage inflation would continue to accelerate or decelerate as w altered w^*, and, in turn, g. Steady wage inflation would be unlikely unless, at the chosen value of X, $S(X)$ was close to zero. In that sense the value of X (or, equivalently, of U) that satisfies $S(X) = 0$ has a special property and may even deserve a special name.

Nonetheless, it must be emphasized once more that any hypothetical experience of freezing a particular utilization rate indefinitely would be bound to alter the system over time in many ways—even if, at the chosen value of X, $S(X) = 0$. Ending the variation of unemployment would exert a profound impact on the parameters of the system (contrary to the assumption underlying the experiment). In a world of a stable unemployment rate, the dispersion of wage offers, the perception of risk, the nature of implicit contracts, the choice between casual and career personnel strategies and between auction and customer marketing would all be affected. Intuitively, I believe that the elimination of variance would raise the utilization rate (lower the unemployment rate) consistent with nonaccelerating inflation. But here again I want to stress the uncertainty rather than to predict the consequence. The unemployment rate which, if maintained indefinitely, would be consistent with nonaccelerating inflation cannot be estimated in a meaningful way from the historical time-series data of a cyclical world.

Another limitation is illuminated by equation 6, which incorporates the cost-of-living influence on wages. It provides a reminder that the perceived secular rate of wage inflation can be altered not only by a prolonged period of high utilization, but also by a set of price-raising supply shocks. There is more reason to focus on w^* than on any U^* as a guide to maintaining stability of the Phillips curve, and that has important implications for the policy strategies that are discussed in chapter 8.

Appendix

In logarithmic form, equations 1 through 3 are

$$\log P_A = \log a + \log Y - \log \bar{Q}_A$$
$$\log P_C + \log Q_C = \log (1 - a) + \log Y$$
$$\log P_C = \log b + \log W_{-1}.$$

If lowercase letters are used to denote $d \log /dt$, these become

(1') $p_A = y$

(2') $p_C + q_C = y$

(3') $p_C = w_{-1}.$

The wage equation (4) is $w = g + S(X)$. When the first-difference is taken, this becomes $w = w_{-1} + S(X) - S(X_{-1})$. If S can be treated as approximately linear in the relevant (small) range,

$$w = w_{-1} + s \frac{\Delta Q_c}{Q_c^*}.$$

If $\Delta Q_c / Q_c^*$ is approximated by $\Delta Q_c / Q_c$, then

(4') $$w = w_{-1} + s q_c.$$

From 2', 3', and 4', it follows that

(7) $$w = w_{-1} + s(y - p_c) = (1 - s)w_{-1} + sy.$$

(8) $$p_c = p_{c_{-1}} + s q_{c_{-1}} = p_{c_{-1}} + s(y_{-1} - p_{c_{-1}}) = (1 - s)p_{c_{-1}} + sy_{-1}.$$

(9) $$q_c = y - w_{-1} = \frac{w - w_{-1}}{s} = (1 - s)q_{c_{-1}} + y - y_{-1}.^5$$

Now 7, 8, and 9 are standard first-order difference equations (for constant y) of the form

$$Z_t = AZ_{t-1} + B,$$

which has a solution

$$Z_t = A^t Z_0 + \frac{1 - A^t}{1 - A} \cdot B.$$

Hence,

(7') $$w_t = (1 - s)^t w_0 + y[1 - (1 - s)^t]$$

(8') $$p_{c_t} = (1 - s)^t p_{c_0} + y[1 - (1 - s)^t]$$

(9') $$q_{c_t} = (1 - s)^t q_{c_0}.$$

For $0 < s < 1$, the solution values are $\bar{w} = y$; $\bar{p}_c = y$; $\bar{q}_c = 0$. Also $p_A = y$ throughout.

Suppose y has been equal to m for a sufficiently long time to establish that solution. But in a period designated as zero, y increases to $(m + h)$, where it remains subsequently. Before the disturbance the levels of the variables are W_{-1}, $P_{C_{-1}}$, $Q_{C_{-1}}$, and $P_{A_{-1}}$. In period zero, their rates of change are altered as follows: $p_{c_0} = m$ (as before); hence $q_{c_0} = h$ (from 2'); $w_0 = m + sh$ (from 4'); and $p_{A_0} = m + h$ (from 1').

5. Because $s q_{c_{-1}} = w_{-1} - w_{-2} = (y - q_c) - (y_{-1} - q_{c_{-1}})$.

The logs of the levels now follow paths described by

$$\log P_{Ct} = \log P_{C-1} + \sum_{\theta=0}^{t} p_{C\theta}$$

$$= \log P_{C-1} + (m + h)(t + 1) - h \sum_{\theta=0}^{t} (1 - s)^{\theta}$$

$$= \log P_{C-1} + (m + h)(t + 1) - \frac{h}{s}[1 - (1 - s)^{t+1}].$$

$$\log P_{At} = \log P_{A-1} + (m + h)(t + 1).$$

$$\log Q_{Ct} = \log Q_{C-1} + \sum_{\theta=0}^{t} (1 - s)^{\theta} \cdot h = \log Q_{C-1} + \frac{h}{s}[1 - (1 - s)^{t+1}].$$

$$\log W_{t} = \log W_{-1} + (m + h)(t + 1) - (1 - s)h \sum_{\theta=0}^{t} (1 - s)^{\theta}$$

$$= \log W_{-1} + (m + h)(t + 1) + h - \frac{h}{s}[1 - (1 - s)^{t+2}].$$

Ultimately, as $(1 - s)^t$ approaches zero,

$$\log Q_{Ct} \to \log Q_{C-1} + \frac{h}{s};$$

the output multiplier is thus $1/s$, as stated in the text;

$$\log P_{Ct} - \log P_{C-1} - (\log P_{At} - \log P_{A-1}) \to -\frac{h}{s},$$

which reflects the ultimate change in relative prices stated in the text;

$$\log W_{t} - \log W_{-1} - (\log P_{Ct} - \log P_{C-1}) \to h,$$

the gain in real product wages,

$$\log W_{t} - \log W_{-1} - (\log P_{At} - \log P_{A-1}) \to -\left(\frac{h}{s} - h\right),$$

the loss of real wages over auction goods.

If, instead, wage equation 5 replaces 4,

(5) $w = ap_A + (1 - a)p_C.$

Since $p_A = y$ and $p_C = w_{-1}$, the equivalent of 7, 8, and 9 above are

(10) $w = (1 - a)w_{-1} + ay;$

(11) $p_C = (1 - a)p_{C-1} + ay_{-1};$

(12) $q_C = (1 - a)q_{C-1} + y - y_{-1}$

(by using $p_C = y - q_C$ in equation 11).

Clearly, these differ from 7, 8, and 9 only by the substitution of a for s. With the wage equation 6, $w = (1 - k)g + kp + S(X)$, where $p = ap_A + (1 - a)p_C$. Taking the first difference and expressing linearly yields

$$w = w_{-1} + k(p - p_{-1}) + sq_C$$

$$= w_{-1} + ka(y - y_{-1}) + k(1 - a)(w_{-1} - w_{-2}) + sq_C$$

$$= w_{-1}[1 + k(1 - a)] - k(1 - a)w_{-2} + s(y - w_{-1}) + ka(y - y_{-1})$$

$$= w_{-1}[1 + k(1 - a) - s] - k(1 - a)w_{-2} + sy + ka(y - y_{-1}).$$

For steady $y = m$, the solution value remains $\bar{w} = m$. Let $z = w - m$ and denote $k(1 - a)$ by v. Then,

$$z - z_{-1}(1 - s + v) + z_{-2} \cdot v = 0.$$

This is exactly the form of the multiplier-accelerator equation.[6] In that case, s is the marginal propensity to save, and v is the accelerator coefficient. The stability and oscillation characteristics are obviously identical.

Bibliographical Notes

The closest intellectual forebears of the model of the inflationary process sketched here are James Duesenberry, "The Mechanics of Inflation," *Review of Economics and Statistics,* vol. 32 (May 1950), pp. 144–49; and the description by Gardner Ackley, "A Third Approach to the Analysis and Control of Inflation," in *The Relationship of Prices to Economic Stability and Growth, Compendium of Papers Submitted by Panelists Appearing before the Joint Economic Committee,* 85 Cong. 2 sess. (Government Printing Office, 1958), pp. 619–36.

Discussions of the cyclical timing of price series go back to Frederick C. Mills, *Price-Quantity Interactions in Business Cycles* (National Bureau of Economic Research, 1946). More recent work by the National Bureau has been led by Geoffrey H. Moore; see, for example, "The Cyclical Behavior of Prices," in Victor Zarnowitz, ed., *The Business Cycle Today,* General Series 96 (National Bureau of Economic Research, 1972), pp. 137–66.

6. See J. R. Hicks, *A Contribution to the Theory of the Trade Cycle* (Oxford: Clarendon, 1950), p. 69.

Studies dealing with cyclical variation in the wage structure include M. W. Reder, "The Theory of Occupational Wage Differentials," *American Economic Review*, vol. 45 (December 1955), pp. 833–52; Pamela Haddy and N. Arnold Tolles, "British and American Changes in Inter-industry Wage Structure under Full Employment," *Review of Economics and Statistics*, vol. 39 (November 1957), pp. 408–14; and Michael L. Wachter, "Cyclical Variation in the Interindustry Wage Structure," *American Economic Review*, vol. 60 (March 1970), pp. 75–84.

My findings on the relation between unemployment and output are reported in Arthur M. Okun, "Potential GNP: Its Measurements and Significance," in American Statistical Association, *1962 Proceedings of the Business and Economic Statistics Section* (Washington, D.C.: ASA), pp. 98–104.

The basic formulation of the inflationary gap model was in John Maynard Keynes, *How To Pay for the War: A Radical Plan for the Chancellor of the Exchequer* (Harcourt, Brace, 1940). One important application to policy is Carl Shoup, Milton Friedman, and Ruth P. Mack, *Taxing to Prevent Inflation: Techniques for Estimating Revenue Requirements* (Columbia University Press, 1943). The analytics are developed by Tjalling Koopmans, "The Dynamics of Inflation," *Review of Economics and Statistics*, vol. 24 (May 1942), pp. 53–65; A. Smithies, "The Behavior of Money National Income under Inflationary Conditions," *Quarterly Journal of Economics*, vol. 57 (November 1942), pp. 113–28; and Ralph Turvey, "Some Aspects of the Theory of Inflation in a Closed Economy," *Economic Journal*, vol. 61 (September 1951), pp. 531–43, and "Period Analysis and Inflation," *Economica*, n.s., vol. 16 (August 194)), pp. 218–27. The frustrations I experienced in my youth with this formulation of the inflationary process are evident in Arthur M. Okun, "The Effects of Open Inflation on Aggregate Consumer Demand" (Ph.D. dissertation, Columbia University, 1956).

The key references relating to the Phillips curve and accelerationist model have been cited in conjunction with chapters 2 and 3.

The literature on supply shocks includes as key contributions, Robert J. Gordon, "Alternative Responses of Policy to External Supply Shocks," *Brookings Papers on Economic Activity, 1:1975*, pp. 183–204; Edmund S. Phelps, "Commodity-Supply Shock and Full-Employment Monetary Policy," *Journal of Money, Credit and Banking*, vol. 10 (May 1978), pp. 206–21; and Edward M. Gramlich, "Macro Policy Responses to Price Shocks," *BPEA, 1:1979*, pp. 125–66.

VII

The Social Trade-off

THROUGHOUT the first six chapters I focused on the descriptive and analytical aspects of price and quantity adjustments and postponed the treatment of the normative aspects for this and the concluding chapter. In this chapter, I first describe how a genuine trade-off between inflation and unemployment emerges in a price-tag economy. I then discuss more specifically the social costs of cyclical unemployment and output losses associated with recession and slack. I turn next to the more difficult task of analyzing the social costs of inflation. Because I argue that the crawl away from money and the search for a "real" unit is a cost of inflation and not a palliative for it, I discuss indexing in considerable detail.

Optimum Output and the Trade-off

The most perplexing problem for macroeconomic policy and social welfare in modern industrial economies is the balancing of the benefits of higher output and employment on the one hand with the costs of inflation on the other. As is often the case, the essential features of the problem are best understood by considering the conditions under which the problem would *not* exist. I begin by explaining why and how the trade-off dilemma is conspicuous by its absence in a world of universal auction markets.

Optimization in an Auction Economy

Consider a hypothetical economy in which all products and factors are traded on fully competitive frictionless auction markets. Then all prices equal marginal costs or, strictly speaking, equal the sellers' estimates of marginal costs. Wages, natural resource depletion, and the user cost of capital enter into the marginal costs of goods. In the labor market the auction process ensures that wages are equated on the margin with the opportunity cost of leisure or other forms of nonworking activity. Then clearly full competitive equilibrium generates an output that can be regarded as ideal. Any output for which buyers are willing to pay a price that exceeds the value of the required inputs to produce it is in fact produced; and no output of lesser value than its input costs is produced.

A number of qualifications must be made to warrant the full optimality of the result. Collective services must be financed by lump-sum taxes because any other taxes necessarily drive a wedge between prices and resource costs, or between wages and the value of home activity, or between the productivity of saving and investment and the income available from them. Any risk aversion must be identical for the individual and the society. Finally, dynamic shifts of the production function through learning by doing or research must not generate externalities (that is, they must be appropriable only by those people undertaking the activity). Restrictive assumptions of these types can be proliferated, but they all seem to be of second-order magnitude; they qualify but do not gravely jeopardize the first approximation of optimality.

Now suppose a full equilibrium of this system is disturbed by some stimulus to aggregate demand, stemming from fiscal or monetary policy or from some private shift of preferences from money to goods. If the stimulus does not change relative demands, clearly another full equilibrium of the system must exist with a simple, across-the-board, proportionate rise of all the initial prices of products and factors, and with no change in any outputs or relative prices. But that equilibrium may not be established immediately. For example, sellers may not recognize the higher factor costs they will have to pay for their inputs; looking at the higher prices posted for their output, they will be induced to augment the supply. Initially for the same reason, workers with a positive elasticity of labor supply in terms of real wages may offer more hours of work in view of the higher nominal wage. These are the misperceptions stressed by the rational expectations theorists. In the case at hand, they generate a higher real GNP. But clearly society has deviated from its optimum; it becomes worse off by producing more. Workers will discover that they have parted with leisure for real wages that are less valuable than the time sacrificed; sellers will find that they have produced more output only by using inputs whose replacement costs exceed the price of the output. (Similarly, any contraction of aggregate demand might push output and employment below their optimum levels while they reduce prices and wages in ways that were not fully perceived initially.)

In this example, as in the price-tag economy described in this book, an increment of nominal GNP is split (at least initially) into an output and a price-level component. Here the gain in output is no gain at all in terms of social welfare. The rise in the price level has no direct implications for social welfare. Even if it is recurrent and generates an inflationary trend, its only social costs are the extra required trips to the bank. The main reason to dislike inflationary surprises in this world is that they are symptoms of disturbances pushing real output away from its equilibrium and optimum level. Public policy should help minimize such surprises so that all changes in prices can be read clearly by sellers as changes in *relative* prices, with no need to ponder whether they may be part of a general uptrend in the price level.

The dynamic properties of such a world can be specified to ensure that equilibrium is ultimately restored at the initial level of aggregate output and the initial set of relative prices and wages, after a single disturbance or even after recurrent upward disturbances of aggregate demand. Then the system will have a vertical Phillips curve if it is viewed over a sufficiently long period. That vertical function protects society from a misguided policy strategy subject to "real GNP illusion," which might try to squeeze out more production than is optimal. Sometimes a vertical Phillips curve is interpreted as a limitation that prevents booms in real activity from lasting, even though they might be attractive. Here the reverse is true: the social welfare cost from an excessively stimulative policy does not stem from encountering the vertical Phillips curve, but rather from not en-countering it soon enough. The cause of the trouble is the incremental real output that emerges during the interval when the Phillips curve is *not* vertical. There is no trade-off of social welfare in the short run any more than in the long run. Price stability (or, equivalently, fully anticipated steady inflation) is a good thing with no regrets; it is desirable, not so much per se, but as a symptom of a system that is not introducing mis-information or misperceptions that will tantalize suppliers into deviations from ideal output.

The plot can be thickened in a number of ways. If suppliers recognize the likely positive relation between surprisingly high prices and surpris-ingly high factor costs, their output will respond less strongly to price sur-prises; that, in turn, reduces the loss of welfare when the source of the surprise is a disturbance of aggregate demand. But there is a cost—a delay in the desired effect—when the source is a shift in relative demands. Risk aversion by sellers would interact with this influence; they would then react to higher prices as though these resulted mainly from rises in ag-gregate demand but react to lower prices primarily as if they reflected downward shifts in relative demand. Risk aversion would also influence the output path if sellers had to determine the quantities to ship into the marketplace on the basis of *expected* prices. The optimal output of risk averters would then be less than the output that maximized expected profits. For the last unit of output that maximized expected profits would expand profits only when the price that actually prevailed matched or exceeded its expected value; that unit would subtract from profits when the price turned out to be surprisingly low. Profits are made higher only if they would be high in any case; so the variability of profits can be reduced by cutting back output.

Finally, the introduction of any elements of monopoly and monopsony power into product or labor markets may have important effects on relative prices or relative wages and relative outputs and employment. The most important macroeconomic consequence of monopoly in product markets and monopsony in labor markets is the introduction of a wedge that forces real wages below the marginal product of labor. If the elasticity of labor supply with respect to the real wage is positive, output and employment are restricted. Any disturbance of aggregate demand that fools the holders of market power into believing that they are offered a higher real marginal return for additional output and employment will reduce effective monopolistic restriction and bring the result closer to a social optimum. Unlike the fully competitive case, monopoly allows misperceptions to produce desirable social results.

The Trade-off in a Price-Tag Economy

In contrast to the pure auction world, an economy in which goods and services are sold by means of price tags necessarily contains elements of monopoly. These in turn generate a restriction of output and a deviation from the social optimum. Because of search and shopping costs, sellers face tilted demand curves in ways that were discussed at length in previous chapters, and they set prices above their short-run marginal costs. Because that monopolistic restriction prevails even in a situation of macroeconomic equilibrium, no optimal properties can be attributed to such an equilibrium. Moreover, even in a macroeconomic equilibrium, relative shifts in demand will be taking place. For firms experiencing adverse shifts in product demand, payrolls are likely to exceed their short-run optimum; yet, because of hiring and firing costs, they may retain underemployed labor if the drop in demand is not clearly permanent. For such firms, the true short-run marginal costs of expanding output may be extremely low. Finally, firms pursuing a pricing strategy oriented toward customer relations may opt to maintain prices and expand output when they perceive a strengthening of demand for goods even though a higher price would increase short-run profits. There are strong grounds for the presumption that in macro equilibrium the output of the price-tag economy is below a social optimum, and that the extra output generated by a strengthening of aggregate demand augments social welfare.

There are even stronger grounds for the presumption that unemployment will be inappropriately high in a labor market that operates through the search process. The social value of search activity lies in improving the match of workers and jobs, thereby increasing productivity. The invisible hand operates effectively when the job seeker rejects an offer and obtains a subsequent one with a higher wage that reflects a higher marginal revenue product in that job. But the individual's incentive to search— its private value—reflects not only the likelihood of finding a more productive job but also of finding a more generous wage offer for a job that is not more productive. The gain to the job seeker from finding an employer who is, for example, especially pessimistic about attracting workers is no net gain to the society. Finally and most significantly, there is a congestion aspect to search that drives a further wedge between its private and social value. By continuing the search for a particularly good job, any person reduces the chances of others in the pool of unemployed of obtaining that job; the cost imposed on them is quite likely to exceed any benefits to employers from the addition to the size of the pool. If the labor market has some amount of buried treasure, each added treasure hunter reduces the expected value of the finds of the others. To take an extreme case, suppose a searcher knew that ten good jobs would become available tomorrow and that nineteen other people would be applying for them. It would be worthwhile for that individual to reject a job offer today in order to join the treasure hunt if the probability of one-half of obtaining that superior job justified the loss of the day's pay. Yet from the point of view of society (and indeed of employers), the pool of job seekers is already redundant.[1]

1. James Tobin develops the congestion argument but notes that it cannot be completely decisive because of externalities on the employer's side. When the employer offers a job to someone who might be even more valuable to another firm, that decision has external effects that operate in reverse. Yet I would argue that if the benefits to that alternative firm stem from using the worker in a more productive job, the pay offer should reflect that and provide the correct incentive to the job seeker who is making the decision. In that case, the costs and benefits are internalized. See Tobin, "Inflation and Unemployment," *American Economic Review,* vol. 62 (March 1972), pp. 1–18.

The optimal properties of macro equilibrium in a competitive auction world and the absence of those properties in a price-tag economy cannot be viewed as a testimonial to the superiority of the auction mechanism. As the analysis in earlier chapters made clear, the distribution of goods (such as eyeglasses) and especially labor through an auction mechanism would be abysmally inefficient. The reliance on search and shopping and on customer and career relations is an efficient adaptation to a world of complex and heterogeneous products and services. A thorough conceptualization of these issues would require the specification of a "transactions function," analogous to the production function, for any economy or any set of goods or services in the economy. The transactions function would specify the resources required for distributing the good or service through hypothetical alternative means of trading. In that perspective, total transactions costs would be viewed, not as components of output, but as a deadweight cost required to convey usable output into the hands of final demanders. The transactions function would specify the various costs that enter into price-tag distribution: search and shopping, managerial systems for determining and communicating prices, and the like. It would also specify the costs of the auction mechanism: stipulating the detailed terms of transactions, grading products, dealing with differences in the subjective evaluation of quality by various demanders, and supplying the services of the auctioneer and traders. These costs should make clear that the optimal properties attributed to the equilibrium in the pure auction world rest on the implicit assumption that all products and services are like wheat and soybeans that can be readily and conveniently traded in auction markets. The price-tag economy is not a reflection of the failure of markets, but of the complexity of goods and services.

Additional important distinctions between price making and auction market clearing emerge when uncertainty and potential surprises in demand are brought into the picture. In the absence of a mechanism to clear markets, the initial impact of any surprise must fall on quantities rather than prices. Disappointingly weak demand entails a lower volume of sales than that expected by sellers, which results in unintended accumulation of inventories and storage costs that cut into social welfare. For perishables and services (especially "unsold labor") that have prohibitive storage costs, the costs are very large. In cases in which fresh fish is tossed into the garbage at the close of business or an airline seat remains empty, that waste represents a full subtraction from the real national product. On the other hand, unexpectedly strong demand may generate frustrated demanders who are unable to obtain goods. Unsold output, unemployed workers, and frustrated demanders are perennial fixtures of the system; their presence cannot be viewed as a disequilibrium that will be ultimately corrected.

When demand and supply have stochastic elements, the resulting phenomena of uncleared markets pose some intriguing puzzles of welfare economics. Some of these issues can be illustrated by a simple example drawn from activity analysis. Consider a newsboy who acquires daily papers at a cost C and gets no refund on unsold papers. The papers are sold at a price P; the daily demand for papers has a probabilistic distribution that is known to the newsboy. To maximize profits, the newsboy will stock enough papers so that the cumulative fraction of the probability distribution of demand will equal C/P. For example, if C is a dime and P is a quarter, the newsboy should operate at the point at which the probability of selling his last newspaper is 0.4. The expected revenue from the sale of the last newspaper (0.4 · 25 cents) precisely matches the cost of 10 cents. From a social point of view, the 60 percent chance that the last newspaper will be unused and discarded cannot be simply interpreted as waste. Rather it represents the cost of making provision for the possible emergence of a demander to whom it will be worth at least 25 cents. In fact, because the reservation price of that potential buyer may exceed 25 cents by an appreciable margin, the social value of making it available must exceed 10 cents. Because the newsboy cannot extract that surplus, the calculations are based on the price of 25 cents. From a welfare point of view, the stock of newspapers is actually inadequate rather than excessive—even accepting the "monopolistic" price of 25 cents.

Now consider a disturbance to the situation whereby a rise in aggregate demand (for example, from a tax reduction) increases the demand for newspapers by one unit a day. Clearly, if the newsboy is aware of the shift in his probabilistic demand curve, he will add one newspaper to his daily order, improving both his income and the welfare of society by providing a newspaper that costs a dime to a buyer for whom it is worth a quarter. In that case, monopolistic restriction is effectively reduced by the increase in demand. Output was undesirably low, and now it is desirably higher.

An interesting possibility emerges if the newsboy fails to recognize the increase in demand immediately and acts on the misperception that the probability distribution of demand is unchanged. During the period in which the shift is not perceived, there will be fewer days of unsold newspapers and more days of frustrated demanders. The social benefits in the reduction of unsold newspapers are obvious. The social costs associated with frustrated demanders require more exploration. Presumably the new customer for a newspaper generated by the tax reduction has a relatively low reservation price, not much above the price tag of 25 cents. But, presumably, frustrated demanders could come from anywhere along the demand curve in the range of reservation prices above 25 cents. If the frustrated demanders are a random sample of all these potential buyers, the social cost of depriving a frustrated demander of a newspaper is the average "surplus" (the average excess of reservation price over actual price). Then, on 40 percent of all days, the tax cut creates a frustrated demander with a loss equal to the average surplus, while 60 percent of the time it supplies a newspaper to a buyer who values the paper at 25 cents. The welfare of society is improved on balance if the average surplus is less than 37.5 cents and worsened otherwise. If this contrived example is taken seriously, the presumption of an improvement in social welfare seems clear. (For a linear demand curve, the intercept would have to exceed a dollar to make average surplus exceed 37.5 cents.)

Of course, the example generated that presumption with a price that far exceeded short-run marginal cost. Suppose instead that the cost of the newspaper was 20 cents with its price remaining 25 cents. In that event, optimization by the newsboy would call for stocking papers at the top of the lowest quintile of the demand distribution. Newspapers would be sold out 80 percent of the time. Under those circumstances a unit rise in demand would rescue a previously wasted newspaper only one-fifth of the time and would create frustrated demanders on four-fifths of all days. In that example an average surplus in excess of 6.25 cents would entail a net loss of social welfare from the unperceived rise in demand.[2]

Even in the original dime-and-quarter example in which price far exceeds marginal cost, successive additions to aggregate demand would ultimately create social losses associated with frustrated demanders that would outweigh the social benefits from the additional papers sold. The story of the newsboy conveys an important lesson: shortages in uncleared markets characterized by excess demand have a social cost. That cost, ap-

2. If the social surplus were evaluated in dollars, the results of the tax cut that raised newspaper demand by one unit would clearly be favorable. An increase in the reservation price of the "old customers" would then be added to the total as a benefit. But that would imply (unreasonably) that the same individual obtains greater utility from a newspaper when after-tax income is increased. In contrast, for a shift in relative demands that favored newspapers, the higher reservation prices would be evidence of increased utility (relative to other consumption items).

propriately weighed against the benefit of increased output, is the one effective short-run ceiling on the socially optimal output, abstracting from inflation. Although one can only guess, I doubt that the U.S. economy has operated at or above that ceiling at anytime since the Second World War. Indeed, in years like 1964 or 1972, when the economy seemed close to a macro equilibrium as judged by its wage and price performance and by standard measures of utilization, the incremental social costs of shortages seemed trivial. Concerns about shortages do become evident when the economy moves into excess demand territory (as in 1966 or 1973), but I would be amazed if the costs associated with them in fact matched the benefits of the increased output.

The effective limitation on the truly optimal output, all things considered, stems from the inflation engendered by excess demand, not from the real costs of factors used in production or from shortages. The trade-off between inflation and unemployment poses a genuine and vexing dilemma. At a time of macro equilibrium, the economy is capable of absorbing additional labor and capital inputs and generating output that is worth more than the costs of the inputs. People with a full perception of the situation are perfectly happy to supply more labor, take jobs sooner, and enter the labor force more readily when additional help-wanted signs reduce the cost and increase the efficiency of job search. Firms are ready to respond to added demands by switching on machines that were previously idle and using labor more fully. But the consequence of stimulating aggregate demand to capture those potential benefits would be inflation.

That dilemma is present even if the long-run Phillips curve is vertical. In such a case, the output and employment bonuses of an excess-demand economy cannot be maintained indefinitely. That does not settle the issue of whether the bonuses over a finite period are greater or less than the ultimate inflationary costs. The warning that the game cannot last forever is not decisive; in principle, it may be worth playing while it lasts. No rational policy can escape the agonizing task of balancing output and employment bonuses with inflation costs. The basic cost of inflation is the impairment of the usefulness of money and the consequent worsening of the economy's transactions function. I have stressed the importance of money previously; I review the costs of inflation in detail in a subsequent section of this chapter. It will become clear that a major difficulty of any analysis or policy strategy aimed at a social optimum stems from the incommensurate character of the benefits of added output and the costs of added inflation.

Social Costs of Recession and Slack

The part of the trade-off that is most readily quantifiable as a social cost measured in dollars is the shortfall of production and employment associated with recession and slack. In a typical U.S. postwar business cycle, such as that depicted in figure 6-1, the recession and recovery generate a trough of output below a prosperity trend line of approximately 12 percent of the real GNP of a single year. In 1979 magnitudes, that amounts to approximately $300 billion. Converting that dollar output loss into a dollar social cost requires a large number of adjustments and corrections. The reduction in working time associated with the recession and slack has a value to the citizenry that is omitted from the measure of real GNP. There is moreover a saving of user costs on capital goods and of depletable natural resources. The elimination of shortages is another benefit. In addition, the cyclical shortfall of output has a variety of favorable and unfavorable effects on the nation's future productive capacity: adverse because of reduced accumulation of both physical and human capital, and beneficial by removing inefficiencies. Finally, there are various distributive aspects of the cycle that are not captured in the measure of real GNP, but that must be reckoned with in any evaluation of social cost.

It is striking that a corrected estimate of social cost does not appear to be significantly smaller than output loss. The real short-run costs of production that are saved by contracting output are very small relative to the value of the output sacrificed. The loss of output is thus a good first approximation in assessing the social costs of recession and slack.

Value of Nonworking Time

The bulge in unemployment during periods of recession and slack is associated with a reduction in time spent working and an increase in time available for seeking other jobs and for the variety of pursuits that may be described as "home activity." The value of that extra time is a partial offset to the losses of output and real income in a depressed economy.

All unemployed persons clearly have the opportunity to search for better jobs than their last positions. If that quest is successful and leads to the acquisition of a job of genuinely higher productivity, it yields a social as well as a private benefit. To that extent, the total social value of search activity is augmented by the increase in the size of the pool of unemployed;

however, it is reduced by the decline in the value per hour of search activity stemming from the prevalence of no-help-wanted signs. The likelihood of improved matches is reduced in a weak labor market. It is impossible to tell which of these effects dominates, but some evidence underlines the magnitude of the reduction in the value of search time. The many dropouts from the labor force in a slack labor market reveal their assessment that the value of search has become so low that it is dominated by exclusive devotion to home activity. Moreover, the unemployed take longer during recession to become reemployed and generally settle for worse jobs, including stopgap jobs in low-paying industries.

Whether the increase in the average duration of a spell of unemployment during recession reflects mainly the increased frequency of no-help-wanted signs (as I argued in chapter 2) or whether it is importantly influenced by misperception of the distribution of wage offers, the verdict that search time is less efficient is on balance identical. That verdict could be upset only by evidence that a significant part of the increase in duration reflects a genuinely wider dispersion of wage offers made by those employers actively hiring during slack periods. In fact, the actual distribution of wages displays more dispersion in a weaker labor market; but the no-help-wanted signs are especially prevalent in high-wage industries and occupations. It is not clear whether the dispersion of wage offers actually obtained by recruits is wider or narrower in a slack labor market. The anecdotal evidence stresses the prevalance of "waiting" rather than searching during a recession as job seekers continue to hope that some wage offer for a good job will be forthcoming. To state the conclusion on this issue cautiously, I see no basis for judging that the aggregate social value of search activity is higher when unemployment is high than when it is low.

In contrast, the value of home activity does offer some significant offset to the real income and output losses of a recession. It is not difficult to estimate the order of magnitude of the loss of after-tax real income from wages and salaries associated with a drop of one percentage point in real GNP. It is frightfully difficult and highly subjective to estimate the fraction by which the value of home activity offsets that loss in real income.

The loss in real employee compensation after taxes can be estimated along the following lines. First, a reduction of real GNP by 1 percentage point is associated cyclically with a decline in labor input of about two-thirds of 1 percentage point, with the remaining one-third reflecting a cyclical decline in productivity (average output per hour worked). Second, because employee compensation amounts to roughly 60 percent oi GNP, a decline in labor input of one percentage point (taken at the national average wage) would reduce employee compensation by 0.6 percentage point of GNP. Third, the marginal tax rate (including federal, state, and local income taxes and payroll taxes levied on employees) can be estimated crudely at 25 percent, leaving 75 percent after tax. The product of these three elements yields the estimate that a reduction of real GNP of 1 percentage point is associated with a loss of real after-tax employee compensation equal to 0.3 percentage point of GNP [(0.667) $\cdot$ (0.6) $\cdot$ (0.75)].

If home activity were fully as valuable as the sacrificed labor income, the appropriate "discount" for its value would thus be 30 percent of the loss of real GNP. But, for several reasons, that would be a gross overestimate. It is reasonable to assume that the disutility of the fortieth hour of work a week for a full-time worker is about equal to the after-tax wage; but the disutility of the first hour of work must be appreciably lower. Moreover, as I pointed out in chapter 3, leisure taken at the initiative of the individual cannot be equated in value with time thrust upon the person as a result of a job loss or a job layoff. In addition, the social stigma and family strains associated with unemployment are a significant deduction from the value of home activity. In his analysis of this issue, Robert Gordon made some reasonable allowances for these factors and concluded that the value of home activity is one-eighth of the loss of real GNP.[3] In effect, he cut by more than half the figure cited above of 30 percent that would apply if the value of home activity equaled that of the lost after-tax wages. I would judge that his estimate is in the right neighborhood.

Effects on Future Productive Capacity

The reduced output associated with recession and recovery tends to decrease the wear and tear on existing capital goods and the extraction of nonrenewable natural resources, such as the products of mining industries. On the other hand, it also reduces the formation of physical and human capital. These aspects need to be taken into account.

In both private and social accounting, depreciation estimates are based on assumptions about the economic lifetimes of assets and generally do not reflect the intensity of use of plant and equipment in the production

3. Robert J. Gordon, "The Welfare Cost of Higher Unemployment," *Brookings Papers on Economic Activity*, 1:1973, pp. 162–63.

of output. In all likelihood, that standard practice of depreciation accounting is a first approximation to reality. The major forces leading to the scrapping of plants, stores, machines, and equipment are obsolescence associated with new technology and aging that has little to do with intensity of utilization. But clearly user costs—the wear and tear associated with the use of capital goods in the productive process—must play some role. It seems reasonable to assign one-third of total depreciation to user costs. Because depreciation on nonresidential fixed capital amounts to approximately 7 percent of GNP, the assignment of one-third of that figure implies that a drop in GNP of one percentage point is associated with an unmeasured, offsetting reduction in user costs of 0.02 percentage point of GNP.

The national accounts record no deduction for depletion, since the value of new discoveries of nonrenewable resources is not measured either. The value of depletion reflected on corporate income statements is substantially less than half of 1 percent of GNP, suggesting that the appropriate correction of social cost for less depletion is trivial.

Another tiny correction that goes in the opposite direction is needed for the cyclical impact on research and development expenditures. These are sharply reduced during recessions. Such cutbacks are not captured as measured declines in real GNP because the outlays are expenses in business accounting and are viewed as an intermediate product in the national accounts. Yet such expenditures clearly do build a stock of knowledge relevant to future productive capabilities of the society.

Outlays by firms on formal training programs for their employees are similarly viewed as expenses; they also are, in fact, reduced during recessions and slack periods, with adverse long-term implications on the stock of knowledge and productive capability. Less obviously but more significantly, the shortfall in employment and slowdown in new hiring reduces the accumulation of experience and of learning by doing and the upward movement of workers into better jobs—losses of human capital that are unmeasurable in any accounting system. On the other side of the ledger, recessions may have a value in jolting inefficient managements and eliminating inefficient employees, as it is often claimed but extremely hard to verify or refute.

The depressing influence of recessions and slack on business fixed investment is reflected in real GNP, but the measurement may not capture the full cost to society. About 20 percent of the cyclical trough of output losses is associated with a shortfall in business expenditures on fixed capital, which is double the average share of such expenditures during prosperity periods. If society is at its optimal margin between consumption and investment, the social cost of the reduction in investment is appropriately measured by the loss of real GNP. But capital formation does have externalities, and these may be only partly compensated by such measures as the investment tax credit (perhaps deliberately undercompensated because tax incentives to investment are regressive in their distributional effects). In that event the loss of capital formation deserves extra weight.

Distributive Costs

Society is concerned about the distribution, as well as the overall magnitude, of the cyclical loss of real income. Programs of unemployment insurance and welfare payments reflect that concern. Because such programs have both administrative and disincentive costs, society does not indemnify the losers in a recession as fully as it might if the transfer were costless, so that the distributive costs must receive extra weight. As Edward Gramlich has shown, the losses of real income associated with recessions and slack are systematically concentrated on particular income and demographic groups.[4] In addition, the haphazard character of job losses and bankruptcies appear as an enforced lottery that detracts from the image of the economic system as reasonable or fair. For good reasons, a lottery that takes 10 percent of real income away from one-tenth of the population is disliked more than a uniform 1 percent loss in real income of the entire population.

Reduction of Shortages

Of the various offsets to the social cost of recessions and slack, the one that I find most difficult to evaluate is the reduction of shortages. A price-tag economy has some shortages even in macro equilibrium. As noted above, these impose social costs to the extent that buyers with relatively low reservation prices obtain products that are unsuccessfully sought by buyers with high reservation prices. Moreover, once the threat of shortages is recognized by buyers, they react in ways that involve costs— ordering further in advance, making commitments that sacrifice flexibility,

4. Edward M. Gramlich, "Macro Policy Responses to Price Shocks," *BPEA*, *1:1979*, pp. 125–66.

and the like. In the labor market, the shortages show up in the form of unfilled vacancies, and the attempts by firms to ensure against them are reflected in hiring ahead of current needs. In the newsboy example, people might awaken earlier to ensure receiving their morning papers. In principle, such adjustments might reduce the social costs of shortages; but they introduce a congestion effect, whereby each person making an effort to avoid being a frustrated demander increases the need for similar costly adjustments by other buyers. In boom periods, many specific shortages last sufficiently long and are perceived clearly enough to induce such behavioral adjustments by buyers. Surely, sellers have even better information. Their decisions to sell at prices that permit prolonged shortages are clear evidence of the inhibitions created by implicit contracts and cannot be attributed to misperception.

Clues to the extent and social costs of shortages are scant. Some information can be gleaned from the time series on orders and backlogs for durable goods manufacture, occasional surveys of job vacancies in manufacturing, reports of purchasing agents, and anecdotes. My own judgmental reading of the evidence is that (apart from energy in the era of the Organization of Petroleum Exporting Countries) shortage phenomena are widespread only in periods of clear overheating of the U.S. economy like 1966 and 1973. A brief list of shortage items appears in years that seem close to macro equilibrium. In years of slack, they do not seem to extend much beyond sellouts for the World Series and for airline flights on Thanksgiving eve. If I were estimating the net social benefit of an excess demand economy, I would make a substantial discount for shortages. But in estimating the net social cost of recessions and slack, I would guess that the offset is only a few percent of the loss in real GNP. But I view this as an area of extreme uncertainty, and I wish I had a better basis for my judgment.

The reduction of shortages is the only element for which the uncertainty about the estimates of offsets is significant. The offset from the value of home activity is appreciable, but seems subject to reasonably satisfactory estimation. Beyond that, user costs of capital, the removal of inefficiencies, the curtailment of growth in human capital and in research and development, and the distributive costs all seem to be of limited significance (as fractions of the forgone GNP). In my view, the adverse influence of the last few items outweighs the offset benefits of the first two. But I do not argue that with conviction. On the whole, I conclude that the net social costs of recessions and slack (apart from alleviation of inflation) are at least 80 percent and may approach 100 percent of the measured loss in real GNP.

Social Costs of Inflation

The preceding conclusion highlights the central proposition that the social cost of inflation is the main reason to avoid strong pressure of aggregate demand—and the only reason for taking a significant risk of recessions or even slack. The efficiency of the transactions mechanism of a price-tag economy depends on some reasonable degree of confidence in the stability of money. Without that confidence, the system could never have progressed beyond the primitive stage of barter. The cost of inflation is the impairment of that confidence and the resulting retrogression toward barter, or the crawl away from money.

I argue that, if one abstracts from variance and predictability, the ideal secular rate of inflation which permits money to accomplish its transactions function must be very low—close to zero. An economy that operates close to that secular optimum is clearly sacrificing a potential bonus of output that it could enjoy for some period of time; in return it obtains a more efficient transactions mechanism for the long run. If the nation should encounter a prolonged recession that makes the secular inflation rate substantially negative, policymakers should aim for a period of excess demand to restore the secular rate to its near-zero optimum and also provide a cyclical bonus of output.

In contrast, if the inflation rate that becomes built into institutions rises far above the secular optimum, the ideal strategy is less obvious. The amount of slack and recession required to restore the optimum secular inflation rate might be more costly, properly discounted, than the permanent acceptance of the new higher rate. Nonetheless, as I argue below, at such a juncture the system must be only partially adapted to a new and higher secular rate; and a policy strategy of letting the economy adapt to that rate would impose significant transitional costs. Indeed, in response to such a strategy, private decisionmakers are bound to be uncertain about the magnitude of the secular inflation rate that ultimately emerges. In particular, when the political process reveals a willingness to tolerate excess inflation, individual decisionmakers may rightly be skeptical about the determination to limit the excess to any specific amount. Uncertainty about the secular rate is bound to increase, and that uncertainty imposes social costs. In short, when demand management is conducted with a reasonable degree of sophistication, policymakers do not, and should not, accept secular deflation. But, on rational grounds, policymakers may be tempted to accept secular inflation. The recognition of that asymmetry imparts an inflationary bias to the economy.

The serious problems of social welfare apply to the *secular* rate of inflation. Cyclical variations in the inflation rate around the secular rate carry less weight. Indeed, in a broader sense, they are automatic stabilizers that reduce the cyclical variation of output and employment in a price-tag economy. Yet the cyclical variations are essentially unpredictable; they are the unanticipated inflation that is often claimed to be especially costly. More generally, in the framework of this analysis, the distinction between high-cost, unanticipated inflation and low-cost, anticipated inflation does not emerge. In the auction world, the minor annoyances of extra trips to the bank are the only costs of anticipated inflation; in a price-tag world, output, employment, and real incomes are affected even when inflation is not a surprise. I discuss these conclusions below in detail.

The Ideal Secular Rate

In a price-tag economy with a given variance of inflation and a given average level and cyclical pattern of resource utilization over time, would any particular secular rate of inflation be ideal? Clearly the information and scorekeeping functions of money would work best with no change in prices. In that event, nominal price tags would provide clear information about changes in relative prices. No buyer or seller would be confused about the implication for relative prices of any change in a price tag. A stable price level permits maximum reliance on historical cost calculations. It also permits intertemporal comparison shopping without adjustments for upward or downward trends. In that world, if I know what I paid for something previously, I do not need to make a logarithmic adjustment for the time elapsed since my last purchase. In short, I can stock in my memory bank the information on *what* I paid, without the information on *when* I paid it.

Even with a horizontal trend to the overall price level, some products and factors will have prices with positive or negative growth trends. In particular, the growth trend of wages will be positive, and the annoying logarithmic adjustment becomes necessary to interpret any observation relative to the norm or to past experience.

To the extent that the implicit contracts and the search process in the labor market are especially important, there may be a case for a horizontal wage trend (and a corresponding negative trend in prices). That was approximated by the actual experience of the United States in the last thirty years of the nineteenth century: apparently workers reaped the benefits of productivity growth mainly from declines in the cost of living rather than increases in nominal wages. I see two reasons to prefer the horizontal price trend to the horizontal wage trend. First, a decision to shift from a horizontal price trend (and rising wages) to a declining price trend (and horizontal wages) would sacrifice some output for a period of time. If these two trends are about equally satisfactory in terms of transactions efficiency, that cost—although transitory—may be decisive. Second, the constraints of a floor on wages and on interest rates make the horizontal price trend preferable. If wages have a horizontal trend, changes in relative wages require many workers to accept falling wages (while other wages rise). The Keynesian wage floor cannot be permitted to develop as an institutional norm in such a world. That deprives society of a benchmark for implicit contracts in the labor market; a floor on changes in nominal wages is useful, and zero is uniquely qualified. That is one advantage of a modest upward trend in wage rates.

The zero floor on the interest rate presumably applies whether the trend of prices is horizontal or downward. But money bears a positive real return when the price level has a downward trend. That return may make money too "good" an asset relative to real capital, impairing social welfare in the long run. The problem of weak incentives for investment may be obviated if the rate of interest is kept close to zero. The flexibility and potency of monetary policy to exert a stimulative influence is especially limited by the zero floor on the interest rate (whether or not liquidity preference sets a higher floor) in a world of a downward price trend.

Concern about the floor on the interest rate generates the argument made by some economists that the ideal secular inflation rate is positive. William Vickrey developed that argument in detail.[5] Monetary policy has more leverage to combat slumps (and no less leverage to combat booms), the higher interest rates are in periods of macro equilibrium. These rates are bound to be higher with a positive inflation rate. Sumner Slichter sounded a related theme when he emphasized that incentives to invest were likely to be bolstered by the higher nominal return to capital (and

5. William S. Vickrey, "Stability Through Inflation," in Kenneth K. Kurihara, ed., *Post-Keynesian Economics* (Rutgers University Press, 1954), pp. 89–122.

higher return relative to that on money) in a world of secularly rising prices.[6]

Another argument for the desirability of a positive secular rate of inflation, which is grounded in public finance analysis, was developed by Edmund Phelps.[7] His point is that no form of taxation is costless and that *some* resort to inflation as a means of financing public services is likely to be optimal. I doubt that such a consideration would have quantitatively important implications in peacetime.

It seems likely that the behavior of prices and wages during the late fifties and mid-sixties in the United States was close to a secular optimum. Wages rose slightly more rapidly than productivity; the prices of *goods* had a nearly horizontal trend; and the prices of those *services* that were labor intensive (and subject to only slow productivity growth) displayed an upward trend. The overall upward trend in prices was between 1 and 2 percent a year, and that in annual labor compensation around 4 percent. I do not believe that a case can be made that 6 percent or 8 percent inflation is inherently better or even as good as that earlier performance. If the 6 percent or 8 percent norm could be established as a secular average with the same year-to-year variability, it might not be drastically inferior but it would be somewhat inferior.

Transition to Lower Rates of Inflation

The simple inequality between the rates of increase in prices and wages has important implications for decisions on whether to roll back or to accept an upward shift in the secular inflation rate once it has occurred. The results are quite different from those of an auction world in which inflation can easily be correctly anticipated and imposes only the costs of extra trips to the bank.

When a price-tag economy has experienced a modest secular rate of inflation, its institutions become adapted to that rate. Experience teaches decisionmakers how much they can and should rely on a nominal yard-

6. See Sumner H. Slichter, "Argument for 'Creeping' Inflation," *New York Times Magazine,* March 8, 1959. The case for secular inflation is somewhat analogous to the "stamped money" proposal of Gesell that Keynes discussed; see John Maynard Keynes, *The General Theory of Employment, Interest, and Money* (Harcourt, Brace, 1936), pp. 357–58. Could Keynes have failed to recognize secular inflation as an alternative way to "stamp" money (and indeed all nominal assets)?

7. Edmund S. Phelps, "Inflation in the Theory of Public Finance," *Swedish Journal of Economics,* vol. 75 (March 1973), pp. 67–82.

stick in price-making and wage-making institutions. Through its norm for wage increases, its bases for calculating costs and applying markups, and the other patterns of behavior discussed in earlier chapters, the society develops a "habitual" rate of inflation, as George Perry has characterized it. In any long-run equilibrium, that habitual rate, the actual secular rate, and the expected secular rate that would be predicted by informed observers must converge.

Suppose that the society encounters a prolonged period of unusually rapid inflation, either because of an extraordinary expansion of aggregate demand or because of repeated adverse supply shocks. As I suggested in chapter 6, that inflationary experience is likely to be interpreted initially by most decisionmakers as transitory. But gradually they will begin to suspect that the secular rate of inflation has risen. These revised expectations will influence auction markets, like those for foreign exchange, bonds, and metals, where the longer-term outlook is highly relevant. But it will take much longer for the habitual rate of inflation that is built into customer and career institutions to adjust upward. The sluggishness of the habitual rate will hold down the actual rate of inflation, although the habitual rate will move up to match the new perceived or expected secular rate. The economy will experience a period of accelerating inflation for any constant set of utilization rates and supply circumstances. That acceleration cannot be ended simply by the elimination of the excess demand or of the supply shock that started the process; it takes on a momentum of its own.

On the other hand, the acceleration will reach a limit; there is likely to be some higher inflation rate at which the habitual rate once again matches the perceived or expected secular rate. That process of transition to a higher secular rate must be costly and subject to uncertainty. Relative prices and incomes must be affected, a reflection of the degree of attachment of various prices and wages to the dollar through implicit and explicit contracts, as I have argued throughout this book. During that transition period, the inflation is likely to be more variable from year to year and from product to product. The shift from a secular inflation rate of, say, 2 percent to 6 percent must raise the variance as perceived by an informed observer, who must recognize the uncertainty about where and when the adaptive process will end.

Once the adaptive process is under way, there are also substantial costs to any strategy of rolling back secular inflation to its earlier rate. Disinflating the economy must also distort relative prices and relative incomes.

Moreover, if the inflation strategy relies solely on demand restraint, it is likely to impose large social costs from recession and prolonged slack. It is entirely conceivable that it may be less costly to accept the higher secular inflation rate on a permanent basis than to pursue a strategy to roll it back. But any acceptance by public policy of that higher secular inflation is clearly an acceptance of the second best over the long run.

The probable reaction to such a decision must be gauged against the general considerations affecting the choice of a secular inflation rate. As I have argued in the preceding sections of this chapter, that choice is always governed by the trade-off of long-run social benefits associated with the transactions efficiencies of lower inflation against the short-term benefits available from higher output and employment. Whenever short-run and long-run considerations conflict, the brief intervals between election days in any democracy may push social discounting in a myopic direction. That problem extends far beyond macroeconomic issues; environmentalists insist that the long-run risks of cancer from pollution and radiation receive an inadequate weight, while national defense enthusiasts contend that the long-run importance of military preparedness is slighted. Indeed, the difficulties of balancing the long run and short run extend to private decisionmaking free of any election day myopia. Individuals find it difficult to put appropriate weights on the dangers of becoming overweight, addicted to alcohol, dependent on borrowing, and the like; many people sense within themselves an irrational tendency to overeat, overdrink, and overspend. Similar considerations create the suspicion of a propensity to overinflate.

There is, moreover, a qualitative difference between the policy actions required to roll back inflation and those required to accept a higher secular rate of inflation. The rollback strategy requires measures that are inherently unpleasant in the short run—whether they take the form of tax increases, cutbacks in public expenditure programs, tighter money, or wage-price restraints. The acceptance of a higher inflation rate avoids these unpleasant alternatives. To an extent, that may be a valid reflection of the point made by Phelps that a little bit of inflationary public finance may be efficient, all things considered. But it may be appealing merely as the easy way out even though it is not socially optimal.

For these reasons, informed private observers are likely to suspect that the resort to a long-run acceptance of a higher secular inflation rate is merely a prelude to the subsequent resort to the third best and then fourth best. Those suspicions must become particularly acute once they begin to be confirmed; and they have been confirmed in the United States, as the nation moved from the implicit acceptance of $1\frac{1}{2}$ percent inflation in the early sixties to 3 percent in the early seventies to 6 percent in the latter seventies. If the president in 1981 were to assure the country that he was utterly determined to stabilize inflation at 8 percent, why would any sensible person believe with any confidence that this assertion marked the final turn of the rachet? Surely, uncertainty would be enhanced and the crawl away from money would be strongly encouraged.

Reasoning along these lines in 1971, I argued that steady inflation at an appreciable rate was a mirage.[8] Events since then have confirmed that conviction. It may well be true that a society should not sacrifice much to achieve a secular inflation rate of 2 percent rather than 6 percent, if it can be fully adjusted to either. But any experience of moving from 2 percent to 6 percent must increase variability and uncertainty and impose heavy social costs.

That general conclusion becomes even clearer in considering the similarities and differences following from a disturbance that pushes the secular inflation rate in a downward direction. Suppose that the inflation rate became negative because of either a repeated supply shock that lowered prices and costs or a prolonged period of weak aggregate demand. Suppose also that the secular inflation rate threatened to be lower than the range consistent with optimal transactions efficiency. In that case, fiscal-monetary management has no dilemma. A stimulative policy that creates some period of excess demand can provide the corrective to bring the secular rate back into the efficient range and also confer a short-run bonus of output and employment. No modern government capable of influencing aggregate demand will live with a negative trend of prices. Such a trend could and did emerge a century ago when policymakers did not have the knowledge or the tools to correct it. But it could not happen today.

Most important, people realize that a negative trend of prices cannot happen in contemporary economic life. The implausibility of secular deflation is a tribute to the recognized effectiveness of Keynesian demand management in avoiding depression. Yet it introduces a bias in the impact of any strategy of demand stabilization, even when it is conducted symmetrically with respect to excess demand and excess supply. In my judgment, the U.S. economy over the past generation has operated in excess-supply territory as much as, or more than, in excess-demand territory:

8. Arthur M. Okun, "The Mirage of Steady Inflation," *BPEA, 2:1971*, pp. 485–98.

clear episodes of excess supply in 1958–63 and 1975–77 easily balance opposite cases in 1966–69 and 1972–73. Yet the recognition of a significant upside risk—and virtually no downside risk—on the secular inflation rate has imparted an inflationary bias to the system. That recognition may help to explain why the inflation rate does not become negative (or even zero) in periods of prolonged slack like 1958–63.

An analogy with dieting comes to mind. A man who becomes underweight during an illness is likely to eat more when he recovers and to regain the weight. What is good for his health in the long run is enjoyable in the short run. But if, instead, he becomes overweight, say, as a result of overindulgence or carelessness, the subsequent requirement to shed the excess poundage for long-run health imposes pain in the short run. The asymmetry produces good reasons to believe that the man is more likely to adjust to overweight than to underweight.

Cyclical Fluctuation in Inflation

Thus far I have focused on the social costs of the *secular* inflation rate. Cyclical fluctuations around that secular average must also be considered, but they pose quite distinct issues. In earlier chapters, I discussed the incentives to increase the predictability of prices and costs and to improve the viability of implicit contracts and the ways in which these incentives lead to arrangements that reduce the responsiveness of prices and wages to cyclical fluctuations in aggregate demand. These considerations operate with different force in different areas and lead to different amounts of smoothing; the result is a systematic cyclical pattern of relative wages and relative prices that does not necessarily reflect the intensity of cyclical fluctuations in the demand for those products and factors. Cyclical fluctuations in the inflation rate introduce an enforced lottery and haphazard redistribution of income and wealth similar to those emerging from a shift in the secular inflation rate. These detract from transactions efficiency and impose social costs.

In the cyclical case, however, there is a presumption that the price and wage fluctuations stabilize output and employment. If, as a first approximation, the time path of nominal GNP is taken as given in light of fiscal and monetary actions and shifts in private propensities to spend, output and employment fluctuate less to the extent that prices and wages fluctuate more in a procyclical manner. In the terms I have used, the split of the deviation in nominal GNP from its trend path then has a smaller component of variation in quantities (and a correspondingly larger component of variation in prices). To put it still another way, cyclical fluctuations in the inflation rate around the secular average are an automatic stabilizer of output and employment. The weaker these cyclical responses in the inflation rate are, the more fiscal and monetary policies are called upon to provide the stabilization.

When customers and suppliers or workers and employers opt for arrangements that tend to smooth the behavior of wages and prices, they calculate the resulting costs to themselves of accepting wider fluctuations in output and employment. They have no reason to take into account the external or "multiplier" effects of those decisions on others in the economy. Even though I have argued that these arrangements are sensible and basically promote efficiency, the externalities make me doubt that they are necessarily ideal. Alternative standards of fairness that could maintain the viability of implicit contracts deserve exploration. The contrast between the Japanese and American labor markets provides an illustration of different arrangements with different implications for wages and employment variability over the cycle. The welfare economics of such differing institutions is a challenging area that I hope will be explored by other economic researchers.

The Information System in a Price-Tag Economy

The analysis of the social costs of inflation presented here does not emphasize the distinction between anticipated and unanticipated inflation, which is the centerpiece of the analysis for an auction world. The nonneutrality of inflation stressed throughout this book applies even to inflation that is anticipated over a short-term and medium-term horizon.

In a price-tag economy, economizing on search and shopping costs is important, and is achieved through establishing customer-supplier and worker-employer relations. For the reasons discussed above, these relations rest heavily on implicit contracts, which are enforced merely by the threat by either party that continuing mutually beneficial transactions may be terminated. The viability of the implicit contract (as well as the enforceability of the explicit contract) depends on each party's knowing what to expect from the other as fair play. However specific or fuzzy those standards may be, they are generally denominated in terms of dollars. They give the majority of income recipients reasonable predictability over their *nominal* incomes for a considerable period, but that predictability of nominal income entails variability of *real* income. The vast majority of wage earners obtain most of their income from career jobs, and they are likely to suffer a loss of real income for a substantial period following an acceleration of inflation. The loss is mitigated but not eliminated for those with wages protected by formal cost-of-living escalators. That escalation is generally partial and is invariably lagged, so accelerated inflation still has some adverse effect on real income. The mean change in real income across the nation may be zero or even positive; but the median change is very likely to be negative. The median matters when opinion polls or election polls are taken. It should be no surprise that, even during 1976 and 1977 when inflation was quite stable at about 6 percent and was well predicted by professional forecasters, it was ranked as public enemy number one by the American citizenry.

The use of nominal magnitudes in a price-tag economy creates transactions costs and information costs of inflation that are not measured in the national income. The dollar is the basic yardstick for planning and scorekeeping. It is the underpinning of cost and financial accounting; it is the heart of the budgeting process for firms and households; it is the measuring rod of economic performance. The nation's investment in the dollar as a meaningful yardstick is a reality, not "money illusion." It is analogous to our investment in the English language. When my friends and colleagues want a chat, they are expressing a desire for a talk and not for a feline pet. Neither the speaker nor the listener is guilty of "English illusion."

It is as much a matter of training and habit to think in dollars as to think in English. People are not taught to store the consumer price index in their memory banks. I once witnessed a group of economists at lunch trying to determine whether academic salaries had risen or fallen in real terms over the past decade. The participants recalled clearly the relevant salary scales from the beginning of their careers. But they did not remember clearly the path of the consumer price index during that period. They needed their data tables to determine how well they had fared in real terms. Most significantly, none of them had found it worthwhile to answer the question before that conversation at lunch.

The language of real units is much more foreign to the general public than to economists. The perception of the typical citizen about the severity of inflation is probably based more on experiences at the supermarket and the gasoline station than on readings of the official indexes. Unless one has a remarkable memory of what prices one paid at what point in time in the past, shopping experiences cannot be readily converted into a numerical estimate of inflation. In a period of 1 percent inflation, people who received pay increases of 4 percent must have recognized clearly that they gained in real terms. In a world of 13 percent inflation of consumer prices, those fortunate enough to receive pay increases of 16 percent are likely to be much less confident about how they are faring and whether they can afford to raise their standard of living. That loss of information is a genuine subtraction from welfare.

Economists who rely on a model of universal auction markets stress an alternative source of the public's dislike of inflation. They argue that most Americans perceive inflation in the form of the higher prices they must pay but do not recognize its contribution to raising nominal income. In effect, people view inflation merely as a purse snatcher or pickpocket because they give it no credit for enlarging their pay increases. Those economists then offer a diagnosis of money illusion and prescribe, as a remedy, an education in thinking in real units.

Any social scientist who alleges that the public is so naive is obliged to explain how that one-sided perception of inflation can arise. This obligation applies with special force to economists who assume, in other contexts, that the typical household is able (and finds it worthwhile) to solve complicated decision problems allocating lifetime income, and to estimate the impact of public debt and deficits on its future tax bills. There may well be some truth in the conjecture that the effects of inflation on receipts and expenditures are perceived asymmetrically by households. But in fact, as I have stressed repeatedly, many households are affected' asymmetrically for significant periods because their incomes do not respond strongly or rapidly to the price level. Like the genuine asymmetry, the alleged misperception asymmetry rests on the dependence of decisions, planning, and scorekeeping on the nominal unit. In particular cases, I doubt that the genuine and the misperception asymmetries can be sharply distinguished, and I do not see much point in attempting to distinguish them. Let me offer a specific example, drawn from a television interview program asking people about their feelings about inflation. One federal executive employee reported that her current income of $28,000 exceeded any hopes she had had at the start of her career, and yet it left her frustrated because she could not afford the living standard that such an income was supposed to provide. Clearly, her comments revealed that she had been thinking in monetary terms. Can anyone fault her for formulating her income expectations and aspirations in nominal terms? Because money incomes today are high relative to aspirations and expectations formed in the past, people who are disappointed about their real incomes naturally and reasonably blame the adversity on an excessive rate of increase in prices rather than an inadequate rate of increase in pay.

The nominal standard has been a habit and a valuable habit in our society. But I do not rest my case on the value—nominal or real—of perpetuating good old habits. There is a genuine issue whether, transition costs apart, education and adaptation could convert implicit and explicit contracts, planning, and scorekeeping into real units. Can the economy escape from its dependence on the dollar and from the costs of inflation that follow from that dependence? That raises the issue of generalized indexing of wages and prices, to which I now turn.

Indexing: Cure or Disease?

If people did learn a new language of real units, could it serve as the equivalent of an economic metric system and solve some of our problems? The attractions of such a new world are powerful and clear. If instability in the value of money could be reduced by shifting the system to one based on a real unit, the difficult task of stabilizing the value of money could be finessed. If the real unit became the standard for explicit and implicit contracts, for cost and financial accounting, and for planning and scorekeeping, fluctuations in the value of the nominal unit might well become unimportant. Workers could evaluate their current jobs by the path of real rather than nominal wages; customers would count on suppliers stabilizing the relative prices of their products (as compared to the general price level) rather than on stabilizing dollar price tags. Interest rates on bonds and mortgages, depreciation allowances, and life insurance policies geared to the real unit might be freed of the distortions of inflation.

Indeed, much can be said in favor of a real-unit standard; and only one thing can be said against it: as I show below, it is an impossible dream. I also demonstrate that the same decisive objection applies to an economy that is fully and promptly indexed to the general price level, which is the equivalent of a real-unit system. I argue furthermore that partial indexing, while feasible, approaches impossibility through instability. The only escape from a monetary economy is retrogression to barter; the challenge to stabilize the value of money must be recognized and accepted.

The Impossibility of a Fully Indexed Economy

Why is it impossible to substitute a real unit or "reallar" for the dollar? Imagine trying to do so in a simple Walrasian world of frictionless auction markets. Suppose that there are only two physical goods (say, oranges and balls) and that they are traded in exchange markets while no production takes place. Markets clear at prices for which the demands for oranges and balls are equal to the fixed supplies of each of the goods. Prices of the two goods are quoted in reallars (the new currency) rather than dollars. There is demand for, and a supply of, reallars, and the market for reallars must also clear. In fact, by a well-known property of Walrasian systems, that market will clear whenever the other two markets clear: the excess supply of reallars is simply the mirror image of the excess demands in the other markets. An excess demand for both oranges and balls entails an excess supply of reallars, for example. The reallar market does not supply an independent third equation for the system to determine the three prices—of balls (P_B), oranges (P_O), and reallars (P_R). That third equation emerges from the designation of the reallar as a numeraire with a price of unity—equivalent to defining both the price of an orange and the price of a ball as relative prices measured in terms of the reallar. There are three equations, which are normally adequate to solve for the three prices:

$$D_O(P_O, P_B, P_R) = S_O$$

$$D_B(P_O, P_B, P_R) = S_B$$

$$P_R = 1.$$

However, the reallar has another important property that must be taken into account. As a real unit, the reallar represents a claim on some market basket of oranges and balls. That means that the unit price of the reallar must equal a weighted sum of the price of an orange and the price of a ball: $1 = \lambda_O P_O + \lambda_B P_B$. To keep things simple, suppose that oranges and balls are of equal economic importance and that a reallar is intended to be a unit of purchasing power over the market basket of one orange plus one ball ($\lambda_O = \lambda_B = 1$). Then the fourth equation that has intruded into the system is: $1 = P_O + P_B$.

The fourth equation destroys the determinacy of the system: in general, no set of values of the three variables will satisfy the four equations. It is easy to see the behavioral significance of that mathematical difficulty.

Business is transacted in the orange market and the ball market, and a pair of equilibrium prices is determined. If, by chance, those market prices add up to unity, all four equations are satisfied. But the two prices can readily sum to 0.90 or 1.2. In that event, the fourth equation is violated. The real unit has been altered in purchasing power, contrary to its definitional characteristics. It turns out to be merely another money subject to appreciation or depreciation in real value just like the dollar it replaced.

To consider how such a system might be made viable, imagine that the government authority responsible for issuing reallars stood ready to *buy* or *sell* a market basket consisting of one orange and one ball for one reallar. Then the reallar would be a commodity reserve currency backed by genuine market baskets. In terms of the Walrasian equation, the stock of reallars would be a variable that expanded or contracted to meet private demands so as to ensure that the fourth equation was satisfied. But it takes some major further innovation, like this hypothetical conversion facility, to provide any verisimilitude for the real-unit system. Put in reverse, the discussion above points to the role that the money equation plays in a Walrasian system: it permits other prices to be set independently.[9]

The same impossibility theorem applies to a price-tag economy governed by universal and instantaneous indexing, because that is precisely equivalent to a real-unit system. Suppose that the sellers of oranges and of balls independently set prices for their respective products in terms of a real unit. Again, only by a wonderful coincidence will P_O and P_B sum to unity so that the reallar can command the defined basket consisting of one ball and one orange.

The problem is no different if instead sellers quote prices in dollars but seek to maintain indexed or real prices by monitoring each other's prices. At a time when $P_O = P_B = 50$ cents, suppose that orange sellers perceive a rise in demand and raise P_O to 60 cents. Ball sellers recognize then that their price of 50 cents now represents only $5/11$ rather than $1/2$ of the standard market basket. If they do not accept the decline in the "real price" of balls and act promptly to raise their dollar price tag, they may start a chase that has no endpoint. Again, only if orange sellers and ball sellers independently accept a compatible set of real prices—reflecting a wonderful coincidence—will there be a determinate set of prices.

9. Actually, the algebra can be handled by allowing any commodity to serve as the numeraire and viewing all other prices as set in terms of that numeraire. Obviously, it is convenient to follow the practice of the marketplace and choose money as the numeraire.

These points are straightforward and traditional. I dwell on them here because they seem to be unrecognized in some writings. Economists who are familiar with these principles and thoroughly capable of counting equations and variables nonetheless present "illustrative" models of the operation of a real-unit or fully indexed economy. As I see it, this is as much of a contradiction in terms as discussing "illustratively" the area of a square circle.

Of course, the impossibility theorems apply solely to cases of instantaneous and universal indexing. The fact that the real-unit or indexing system cannot work in a pure or logically extreme form does not necessarily prove that it would be unfeasible or undesirable in diluted form. For example, the introduction of any lag in the indexing of orange prices and ball prices in the dollar price-tag economy permits determinacy. The system does not explode if the ball sellers adjust to the actions of the orange sellers with a lag of five minutes, but that degree of dynamic instability is so close to explosiveness that it may be indistinguishable in practice. Nor does the basic problem of the need to agree on real prices vanish, even when the lag is appreciable.

Consider a case in which orange sellers set new prices each Monday. Meanwhile, ball sellers change their price tags only on Friday, but also stipulate an indexing provision whereby the price of balls on Tuesday, Wednesday, and Thursday reflects proportionately any change in the orange price posted on Monday. Suppose that the system has been operating in equilibrium with $P_O = P_B = 50$ cents. Over the weekend orange sellers correctly perceive an increase in demand that calls for a higher price of 60 cents. On Tuesday the indexing formula pushes the price of balls to 60 cents, thereby matching the price of oranges.

The consequences of that indexing must be evaluated in light of the source of the disturbance that raised the price of oranges. The indexing is constructive when the initial disturbance is a general decline in the demand for money or an unwanted increase in the supply of money that calls for no relative price adjustment between oranges and balls. Suppose the shadow equilibrium is $P_O = P_B = 60$ cents. The indexing then promptly corrects the inappropriate shift in relative prices that occurs merely because oranges are priced on Monday and balls on Friday. Suppose, however, that the rise in the demand for oranges was a relative shift associated with a decline in the demand for balls, and that a new equilibrium could have been established with P_O at 60 cents and P_B at 40 cents. Then clearly the indexing is perverse and enlarges the disequilibria of quantities on Tuesday, Wednesday, and Thursday. The same adverse effects apply if the initial disturbance was a shift toward oranges away from money, where the new "shadow" equilibrium would have had P_O at 60 cents and P_B at 50 cents. Indexing resists changes in relative prices, and it is constructive when the changes are inappropriate. The purely monetary disturbance that raises demands for both commodities equally and calls for no relative price adjustment is an example of the wonderful coincidence in which sellers agree on relative prices. Both groups are, in effect, ready to swap balls for oranges, one for one. The indexing imposes that barter arrangement, in effect, as a substitute for monetary arrangements.

Indexing in a More Realistic Model

This parable from the simple hypothetical economy has clear implications for the more realistic world that was outlined in chapter 6. To begin the translation into the more realistic model, suppose that oranges are the prototype auction good, while balls are a customer good. Both are produced as well as exchanged. The price of balls does not adjust to clear the ball market; that is the source of the cycle in output and employment in this world and also the reason why inflation is a real and nonneutral process.

Suppose that initially the system enjoys an equilibrium state with constant output and constant prices of both auction and customer products. A disturbance occurs and the deviations from the equilibrium path are linked by the following equation: $y = a (p_A + q_A) + (1 - a) (p_C + q_C)$, where p_A and q_A are rates of change in prices and quantities in an auction goods sector, p_C and q_C are rates of change in prices and quantities in a customer goods sector, and a is the weight of the auction sector $(0 < a < 1)$. If the source of that disturbance is a shift upward in aggregate demand, as reflected in y, the system could be equilibrated with no change in quantities and with both prices moving up in proportion: $p_A = p_C = y$; $q_A = q_C = 0$. The normal cyclical problem analyzed throughout this book arises because customer prices are not fully responsive and hence customer output must vary. But if the customer price is indexed to the auction price, the equilibrium with no quantity adjustments is clearly facilitated.[10]

For any other type of disturbance that requires a change in relative prices, however, indexing renders equilibration impossible. If there is a

10. If p_C equals p_A, $y = p_A + a q_A + (1 - a) q_C$.

shift in the relative demands for the two goods, or a change in supply conditions for either product, a change in relative prices is needed and cannot occur. The system, in effect, has only one price when it needs two.

For example, a poor crop, which pushes up the auction price, necessarily also pushes up the customer price and forces a contraction of customer goods output. For such an auction supply shock, the "shadow" equilibrium is $p_A = -q_A$; $p_C = q_C = y = 0$ on the convenient but highly unrealistic assumptions of unitary price and income elasticities for auction goods. Under those circumstances, any indexing of customer prices following supply shocks in the auction area is perverse (because the price of the customer good should not change at all). For that case, the optimal amount of indexing is precisely zero. It actually becomes negative on the more realistic assumption that the price elasticity of demand for the auction goods, e, is less than unity in absolute value. Then the poor crop increases the total expenditures on auction goods: $p_A + q_A = [1 - (1/e)]\bar{q}_A$, where $\bar{q}_A$ would be negative for the poor crop. A decline in the customer price is then required to maintain customer output, given nominal income. That is, to allow $y = q_C = 0$, p_C must be

$$\frac{-a\bar{q}_A}{1 - a}\left[1 - \left(\frac{1}{e}\right)\right].$$

The indexing of customer prices in this discussion stands as a proxy for the indexing of wages. Customer prices are the product of wage costs and a markup ratio, and indexed wages produce indexed prices insofar as the markup ratio is stable and applied with no appreciable lag. Clearly, indexing of wages to consumer prices converts an adverse supply shock in oil or grain into a depressant of output and employment in the customer goods sector. Wage indexing also has severe adverse consequences when the source of the disturbance is an autonomous change in the wage level itself or in the markup ratio. With indexing, such initial shifts in the price and cost structure magnify the downward pressure on output and employment. There are further cases in which optimal indexing is negative. For example, if markups widen, customer goods output can be maintained at a given nominal income only if nominal wages decline. Conversely, if wages make an autonomous jump, markups must be squeezed in order to maintain customer output at given nominal income. The deviation of the customer price from equilibrium is $dw + dm$, where dw is the wage deviation and dm the markup deviation. If p_C is to equal zero, dm must equal $-dw$. The problems of some European countries in the seventies, as described by some observers, are related to the complications of essentially complete wage indexing following an initial wage push. That would be the translation into the terms of this model of the structural thesis about excessive real wages developed by Herbert Giersch and elaborated by Jeffrey Sachs.[11]

In short, indexing contributes to social welfare only when the disturbance is a shift in aggregate demand that should not change relative prices or quantities. Any other disturbance, which should alter relative prices, is translated by indexing into greater instability of both the price level and output. The case of oil prices is the most egregious example of indexing that works contrary to social welfare, but it is far from the only case. Most of the disturbances of the real world apply to relative demands and relative supplies, although disturbances in aggregate demand are clearly of major importance. Given the mix of disturbances, it is not clear whether the optimum amount of wage indexing would be positive or negative, and it is quite unlikely to be significantly positive.[12]

Indexing of wages is sometimes also recommended as a way to improve equity. That argument recognizes the point, stressed repeatedly here, that the effects of inflation on the real income of various groups depend in an arbitrary and haphazard way on the extent to which their nominal incomes are tied to the dollar. If nominal standards in implicit and explicit contracts were converted into real standards, the haphazard nominal element should be reduced. But that line of reasoning ignores the fact that, if additional workers are granted indexed wages, the prices of the goods they produce will respond much more to any acceleration or deceleration of consumer prices. As a result, the disturbances in real incomes for the workers who are not indexed will be magnified. Everybody who obtains

11. See Herbert Giersch, "Aspects of Growth, Structural Change and Employment—A Schumpeterian Perspective," *Weltwirtschaftliches Archiv,* vol. 115, no. 4 (1979), pp. 629–52; and Jeffrey D. Sachs, "Wages, Profits and Macroeconomic Adjustment: A Comparative Study," *BPEA, 2:1979,* pp. 269–319.

12. In her incisive analysis of this issue, on which I draw heavily, Jo Anna Gray develops a model in which the optimal amount of indexing must be positive (although clearly less than complete). See her "On Indexation and Contract Length," *Journal of Political Economy,* vol. 86 (February 1978), pp. 1–18, and "Wage Indexation: A Macroeconomic Approach," *Journal of Monetary Economics,* vol. 2 (April 1976), pp. 211–35. Gray's results differ from mine because she considers only aggregate demand shocks and productivity shocks. There is no room in her model for supply shocks in the auction sector or autonomous wage and profit pushes, for all of which the optimum indexing would be *negative.* An obvious, but quite unimportant, additional source of different results is that she assumes the elasticity of labor supply is positive while I take it to be zero.

the insurance policy of keeping up with the cost of living creates added price-level risk for those who remain uninsured. If customer prices follow wages with a short lag, it is not clear whether the distributional consequences from extending the scope of indexing will on balance be favorable or unfavorable. Even indexing that applies to all earners of labor income has an ambiguous result, given the added price-level risk imposed on recipients of property income. Indexing creates a hot potato that can be shifted from one group to another but cannot be cooled off. That is the dynamic counterpart of the impossibility theorem. Indexing that applies to all forms of income and balance-sheet items runs into the static impossibility theorem with which this section began.

VIII

Policies to Combat Inflation and Unemployment

BECAUSE indexing offers no escape from the inflation problem, public policy must face the challenge of stabilizing the value of money and the conflicts between stable prices and maximum production. I address this question in this final chapter. I first consider the scope and limitations of fiscal and monetary instruments for resolving the price-quantity dilemmas. I then suggest other instruments—various types of cost-reducing actions and incomes policies—that would help reconcile the price and employment objectives.

Strategic Issues of Demand Management

To set the stage for the discussion of fiscal and monetary strategies, I summarize and formalize some of the earlier analysis concerning the social loss function, the short-run Phillips curve, and the Phillips-curve adaptation or shift function, which define the objectives of and constraints on demand management.

The Social Loss Function

Society is made worse off by (1) a greater deviation of the unemployment rate, U, from the rate associated with critical shortages, U_s; (2) a higher level of the adapted (or norm or habitual) inflation rate, p^a, and greater variability of that rate, σ_{p^a}; (3) a greater deviation of the actual inflation rate, p, from the adapted rate. The social loss, L, can be expressed as

$$L = L(|U - U_s|, p^a, \sigma_{p^a}, |p - p^a|).$$

Moreover, assuming positive values of p^a, the partial derivative of L is positive with respect to each of its arguments.

The unemployment rate enters in this way because both slack and shortages mean social loss. Prices normally exceed short-run marginal costs in the price-tag economy, so that, other things being equal, society is generally better off when it produces more output and experiences lower unemployment. But extremely high rates of utilization create shortages and impose costs on frustrated demanders. Hence, below some low rate of unemployment, the cost of the incremental shortages would exceed the benefits of the added output.

The height and perceived variability of the adapted inflation rate are social burdens reflecting the loss of transactions efficiency associated with a shrinking and uncertain value of the dollar yardstick. The final term of the loss function reflects the misallocations stemming from an inflation rate higher or lower than the one to which the system is adapted.

The loss function presented here differs in several ways from that associated with the view that focuses on the natural unemployment rate. That function can be expressed as $L = L\,(|U - U^*|, |p - p^e|)$, where U^* is the unemployment rate at which the labor market is in equilibrium and p^e is the expected inflation rate. I have explained above why U_s is likely to be far below U^*; this implies that, apart from their inflationary consequences, unemployment rates associated with excess demand are beneficial. The difference between U^* and U_s could not emerge in the competitive auction world that underlies the natural rate model, and so U_s does not enter that loss function. In a sense, p^e and p^a are counterparts—both serve as benchmarks for a "nondistorting" rate of inflation. In the price-tag economy, the adapted rate reflects a set of behavioral patterns that cannot be instantly or costlessly abandoned even when a consensus of expected inflation diverges from the adapted rate.

In the competitive auction model, the loss function includes the actual inflation rate only insofar as it diverges from the expected rate. The price-tag formulation attributes costs to the speed of inflation that go beyond annoying trips to the bank, and so cannot be ignored—even when the system is fully adapted. In the price-tag model, the achievement of a low and reliable adapted inflation rate requires the acceptance of an unemployment rate above that associated with critical shortages, and there is a continuing trade-off between inflation and unemployment that creates a dilemma and a constraint for economic policy. This is a sharp contrast with the competitive auction model. There the behavioral equations specify that $U = U^*$ whenever $p = p^e$. Real disequilibria occur only because of mistaken price expectations. A macro equilibrium is a stabilization bliss point, with both arguments of L taking on a zero value. The value of U at such a bliss point is unique; the value of p is not. Clearly, there is no trade-off in that world.

The Short-Run Phillips Curve

The rate of inflation in the price-tag economy depends on the unemployment rate and on the adapted inflation rate[1]

$$p = F(U, p^a),$$

where $F_U < 0$ and $F_{p^a} > 0$. The higher the rate to which the system is adapted, the higher is the actual inflation rate any given level of unemployment, other things being equal. The menu currently available to the policymaker reflects the past experience of the system. Depending on history, any member of a family of short-term Phillips curves might be observed, and each one is associated with a different adapted rate.

If an increase of 1 percentage point in the adapted rate generates a vertical upward shift of 1 percentage point in the function, the function can be separated as

$$p = p^a + F_1(U).$$

According to the second term, the level of the unemployment rate determines whether the current inflation rate is greater than, equal to, or less than the adapted rate. Presumably at some unemployment rate, $F_1 = 0$ and $p = p^a$. In this form, the unemployment rate, which may be denoted U^0, has the same value for all values of p^a.

If the function has these properties, it is analogous to the natural rate version of the short-run Phillips curve that expresses the same relation in terms of the expected inflation rate and the natural unemployment rate: $p = p^e + F(U^* - U)$. However, because of differences in the loss function noted above and differences in the adaptation function discussed below, U^0 is different from U^* and deserves no special title like "natural." A family of Phillips curves associated with different adapted rates is illustrated in figure 8-1. The figure is drawn on the assumption that U^0 is constant; the long-run locus of points associated with $p = p^a$ is vertical, which is consistent with the accelerationist view.

1. The role of supply disturbances in affecting this function and the adaptation function is ignored in this section, but will be considered in detail below.

Figure 8-1. *The Phillips Curve Trade-off at Different Adapted Rates of Inflation*

Rate of price inflation (percent)

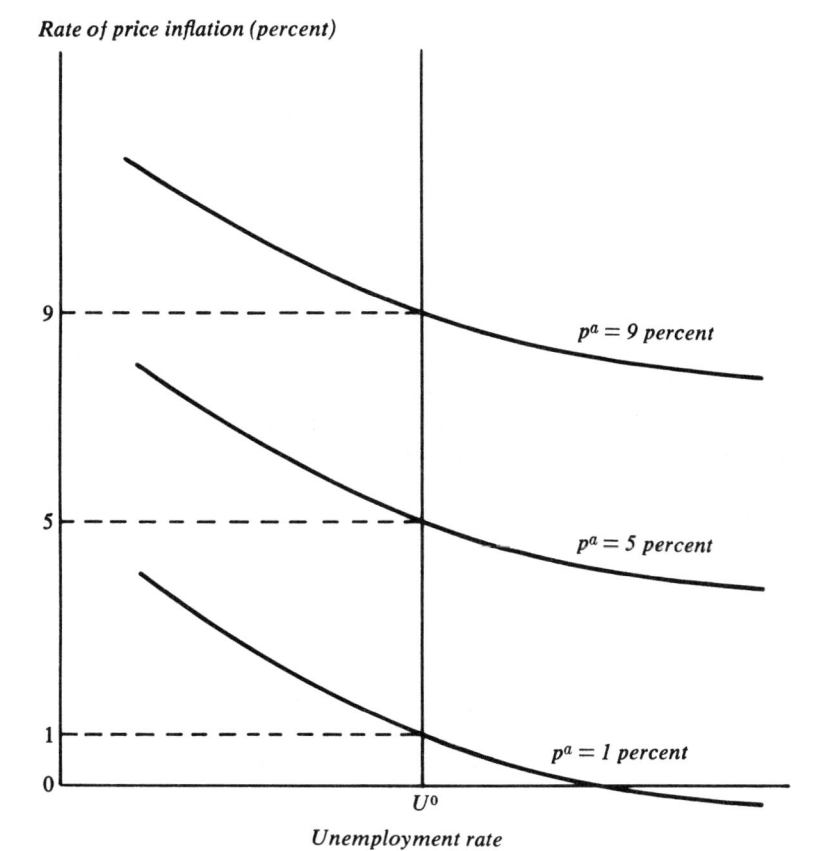

Unemployment rate

The Adaptation Function

Completing the system requires a specification of how the adapted rate changes over time. That can be expressed as

$$\dot{p}^a \; = \; G(\bar{p} - p^a),$$

where $G' > 0$, $G(0) = 0$, and $\bar{p}$ is the perceived value of the cycle average (or secular inflation) rate. It is a consensus perception or expectation about some unspecified long-term horizon for the future. When the majority of people believe the long-run rate of inflation that the system is likely to generate exceeds the rate to which it is currently adapted, they take steps to protect themselves against inflation in a way that increases the adapted rate. A shortening of price periods and wage intervals and the institution of indexing arrangements have been discussed above as illustrations of adaptive acceleration.

The adapted inflation rate reflects the way people conduct business with each other, the way they communicate, and the way they do their own scorekeeping and planning for the future. Changes in those practices are likely to be motivated by consideration of the inflation outlook over a long-term horizon. The key issue is not whether the inflation rate of next quarter or next year is likely to be influenced by boom or slack and favorable or unfavorable supply shifts, but whether the performance over the next several cycles is likely to be quite different from the one that would justify current price-making and wage-making practices.

The perceived secular rate is not derived mechanically from any particular past experience. It reflects forward-looking as well as backward-looking elements. Any indications that the recent past is atypical and not likely to be repeated in the future will reduce the weight attached to that experience in the perception of the secular rate. In fact, the secular rate may not be formulated as a single number. A sense of greater variability (less reliability) in estimates of the inflation outlook will affect behavior in much the same way as an upward revision in the point estimate of the long-run outlook. Both induce people to alter practices and change conventions so that they rely less heavily on the stability of the purchasing power of money.

The proposition I want to stress is that the short-term Phillips curve shifts upward when $\bar{p} > p^a$ and *not necessarily* when $p > p^e$ (or, equivalently, when $U < U^*$). The essence of the distinction is that any shift in aggregate demand affecting p (and U) will have a long chain of real consequences:

$$p \text{ and } U \to p^e \to \bar{p} \to p^a.$$

The initial cyclical disturbance will be digested promptly into inflationary expectations for the near term (p^e). That, in turn, will have prompt and sizable effects on the prices of storable auction commodities as well as on short-term interest rates. If the disturbance is perceived as a change in the shape of the current (and only the current) cycle, however, it may have very limited effects on career wages and markups of customer goods. The perceived secular rate changes only when people begin to suspect strongly that the long-run profile of prices has changed—that, as I mentioned previously, the drawings are coming out of a different urn. The long-run expectation or perception embodied in an altered $\bar{p}$ must be fuzzier and more subjective than those underlying p^e precisely because people are not familiar with the new urn. Changing long-term expectations is a different and more time-consuming matter than changing short-term expectations.

The link in the chain between $\bar{p}$ and p^a implies that changing behavior is different from and more time-consuming than changing long-term expectations. The behavioral relations embodied in the adapted rate involve systems of communication and information. It is costly to surprise workers, customers, and suppliers; it is painful to reformulate the unwritten and written rules of the game; it is risky to get out of step with one's competitors; it is troublesome for managers, shareholders, and government agencies (including tax collectors) to develop and agree on a new accounting system. So the gap between the perceived secular and the adapted rate is closed only gradually over years and perhaps decades, even when nobody is fooled by inflation. Throughout the entire process, the nominal disturbance continues to have real effects.

In this world, the shifting of the short-run Phillips curve is not determined solely or simply by the difference between U and U^0. On the one hand, the particularly strong but transitory boom when U is smaller than U^0 need not alter $\bar{p}$ and may leave the short-term curve intact. On the other hand, once $\bar{p}$ is affected and p^a has begun to rise, a temporary jump in unemployment above U^0 provides no guarantee of ending that rise. Economic actors are wise enough to recognize that the peak of unemployment reached during a recession is not likely to be maintained, and consequently they give it little or no weight in their estimate of the secular inflation rate. In figure 8-1 the economy may operate to the right of U^0 and still experience a continuing deterioration of the short-term trade-off. Even in that formulation, which assumes a vertical long-run Phillips curve, U^0 has no instant magic. Accelerating inflation can last for some time, although not indefinitely, while $U > U^0$. It cannot last indefinitely because p, $\bar{p}$, and p^a will ultimately reach equality if U is kept at U^0, so long as the system has the vertical property illustrated in figure 8-1.

As an example of the process at work, suppose that a prolonged boom (or a series of recurrent adverse supply shocks) that generates an unusually high inflation rate over a substantial period begins to raise $\bar{p}$. That, in turn, begins to pull p^a upward. While the boom continues, U is less than

U^0 and $\bar{p}$ is greater than p^a. Now suppose that demand is restrained enough to end the boom and make U equal to U^0. That should slow the actual inflation rate so that it equals the adapted rate. But at this point (call it period T), the perceived secular rate is likely to remain higher than the adapted rate and the actual rate. Because $\bar{p}_T$ is greater than p^a_T, the adaptation function continues to worsen the trade-off, raising both the actual and adapted rates while $U = U^0$. Thereafter, p^a and p move increasingly closer to $\bar{p}_T$. Both p^a and p are less than $\bar{p}$, and the U^0 value of unemployment is likely to be perceived as sustainable; so it is reasonable to suppose that $\bar{p}$ will not rise above $\bar{p}_T$. In that event, all three inflation rates would ultimately reach equality and at values above p^a_T, although no value higher than $\bar{p}_T$. Clearly, a strategy of demand management that seeks to end a boom and avoid any further acceleration above the prevailing level of the adapted rate must be more restrictive than merely achieving U^0. If the strategy is determined to roll back the adapted rate, it must be even more restrictive.

Conditions of Precise Control Over Aggregate Demand

The basic dilemma of the policymaker may be seen most vividly in an unrealistic hypothetical setting. Assume that the social loss function, the Phillips curve, and the adaptation function are known precisely and that the policymaker has complete control over aggregate demand (but no other instruments to affect the functions).

For such a world there is a pure anti-inflation strategy of demand management. It consists of choosing the secular rate that optimizes transactions efficiency, which for simplicity I take to be zero inflation. Once the price level is stable for some considerable period of time, a high degree of certainty is likely to be attached to that zero secular inflation rate when decisionmakers recognize the system's consistent performance and attach more reliability to their nominal arrangements. So $p = p^a = \sigma_{p^a} = 0$. The policymaker must accept the unemployment rate associated with zero inflation. Because that unemployment rate is higher than U_s, the sacrificed output and employment reflect a genuine social loss.

That loss, in turn, raises questions about the optimality of the pure anti-inflationary strategy. Indeed, on some simple and rather reasonable assumptions about continuity and separability of the loss function, the uncompromising, pure anti-inflation strategy becomes inferior to a compromise strategy that accepts some inflation in order to obtain somewhat

Figure 8-2. *The Social Loss Function*

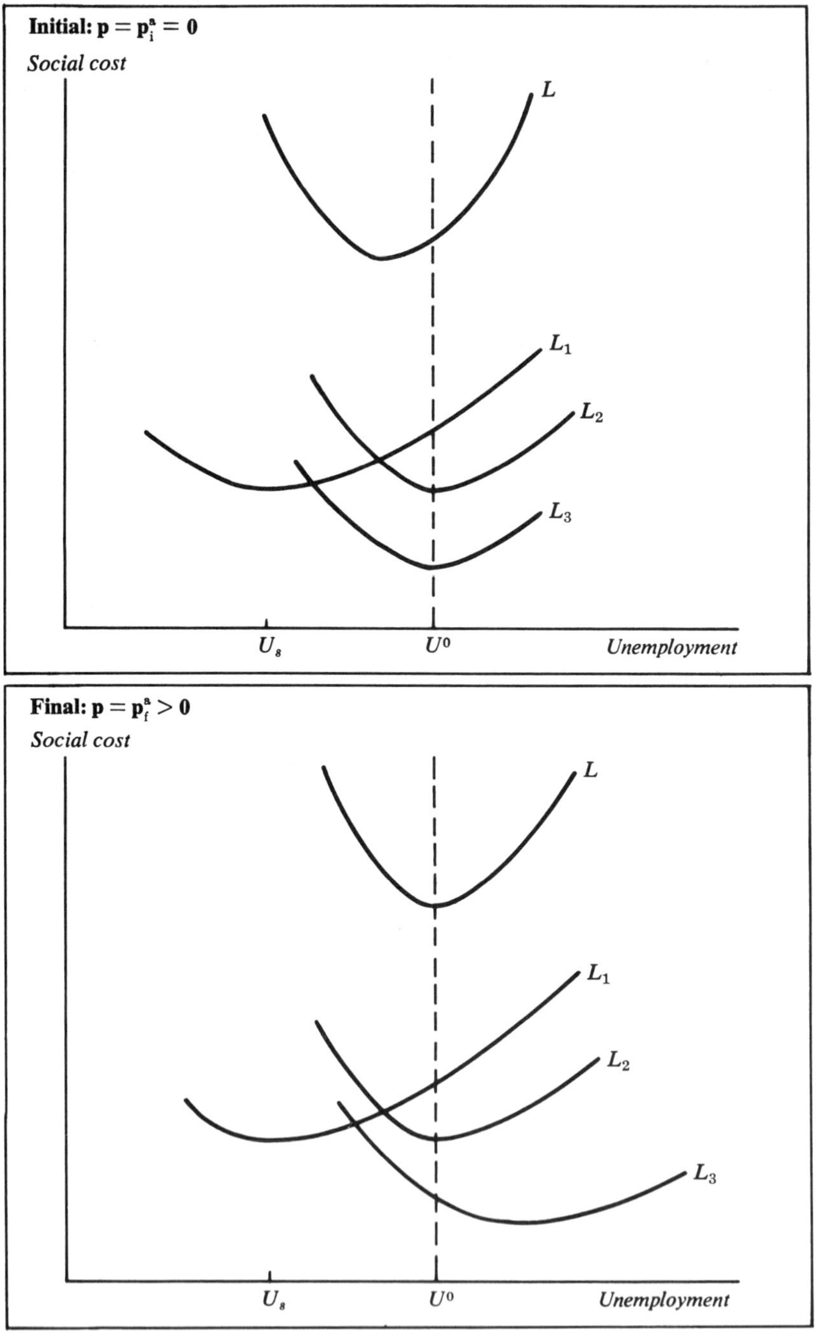

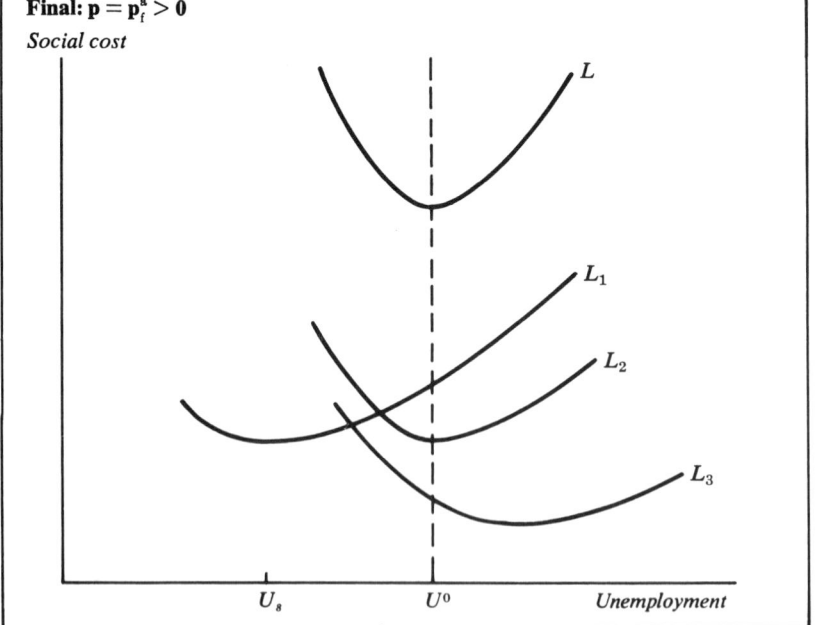

lower unemployment—even transitorily. Figure 8-2 depicts such a condition in which the pure anti-inflationary strategy cannot represent the social optimum. The figure is drawn on the assumption that the social loss function can be partitioned into three parts: L_1, the loss associated with unemployment that deviates from U_s; L_2, the cost associated with a current rate of inflation different from the adapted rate; and L_3, the current discounted cost of the long-run consequences for the adapted rate (and confidence in the adapted rate) that stems from any present inflation. The figure also assumes that a pure anti-inflationary strategy has been pursued so that the adapted inflation rate is initially zero and the unemployment rate is initially U^0. The short-term and the long-term inflation costs (L_2 and L_3) are minimized by maintaining that unemployment rate and zero inflation. Both higher and lower unemployment rates would raise L_2 and L_3—rises or declines in the price level would have disruptive effects on resource allocation and distribution in the short term and on confidence in the stability of the purchasing power of money in the longer term. Reflecting the empirical view that the short-term Phillips curve is nonlinear, L_2 and L_3 are shown rising faster at unemployment rates below U^0. Meanwhile, L_1 rises everywhere to the right of U_s. If the slope of L_2 and L_3 is zero at U^0 but the slope of L_1 is positive, the slope of L (the sum of L_1, L_2, and L_3) must be positive. If there is a unique minimum for a continuous loss function, the slope of L at that point must be zero. Then L_2 and L_3 must have negative slopes to offset the positive slope of L_1. The loss function must be minimized at an unemployment rate less than U^0, involving some positive rate of inflation. As long as a small amount of inflation hurts only a little, L_2 and L_3 must have slightly negative slopes just to the left of U^0, which must be outweighed over some finite interval by the positive slope of L_1. Some compromise toward accepting inflation is required for an optimum.[2]

That compromise may be a small adjustment if the long-run Phillips curve is vertical and if the long-run cost associated with a disturbance to the adapted inflation rate is at all significant. The principle of compromise does not depend on a negative slope of the long-run Phillips curve, how-

2. Note that the loss function described here is derived from, but is not the same as, the four-argument function given earlier. In the present discussion the loss function incorporates all future consequences of a given policy choice. It takes into account the discounted cost of the long-run consequences for the adapted rate that stems from current inflation. Note also that the inferiority of the pure anti-inflation strategy is unambiguous only when actual and adapted inflation are initially zero because that is the only time that the minimum of L is unambiguously to the left of U^0.

ever. Even if unemployment can be kept below U^0 for only a limited time, the benefits of a small boom are likely to exceed its permanent costs.

The case for the pure anti-inflation strategy requires that any amount of inflation is qualitatively different from no inflation—that L_1 or L_2 is not continuous in the neighborhood of its minimum. In effect, inflation has to be viewed as inherently bad. Indeed, some views of the trade-off develop such a position. Unless the government follows a consistent policy of price stability, it violates its implicit contract with those members of the public who place their confidence in the money it prints. The government's commitment to the stability of money is viewed as the implicit grandfather contract that permits other implicit contracts to be maintained.

Even in that formulation, wartime can be identified as a possible exception to the commitment to a pure anti-inflationary strategy. The extra output that might be needed to save the nation has a particularly high value, which is likely to outweigh the cost of somewhat lesser transaction efficiency in the future. Moreover, for that reason the adoption of a high-pressure demand-management strategy in time of war is likely to have a much smaller destabilizing effect on the size and the variance of the perceived secular inflation rate than it would under conditions that are less clearly justified and seemingly more capricious.

I would expect some dilution of the pure anti-inflation strategy to be optimal, but only a modest dilution. If a pure anti-inflation strategy had been pursued in the past, policymakers would find that some period of excess demand was worthwhile if they took full account of the long-run inflation costs stemming from this temporary venture into lower unemployment. Once that venture is undertaken, the perceived secular inflation rate and the adapted rate move upward. That, in turn, shifts L_3 to the right in unemployment space (as shown in the bottom panel of figure 8-2); indeed, the slope of L_3 becomes negative even at U^0 (because a move back to U^0 would leave p^a positive indefinitely). That means that, at some unemployment rate U^1 that is smaller than U^0, the negative slope of L_3 keeps growing in absolute value. To stay at an optimum, the economy must be moved to a higher unemployment rate (closer to U^0), where the negative slope of L_2 is smaller in absolute value and the combined slope of L_1, L_2, and L_3 remains zero. Eventually the "optimal boom" ends when p^a is sufficiently high so that the negative slope of L_3 exactly matches the positive slope of L_1 and the slope of L_2 is zero (because $p = p^a$). Then society has done its compromising and experiences some long-run inflation cost. There is no reason to opt for a higher or lower unemployment than U^0 from that point on.[3]

Imperfect Control of Aggregate Demand

The plot thickens when a realistic allowance is made for uncertainty about the course of nominal aggregate demand. While still assuming that the government has complete and accurate knowledge of the three functions specified above, I now concede that no monetary and fiscal strategy (whether conducted by rules or by discretion) can keep the economy on a predictable path of nominal GNP. At best, the government can aim for a particular target of nominal GNP, and must accept the consequences if it misses. If it overshoots the target, the resulting increment of nominal GNP is split into some extra output (and added employment) and some additional inflation. Conversely, if it falls short of the target, the shortfall of nominal GNP is split into an output and an inflation decrement, governed by the short-term Phillips curve. The recognition of this one dimension of uncertainty on the part of the policymaker forces a number of amendments to the discussion above in which certainty was assumed.

First, the concept of a pure anti-inflation strategy, which served as a useful benchmark in the world of certainty, loses meaning in the face of uncertainty. Purity would imply taking zero risk of any inflation for any period; such a strategy would produce both persistently high unemployment and a negative trend of prices that serve no useful social purpose. A strategy that maintains an *expected* inflation rate of zero may make sense but will have to accept some positive inflation half the time.

Second, the optimum policy now becomes dependent, not only on the minimum point of the loss function, but also on any asymmetry in the way the loss function rises on the two sides of its minimum. Expected social loss must be minimized, and that depends on the distribution of "misses" around a target and on the social losses associated with positive and negative misses. I see no reason why the policymaker's aim at the nominal GNP target should be biased upward or downward; but I see a number of reasons to believe that the loss function is not completely symmetrical

3. The proposition that some amount of "partying" is worthwhile over the lifetime of the nation leaves open the issue of when to hold the party. The long-term costs in transactional efficiency are equivalent to some loss of output for the future, which is weighed against the additional current beneficial output (net of shortage costs) from the boom. It takes discounting to establish the rationale for taking the optimal boom currently rather than deferring it indefinitely.

on both sides. The nonlinearity of the short-term Phillips curve suggests that a surprise reduction of one percentage point in the unemployment rate *below* its implied target is likely to generate a bigger positive inflation surprise than the negative inflation surprise generated by an unexpected extra point of unemployment. Taken alone, that asymmetry would argue for aiming a little below the target of nominal GNP appropriate to a world of certainty. On the other hand, for very large misses below the objective, society may bear the burden of both high unemployment and surprising declines in prices—the fact that deflation as well as inflation is costly argues for aiming above the certainty target. I see no basis for a clear verdict on whether the overshoot or undershoot is, on balance, more risky.

Third, and most important, because the economy can go off track in the presence of uncertainty, a strategy is needed for policy reactions to such a departure from the desired track. This has been a critical issue in the recent era of chronic inflation. I examine it in detail by working through a rather lengthy example.

Suppose an economy that was initially optimized with some particular unemployment rate and a relatively low adapted rate of inflation experiences either a prolonged boom or a depression through the mistakes or the misfortunes of the policymakers. Suppose further that this experience changes perceptions of the secular rate of inflation and begins to affect the adapted rate. Consider first how policymakers act if their strategy is employment-oriented, that is, seeking to control nominal GNP in an effort to return promptly to the unemployment rate that was initially regarded as optimal (U^0). In the case of the boom, that policy calls for raising unemployment, but not above the secularly ideal rate. Now the policy to stop the boom is initiated when the actual rate of inflation exceeds the perceived secular rate, which, in turn, exceeds the adapted rate. As I argued above, the adaptation continues (although not without limit) until the secular and the adapted rate are once again equated. Stopping the boom still permits the establishment of a new higher adapted rate— higher not only than it was before the boom but also higher than when the boom in real activity was ended. For a depression, the reverse is the case: the restoration of the initially optimal unemployment rate permits a ratcheting down of the adapted rate below its rate when U^0 was restored and presumably far below its initial predepression rate. In both the boom and the recession the employment-oriented strategy reestablishes U^0 promptly at the expense of accepting permanently a higher or lower p^a than was initially regarded as optimal.

Now consider the different results that emerge from a price-oriented strategy that seeks to restore the initially optimal p^a. In the case of the boom, that fiscal-monetary strategy must accept a period of unusually higher unemployment sufficient to lower the secular and adapted rates to their initial value. In effect, the high unemployment of this transition period is required to average out the particularly low unemployment of the boom. Similarly, ending a depression requires an overshoot—a period of especially low unemployment to reverse the decline of p^a and restore its initial value. To stabilize the secular inflation rate, the price-oriented strategy tends to accept additional short-run variability of output and employment with its compensatory boom and slumps. It even accepts greater variability of inflation around its cycle-average rate in order to reduce the variability of the cycle average.

What can be said about the relative merits of these two pure strategies (abstracting from the obvious possibility of compromise strategies)? The verdict is straightforward only for the case of deep depression that brings the secular inflation rate below the rate that is optimal for transactional efficiency. The price-oriented strategy is then clearly superior. Why endure deflationary distortions permanently, as the employment-oriented strategy does, when the price-oriented strategy can eliminate them *and* obtain extra output—achieving two good outcomes simultaneously?

In the case of ending a boom, however, the price-oriented strategy can end inflationary distortions only by sacrificing output and unemployment, that is, buying one good outcome by giving up another. The boom was undesired and unwanted (by assumption); its benefits (extra output and employment) are less than its costs (short-run and long-run inflationary distortions). But a price-oriented strategy initiated once a boom has taken hold cannot simply reverse benefits and costs. Because the Phillips curve is likely to be nonlinear in U and the social loss function nonlinear in $(U - U_s)$, the output and employment costs of the needed compensatory recession are likely to exceed the output and employment benefits from the boom. Because p^a has begun to rise by the time the curative policy is put in place (by assumption) and because neither the rise in p^a nor the increase in σ_{p^a} can be halted immediately, the anti-inflationary benefits of the price-oriented strategy are likely to lie below the inflation costs of the boom. The employment-oriented strategy therefore may be superior in ending the boom. The cost of putting the cork back into the bottle may be too great to justify that action, even if it is deeply regrettable that the cork escaped from the bottle.

All in all, if the economy occasionally encounters serious recessions and prolonged booms, the optimal strategy could conceivably be asymmetrical—price-oriented in dealing with deep recessions and employment-oriented in dealing with booms. But once private decisionmakers recognize such an asymmetrical strategy, it must affect their behavior. If the cycle-average inflation rate is quite unlikely to be allowed to drift downward and remain low, but less unlikely to drift upward and stay high, the expected value of the secular rate must be increased and the confidence in that expected value reduced. That shift in expectations impairs transactional efficiency. The behavioral patterns that require confidence in money are weakened, so that the adaptation function is altered. The translation of inflation surprises into $\bar{p}$ may incorporate an asymmetry: it becomes reasonable for people to change their secular inflation expectations less in response to periods of prolonged slack (like 1958–63) than to periods of prolonged boom (like 1965–69).

The possible consequences of an asymmetrical strategy for the behavioral functions underlie the case articulated by William Fellner and others for the adoption of a symmetrical and consistent price-oriented strategy.[4] With that strategy disturbances still occur, and they affect the current inflation rate and the inflation rate expected over the short term, but any disturbance has smaller effects on the secular inflation rate and encounters a more firmly entrenched adapted rate. The fundamental confidence in the money and monetary arrangements is strengthened. Moreover, this line of reasoning is sometimes reinforced by the philosophical view that it is not surprising or inappropriate that society needs to accept unusually high unemployment for a period after it has deviated from its optimal track with a period of unusually low unemployment. The issues raised here extend beyond demand disturbances and indeed beyond aggregate demand management; in particular, they apply also to cases of Phillips curve disturbances.

Disturbances in the Short-Term Phillips Curve

The policymakers cannot predict with complete accuracy the rate of inflation that will be associated with any particular unemployment rate. To focus on this single element of uncertainty, I temporarily restore the assumption that the policymakers have perfect control over nominal

4. See, for example, William Fellner, *Towards a Reconstruction of Macroeconomics: Problems of Theory and Policy* (American Enterprise Institute, 1976); and "The Credibility Effect and Rational Expectations: Implications of the Gramlich Study," *Brookings Papers on Economic Activity, 1:1979*, pp. 167–78.

aggregate demand through fiscal and monetary instruments. In addition, I continue to assume that they have no other instruments with which to influence the Phillips curve, the adaptation function, or the social loss function.

At this point I introduce a stochastic element into the simplest version of the Phillips equation,

$$p = p^a + F_1(U) + v,$$

where the disturbance term, v, has an expected value of zero. The disturbance does not alter the economy's production function; it may be an autonomous shift in the foreign exchange rate or the price markup or wage norm such as those discussed in chapter 6.

If the disturbance is in an upward direction ($v > 0$), it leads to higher prices, higher unemployment, or some combination of both. It may also affect aggregate demand and nominal GNP for given fiscal-monetary policies. For example, by redistributing income and wealth, the disturbance may alter aggregate demands for goods and services or for money. Nonetheless, focusing on the supply-side effects, I suppose that the economy remains on the nominal GNP track that it would have otherwise maintained, unless some deliberate changes in monetary and fiscal policy are made. To maintain the paths of output and employment in the presence of the disturbance, the rate of growth of nominal GNP would have to be enlarged by the fraction v.

Without that incremental nominal GNP, something has to give. In the world of universal auction markets with no frictions, prices do all the adjusting, generating cleared markets with no change in either the general price level or in the paths of output and employment (abstracting from conceivable effects on the labor supply operating through real wages). That is not the case in this model. Indeed, the consequence of the cost disturbance for output is equivalent to that of a decline in aggregate demand that reduced the rate of growth of nominal GNP by v. The "split" of such a decrement in nominal GNP consists primarily of reduced output in the short run. During the period in which the fraction of the split that applies to the price level is s, the fractional loss of output associated with the disturbance would be $v(1 - s)$, and the increment to prices would be equal in absolute size. The consequences of the shock are even more adverse if the disturbance lasts long enough (or creates anxieties that it may last long enough) to affect the perceived secular rate and the adapted rate of inflation. If the change in the adapted rate is a fraction j of the incre-

Figure 8-3. *Price Level and Output Path from a Nonaccommodating Response to a One-Shot Disturbance*

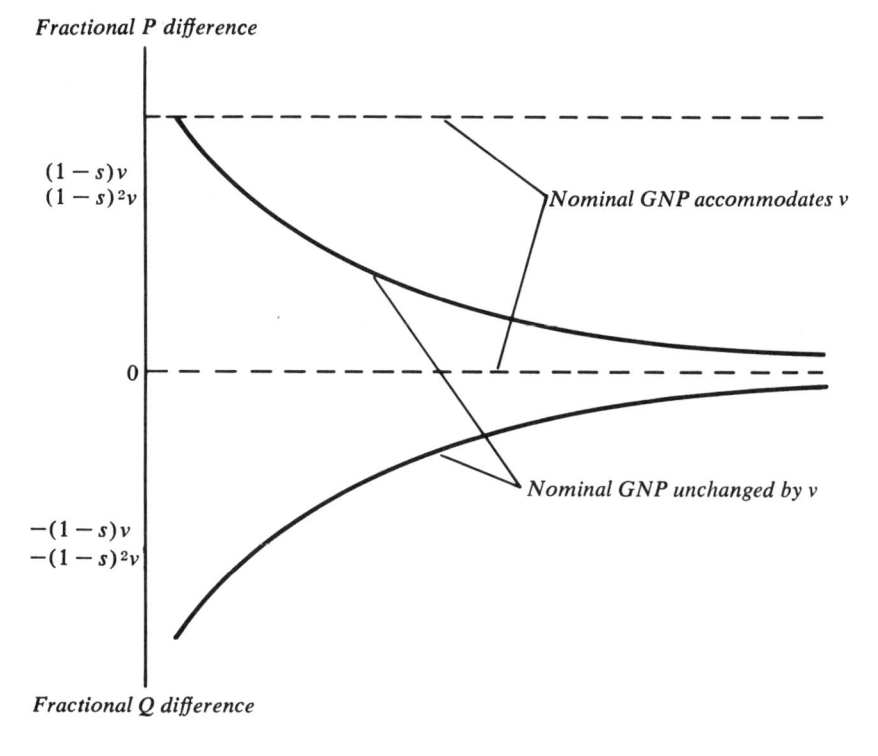

Fractional P difference

$(1-s)v$
$(1-s)^2v$

Nominal GNP accommodates v

0

Nominal GNP unchanged by v

$-(1-s)v$
$-(1-s)^2v$

Fractional Q difference

ment in the actual rate of inflation and if one abstracts from time lags, the price bulge (and, equivalently, the output dent) is $v\,(1-s)/(1-j)$.

If the disturbance lasts for a single period and then disappears (but does not reverse itself), the bulge in the price level that developed in that initial period continues to depress the level of output and employment for some time along an unchanged path of nominal GNP. Indeed, output must remain below the track that it would have followed in the absence of the disturbance as long as the price level remains above its corresponding benchmark track. Eliminating the price bulge requires a period of slack in which the actual inflation rate is below the adapted rate. As illustrated in figure 8-3, the benchmark tracks of both output and price level are approached asymptotically, given the unchanged track of nominal GNP. The deviation in successive periods is $v(1-s)$, $v(1-s)^2$,

$v(1 - s)^3$, and so forth. During the entire adjustment there is a cumulative output loss equal to v/s (as a fraction of a year's real GNP) and a bulge in the price level cumulating to the same fractional magnitude.

The disturbance clearly imposes social costs. The loss of output—or, equivalently, the extra unemployment—swells L_1. Assuming that before the disturbance p was equal to p^a, both the initial spurt in inflation and the subsequent correction in which p is less than p^a enlarge L_2. Finally, L_3 is adversely affected to the extent that the shock is viewed as having longer-run implications for price performance.

If the fiscal and monetary authorities can diagnose and respond to the disturbance promptly and alter the course of nominal GNP, they can influence the character of the social losses. But they cannot prevent the entire loss, and there is no clear operational verdict on what demand-management strategy minimizes the social loss associated with the disturbance.

One possible strategy is employment-oriented. Assuming that the policymaker can diagnose and respond to the disturbance as soon as it emerges, a fractional increment v to nominal GNP during the initial period will permit output and employment to be maintained. Without the lags and feedbacks and the influence of the temporarily higher actual inflation rate on the adapted rate, the price level must remain permanently higher than its benchmark magnitude immediately after the first period (assuming throughout that the disturbance lasts for only a single period). That case is illustrated by the dotted lines in figure 8-3. With lags, price-wage feedbacks, or effects on the adapted rate, some further increment in nominal GNP may be necessary in subsequent periods, permitting a longer period of maintained extra inflation and a larger total price bulge.

Analysis of the loss function suggests that such a pure employment-oriented strategy is unlikely to be optimal. Assuming that the position of the economy was optimized before the shock, the sum of the slopes of the three elements of the loss function viewed in unemployment space must have summed to zero, as in bottom panel of figure 8-2. In the presence of the shock and with the maintenance of the initial unemployment rate U^0, L_2 shifts to the right because the actual inflation rate during the period of the disturbance exceeds the adapted rate. Moreover, L_3 may shift upward and to the right, insofar as the disturbance (and the employment-oriented policy) may have unsettling effects on long-run price expectations. Meanwhile, there is no reason to expect L_1 to shift; for a given unemployment rate, the social costs of unemployment remain unchanged.

But U^0 (and the corresponding output level) can remain an optimum only if the slopes of L_2 and L_3 at U^0 are no steeper than initially. The shapes of the curves illustrated in figure 8-2 imply that they do become steeper at higher inflation rates. Indeed, if L_2 is initially minimized so that its slope is zero at U^0, its slope must become negative at U^0 when it shifts.

This reasoning about the slope of the loss functions presumes that, if the unemployment rate is unchanged and the inflation rate increases, the marginal social cost of an added point of inflation increases relative to that of an added point of unemployment. Intuitively I believe there is bound to be such a changing marginal rate of substitution in the minds of the public, although Edward Gramlich could find no evidence of it in survey data. (Both he and Franco Modigliani and Lucas Papademos have outlined models in which the employment-oriented response to a cost shock is optimal.)[5] If people suffer more by extra inflation when inflation is a more serious problem, some compromise is required that accepts at least a little more unemployment in the face of cost inflation.

At the other extreme is a price-oriented strategy that restrains aggregate demand sufficiently to head off *any* additional inflation from the disturbance (assuming that the policymaker is capable of diagnosing and responding to the disturbance at once). To hold the price level constant in the initial period, policy must induce a fractional reduction in nominal GNP and then in real GNP, amounting to v/s. This severe approach, which Gramlich has labeled "cold turkey," is unlikely to be optimal, as an inspection of the components of the loss function suggests.[6] Consider now L_1, L_2, and L_3 as they would emerge in inflation space rather than in unemployment space, illustrated in figure 8-4. Because no added inflation is permitted by the cold-turkey strategy, L_2 and L_3 do not shift. However, because a given inflation rate entails higher unemployment (and greater social costs) during the period of the disturbance, L_1 shifts to the right (becoming L_1'). The shift is likely to make L_1' steeper (in absolute value) because the social benefits of lower unemployment from an extra point of inflation will weigh more heavily. In that case, the cold-turkey strategy cannot be optimal. The same presumption about uncompromising strategies emerges: at a higher unemployment rate and an unchanged inflation

5. See Edward M. Gramlich, "Macro Policy Responses to Price Shocks," *BPEA*, 1:1979, pp. 125–66; and Franco Modigliani and Lucas Papademos, "Optimal Demand Policies against Stagflation," *Weltwirtschaftliches Archiv*, voll. 114, no. 4 (1978), pp. 736–82.

6. Gramlich, "Macro Policy Responses to Price Shocks," p. 51.

Figure 8-4. *The "Cold-Turkey" Strategy and Its Effect on the Unemployment Loss Function*

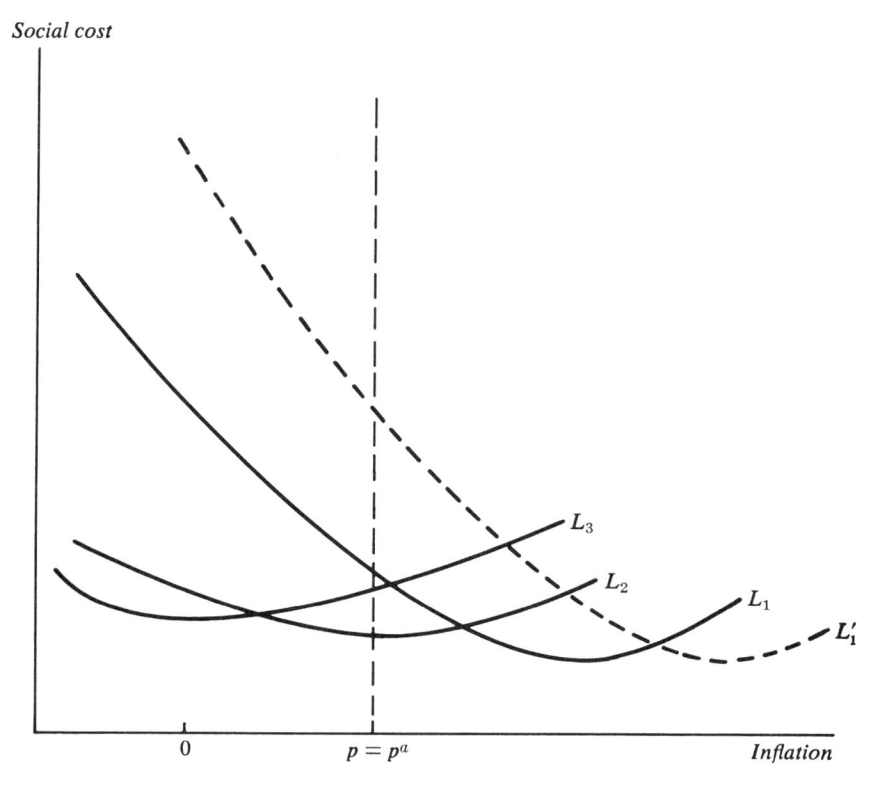

rate, the marginal social cost of added unemployment rises relative to that of added inflation. Only an implausible linear construction of these functions would make either of the "pure" strategies a serious contender for optimality.

A strategy of maintaining an unchanged path of nominal GNP, like the cold-turkey strategy, is price-oriented and is also unlikely to be optimal. Although this strategy operates with a considerable delay, it insists on restoring the initial track of the price level eventually. Insofar as s is smaller at lower output and higher unemployment rates (reflecting the nonlinearity of the Phillips curve), the total cost in output or unemployment (measured in "point-years") is smaller with constant nominal GNP than with the cold-turkey strategy. The nonlinearity of L_1 implies that the social loss imposed by the gradualist strategy is smaller per point of unemployment. (Three years with an extra point of unemployment is less burdensome than one year with three extra points, for example.) On the other hand, the gradualist strategy may impose some L_3 costs and definitely imposes L_2 costs both initially and during the subsequent corrective recession. In particular, that corrective recession with the constant nominal GNP path seems likely to add to social costs, on balance. In the case of prolonged demand disturbances discussed above, the price-oriented strategy that had to be taken seriously required restoring the initial *inflation rate,* but not on rolling back the *price level* to its benchmark path. I find it hard to imagine plausible values of parameters that would make the L_3 benefits of the corrective recession match the L_1 and L_2 costs.

So it appears that the optimal compromise strategy in response to an upward cost disturbance is likely to accept a permanent bulge in the price level, a temporarily higher inflation rate, and a temporarily higher unemployment rate. The precise optimal division in the temporary increments between inflation and unemployment depends on the degree of curvature (or nonlinearity) of several functions. I see no way to form a reasonable guess about that division from either a priori reasoning or intuition.

Does the acceptance of a price level bulge in response to upward cost disturbances represent a degree of laxity in the pursuit of long-term stability? That depends on the mix of upward and downward cost disturbances and on the nature of the policy response to the latter. If the probability distribution of disturbances is symmetrical and the policy response is consistently symmetrical, even a fully employment-oriented strategy should not be expected to raise the long-run path of the price level. But there are reasons to question each of these premises. The distribution of disturbances is not likely to be symmetrical and may well have a long upper tail. Natural catastrophes, wartime dislocations, and strikes are examples of changes in the cost structure that operate only in an upward direction. Moreover, many other sources of cost disturbances are not necessarily symmetrical: crop failures are not merely bumper crops in reverse, and cartelization is not just a price war in reverse. Some disturbances that emanate from the concerted behavior of groups, like a surprising change in union wage demands or in business markups, are more likely to be upward than downward. As long as the expected value of the distribution of cost disturbances is zero (as it must be by definition of "disturbance"), the asymmetry has no necessary inflationary bias. If, however, the policy response is confined to the large, visible disturbances while small disturbances are ignored, the asymmetry with the long upper tail and a compromise policy strategy will put more bumps than dents in the path of nominal GNP and create an upward bias in the path of the price level.

Even if disturbances were symmetrically distributed and as readily diagnosed in a downward as an upward direction, policymakers might not in fact respond symmetrically to them. If they tried to optimize consistently, one should expect a similar compromise to a downward cost shock as to an upward one of equal size and duration; some of the benefits of the downward shock should be taken in the form of lower inflation and some in the form of lower unemployment. If the policymaking authorities are strongly influenced by election-year myopia, they may choose to let the downward disturbances generate brief "noninflationary booms," while letting the upward disturbances create bumps in the price level (without subsequent offsetting dents). That would produce an inflationary bias over the long run. People who are skeptical about the political process and who stress the reasons for distrust and suspicion of the policymaking authorities would want to narrow their discretion in responding to shocks and hold them to a strict implicit contract to stabilize the price level. In a sense, that view of the policymaker is analogous to the worker's view of a career employer. In responding to a slump, the firm might prefer to hold down wages rather than to engage in layoffs, and might legitimately believe that the employees would also fare better with the strategy of keeping wages low. Because the firm is suspected of looking for excuses to cut wages, it cannot implement that strategy without antagonizing its workers. Here, the policymakers who are suspected of generally wanting to impose more inflation than is ideal for the society will antagonize critics if they respond to an upward cost disturbance by imposing a temporary inflation bump that in fact is a lesser evil for the nation. Instead, the policymakers are asked to show grim determination to maintain the price level despite the upward cost disturbance; in that way it is argued that they can allay distrust and suspicion, build confidence in the stability of the secular rate, and achieve a net reduction in L_3.

In general, the case for a pure (or even nearly pure) price-oriented strategy must rest on some peculiar asymmetry somewhere in the system —such as the policymaker's proclivity to inflate, an extremely lopsided distribution of disturbances, or conceivably an asymmetrical and sensitive response of the adapted rate of inflation (through price-wage feedbacks) to upward movements of the actual rate. As I noted earlier, the case for an employment-oriented strategy must rest on alleged properties of the loss function that I find to be rather implausible. In fact, because the policymakers are unlikely to be able to diagnose and respond to disturbances instantaneously, some compromise from the employment-oriented strategy is inevitable. To the extent that they can make prompt diagnoses and responses, the best rule is to compromise. There is a strong presumption against any price-oriented strategy, whether it focuses on a price-level track, the adapted rate, or a nominal GNP path. The presumption is equally strong against an employment-oriented strategy, whether it is formulated as maintaining full employment or the natural unemployment rate.

The most important conclusion of this section concerns what fiscal-monetary policies cannot do about disturbances, rather than what they should do. Large upward cost disturbances impose heavy social costs that cannot be eliminated by demand management even if the policymakers have immediate and complete control over the path of nominal GNP.

This analytical framework allows cost disturbances to be important, as they have been during the decade of the seventies. Indeed, the insistence by many economists that food shocks and fuel shocks could not create a stabilization problem was an outstanding failure that revealed the serious flaws of some economic theory. Strikingly, that error was particularly egregious among economists who had triumphed in the late sixties by predicting the instability of the short-term Phillips curve. The same model that generated the correct conclusion that the trade-off would worsen as the result of a prolonged boom also produced the erroneous conclusion that oil price escalation would *not* worsen the trade-off.

The macroeconomics and microeconomics of rising energy prices have still not been integrated in most professional or popular discussion. The allocation of energy resources can be improved by more rapid increases in prices of energy products, through both demand conservation and supply incentives. But those price increases translate into inflation, which has significant costs in terms of macroeconomic stabilization. Otherwise thoughtful politicians and editorial writers can demand higher gasoline prices and more effective measures to achieve price stability, without ever seeing the conflict.

Why and how does traditional economic modeling submerge the macroeconomic importance of cost disturbances? First, the random-walk character (or caricature, as I argued in chapter 4) of efficient markets implies that cost disturbances for a particular commodity will be serially uncorrelated through time. Given a change in the strength of either demand or supply for grain, fuel, or metals, the price immediately after the shift will reflect the assessment by market participants of the implications of that shift for all subsequent periods. Once that assessment is incorporated in the price, no significant further change in the relative price is to be expected. With that view of the world, no one needs to be concerned about long-run inflation distortions (L_3 costs) from food or fuel shocks. Indeed, such changes in relative prices are often characterized as "one-shot" movements and thus are distinguished from inflationary developments. Even for competitive markets, that view is a caricature. Over the decades, the relative price of haircuts has risen, that of travel has fallen, and the wage differential between skilled and unskilled labor has narrowed; those movements are not symptoms of the inefficiency of markets but rather of the persistence of various long-term forces that underlie relative shifts in demand and supply. It is entirely possible, within the framework of efficient markets, for a major auction product like grain to develop a trend of rising relative prices (say, as compared to labor costs) with adverse implications for the rate of inflation.

In the case of the Organization of Petroleum Exporting Countries, the random-walk view palpably misses the point. The efficient cartel will use its power in setting prices to promote expectations by its members of a rising long-run trend of real prices; with that expectation, the members will be patient about increasing production and will have less of a tendency to create gluts or offer secret discounts that would weaken the viability of the cartel. Such a cost disturbance cannot be dismissed as short-lived or serially uncorrelated. In ways that are similar to OPEC pricing policy, certain actions by the U.S. government, such as increasing minimum wages, payroll tax rates, and regulatory compliance costs, seem to represent elements in a consistent long-term trend.

Disturbances that cannot be dismissed as transitory may generate revised expectations and increased uncertainty about the secular rate of inflation. Indeed, I see no reason to distinguish, in principle, between a cost disturbance and a demand disturbance on those grounds. If an interval of particularly severe excess demand were known to be purely transitory, it presumably would have no effect on people's expectations and attitudes toward inflation rates for the longer run. There may be different perceptions of the likely duration of various types of disturbances, but that cannot justify the implication built into the standard "natural rate" model that any cyclical deviation has lasting effects on the inflation rate while any cost disturbance has only a one-shot influence.

Moreover, in most macro analytical models, all prices are viewed as equally flexible. In such a world, changes in relative supplies or relative demands cannot affect the general price level. From that vantage point, which is shared by many Keynesians as well as by monetarists and rational expectations theorists, it is a crude and vulgar fallacy to believe that inflation is influenced by falling prices for hand calculators or rising prices for haircuts. In a world of universal auction markets, all prices are perfectly flexible, and relative shifts in supplies and demands cannot be destabilizing to the general price level. A change in the supply of raw materials—and particularly imported raw materials—can affect the economy's production function or its consumption-possibility curve. Such developments create no macroeconomic stabilization problem, however. If prices must go up in one area, the auctioneer will ensure that they go down in most other areas. In effect, universal auction markets automatically produce "negative indexing": higher oil prices bring lower wages without any weakening of the labor market or any deviation from a given path of nominal GNP. Obviously, that is not what happens in the price-tag economy; indeed, given the existence of any consumer price-wage feedback, higher oil prices generate higher wages at an unchanged degree of tightness in the labor market.

Finally, those who live by the creed that inflation is always a monetary phenomenon can point to the existence of some strategy of demand management that would keep the price level on track despite any upward disturbance. That is a semantic rather than a substantive defense. A cold-turkey strategy can convert any problem of additional inflation into additional unemployment. Such a price-oriented strategy is not optimal. Moreover, it is a "fine-tuning" strategy that cannot be implemented by constant money growth and steady fiscal settings. It *must* create extra unemployment even if everyone knows what the policymaker will do, because commitments and arrangements for wages and price making do not permit the perfect negative indexing that characterizes the auction world.

Cost-Reducing Policy Instruments

Because upward cost disturbances impose large social losses that cannot be avoided by any strategy of demand management, broader questions arise about the tools of policy. Must cost disturbances be viewed as entirely exogenous and beyond the control of any policy action? In particular, are there any constructive preventive measures or analogies to automatic stabilizers with respect to cost disturbances? Could deliberate downward cost disturbances be generated to offset upward ones?

In addressing these questions, it will be important to recognize the analytic symmetry of the two main agonies of the seventies—inflationary adaptation and upward cost disturbances. Both represent a deterioration in the menu facing the policymaker. In the simplified Phillips equation a positive v that persists and a jump in p^a are equivalent. As a result of either, the same unemployment rate (or, more generally, utilization rate) implies a more rapid increase in the price level. Equivalently, maintaining the same inflation rate through demand restraint requires slack and extra unemployment in the price-tag economy. The trade-off in both these cases is genuine and vexing, as long as the only tools available are those of demand management.

I now want to discuss the potential benefits of other tools, and I begin this analysis with a fantasy. Suppose that the policymakers have a limited private stock of downward cost disturbances or negative v that they can impose on the system at their discretion. To put it concretely, suppose that the inflation rate reflected in the short-term Phillips curve can be shifted downward by 5 percentage points during the course of any generation. Apart from time preference, the policymakers might find it most constructive to use this manna from heaven in small amounts consistently ·through time, for example by 0.2 percentage point every year. The nonlinearities of both the Phillips curve and the various components of the social loss function may encourage the policymakers to use this divine gift most liberally either to neutralize upward cost disturbances that would otherwise generate upward shifts in the Phillips curve, or else to ease the agonizing task of reversing an upward shift in the adapted rate of inflation following a prolonged period of upward disturbances in either costs or demand. For example, if developments in the private marketplace create an emerging positive v of 1 percentage point, the application of a negative v of equal magnitude through policy action is a perfect offset. If the policymakers had no such offset and instead followed a price-oriented demand strategy, they would sacrifice $1/s$ point-years of output to avoid the cost inflation, with a substantial social loss reflected in L_1. The pursuit of the optimal compromise demand strategy means a somewhat smaller— but only slightly smaller—social loss. The benefit of the divine gift per percentage point of negative v is then a magnitude approaching $1/s$ of the nation's annual real GNP. Just as disturbances that raise the aggregate price structure have a macroeconomic cost, the ability to neutralize them has a distinct and important macroeconomic value.

To translate this fantasy into operational and concrete terms, it is necessary to consider the nature of the cost disturbances that are actually encountered and the possibilities for constructing offsetting cost reductions to serve as neutralizers. Any increment to the price level associated with a given output (and a given unemployment rate) that stems from sources other than an increment to nominal aggregate demand can be regarded as an upward cost disturbance. More specifically, such a development may stem from (1) a reduction in the supply of auction products; (2) a shift in demand toward auction products and away from customer products; (3) a depreciation of the national currency; (4) a rise in rates of taxes that are shifted forward and raise market prices relative to factor costs; (5) an increase in the wage norm or, equivalently, a reduction in the productivity of labor at a given wage norm; or (6) an increase in business markups at a given intensity of aggregate demand. I discuss these disturbances and the possible neutralizers under four categories: shifts in auction markets, foreign trade and exchange rates, indirect taxation, and wage behavior.

Shifts in Auction Markets

I developed a model of a two-product economy in chapter 6. The auction good had completely inelastic supply and involved no labor costs; the price of the customer good was based on a fixed percentage markup applied to labor costs and reflected shifts in demand only to the extent that the tightness of the labor market affected wages. The analysis of various disturbances in that world revealed that, given the level of nominal GNP, an exogenous reduction in the supply of the auction good (for example, as the result of a crop failure) raised the aggregate price level (a weighted average of the price of the auction good and that of the customer good). The magnitude of that increment in the price level varied inversely with the price elasticity of demand for the auction product, directly with the influence of the cost of living on money wages, and inversely with the magnitude of the influence of unemployment on wages. Given nominal GNP, the same factors that magnify the increment to the price level also magnify the reduction in the output of customer goods stemming from a given drop in the supply of the auction good. Alternatively, they also magnify the increment in nominal GNP required to avoid a decline in the output of the customer good.

Major auction items like grain have a very low price elasticity of demand and display extremely volatile prices that can impose substantial macroeconomic stabilization costs. The bumper crop is worth far more to society than the value of the extra grain, and the crop failure costs society far more than the loss of that harvest. The size of the macroeconomic externality can be startling. Abstracting from stocks of grain and foreign trade, if the price elasticity of demand for grain is 0.2, the loss of output of one bushel worth $5 adds $20 to grain costs; that is, $P_G \cdot [(1/e) - 1]$. If the policymakers do not alter the settings for fiscal and monetary policies and, moreover, if redistribution of income and changes in relative prices do not alter aggregate demand, nominal GNP should be unchanged. Hence expenditures on nonfarm GNP must be reduced by $20. How that $20 reduction is split between a change in output and a change in prices depends on the responsiveness of wages to slack (the size of s) and on the magnitude of the consumer price effect on wages (k in the algebraic notation of chapter 6). Over an annual interval, most empirical estimates for the United States suggest that the price-reducing influence operating through s is at least fully offset by the price-raising influence through k. In that event, the entire $20 (or more) is a decrement in output. So the loss of a $5 bushel of grain costs the society $25 in total production!

The existence of reserve stocks of grain acts to moderate that huge effect; sales from those stocks by traders will enhance the available supply to consumers in the event of a crop failure that is generally regarded as transitory. Such sales act as the equivalent of an increase in the price elasticity of demand. But the private incentives to hold inventories of grain reflect assessments of the probability distribution of grain prices and the costs of storage; they do not incorporate the macroeconomic externalities on which the traders cannot collect a profit. A clear case emerges for a social policy to subsidize the holding of stocks of grain and similar auction items. If, through a government subsidy, the cost of holding stocks is reduced, traders will accumulate more stocks during periods when grain prices are generally considered to be below normal; they will have larger stocks from which to make sales and capture profits when prices are especially high. The result will be a reduction in the amplitude of fluctuations in grain prices and in the size of cost disturbances affecting macroeconomic activity. As the rising L_2 costs on both sides of p^a signify, society dislikes variability in the inflation rate. Even if the probability distribution of grain prices is symmetrical about its mean, a stock subsidy can contribute to social welfare by reducing the variance of that distribution without changing the mean. In fact, that distribution is likely to be asymmetrical with a long upward tail, both because a crop failure can push output below the average more than a bumper crop can raise output above its average and because prices are much more responsive to current output when stocks are depleted by crop failure. As is so often the case, the nonnegativity of stocks is the source of an important asymmetry. If a stock subsidy can reduce significantly the probability of major upward cost disturbances that would add points to the overall inflation rate, it is a valuable insurance policy. As an added bonus, the stock subsidy may lower the mean of grain prices insofar as the price responds asymmetrically to surprises in available supply and insofar as farmers are risk-averse and produce more with less volatile prices.

If the government actually managed stocks of grain rather than subsidizing private holders, it might in principle wish to sell stocks at times when grain prices were not above normal if there was a need to counter other upward cost disturbances (for example, in oil) or to combat inflationary adaptation. But such actions seem to punish farmers for the sins of oil producers or the sins of previous fiscal and monetary authorities, and so are politically unattractive. When the elasticity of supply is significant, subsidies to producers may accomplish the cost-reduction objective through the use of a carrot rather than a stick. For the short-run horizon in which supply is essentially inelastic, a subsidy to either producers or consumers must drive up the rents of producers rather than lower the prices paid by the consumer in the marketplace. For a grain-exporting nation, the domestic supply is elastic given the world price; and a subsidy to domestic buyers (or to producers on domestic sales) can have a decided cost-reducing effect. Such actions can take a more drastic form, like the sudden U.S. embargo on soybean exports in 1973, that can strain customer relations between the exporting country and its importing trading partners. More frequently, countries take opposite steps to provide extra protection to domestic agriculture and raise prices paid by consumers, even in the midst of crusades against inflation. These actions in farm policy are examples of the many self-inflicted wounds in the form of adverse cost disturbances that policymakers incur for microeconomic and distributive reasons.

Although the stock subsidy is an effective stabilizer in response to a cost disturbance, the measure must be given lower grades for its performance during purely cyclical disturbances that take the form of shifts in nominal aggregate demand. As I noted in chapter 4, prices of auction goods, even those that have low income elasticities of demand, outrun the general price level in recessions. The price sensitivity of these goods makes the aggregate economy more "auction-like"; it increases the price component of the split in increments of nominal GNP. The volatility of auction prices has a macroeconomic effect in the upswing by raising interest rates for a given stock of money, which drives up wages to the extent that they are influenced by consumer prices, and by increasing real fiscal restraint (insofar as the response of government outlays to the price level in the short run is smaller than that of tax revenues). The interest and fiscal effects may actually serve as automatic stabilizers on the size of the *nominal* GNP disturbance; moreover, all three effects entail greater stability of output and employment (and more price-level variation) for a given nominal GNP disturbance. On the whole, the benefit of greater real stability must be weighed against the L_2 costs associated with more variability in short-run inflation rates.

When subsidized holdings of stocks enter this story, the subsidy leads traders who correctly diagnose the temporary character of cyclical swings in auction prices to make extra sales from their enlarged stocks in the boom and extra purchases of stocks during the slump. By evening out the fluctuation in prices over time, the subsidy may exacerbate the amplitude of real cyclical swings. For example, if prices of farm and mineral products had fallen to a greater extent during 1974–75, the unemployment rate might not have reached 9 percent. Thus the stock subsidy may be harmful in cases of purely cyclical disturbances.

The effects of the stock subsidy and those of wage indexing provide an interesting contrast. Indexing increases the response of the price level to upward disturbances in aggregate demand and also to upward cost disturbances. The latter is clearly a socially undesirable influence. The stock subsidy, on the other hand, is intended to and is likely to reduce the positive response of the price level to cost disturbances. In the process, however, the subsidy also reduces the positive response of the price level to aggregate demand disturbances.

That defect of the stock subsidy raises questions about designing the instrument. Should government managers of grain stocks be instructed to respond differently to price changes that are diagnosed as cyclical than to those attributed to surprises in crops? Could a subsidy create similar incentives for private grain traders?

Foreign Trade and Exchange Rates

In the discussion of the prototype case of grain it became clear that the international character of the grain market affects both the nature of disturbances and the effectiveness of national policies to address them. The implications of international trade deserve more careful and detailed inspection.

The major auction goods are traded in world markets, and their prices in any nation reflect world supply and demand. The fact that grain is grown in many countries with imperfect correlation of weather conditions leads to a geographical averaging of supply that should reduce the volatility of grain prices in any nation. The same worldwide interdependence also limits the ability of a single nation to insulate itself from its own domestic supply (or demand) disturbances. When countries are frustrated by the constraints imposed by world markets, they tend to interfere with those markets with such techniques as varying the degree of import protection, shifting between export subsidies and export disincentives, and the like. Many of the considerations affecting world grain markets point to the desirability of international coordination to develop jointly managed international stocks of grain or coordinated subsidies to private stockholders in various capitalistic nations. The negotiation of such coordinated multinational policies often founders on issues of how to share the responsibility, authority, and costs.

To analyze the effects on one nation's performance and policy of a disturbance originating abroad in the cost of a traded good, three distinct effects need to be distinguished: terms of trade, nominal aggregate demand, and the price level; these effects may depend on whether exchange rates are fixed or flexible. I begin by turning the clock back to a regime of fixed (or, more accurately, pegged) exchange rates. I then examine the effects from the vantage point of the United States buying an import (like coffee) and selling an export (like grain).

TERMS OF TRADE. The terms-of-trade effect is straightforward. It represents the shift in the menu of consumption possibilities at a given utilization rate associated with the exogenous change in the price of the traded commodity. An upward cost disturbance in coffee, such as a freeze in Brazil that raises the world price, shifts the terms of trade against the

United States. It reduces the contents of the market basket that American consumers can purchase with their incomes (at a given domestic output level). Whatever in fact happens to real GNP, the trade balance, or any other variable, because of the higher price of coffee, Americans would have to incur a larger deficit (or smaller surplus) on current account and accumulate less wealth if their physical production, consumption, and domestic investment were completely unchanged.

In the case of an exogenous rise in U.S. grain prices, stemming, say, from a crop failure abroad, the terms of trade shift in favor of the United States. There is a shift in the consumption-possibility frontier that is not recorded in the real GNP as traditionally deflated. This means that the same real activity generates a larger accumulation of wealth by Americans.

AGGREGATE DEMAND. For a given fiscal program and a given money stock, any change in nominal GNP that results from the cost disturbance is the aggregate demand effect. It could be safely regarded as negligible if the demand for coffee had unitary price elasticity (as I noted in chapter 6). But because the price elasticity of demand is much less than unity, the upward cost disturbance is likely to exert a downward effect on nominal aggregate demand for domestic output. The increase of outlays on coffee tends to reduce expenditures on other items and on saving by consumers from a given nominal income, so consumer demand for domestic goods ·and services falls. The increased proceeds of the coffee exporters tends to raise their purchases from the United States, but they are not likely to be such good customers for American goods per dollar of incremental income as are American consumers. The net effect is likely to be a downward shift in the Hicksian investment-saving (*IS*) curve. The upward cost disturbance in grain prices originating abroad is likely to shift the *IS* curve upward, reflecting the extra proceeds obtained by American farmers from foreigners.

How much any shift in the *IS* curve actually changes nominal GNP for a given money stock and a given fiscal program (as opposed merely to changing interest rates) depends largely on the interest elasticity of the demand for money. The greater the elasticity, the flatter is the *LM* curve and the larger the decline in GNP. In addition, the disturbance may alter the transactions demand for money at a given nominal GNP. In particular, the increase in the dollar value of coffee imports could produce such a shift in the money-demand function because imports (as well as domestic value-added) generate transactions requirements for dollars. In that case, the added demand for money could exacerbate the probable decline in nominal GNP.

PRICE LEVEL. An upward cost disturbance in coffee raises the level of consumer prices in the United States. Although one can imagine a variety of possible ripple effects on the GNP deflator, the main influence at a given unemployment rate is likely to be the positive effect on wages from consumer prices.

The upward cost disturbance in the imported good is troublesome on all fronts, with an adverse terms-of-trade effect, some destabilizing reduction of nominal aggregate demand, and an inflationary impact on consumer prices, and, most likely, on the GNP prices. For a decline in the price of coffee, the terms-of-trade effect and the price-level effect are turned around; the aggregate demand effect is also reversed in sign but it must continue to be regarded as destabilizing and unfavorable. Volatile prices of a major import are a matter of macroeconomic concern, which warrants efforts to create domestic stockpiles or to negotiate long-term stabilizing trade and commodity agreements.

In the case of the rising grain price, the upward thrust on the price level works directly on the GNP deflator as well as indirectly through consumer prices and wages. Other things being equal, is a given upward push on consumer prices from grain more serious than one from coffee because of the direct inclusion of the grain prices in the GNP deflator? I think not. The concerns about the stability of the purchasing power of money and its usefulness as a yardstick and a basis for implicit and explicit contracts apply to the value of money in buying goods and services from abroad as well as at home. In that sense, the L_2 and L_3 component of the social loss function should be regarded as applying to the price behavior of GNP plus imports.

The upward cost disturbance from grain may not be more serious than that from coffee, but it is no less serious. The upward push on the price level is likely to be larger than the increase in nominal aggregate demand, which results in downward pressure on real GNP outside the grain area (or, more specifically, on customer goods), for given fiscal-monetary settings. The country is then likely to produce fewer automobiles and fewer homes and to experience higher unemployment. Or, as discussed above, the policymakers may be able to diagnose the event as it emerges, "accommodate" the extra grain-induced inflation, and maintain output and employment, but only at the expense of accepting more inflation. So the paradox emerges that the benefit in the terms of trade from the foreign crop failure may be swamped by the losses in macro stability. The United States may well be worse off despite the increased earnings from its grain. The government may wish to insulate the domestic consumer from the impact of higher food prices, not because it gives preference to urban consumers rather than to farmers, but because it strives for stability of the price level.

How would the three effects in the coffee example be altered if the United States produced a large amount of coffee at home and imported only half of its requirements? The terms-of-trade effect associated with any given increase in the price of coffee would be cut in half and any aggregate demand effect would probably be trimmed (although it would be complicated by the redistribution of income and wealth from American coffee consumers to the hypothetical domestic producers). But the effect would be just as large on the consumer price index and much larger on the GNP deflator. Indeed, if the nation were fully self-sufficient in coffee but the price of coffee were nonetheless determined in a world auction market (or by a world cartel), the effects on consumer prices would be as large, and that on the GNP deflator still larger.

This result is directly relevant to the problem posed by OPEC. Because the United States produces much of the petroleum (and most of the total energy) that it consumes, the adverse effect on U.S. terms of trade from OPEC price increases is smaller than that on other nations like Japan that rely almost entirely on imports. The cost-raising pressure is no smaller for consumer prices and is larger for the GNP deflator. If the United States became entirely self-sufficient in energy, it would enjoy large benefits in the terms of trade. Its self-sufficiency would weaken the power of the cartel to continue the rapid escalation of world energy prices. But to the extent that OPEC still had enough market power to set world oil prices in a discretionary fashion, the United States would still be vulnerable to macro destabilization from a hike in oil prices by the cartel. Self-sufficiency achieved by conservation would lower the weight of energy in the national market basket. However, a large adverse effect from a rise in oil prices would still be possible. There would remain a strong case on social welfare grounds for providing some insulation of the domestic price from the world price and stimulating a public interest in moderating the increase in the price of energy.

FLEXIBLE EXCHANGE RATES. The results discussed above must be modified when a regime of flexible exchange rates is recognized. For example, the likelihood of the grain paradox is reduced. The increase in the demand by foreigners for U.S. grain is also an increase in the demand for dollars and tends to raise the foreign exchange value of the dollar. To the extent that there is appreciation of the dollar (tiny or sizable), prices paid by Americans for imports and import-competitive domestic products are reduced. That helps to offset the increase in consumer prices due to the rise in grain prices. In general, induced changes in dollar exchange rates push consumer prices down when export prices rise in response to a cost disturbance originating outside the United States and push consumer prices up when the disturbance is a rise in the world price of imports. That is stabilizing for the grain example, in which the increased price for exports would otherwise be associated with upward pressure on the price level. However, the exchange rate change exacerbates the macro instability associated with the coffee example, in which the initial cost disturbance is an adverse shift in the relative prices of American exports and imports. Other things being equal, the increased outlays on coffee by the United States weaken the dollar and thereby raise the dollar prices of other imports and domestically produced tradable goods.[7] Flexible exchange rates tend to make the volatility of the grain or other export prices less troublesome to the United States, but the volatility of prices of coffee or other imports (and, most seriously, oil) become more worrisome.

Any appreciation of a nation's currency, which results from exogenous disturbances and originates outside the United States or in the private sector at home, is the equivalent of a negative v or downward cost disturbance with favorable macroeconomic consequences. For example, the British development of oil in the North Sea bolstered sterling and held down prices of imports and tradable goods produced at home. The exchange rate need not be taken as exogenous, however. It can be influenced by conscious policy, particularly through monetary policy. A combination of tighter monetary policy and easier fiscal policy that leaves nominal aggregate demand unchanged is likely to produce a currency appreciation and a downward shift in the short-term Phillips curve. Such a strategy is particularly attractive to a nation that is trying to end chronic inflation, and, in particular, to halt and reverse inflationary adaptation. Indeed, it was practiced diligently by some countries during the late seventies. Be-

7. In all cases the effects on aggregate demand seem likely to be stabilizing. The depreciation following the rise in the price of coffee often bolsters aggregate demand, while the appreciation following the rise in the price of grain is likely to dampen aggregate demand.

cause exchange rates are always a relative matter, such a policy by any country is an "inflate-my-neighbor" strategy, imposing upward cost disturbances on other countries. Only a few nations can win this game, but it is surprising that so few played. Why was inflate-my-neighbor policy not as much of a global plague in the seventies as "beggar my neighbor" was in the thirties? Perhaps the strategy was limited by the political power of export and import competitors, the two interest groups that are adversely affected by the inflate-my-neighbor policy. Perhaps it was too new and too unsuitable for most political leaders after generations in which countries (unlike firms or families) sought consistently to sell cheap and buy dear.

The attractiveness of a shift in the fiscal-monetary mix in pursuit of currency appreciation varies among countries. It is particularly great for a small, open economy because an appreciation of given size is likely to have a larger downward impact on consumer prices and to be accompanied by a smaller increase in interest rates. The United States would encounter major increases in interest rates if it pursued such a strategy, both by raising foreign interest rates and by widening the differential between domestic and foreign rates. To the extent that the short-term interest costs of sellers in a price-tag economy enter into their pricing, the resulting upward cost disturbance might offset much of the downward cost benefits of the currency appreciation. The desire to avoid a rise in interest rates may actually be a good economic reason why the United States adopted the least stimulative fiscal policy of any major nation in the late seventies.

In addition, currency appreciation is particularly beneficial to a country in which consumer prices exert a major influence on wages. For such a country, the appreciation may have lasting and indeed cumulative effects. The reduction in prices of imports provided by the initial appreciation then slows wages significantly. The wage slowdown, in turn, produces favorable price developments that make the country's currency more attractive as an asset. That may lead to a further appreciation, which reinforces the stability of wages and prices and generates a "virtuous circle" from the point of view of combating inflation.

PRICE-TAG SECTOR. In the discussion of international trade and exchange rates, I concentrated on auction markets. A few implications of international trade for the price-tag sector also deserve mention.

A greater degree of openness in an economy makes the behavior of this sector more "auction-like." Indeed, markups on manufactured goods that have strong import competition tend to shrink more in response to weak demand from a loss of market shares to foreign sellers than to weak demand from a recession in which the foreign share of the market is unchanged. For example, the pricing of U.S. small automobiles responds more to the loss of sales to imported Japanese automobiles than to the loss of sales due to a recession. The customer-market paradigm supplies a good reason. Japanese cars threaten to divert customers to a competitor; a recession takes away sales temporarily, but the customer may return on a brighter day.

The sensitivity to foreign competition should also be reflected in wage determination. In the absence of import protection, foreign competition would be expected to hold down wages as well as markups in American industry. For an industry that is export-oriented, both markups and wages could be affected by the pricing of foreign sellers who compete in third markets. I understand that such effects are evident in the data of small industrial countries; they are stressed particularly by Scandinavian economists. They are perhaps clearest in reverse in U.S. examples: industries that have received import protection have exploited these benefits through higher prices (and higher wages) as well as higher volumes of output and employment. The understandable joint support for import protection by career workers and their employers in many industries conflicts with the public interest in price stability as well as efficient allocation.

Indirect Taxation

The cost-raising aspects of increases in oil prices are analogous to those of increases in indirect taxes, and they can be neutralized by reductions in actual indirect taxes. The equivalence of oil prices to indirect taxation can be seen if OPEC is viewed as a hypothetical public finance entity. Imagine that a new nationwide governmental unit was created and that it levied indirect taxes on crude petroleum and spent part of the revenues on the purchase of domestically produced output. The excise tax on oil would be shifted forward into higher prices of petroleum products. In the absence of any adjustment in other prices, the dollar value associated with a given output or a given market basket would be increased. Thus the tax has a cost-raising effect. Because the price-tag economy does not have a mechanism for "negative indexing," the adjustment to the initial upward push on the price level cannot be limited to prices and wages, but must involve a decline in real activity, if the fiscal-monetary settings are unchanged.

The cost-raising effects of this example are replicated when federal, state, or local governmental units actually raise indirect taxes that are shifted forward into prices. By the same token, the rate of indirect taxation is a policy instrument that can be applied in a downward direction to produce favorable effects that neutralize the cost-raising actions of OPEC or other exogenous forces.

The cost-raising or cost-lowering influence follows from changes in any taxes that are shifted forward into prices. Many indirect taxes are part of the direct costs of producers; sellers in a price-tag economy have no reason to distinguish such levies from labor or raw material costs in totaling the costs to which they apply their markups. Such a characterization applies to most indirect taxes that are actually in use—general sales taxes, payroll taxes on employers, most forms of specific excises, tariffs, and value-added taxes (which are common in Europe). It also applies to several types of governmental regulatory measures that are equivalent to indirect taxes although they raise no tax revenue. These include the minimum wage and a variety of mandated actions to promote safety, health, and environmental objectives. But some indirect taxes fall on rents and are likely to be absorbed by the producer, rather than shifted forward to the consumer. The classic example is the taxation of land values. A new example is the "windfall" excise tax on U.S. production of crude petroleum; insofar as the domestic price is fixed by the world market, the windfall tax absorbs rent that would otherwise accrue to U.S. producers. ·Somewhere in between the tax that is part of direct costs and the tax that falls purely on rent are such examples as property taxation on the value of business structures. That tax falls on quasi-rents and is part of overhead costs. The issues determining the extent and speed of forward shifting of business overheads in general (discussed in chapter 4) are relevant here.

To the extent that direct taxes primarily affect rents, they are unlikely to be shifted forward into product prices. A standard elementary analysis of the corporate income tax demonstrates that, for a firm engaged in short-term profit maximization, the marginal unit of output has zero incremental profit and hence zero marginal tax liability. The supply price of that marginal unit is unaffected by the rate of tax. Some features of a price-tag economy limit the applicability of that clear verdict. One is that rules of public utility regulation that are geared to *after-tax* profit rates lead to forward shifting of changes in the rate of corporate income taxation. Moreover, the strategies of longer-run profit maximization appropriate to customer markets may have similar consequences and generate some forward shifting. Empirical research on the extent of forward shifting of the corporate income tax has yielded conflicting and somewhat indecisive results. At a minimum, it would be unwise to rely on cuts in the corporate income tax as a cost-reducing measure.

If the supply of labor is completely inelastic with respect to the real wage, the personal income tax on wage and salary income is not shifted to employers in the form of higher wages. That conclusion is robust whether the labor market operates through an auction, search, or toll mechanism. As long as workers' decisions are based on a comparison of relative wages among various jobs, a change in the rate of income taxation does not alter the scale.[8] Although the empirical evidence for the United States is consistent with the verdict of no shift, that is not the case for other countries.

This line of reasoning is not totally reassuring because any model with an exclusive emphasis on wage-wage comparisons implies that consumer prices (and income taxes) have no effect on wages. In chapter 3, I interpreted the cost-of-living escalator on wages as a type of insurance for risk-averse workers that firms may accept as a worthwhile fringe benefit. If workers regarded potential surprises in income tax rates as a major source of uncertainty about their real after-tax income, they might seek insurance against that contingency as well. In modern U.S. historical experience, that has been an unimportant risk. In peacetime, federal income tax rates have moved sluggishly and have been lowered more often than raised by new legislation. Only recently has the unlegislated inflation-induced movement to higher brackets become a matter of any quantitative significance.

Because management and labor accept the consumer price index as the benchmark for escalators, indexing protects the covered employees from increases in indirect taxes but not from increases in income tax rates. As a measure of the purchasing power of money over the household market basket, the consumer price index correctly reflects rising sales taxes and other indirect taxes that are shifted forward, and correctly ignores changes in the income tax. But what is right for that index may not be right for the objectives of wage indexing. If the rate of income taxation moved upward persistently, I would expect escalators adopted under collective bargain-

8. The only important analytical qualification is that relative money wages on those jobs that have large nonpecuniary benefits (which go untaxed) will be lowered by an increased rate of income taxation. The reason is that the increase in the tax rate initially makes the jobs with large nonpecuniary benefits relatively more attractive and thereby induces a shift of labor to those jobs from jobs with small nonpecuniary benefits.

ing to begin to cover that contingency also by embracing some new index of the real after-tax value of a dollar of before-tax wages. However, any move in that direction is purely conjectural and obviously not imminent.

Under present circumstances in the United States, reductions in forward-shifted indirect taxes will operate to lower the price level directly and also indirectly through the linkage of consumer prices to wages. Robert Crandall has identified a large arsenal of such potential tax cuts (and of changes in regulations that are the equivalent of cuts in indirect taxes).[9] One could imagine going beyond the contents of that arsenal by the adoption of subsidies, which are simply negative indirect taxes. But the application of these measures to neutralize upward cost disturbances or to combat inflationary adaptation is neither simple nor free of side effects. First, if the initial upward cost disturbance arises in the price of a traded good, the policymaker must decide whether to attempt to offset the effect on consumer prices, on the GNP deflator, or on the price of the national market basket that consists of GNP plus imports. Second, the neutralizing policy action should be designed to have, in combination with the initial cost disturbance, no significant net impact on nominal aggregate demand. Taken alone, a reduction in indirect taxation would provide a fiscal stimulus that would be appropriate only if the initial cost disturbance had a significant sedative effect on aggregate demand. Otherwise, a reduction in indirect taxes requires an increase in direct taxes (or the sacrifice of an opportunity to lower direct taxes) or else a reduction in transfer payments or government purchases.

Third, the required neutrality for demand may force costly adjustments in public finance. If the tax structure and the allocation between public and private goods are viewed as initially close to an optimum, cutting indirect taxes imposes a distortion. It is easy to exaggerate that distortion: when I observe the movement in the composition of taxes over time that has been generated by the growing importance of the social security program and the changing mix of responsibilities among federal, state, and local governments, I doubt the existence of even a crude optimization that would be costly to upset. On the other hand, even if the distortions are minor, it is the present value of them over a long-term horizon that must be weighed against the essentially short-term stabilization benefits of the neutralization. That is because only a *permanent* reduction in the rate of

9. Robert W. Crandall, "Federal Government Initiatives to Reduce the Price Level," *BPEA, 2:1978*, pp. 401–40, reprinted in Arthur M. Okun and George L. Perry, eds., *Curing Chronic Inflation* (Brookings, 1978), pp. 165–204.

indirect taxation can fully offset a single (but unreversed) upward cost disturbance. For example, if grain prices jump by the equivalent of 1 percent of GNP but are expected to follow a random walk subsequently, the rate of indirect taxation must be lowered by 1 percent of GNP and maintained at that lower level thereafter. Finally, although a compensatory increase in income taxes would be unlikely to vitiate the downward cost impact of a reduction in indirect taxes, there is a danger that repeated reliance on this prescription could lead to the incorporation of income taxes into escalators (or equivalent institutional changes), as I suggested above.

Because of these considerations, tax cuts for reducing costs should be made with caution and not be regarded as a device for fine tuning. Instead they should be reserved for countering major shocks (like that of energy in 1974 and 1979 or of grain in 1972–73) or for combating a serious case of inflationary adaptation. Even then, the social benefits and costs of such tax cuts must be compared with those of alternative neutralizers, a subject that I explore more thoroughly below.

No matter how one assesses the potential value of reductions in indirect taxes as an anti-inflationary instrument, the risk of increasing inflation by raising these taxes (and their regulatory equivalents) is clear. Yet such self-inflicted wounds are common: major increases in employer payroll taxes and in the minimum wage were enacted in the United States in 1977 and the initiation of a value-added tax was seriously suggested by influential members of Congress in 1979.

Restraining Wages and Markups

The micro analysis of the price-tag economy showed that private decisionmakers have a range of choices in determining markups and wages and that there are important externalities in these choices. Decisions at one extreme introduce a positive v into the price equation; when firms or unions behave that way, they act as mini-OPECs, imposing cost-raising losses on society. By the same token, decisions at the other extreme confer the social benefits associated with any negative v. The magnitude of the potential social benefits or losses associated with such favorable and unfavorable outcomes depends on the extent of price-wage and wage-wage feedbacks in the system and on the sensitivity of the adapted rate of inflation to current price and wage behavior. An increase in business markups, like a jump in the price of coffee, has a greater inflationary influence on consumer prices when consumer prices have a larger effect on wages and when any bulge in the price level has a greater influence on the adapted rate of inflation. Like an incremental markup, a wage increment affects the entire system through the feedbacks from wages to consumer prices and from the actual inflation rate to the adapted rate. But, unlike the markup, the wage increment has an additional channel of influence on the price level through the wage-wage linkage or wage emulation process that I stressed in chapter 3. An incremental wage is potentially a stronger inflationary force than an incremental markup of equal size and requires a stronger antidote.

RELATIVE POTENCY. This important distinction between the effects of wage behavior and of markup behavior can be illuminated by a bit of algebra. Suppose that the overall rate of price increase in the economy is equal to the rate of wage increase plus the disturbance term, $p = w + v$. This disturbance term reflects changes in the markups, changes in the rate of indirect taxes that are shifted forward, and disproportionate changes in import and auction prices. To simplify matters, I omit the markup lag and truncate the auction sector into v. Wage inflation in this world is assumed to be a function of lagged wage inflation, lagged price inflation, and the utilization rate, X, with a disturbance term, z, and an arbitrary constant, c_0:

$$w = c_0 + nw_{-1} + kp_{-1} + s(X - X_0) + z,$$

where the X_0 term is the value of X at which the utilization rate exerts neither upward nor downward pressure on the wage rate. The system can be solved as a reduced form for the rate of price increase, which yields

$$p = c_0 + (n + k)p_{-1} + s(X - X_0) + z + v - nv_{-1}.$$

Now in such a system suppose that v is positive for a single period and then returns to a value of zero thereafter. That would occur, for example, if markups widen and then remain permanently at their higher percentage level. Suppose for simplicity that the system had been experiencing no wage or price inflation previously $(c_0 = 0)$; and assume further that the utilization rate is unchanged at X throughout (for example, the increase in the markup is fully accommodated by a fiscal-monetary adjustment). Following the disturbance in period one, the inflation rate is given by

$$p_1 = v_1; \qquad p_2 = (n + k)v_1 - nv_1 = kv_1;$$

$$p_3 = (n + k)kv_1;$$

and, in general,

$$p_t = (n + k)^{t-2}(kv_1).$$

The last equation is also relevant to wage inflation, once wages reflect the price inflation with a lag of one period. As long as $n + k$, the sum of wage-wage and price-wage feedback coefficients, is less than unity, the inflation rate diminishes over time. Ultimately the price level is permanently higher (if continuous compounding is ignored) because of this disturbance by a percentage increment of $v_1(1 - n)/(1 - n - k)$.

Suppose instead that an upward disturbance emerges in the wage equation: $(z_1 > 0)$, and that it, too, lasts only a single period and is not reversed thereafter $(z_i = 0 \text{ for } i \neq 1)$. Then the inflation rate for prices and wages alike is given by

$$p_t = w_t = z_1(n + k)^{t-1}.$$

As long as $n > 0$ (the existence of some wage-wage feedback), the inflation generated by the wage disturbance is larger than that stemming from a price disturbance of equal magnitude. In a model with full short-run acceleration, $(n + k)$ would equal unity, and the one-shot disturbance equal to z_1 in the rate of wage increase would, at a given utilization rate, produce a permanent increment of z_1 in the inflation *rate* and an indefinitely widening increment to the price level. If, however, $(n + k) < 1$, the inflation rate diminishes and the ultimate increment to the price level is $z_1/(1 - n - k)$—again, ignoring continuous compounding.

Like a wage disturbance, a temporary increase in the utilization rate generates more inflation than that resulting from a price disturbance of equal magnitude. Suppose that

$$X_1 = X_0 + x_1, \text{ while } X_i = X_0 \text{ for } i \neq 1.$$

Then

$$p_t = w_t = sx_1(n + k)^{t-1},$$

which matches the previous result for $x_1 = z_1/s$.

In a full analysis of such disturbances, I would allow for a dynamic influence on the constant term of the wage equation (c_0) as the additional current inflation raised the perceived secular rate and the adapted rate. The effect on the adapted rate per point of short-term inflation may conceivably vary for different types of disturbances. For example, I noted previously that fluctuations in utilization (or unemployment) that are viewed as "normal" cyclical movements are likely to be discounted especially heavily. Nonetheless, I doubt that the dynamics of the adapted rate would alter the conclusions about the relative inflationary effects of the various disturbances. If it can be assumed, as a first approximation, that the effect on the adapted rate from increments to current inflation is identical regardless of the source of the disturbance, I can offer two conclusions. First, a wage disturbance is a more powerful destabilizer than a markup disturbance of equal size. The extra power depends on the size of the wage-wage coefficient relative to the price-wage coefficient. Second, a wage disturbance of given size has the same inflationary effect as a substantially larger increase in the utilization rate ($x = z/s$) lasting for an equal period of time.

These results respectively imply that an instrument of public policy that could alter the disturbance term in the wage equation by a given amount would be a more potent tool of stabilization than one that exerted equal control on the disturbance term in the price equation, and that the hypothetical instrument of wage-influence would be an excellent substitute for slack (and extra unemployment) as a means of combating upward cost disturbances or inflationary adaptation. At this point, I have not identified the hypothetical wage lever, nor have I reckoned the costs of applying it. As William Brainard shows, the correct choice of policy instruments depends heavily on these costs, such as distorting the tax structure in the case of indirect tax cuts or distorting labor allocation and wage determination with the wage lever.[10] For any given set of instrument costs per unit of v or z, the wage lever is more attractive than the markup lever (or indirect tax cut), and its margin of attractiveness widens the larger the role of wage-wage linkage relative to price-wage linkage.

ENDOGENEITY OF WAGE AND MARKUP SHIFTS. The wage lever may be a valuable policy instrument even in a system marked exclusively by a price-wage feedback. Not all shifts in the wage or markup functions are exogenous to the economic system. Some disturbances may be generated by interest groups with market or political power, and the likelihood of their emergence will depend on how the government is expected to react to them. Suppose a group of labor organizations is sufficiently powerful to create at their discretion an upward disturbance in the wage equation. They can obtain an acceleration in wages for their members, although only at a cost of some loss of jobs. As long as the incremental wages are not immediately and fully emulated by all employers for all workers, the members who keep their jobs gain at least a temporary bonus in relative wages and in real wages. They would obtain a bonus in the real consumer

10. William Brainard, "Uncertainty and the Effectiveness of Policy," *American Economic Review*, vol. 57 (May 1967, *Papers and Proceedings, 1966*), pp. 411–25.

value of total wages even if their wages, measured in the quantity of their own product, were held constant by an immediate and proportionate acceleration of the prices of the output they produce. In fact, as I emphasized in the models of chapter 6, the prices of workers' output are likely to lag behind labor costs, and that lag provides a temporary bonus in real product wages also.

Obviously the prospect of losing jobs to nonmembers (or to labor-saving machines) is a deterrent of some significance against the exercise of market power. It will not be an effective deterrent, however, if the possibilities for such substitution are sharply limited in the short run. For some small, highly specialized occupational groups (for example, a union of airline mechanics), substitution is a minor threat. Such groups may use their monopoly power in ways that pose a social problem of allocation and distribution, but they are unlikely to create significant macroeconomic problems.

For a very large group, the danger of adverse macroeconomic consequences may serve as a significant deterrent on the exercise of monopoly power because the members share those social costs with the rest of the citizenry. If the monopoly group consisted of all members of the labor force, that deterrent would be quite effective; workers could not want to generate an inflationary recession merely to gain a temporary advantage associated with the lag in the transmission of wages into prices. If the membership amounts to, say, one-fourth of the labor force, the social costs have some deterrent value, but they do not prevent a range of action by members that advance their self-interest by grabbing a sufficiently larger slice of a shrunken pie. The same set of considerations would arise in the event that a sizable fraction of business firms developed a means of tacit collusion that could be exercised to widen their markups.

Macroeconomic policy faces a dilemma because effective measures to limit the macroeconomic social losses from wage acceleration or markup widening remove an important deterrent against such actions. Suppose the government routinely applied a perfect neutralizer of upward cost disturbances (for example, a value-added subsidy in a system with a pure price-wage feedback); then the monopoly groups could exercise their push with confidence that they would not suffer from recession or inflation. On the other hand, if the government is committed not to use neutralizing instruments in response to a wage acceleration or markup widening that stems from the exercise of monopoly power, the commitment can be only a partial deterrent. If the monopoly power is nonetheless exercised, inaction by the government imposes losses on the other citizens who are innocent victims of the power group. The government can function effectively only if it has a specific instrument to restrain such action, presumably a measure of antitrust policy or incomes policy.

This example of a macroeconomic externality has many microeconomic analogues. If some firms use a production process that belches forth noxious smoke when they minimize their internal costs, they impose costs on the entire citizenry. The costs to the community must be of some concern to the managers—because of anxiety about their own health or that of their workers, about bad public relations, or about restrictive legislation. If the government reacts to the smoke as an exogenous force and takes effective measures to clean the air with smoke antidotes, that program must reduce the inhibitions on the smoke creators. If it fails to use the antidotes, it may impose large losses on most citizens and yet strengthen only marginally the disincentives to pollute. The government needs an instrument to convert the social costs of the smoke into private costs for those whose decisions determine the amount of emission. In these respects, inflation pollution is analogous to smoke pollution.

THE GENERALIZED EXTERNALITY. In a price-tag economy the typical firm and typical labor union are potential creators of inflation pollution. Short-run market power is a universal feature of career labor markets and customer markets. A measure of restraint on the exercise of that short-run market power is normally optimal for decisionmakers who are appropriately concerned about long-term profit maximization or lifetime income maximization. Different managers (or different union leaders), however, apply varying subjective discount rates and make contrasting estimates of the relevant short-run and long-run elasticities. There is a range of discretion and judgment that can result in an increased or decreased exploitation of short-run market power.

Any firm or union that alters its choice in the range of discretion toward higher markups or higher wages raises the dollar total of given real GNP and thereby imposes costs on society in the form of reduced output, a higher price level, or both. The presence of price-wage and wage-wage feedbacks magnifies these social costs. The micro unit in a price-tag economy can become a mini-OPEC at its discretion; and its calculation of its own net benefits from such action incorporates only its small share of the macro externalities. In the absence of an instrument of public policy to internalize the social costs, a price-tag economy suffers from a market failure.

Can these macro externalities be reflected efficiently? It is not obvious that the costs of correcting the market failure are less than the costs of leaving them uncorrected. There is a strong case, resting on solid theoretical ground, for exploring the possibilities of incentives (and disincentives) for the discretionary use of market power to lower (and avoid raising) costs.

COMPETITIVE STRATEGY. One set of such measures might seek to increase the effectiveness of price and wage competition. On the labor side, such measures might repeal various floors on wages (like those set by the Davis-Bacon Act); or might try to weaken the strike weapon in collective bargaining. On the business side, steps might be taken to develop more stringent antitrust legislation or more effective enforcement of existing antitrust laws, or to promote the effectiveness of import competition with a more liberal trade policy. To the extent that these measures can remove some of the monopoly element in certain wages or prices, they are capable of providing a one-time reduction in the cost structure in a manner similar to cuts in indirect taxes. Furthermore, if such policies make the demand curves of individual firms more elastic in the short run, they narrow the range of discretion that is a source of cost disturbances. Finally, the procompetitive strategy tends to make the whole system more auction-like by enlarging the price component and reducing the quantity component of the change in nominal aggregate demand.

I believe that the effective scope of this strategy is limited because the appropriate functioning of customer markets and career labor markets requires a marked departure from the price flexibility of the competitive model. Customers and suppliers, employees and firms develop methods of reducing price variation that help perpetuate relations and minimize transactions costs over the long run. An attempt to make all markets behave like auction markets might impose significant social costs.

WAGE-PRICE GUIDELINES. Another major category of cost-reducing measures seeks to influence more directly the decisions of the private sector on wages and markups. Programs of price-wage restraint can be implemented by voluntary or semivoluntary guidelines, by mandatory controls, or by tax incentives. I focus first on the programs typically associated with the nonmandatory guideline approach by inspecting wages and then prices.

In a typical program the government enunciates a ceiling rate of wage increase from some benchmark period and attempts to enlist the cooperation of firms and employees to accept that constraint. The ceiling, or numerical standard, is usually set as a percentage, although some countries have at times used dollar-and-cent ceilings (obviously, in the relevant currency unit) in an effort to favor low-wage workers. In general, the numerical standard is applied to the average pay raise awarded by any employer; it deliberately seeks not to restrain changes in the relative pay structure within the firm.

When the program is initiated and the numerical standard first promulgated, the policymakers must decide how much of a deceleration in wages they seek relative to the recent pace of pay increases. The attractions of a large deceleration are obvious from the point of view of the anti-inflationary objective. A major and abrupt deceleration, however, would ask workers about to receive their pay increases in the staggered schedule of wage setting to accept a serious disadvantage relative to those who received pay increases immediately before the program. Overly ambitious targets for deceleration can create perceived inequities that are bound to impair compliance.

As I read the evidence of the Kennedy-Johnson guidelines in the early sixties, the Nixon Phase II of the early seventies, and the Carter guidelines in 1979, numerical standards—whether enforced by legislation or not—have had a noticeable restraining influence on actual wage increases. Why would employers who were about to award an average raise of 9 percent to their workers lower that figure to 7 percent merely because the government implored them to do so? If the wage is set through collective bargaining, why would the union accept that lower figure? The answer is that any voluntary program has some sanctions; large firms and large unions are concerned about their relations and their image with the public and with the government, and they attach costs to being identified as unpatriotic violators of a cooperative effort. Moreover, and I believe most important, the government's patriotic appeal modifies the attitude of workers to what might otherwise be regarded as unfair treatment. The workers in a nonunion firm understand the constraint placed on their employer by the appeal for cooperation. That recognition reduces the antagonism toward holding wages down that might otherwise swell the quit rate. In effect, the guideline relieves employers of that burden: they are able to reduce slightly any implicit contract that would otherwise have required larger pay increases than are needed to elicit the required supply of labor in the short run. In a large unionized firm, the prospect that the government would support the firm (at least, by not intervening) in a strike designed to achieve a guideline-busting settlement blunts the union's strike weapon. In addition, the perceived changes in the benefits and costs of pay increases as viewed by employers are reinforced by the expectations that other firms will also slow their wage increases. Looking ahead over the next year, the firm sees its workers less disadvantaged in terms of relative wages by a pay slowdown if it expects many other employers to institute a comparable slowdown.

The numerical wage standard fits into the analytical view of a wage emulation process in the labor market. When wages are influenced by the recent pattern of wage increases through a norm or a descriptive guideline, it is understandable that the government's prescriptive guideline can put downward pressure on the average rate of wage increases. The numerical standard operates to reduce the average mainly by pushing down on the upper end of the distribution of wage increases that would have taken place in the absence of the program. The government can also exert some restrictive influence on increases that are below average. Firms that were prepared to raise pay by only 7 percent when the prevailing average was 9 percent would presumably opt for a figure below 7 percent if the program pushed the prevailing average down to 7 percent. Nonetheless, the visibility and publicity of the numerical standard may make career workers more antagonistic toward pay raises of 5 percent when there is a 7 percent guideline than they would have been toward 7 percent raises when the prevailing average was 9 percent. For these reasons, any program with significant effects is likely to compress the dispersion of pay increases (on both the high and low ends of the salary scale) in the process of lowering the mean.

The focus of the restraint on pay increases that would otherwise have been particularly high has additional social benefits to the extent that exceptionally large increases act as pacesetters with important emulative effects on other wages. On the other hand, if the restraint on large wage increases impinges on rapidly growing firms that require increases in relative pay to fulfill their recruiting needs, the program would misallocate resources. When the labor market is not tight, I suspect that such cases are exceptional. Moreover, in informal programs, employers can usually find loopholes, such as nonpecuniary or deferred benefits, if they wish to evade the intended restraint without being identified as flagrant violators. These are not fully exploited because employers have strong incentives to cooperate in their own self-interest. As George Meany complained in some perceptive economic theorizing, every employer is potentially a volunteer enforcement agent in a wage-restraint program.

Even with a modest target for deceleration, the program is likely in its initial stages to upset established practices of wage emulation. Indeed, that is inescapable in any successful effort that breaks a wage-wage spiral. Certain "relativities" are fondly cherished by personnel managers and other practitioners in the area of industrial relations. These distortions can disturb the institutions of collective bargaining and the reliance on implicit contracts. Concerns about undermining these institutions are reflected in the strong opposition of labor experts against a wage program that puts heavy reliance on a numerical standard.[11] In their view, any successful wage program that conserves present labor market institutions must work through a case-by-case administrative process that is sympathetic toward normal wage-wage emulation.

Despite the incentives that operate in favor of compliance, neither the sanctions nor the expectations are sufficient to make it universal. When major examples of violation become visible, the ability of the individual employer to comply and the willingness of workers to accept restraint erode. In 1966 the wage guideline was swept away by the tides of excess demand, when large increases in the pay of low-wage casual jobs undermined the appeal for restraint in the union sector. In 1979 a few major contract settlements exceeded the guidelines in a highly visible way, reflecting the desire of unions to defeat the program and the failure of government to give sufficient encouragement to firms to resist those demands. The result was wide disparity between wages in major union contracts and the pattern of wage increases elsewhere. Undoubtedly the acceleration of consumer prices accompanying the energy price explosion also added to the pressure on the Carter administration to raise and relax its wage standard for 1980. Similarly, the squeeze on real wages in the United Kingdom associated with sharp increases in import prices, which stemmed in turn from a devaluation of sterling, eroded the acceptance by workers of restraints on pay increases in 1977. Remarkably, to the best of my knowledge, wage restraint programs have never been seriously damaged by any emerging trend of wider markups by domestic employers. In attempting to offer an overall appraisal of informal programs of wage restraint, I am reminded of P. T. Barnum's statement that a lamb can be kept in a lion's cage if one has an adequate supply of lambs. I believe

11. See John T. Dunlop, "Inflation And Income Policies: The Political Economy of Recent U.S. Experience," *Public Policy*, vol. 23, (Spring 1975), pp. 135–66, and "Wages and Price Controls as Seen by Controller," *Labor Law Journal*, vol. 26 (August 1975), pp. 457–63.

these programs can make a noticeable contribution for a substantial period of time, but they are ultimately consumed by various types of lions —excess demand, people determined to be noncooperative, or unrelated cost disturbances.

Informal programs invariably have a price and a wage side, but the former is generally less significant. The variability of price increases among firms in the cost-markup industries is so large that no numerical standard can be reasonably applied. The program operates most directly by appealing for price increases that do not exceed cost increases, which is equivalent to a rule against widening markup. The objectives may become slightly more ambitious if the target for cost pass-through is limited to dollars and cents, rather than a percentage, if it is delayed in time, or if it is held to some ceiling on profit margins. Basically, however, the opportunities for squeezing markups under a voluntary program are limited for several reasons: it is difficult for the government or any other outsider to calculate a firm's markup above direct costs; on average, markups in the customer market sector are sufficiently stable that they are not a matter of major concern; even a significant squeeze on markups would have only a small effect on the overall inflation rate. Meany's complaint is obviously asymmetrical: consumers cannot monitor prices or markups in a manner that enables them to enforce restraint on firms in the same way that employers can enforce restraint on workers. Moreover, because compensation of employees represents three-fourths of the national income, wages are inevitably the prime target of a guideline policy. The markup standard really is a way of helping to transmit a slowdown in labor costs reasonably promptly and fully into a slowdown in prices. Because the transmission of labor cost increases into price increases is the normal behavior in customer markets, the program is largely a means of ensuring that the transmission belt operates as well as it would in the absence of the program.

There is also some room for encouraging businessmen to operate at the lower end of the range of discretion. In the process of jawboning, the government official learns that many firms have major internal differences among top management on their own ideal markup strategy, with sales and production people generally opting for a high-volume, low-markup posture in opposition to financial officers. Sometimes the government's plea for patriotism can tip the scales in favor of the people who are already inclined to move in that direction.

If the transmission belt operates in its normal fashion, the concentration on wage restraint has only a temporary bias against the welfare of workers. The wage slowdown, if it is achieved, is translated into a price slowdown, but only after some lag during which an effective wage standard is likely to redistribute income from labor to business. Reliance on legislative authority rather than moral suasion is of course a means of obtaining greater compliance with a program of price and wage restraint. The expectation of greater compliance at the outset is a definite advantage. On the other hand, techniques to close the loopholes for subtle violations of a voluntary program exacerbate the misallocation of resources likely to be caused by the program.

Because of its clear and substantial sanctions of legal redress, a controls program can promote a more ambitious deceleration of wages than is possible under a voluntary program—providing that society is willing to accept or indemnify the transitory redistribution that is adverse to workers. Such a program also permits a more ambitious effort to restrain markups and even to hold down auction prices. A process whereby price increases must be approved in advance necessarily slows the transmission of cost increases into prices and thereby squeezes markups. By enforcing at least a temporary absorption of increases in raw materials costs, the program can exert some downward pressure on auction prices through the resistance of fabricators and distributors. Indeed, some mandatory controls programs have established ceilings on auction prices, thereby deliberately preventing market clearing. The legal authority encourages the government to cast its net widely in order to constrain the behavior of small units and groups that would not come under the surveillance of a voluntary program. Moreover, the political atmosphere surrounding the adoption of mandatory controls tends to emphasize the need for sacrifices by all groups, even when the sacrifice required has little to do with restraining inflation. A typical example is the inclusion of a restraint on corporate dividend increases in a mandatory controls program. Such instances illustrate the broader problem—that a mandatory controls program tends to politicize the entire economic process. That may be its largest social cost.

Although every experience with mandatory controls has produced some examples of resource misallocation, it is not obvious that they aggregate to a social loss that is comparable to the benefits of relief from inflation without recession. The misallocations would grow increasingly costly and worrisome with a controls program of long duration. This highlights the complexities of the process of phasing out a program of mandatory controls. The phasing out of the Nixon controls program in 1973–74 was disastrous in part because the program had been used to suppress excess demand and permit a degree of fiscal and monetary stimulation that in retrospect was clearly inappropriate. The phase-out also coincided with the food and fuel shocks of 1973–74. In principle, a period of mandatory wage and price controls in peacetime should be accompanied by some margin of slack to ensure that the program is swimming with the tides of the marketplace. If that margin is very large, it defeats the purpose of the restraint program, which is to achieve a reduction in the inflation rate with much smaller doses of slack and unemployment than would be required in the absence of a direct restraint on prices and wages. If nominal GNP growth is appropriately decelerated during the course of the program and if perceptions and expectations about the secular rate of inflation are changed for the better, there is no reason why a phase-out of the program should be accompanied by a major bubble of pent-up price and wage increases. What is true in principle in these cases, however, has never been achieved in practice as far as I know.

TAX-BASED INCOMES POLICIES. Proposals to use the tax system to provide incentives for wage and price restraint represent a logical extension of the economist's standard prescription for dealing with externalities: internalize them into the cost and benefit calculations of the individual decisionmakers. Because accelerating wages or widening markups generate inflationary pollution that is unpleasant for other members of society, and if restraint on wages and markups helps to relieve the burden for all, the decisionmakers who determine wages and markups should be confronted with a range of opportunities that reflects the cost or benefits imposed on others. A tax surcharge or subsidy associated with less or more wage and price restraint introduces a penalty or reward that is definite and calculable. If that penalty or reward approximates the external effects of alternative actions, the balance is set correctly for the decisionmaker. Unlike mandatory controls, taxes or subsidies do not forbid any particular outcome; unlike the voluntary program, they do not excoriate any action as antisocial.

The prototype of tax-based incomes policies is the Wallich-Weintraub proposal.[12] Like other approaches, it sets a ceiling or numerical standard

12. Henry C. Wallich and Sidney Weintraub, "A Tax-Based Incomes Policy," *Journal of Economic Issues*, vol. 5 (June 1971), pp. 1–19. For a thorough analysis of this and other tax-based incomes policies, see Okun and Perry, eds., *Curing Chronic Inflation.*

for wage increases; its distinguishing feature is the character of the sanction, specifically a schedule of surcharge rates applied to the corporate income tax for firms awarding pay increases that exceed the standard. For example, if the standard is 6 percent and the basic rate of corporate income taxation is 45 percent, a firm that increases wages by 7 percent might be subject to a corporate tax rate of 50 percent; one with wage increases of 8 percent might be required to pay 55 percent; and so forth.

The tax-based incomes policy with a penalty is potentially effective as an anti-inflationary device only in career labor markets and customer markets. For any nonunion employer who would otherwise raise pay by more than the standard, the penalty acts as an extra tax on wage increases and makes the firm opt for a smaller wage increment. In the traditional model of short-run optimization, that is no blessing. If, for example, the firm faces an upward-sloping short-run supply curve of labor, its choice of a lower wage forces it to settle for a lower level of employment. That, in turn, implies a lower level of output. If the product demand curve is constant, the market-clearing, short-run profit-maximizing price is higher, and not lower! This point is illustrated in figure 8-5. If many firms reduce employment, the product demand curves will shift down and so may the price. Even then, the tax-based incomes policy with a penalty is merely contractionary rather than distinctly disinflationary.

The logic of this policy is clear for firms that operate in a toll labor market and engage in the cost-based pricing characteristic of customer markets. To protect their investments in the tolls, such firms typically pay a higher wage than that required to obtain the number of workers needed currently; they operate *inside* their short-run labor supply curve. The tax-based incomes policy with a penalty, reinforced by the expectations produced by the guideline and its fairness provisions, leads the firm to choose a lower wage than otherwise. But it may still elicit as large a labor supply as it would have employed in any case; and thus it has no reason to reduce employment. Moreover, the lower wage translates into lower prices through any markup pricing formula. If the firm opts for a wage increase above the standard and becomes subject to a corporate income tax surcharge, whether it shifts that forward into prices depends on whether it charges its corporate tax liability to direct costs. The choice of the corporate income tax (rather than a payroll tax) is meant to reduce the likelihood of forward shifting.

In the context of collective bargaining, the tax-based incomes policy with a penalty increases the cost to the firm of yielding to demands for

Figure 8-5. *The Contractionary Effect of a Tax-Based Penalty Plan outside the Career Labor Market*

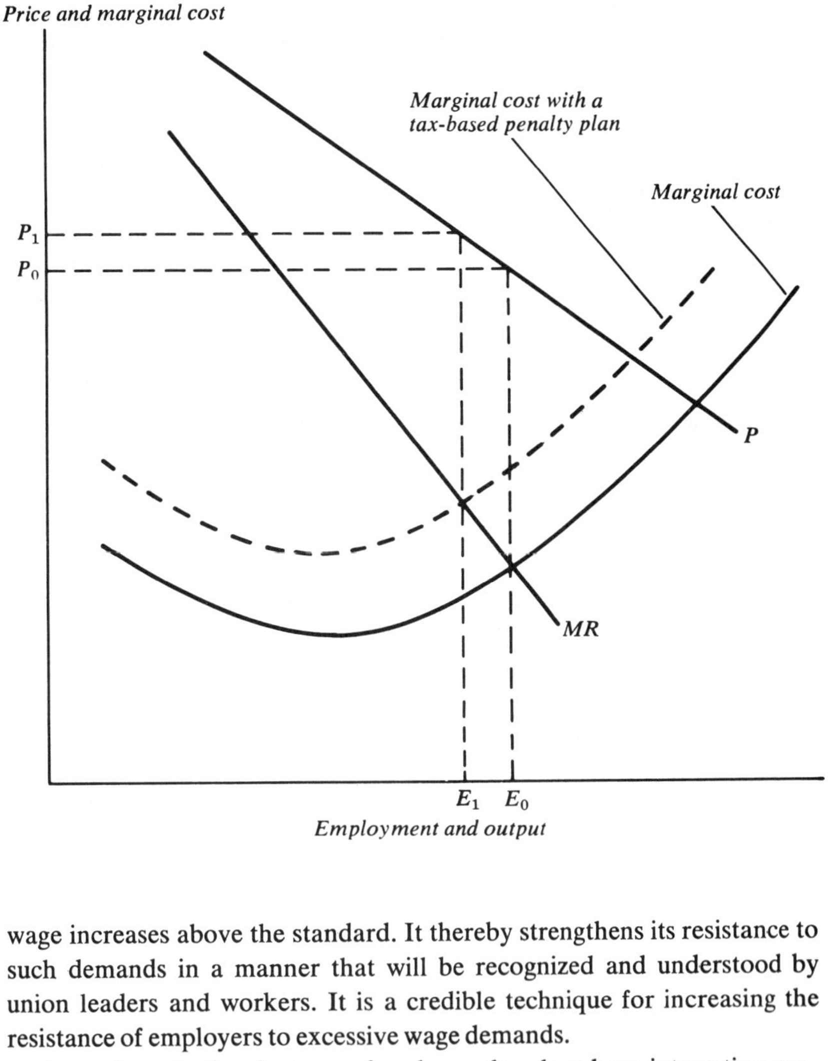
Price and marginal cost
Marginal cost with a
tax-based penalty plan
Marginal cost
P1
P0
P
MR
E1
E0
Employment and output

wage increases above the standard. It thereby strengthens its resistance to such demands in a manner that will be recognized and understood by union leaders and workers. It is a credible technique for increasing the resistance of employers to excessive wage demands.

A number of other features of such penalty plans have interesting analytical aspects. First, the program is intended to be limited in application to large firms in order to economize on administrative complexity. How much potential effectiveness is reduced by such selectivity depends on the role of wages set by large firms as pacesetters in the wage emulation process. Second, a penalty plan is not intended to be a prohibitive tax. It is expected that some rapidly growing firms that need major increases in relative wages to meet their recruitment needs will find it worthwhile to pay the penalty. For them, some distorting effect will stem from the penalty, but one that is less serious than that produced by the absolute prohibition under controls. Finally, a penalty plan need not be a substitute for moral suasion, but may be designed to reinforce a numerical wage standard and, indeed, to record by legislation the social consensus in support of that standard.

Business executives have generally opposed a penalty plan because of the fear that they would be unable to restrain wages adequately (particularly in collective bargaining) and would be subject to additional tax burdens. Labor groups are even more fearful of the exclusive focus on wage restraint, of reduced flexibility in bargaining, and of lower real wages. Understandably, they are not entirely reassured by the econometric finding that wage slowdowns have been followed by commensurate price slowdowns in past experience. Proponents of penalty plans have offered additional forms of reassurance, such as a proposal for a general surcharge on the corporate income tax in the event of an aggregate widening of markups. Indeed, in light of past experience, a temporary widening of markups seems probable for the first year of the program as the wage slowdown is gradually transmitted into a price slowdown.

In view of the general political hostility that greeted the proposal for a penalty plan and the particular widespread concern about its antilabor bias, I suggested a reward approach designed to achieve the same objectives. The tax-based incomes policy with a reward also relies on a numerical standard (ceiling) for wage increases; it offers a tax credit to employees of firms that hold average wage increase within the standard. The tax credit would be paid to workers; the eligibility for the credit and its certification would depend on the behavior of the employing firm. Although it may seem paradoxical to refuse to reward workers who receive a 3 percent pay increase in a noncompliant firm that averages 10 percent, that is an entirely sensible approach: the firm is making a statement about the relative merits of those workers, and any inequity felt by them should be expressed to their firms and not to the Department of the Treasury. Basically, while the penalty plan seeks to strengthen the resistance of employers to large wage increases, the reward approach is designed to reduce the resistance of workers to wage slowdowns.

In my judgment, the reward approach has a number of advantages and a number of disadvantages relative to the penalty method. First, the reward approach avoids the actual likelihood of squeezing real wages during the initial phase of the program and more generally avoids the image of squeezing labor exclusively. Second, the reward approach eliminates any danger of forward shifting of the tax adjustment into prices. Third, by requiring the employer certification for eligibility, it creates proper incentives against cheating and in favor of translating the tax benefit into wage restraint.

On the other hand, the reward approach uses up federal revenues and creates the same problems associated with reductions in indirect taxes discussed above. Moreover, the compensating fiscal adjustment is obliged to avoid taxing workers' incomes in order to finance the tax credit. Another disadvantage of the reward approach is that it cannot be applied selectively; although small firms can be exempted from liability for a penalty, their workers cannot reasonably be excluded from eligibility for reward. Although some economists whose judgment I respect view the administrative cost and complexities of a reward plan with anxiety, I regard these complexities as comparable with present provisions for capital gains and business entertainment and travel expenses, which are currently enforced purely by the selective auditing of returns. If the compliance costs of small businesses are viewed as onerous, they could be allowed to qualify their employees for the reward by a mere pledge of good faith to restrain wages, with little loss in the program's effectiveness or in the revenue impact of the reward.[13]

When general tax reductions are contemplated, they can be designed to reap the benefits of the reward approach and simultaneously to use the selectivity of the penalty plan. For example, a tax reduction on wage and salary income could be made universal, except for employees of large firms that had conferred average wage increases above some numerical standard. Alternatively, a reduction in the corporate tax rate (or provisions for more rapid depreciation) could be enacted with the requirement that large firms could benefit from the tax cut by more than some dollar amount only if they certified their compliance with standards for wage and price restraint.

The reward approach to tax-based incomes policy also shades into proposals for tax reductions as a way to lubricate a social contract and increase the acceptability of voluntary (or mandatory) standards for restraint on wages and markups. The budget of the United Kingdom in 1977

---

13. Although I once tentatively advanced a proposal for a reward plan to be paid to firms practicing markup restraint, I now doubt whether that approach is administratively or even conceptually feasible in light of the problems that Gardner Ackley identifies. See his remarks in "Implications for Policy: A Symposium," in Okun and Perry, eds., *Curing Chronic Inflation*, pp. 271–74.

provided for a tax cut on wage and salary income that was explicitly contingent on the acceptance of a specified pay hold-down by the Trades Union Congress. That particular arrangement was geared to the parliamentary form of the British government and highly centralized character of the British union movement, but the fabric of that idea could be tailored to fit American institutions. In fact, a proposal long these lines for the United States was offered in 1974 by George Perry.[14]

In my judgment, a tax-based incomes policy stands attractively on a middle ground between moral suasion and price-wage controls. It is a market-oriented strategy appropriate to deal with an externality, although it cannot be designed with the current state of knowledge to provide a precise or even approximate offset to the externality. The operation of alternative forms of tax-based incomes programs poses important unanswered questions that deserve serious study. Undoubtedly, even the most wisely conceived tax-based incomes policies are likely to be subject to considerable leakages and significant administrative costs. But I would expect them to shine as a paragon of efficiency in comparison to the social costs of unemployment and slack as a cure for chronic inflation.

An Efficient Macroeconomic Strategy

Earlier in this chapter, I discussed the scope and limitations of policies to influence aggregate demand and of policies to influence the aggregate cost or supply function. A comprehensive stabilization approach must blend the two sets of instruments.[15] With the monetary and fiscal tools

14. Statement of George L. Perry, *The 1974 Economic Report of the President,* Hearings before the Joint Economic Committee, 93 Cong. 2 sess. (U.S. Government Printing Office, 1974), pt. 2, pp. 540–47.

15. As I explained in chapter 1, the supply considerations of this book have been limited to an analysis of the price level associated with various possible levels of aggregate output for a given productive capacity of the economy. What has recently come to be known as supply-side economics is an analysis of the determinants of changes in the production function. Some prescriptions for policy actions that have a reasonable prospect of increasing the growth of productive capacity and productivity have been advanced by enthusiastic exponents as cures for inflation also. Their position simply cannot be taken seriously. The links in the chain—from increased capital formation, to increased productivity, to competitive forces that lower prices, and to the consequent feedback on wages—are too long and too fractional to expect such policies to affect the inflation rate by as much as a percentage point over a five-year period, even for the most ambitious program. I suspect that curbing inflation would do more to revive productivity than a direct stimulus to productivity could do to slow inflation.

that influence nominal aggregate demand, public policy can keep the economy reasonably close to a target for the price level or to a target for output (and unemployment), but not to both.

If policymakers operate with only the instruments of demand management, they must choose between real targets and price targets. They do not serve the nation well if they concentrate on output and employment targets—whether the objective is set forth as achieving full employment, the natural unemployment rate, or potential GNP. In a world of demand and cost disturbances, such a strategy permits significant and even cumulative deviations from any desirable price level path. In the event of mistakes or misfortunes that generate a prolonged boom, a policy that responds simply by trying to roll back unemployment to its target cannot hope to roll back inflation and may not even end its acceleration. After an experience of unusual and mounting inflation, people begin to change the way they form price and wage decisions and to alter their commitments so as to adapt to a new environment in which they expect a more rapid upward trend in the price level but feel less confident. It takes time for people to change their minds about the secular inflation rate; once they do, it takes even longer to change their behavior to accord with their new perception. While these changes are taking place, inflation at any given unemployment rate is intensified. That process cannot be ended simply by removing the excess demand that may have been the initial cause of the mounting inflation. The dynamics of the inflationary process mean that it is continuing and cannot be treated as a phenomenon that will disappear. A thoroughgoing commitment to employment targets is an invitation to large and cumulative fluctuations in the price level.

Even if demand and cost disturbances are symmetrical in the long run, the variability in prices resulting from an employment-oriented strategy would impose social losses; it would impair planning, destroy information, and impose higher risk premiums on lenders and borrowers, firms and career employees, customers and suppliers. Asymmetry is likely to compound the problem. The biggest surprises in the distribution of cost disturbances are likely to raise costs. The policy responses to demand disturbances—if not the disturbances themselves—are also likely to be asymmetrical with firmer and prompter responses to recession than to boom. Policymakers are subject to election-day myopia; they are confronted with enormous political costs in administering the unpleasant medicine of demand restraint, and they are tempted to engage in benevolent fooling. The agonizing truth is that the public can be better off in the

short run if it believes a lie. If the public can be convinced that a prolonged expansion is merely a transitory cyclical episode, that conviction
will hold down the long-term inflation losses and enable the nation to
enjoy the boom without suffering a serious impairment of the dollar yardstick. But at the end of that road, responsible democratic government goes
over a cliff.

All these considerations enhance the attractiveness of a strategy that
aims at the price level. The authorities are then required to fulfill their
implicit grandfather contract; they must maintain the purchasing power of
money and the efficient functioning of a monetary economy. However, a
commitment to price targets implemented solely by demand management
is costly and inefficient, particularly when it encounters cost disturbances
or inflationary adaptation. When, as in 1979, OPEC adds about 3 percentage points to U.S. consumer prices, the government's determination
to maintain the target for the price level (or nominal GNP) generates a
costly recession. People will be wise enough to expect a recession; they
will respond, as they do to an actual recession, with large cutbacks in
output and employment and limited slowdowns in prices and wages. Ongoing commitments to prices and pricing methods and positive indexing
arrangements determine the response and provide a sharp contrast to the
negative indexing that would solve the problem in a pure, frictionless
auction world.

Similarly, a price-oriented strategy armed solely with tools of demand
restraint is an inefficient and high-cost cure for an inflation that has begun
to generate adaptations. The price-oriented strategy linked to a nominal
GNP target offers people a threat of recession and a hope of diminishing
inflation. It tells them that the more they act collectively to reduce inflation, the less they will suffer from slack and recession. Economists must
be uncertain about how people would respond to such a strategy, however, no matter how firmly they may be convinced of the government's
determination.

In making judgments about the demand restraint strategy, one must
start with knowledge about how decisionmakers respond to actual recessions. In auction markets, expectations call the tune; prices and interest
rates respond sensitively to slack and recessions. In 1974–75 even long-
term assets with auction features—like bonds and real estate—displayed
a flexible response. It is inconceivable that participants in those markets
had different expectations about the future course of the price level or
fiscal and monetary policies from those of participants in labor markets

and product markets for finished goods. Yet in those latter categories of markets, prices kept rising at a barely diminished pace, while output and employment fell back sharply. The problem is not expectations but commitments to price making and wage making that create the insensitivity of such prices and wages. Changing expectations is one link in the chain of altering behavior, but it is only a single link. When an actual severe recession that drives operating rates in industry below 70 percent and unemployment rates to 9 percent has so little effect on industrial markups and on the wages of major categories of career workers in union and non-union areas, how confident can anyone be that these prices and wages will respond sensitively to the mere *threat* of such adversity? Those prices and wages are not the result of precise forecasts: indeed, they reflect arrangements that people have sensibly adopted to reduce their dependence on forecasts. So the firm operating in a customer market and in a career labor market will stand ready to hold down its prices when its costs slow down, and to enforce a slower wage trend for its employees when the cost of living stabilizes or when the wages set by its competitors slow down. But the record of experience suggests that the firm will not take such actions readily merely on the basis of a forecast. It is highly risky to formulate a policy predicated on the assumption that enunciation of a new price-oriented strategy will alter established patterns of behavior and responses in a dramatic way.

The cost-reducing tools are potentially the great reconciler of employment targets and price level (or nominal GNP) targets. In response to OPEC price increases or wage adaptation, cuts in indirect taxes and tax-based incomes policies provide important opportunities for staying close to the price target without major shortfalls from desirable utilization rates. These options avoid the destructive losses of severe recessions and prolonged slack and also those of the impairment of the value of money. The cost-influencing measures should become part of the standard arsenal of government policies. They are not instruments for fine tuning. However, they should be used as routinely to combat major upward cost disturbances or inflationary adaptation as tax cuts are now used to combat serious recessions.

With a combined arsenal of demand-influencing and cost-influencing instruments, a price-oriented strategy becomes feasible. Targets for nominal GNP deserve priority over employment targets in that context. The uncertainty about the price level is more costly for the long run, and can be most readily controlled by the policy strategy. A credible commitment to the price path is essential, as William Fellner has argued persuasively. Given that commitment, the best target for the unemployment rate at any time is the lowest rate consistent with remaining at the chosen price level, with appropriate reliance on the instruments. The only useful general rule for macroeconomic policy is to aim at the lowest unemployment rate consistent with a stable price level.

The pursuit of a target path for nominal GNP has obvious implications for fiscal and monetary policies. It is clear, for example, that an objective of 5 percent growth for nominal GNP is inconsistent with large federal deficits and a 10 percent growth of monetary aggregates. There is no particular prescription, however, that can be written for the instruments that will always be optimal for the pursuit of the nominal GNP path. No fixed settings for the instruments can be efficient.

The adoption of the objective of growth in nominal GNP leaves open a wide range of important issues about the mix of policies and the optimum method of control. The primary focus should be on the question of how fast nominal GNP is intended to grow. Settings of the various instruments for influencing demand are a secondary question that should be discussed only in the context of the answer to the first. In particular, the needed long-term strategy to cure chronic inflation must begin by drawing a path of slowing nominal GNP from the rates of about 11 percent that were experienced in the late seventies to an ultimate goal of, say, 5 percent. The adoption of 1 percentage point reduction a year is a simple and understandable and probably sensible objective. That requires fewer expansionary fiscal and monetary policies than were applied during the decade of the seventies. Measures to lower the cost structure and to establish a tax-based incomes policy are no substitute for demand restraint, but rather a complement in an overall efficient strategy to shift the balance in the reductions in growth of nominal GNP from output loss to inflation slowdown.

A definite commitment to a path of decelerating growth for nominal GNP would be a valuable and important step in the conquest of chronic inflation. As I have argued, taken alone, such a commitment would do little to change current wage or markup behavior. It would, however, support bond prices, affect the premium to protect against inflation in the prices of precious metals and real estate, and otherwise help to renew the economy's dependence on money. Most important, I expect it to help immediately in slowing the crawl away from money and perhaps turning it around. A change in long-term expectations about the secular rate, if held with conviction, would arrest the process of inflationary adaptation. I expect to see less pressure toward cost-of-living escalators, fewer shifts to replacement-cost accounting and replacement-cost pricing, and a greater willingness to make longer-term nominal commitments. To obtain those benefits, the credibility of the government's stance is a critical element if I may again echo Fellner. But to take issue with him, a policy that accepts a significant risk of catastrophe and permits the government to do nothing in the event of that catastrophe must be subject to important doubts. If the response of price and wage decisionmakers to the new posture is not dramatically different from their response to past episodes of reduced demand, the strategy that relies on demand restraint alone would entail drastic increases in unemployment and cutbacks in capital formation for prolonged periods. Once the benefits of measures that can directly reduce costs and provide incentives for wage and markup restraint are added to the package, the entire commitment becomes far more credible and convincing.

If the combined strategy that I recommend is implemented and if it is successful, economists would have grave difficulties disentangling the contributions made by demand restraint and those made by the cost neutralizers and the incomes policy. I sometimes think that the preference of many economists for an undiversified, single-shot approach for curing inflation reflects, perhaps unconsciously, a desire for a controlled experiment that will establish decisively who is right and who is wrong. In my judgment, the good of the country requires that the profession sacrifice that opportunity for scientific inquiry. In any case, we should cherish the opportunity to continue our debates in the years ahead.

I do think that issues of broad social philosophy enter into differences in viewpoints. Some fear that a broader and more comprehensive strategy will turn into greater involvement by government and an excuse for ever more regulation of and interference with the market system. What they see as the danger of tampering, I see as the possibility for correcting an externality that no efficient system should tolerate. What they see as a minimal exercise of the power and authority of government, I see as an aloof authoritarianism and stern paternalism. I would be morally outraged by a local ordinance designed to promote fire prevention by prohibiting the fire department from responding to any alarms for a month. This is a strong analogy to attempting to prevent inflation by committing the government not to deal with a recession no matter how deep it becomes. A democratic society must have better cooperative ways to instill such socially desirable efforts than by threat and fear. Indeed, constraint and discipline are part of the program, just as the stop signs and speed limits are part of a program of traffic safety. In the economic program the groups that will be constrained should be alerted to the options and to the possibilities of easing their transition to a noninflationary environment. I suspect that, if labor unions recognize that the nation is committed to a path for GNP that precludes wage increases of more than 4 percent a year five years from now and businessmen recognize that their markups will be constrained, they will understand the need for a coordinated approach with the help of government to provide the cost reductions and the social compact that can implement the program without the risk of deep recession.

I expect the era of chronic inflation to end in the eighties. I am not particularly optimistic, however, that the era will be terminated by a coordinated program that combines a deceleration of nominal income growth with the cost-reducing elements and the incentives to wage and price restraint that the analysis of this book has highlighted. Viewing the world objectively, I believe it is more probable that the era of chronic inflation will end with a deep and prolonged recession or with a protracted period of rigid mandatory price and wage controls. I am not resigned to that conclusion, and I hope economists will work hard to prevent it.

Over the longer run, I am confident that the next generation of economics students will be able to explain the seventies—a period when economists had so much difficulty understanding why even fully perceived nominal disturbances could have had real effects, and why inflation loomed so large in the minds of the public when, in the economists' models, it posed nothing more than annoying extra trips to the banks. Those students will also develop a better understanding of what went wrong when politicians seriously espoused the initiation of value-added taxes in a time of mounting inflation or believed they were dealing decisively with the inflation problem by promising to balance the budget. I hope this book contributes in a small way toward hastening that day.

Index

Aaron, Henry J., 222

Abramovitz, Moses, 33n

Accelerationist theory: approach to inflation, 38–39, 118–21, 237–38; auction-customer approach to, 257–58; compared with other theories, 239–44

Acceptance quality standard, 66–67, 68, 77, 79

Acceptance wages: acceptance quality standard and, 66; based on relative wages, 36–37; factors influencing, 28–30; to increase employment, 46; and workers' horizons, 46–47

Accounting, inventory, 157–60

Ackley, Gardner, 23, 261, 352n

Adaptation function, 300–03

Administered price thesis, 173–78, 181

Aggregate demand, 4–5, 10; and GNP, 4, 264, 311, 323, 327; imperfect control over, 307–10; inflationary effect of, 271, 278, 284; for labor, 35; and monopoly, 266, 269; precise control over, 303–06, 310–11; price sensitivity to, 136, 144–45, 147, 148–50, 173–74; social loss from additions to, 270

Aggregate supply function, 4, 5, 13, 21. *See also* Supply; Supply shock

Agricultural products, auction market for, 134–36

Anti-inflation strategy: cold-turkey, 314, 315, 320; comprehensive macroeconomic, 353–59; cost-reducing policies as, 320–22, 356; demand management, 297, 303–10, 313, 353–54; employment-oriented, 308, 309, 317–18; fiscal-monetary, 307, 309; foreign trade implications for, 326–32; indirect taxation as, 332–36; from maintaining GNP, 307–08, 311–18, 320, 357, 359; optimal compromise, 316–17; price-oriented, 309, 310, 318, 320, 336–37, 341–42, 356; pure, 303, 305, 306, 309, 315, 317; wage restraints as, 336–37, 339–48

Arrow, Kenneth J., 33, 79–80

Ashenfelter, O. C., 133

Assets: break-even horizon for, 186; fixed production capital, 200–03; inflationary effect on, 206–08; as inflation hedges, 203–04, 214–15; liquidity, 183, 187, 190; loan market and, 188–89; markets for, 182–83; nominal, 199, 216; portfolio choice for, 190–91; purchasing-power risk of, 203, 211; real, 199, 214; transaction costs of, 183–86. *See also* Bonds; Money; Saving

Auction-customer model, 223–24, 244–46; conversion to simple accelerationist model, 257–58; customer price relation to wages in, 251–53; fiscal-monetary policymaking in, 246–48; international trade effects in, 255–56; productivity growth in, 249–50; supply in, 253–55; wage norm changes and, 250–51

Auction labor market: compared with search market, 26–27, 32–35; marginal labor cost in, 31; toll in, 76; worker training in, 71

Auction product market: anticipated inflation in, 281, 286; competitive equilibrium in, 143–44; efficient market theory applied to, 137–38; inflation sensitivity of, 213–14; inventories, 135, 136; nominal GNP impact on, 224; participants, 135; prices, 134–36; stock subsidies in, 322–25; trade-off between inflation and unemployment in, 263–65; transaction costs of, 184–85

Azariadis, Costas, 130, 133

Baily, Martin N., 111n, 130

Bakke, E. Wight, 131–32

Banks, in loan market, 192–94

Barro, Robert J., 25

Barter, 217, 220

Baumol, William J., 186, 220

Becker, Gary S., 71, 79, 82

Berle, Adolf A., Jr., 173, 181

Bernstein, E. M., 222

Bilateral mononoly: and career labor